D1248737

PERSPECTIVES IN SOCIOLOGY
Herman R. Lantz, *General Editor*

ADVISORY EDITORS

Alvin W. Gouldner, *Washington University*
Robert A. Nisbet, *Columbia University*
Melvin M. Tumin, *Princeton University*
Jerry Gaston, *Southern Illinois University*

The Sociology
of Science
in Europe

Edited by

Robert K. Merton
and
Jerry Gaston

Southern Illinois University Press

CARBONDALE AND EDWARDSVILLE

Feffer & Simons, Inc.

LONDON AND AMSTERDAM

Library of Congress Cataloging in Publication Data
Main entry under title:

The Sociology of science in Europe.

(Perspectives in sociology)
Bibliography: p.
Includes index.
1. Science—Social aspects—Europe. I. Merton,
Robert King, 1910-   II.   Gaston, Jerry.
III. Series.
Q175.52.E85S66   1977   301.5   77-2996
ISBN 0-8093-0633-6

REF
Q
175.52
.E85
S66
1977
Cop.1

To Our Colleagues
IN THE
SOCIOLOGY OF SCIENCE

CONTENTS

Preface

THE PAST two decades have witnessed the increasingly rapid development of the sociology of science. That development did not occur in isolation, either from cognate disciplines or from changing social contexts. It derived in no small part from a confluence of scholarly interests in science as a cognitive, social, and historical phenomenon that joined the sociology of science at first with the history, philosophy, and politics of science and then in growing measure with science policy studies, information science, and the psychology and economics of science. The convergence of disciplinary perspectives has led anew to the interdisciplinary field known as "social studies of science" in some countries and by kindred terms, such as the "science of science," in others.

Just as the sociology of science has come to avoid the parochialism of impermeable disciplinary boundaries, so it had some time before avoided the parochialism of national boundaries. Beginning with the Fifth World Congress of the International Sociological Association held in 1962 at Washington and continuing on an enlarged scale with the Sixth Congress at Évian, the Seventh at Varna and the Eighth at Toronto in 1974, sociologists of science from numerous countries have engaged in periodic interchanges and occasional collaboration. On these quadrennial occasions, it became evident that the emergence of English as an ecumenical language was a mixed blessing, not least for those brought up in English-speaking societies. Its widespread use appeared to make for an asymmetrical flow of information, with research published in English tending to be widely known to the international community of scholars while research published in the other European languages—particularly languages other than French and German—being less widely known.

This circumstance, oftèn discussed at the international meetings, led to the idea of having a volume that would inform the growing numbers of scholars in the sociology of science about work being variously developed in European countries. In the course of a wide-ranging inquiry among colleagues in those countries, we were advised by some that research in their own country had not yet reached a point warranting a distinct chapter in this volume although in a good number of cases, such as the Netherlands, Czechoslovakia, East Germany, Bulgaria, Romania and Yugoslavia, it was evident that a subsequent volume will call for chapters specific to each.

Two correlative papers should be mentioned here. The one, prepared as though in anticipation of this volume, is an account, published in English, of research developments in Hungary, written by Sándor Szalai and János Farkas ("Sociology of Science and Research," *Szociólogia* 5, Supplement, 1974:105–10). Professor Szalai and Dr. Farkas have kindly allowed us to include their bibliography along with the bibliographies for other European countries so all is not lost. The other paper complements this volume by providing an analytical account of the emergence and development of the sociology of science chiefly in the United States: Jonathan R. Cole and Harriet Zuckerman, "The Emergence of a Scientific Specialty: The Self-Exemplifying Case of the Sociology of Science," pp. 139–74 in Lewis A. Coser, ed., *The Idea of Social Structure* (New York: Harcourt Brace Jovanovich, 1975).

Contributors to the volume were asked to provide accounts of the beginnings of the sociology of science in their respective countries and of research developed there to the relatively recent past. It is the latter, penultimate period in the history of disciplines and specialties —the period of the academic generation or two *ante me*—that often seems to become a blind spot for successive cohorts of newcomers to the discipline. The more distant past of the subject is known to them through its being a matter of prescribed study—"the history of the subject"—while their immediate research interests make for their acquiring a close knowledge of the moving frontiers of inquiry. But the period just preceding the immediate present, seldom recorded in conventional histories of the subject, needs to be illuminated by overviews of the kind set out in this volume. It is our hope that periodic audits of this kind will continue to serve the same purpose.

Part One, written with the encouragement of Professor Herman R. Lantz, general editor of the series, Perspectives in Sociology, in which this volume appears, is an episodic memoir in the sense of treating selected aspects of the sociology of science that have come within the personal experience or knowledge of the author. It examines only a few moments in the distant antecedents and near past of the sociology of science that provide contexts for some recently developing ideas and research programs in the field.

Part Two, which gives the book its title and forms its chief substance, consists of the indicated overviews of the sociology of science in various European countries. From those overviews, it appears that no monochromatic sociology of science uniformly cuts across national borders; rather, the work in each country tends to have its own composite character. But it also appears to be the case that, along with these differences, the sociology of science practiced in these national societies exhibits strong commonalties of problematics and methodology and far from negligible commonalties of theoretical orientation and techniques of investigation.

A collaborative venture of this sort places the editors in the happily acknowledged debt of many. Most of all, we owe thanks to our collaborators who, sometimes with misgivings, undertook the difficult task of surveying the field as cultivated in their own countries and, for the most part, providing comprehensive bibliographic references. (It should be noted here that the author of the chapter on France is a scholar who sometimes prefers to write under a pseudonym.)

Our thanks go also to Professor Adam Podgórecki who gave us valuable advice in the early phases of this undertaking and to Professor Lantz who, as we have said, encouraged us to prepare this volume for the series which he edits. We thank the others who helped us to bring this volume into print: Tia Powell for editorial assistance and for typing the final draft of the manuscript; Evelyn Geller for providing editorial aid to several authors; Mary Wilson Miles and Dorothy Brothers for transcribing Part One of the volume; Mary Gaston, Thomas F. Gieryn and William Koerber for assistance in what turned out to be an arduous task of reading proofs; and Beatrice Moore especially for her sustained attention to the subtleties of diverse national styles of expression and for her unfailing patience in coping with the faults of the editors. The senior editor acknowledges aid from the National Science Foundation in the form of a grant to the Columbia University Program in the Sociology of Science.

The regrettable errors that remain after all this help are plainly ours.

Columbia University   R. K. M.
Southern Illinois University   J. G.

LIST OF CONTRIBUTORS

FILIPPO BARBANO is Professore Ordinario di Sociologia, Faculty of Political Science at the University of Turin, and Director of the Institute of Political Science. He is the author of numerous monographs in theoretical sociology.

GENNADY M. DOBROV is Professor and Deputy Director, Institute of Cybernetics at the Ukrainian SSR Academy of Sciences, USSR. His books on science policy have been supplemented by specialized papers in the field.

PAUL FRANK, the pseudonym of an American scholar and observer of the French scene for several years.

JERRY GASTON is Associate Professor of Sociology and Chairman of the Department of Sociology, Southern Illinois University at Carbondale. His most recent book is *Originality and Competition in Science* (Chicago: University of Chicago Press, 1973).

ANDREW JAMISON, now in the Department of Sociology, University of Lund, has taught courses on science and society there and at the University of Copenhagen. He is the author of *The Steam Powered Automobile: An Answer to Air Pollution* (Bloomington: University of Indiana Press, 1970).

ROLF KLIMA is Researcher and Lecturer in Sociology and Philosophy of Science, Faculty of Sociology, at the University of Bielefeld. His publications have appeared as chapters in books, in *Social Science Information*, and in the *Zeitschrift für Soziologie*.

ZDISLAW KOWALEWSKI, a specialist in the sociology of science, is affiliated with the Polish Academy of Sciences in Warsaw.

TADEUSZ KRAUZE is Research Associate of Social Analysis of Science Systems at Cornell University, and a specialist in mathematical approaches to the study of the sociology of science.

ROBERT K. MERTON is University Professor at Columbia University. His recent books are *Sociology of Science: Theoretical and Empirical Investigations*, edited by Norman W. Storer (Chicago: University of Chicago Press, 1973), and *Sociological Ambivalence* (New York: Free Press, 1976).

MICHAEL J. MULKAY is Reader in Sociology at the University of York (England). Author of *Functionalism, Exchange, and Theoretical Strategy* (London: Routledge and Kegan Paul, 1971) and *The Social Process of Innovation: A Study in the Sociology of Science* (New York: Macmillan, 1972); his newest book (with D. O. Edge) is *Astronomy Transformed* (New York: Wiley-Interscience, 1976).

ADAM PODGÓRECKI is Professor at the University of Warsaw. A specialist in sociotechnics and the sociology of law, his latest books include *Law and Society* (London: Routledge and Kegan Paul, 1974) and *Practical Social Sciences* (London: Routledge and Kegan Paul, 1975).

LUDGER VIEHOFF is a Research Fellow at the Science Studies Center, University of Bielefeld.

Part One

THE SOCIOLOGY OF SCIENCE

An Episodic Memoir

Robert K. Merton

THE DANISH POLYMATH, PIET HEIN—physicist, poet, city-planner, inventor of the verse form known as Grooks and the geometrical form known as the super-egg, resistance-fighter against Nazi tyranny, and man of much wisdom—once remarked to a group of his friends that "art is the solving of problems that cannot be expressed until they are solved." Much the same can be said for the art of inquiry in other humanistic and scientific disciplines. For if the formulation of a problem includes its implications and consequences, then each (temporary) solution enables us to express it more fully. To develop the problematics of a field of inquiry, such as the sociology of science, may be as demanding a task as the solution of a particular problem.

It is fitting, for another reason, to draw upon Piet Hein when introducing this volume devoted to the state of the art of that emerging sociological specialty, the sociology of science, as it is practiced in a variety of European societies. True, Piet Hein likes to describe himself as a "specialist in anti-specialization." But he is quick to add that only when a field of inquiry is specially cultivated by people who devote themselves wholly to it does it generate deep knowledge and understanding. True also, like other virtues become vices through great excess, extreme specialization in any branch of learning runs the risk of defeating its function by isolating knowledge from its contexts and thus fragmenting it. In short, there really can be too much of a good thing, as the Nobel laureate in physiology, Dickinson Richards (1953), demonstrated in examining the generic phenomenon of hyperexis ("the excess response, a homeostatic effort that overreaches itself"). But clearly, the nascent specialty of the sociology of science is still far removed from the danger of such excessive specialization.

As several papers in this volume testify, the study of how scientific specialties emerge, evolve, and affect the development of scientific knowledge has become a focus of inquiry in the sociology of science itself. Garvey and Griffith (1964, 1966), Hagstrom (1965), Ben-David and Collins (1966), Fisher (1966), Crane (1969, 1972), Griffith and Miller (1970), Mullins (1972, 1973a, 1973b), Griffith and Mullins (1972), Thackray and Merton (1972), Law (1973), Small (1973), Mulkay and Edge (1974), Small and Griffith (1974), Griffith, Small, Stonehill, and Dey (1974), Mulkay, Gilbert, and Woolgar (1975) and Edge and Mulkay (1975, 1976) are among those who have provided the instructive beginnings of a sociological understanding of specialty-formation and development in a variety of scientific disciplines. Something of a departure in this gathering of studies is Mullins's (1968, 1973b) use of network analysis which relates social indicators such as coauthorship, communications networks, and teacher-student lineage to such cognitive indicators as citation analysis provides.

J. Cole and Zuckerman (1975)—from whom I have looted most of the foregoing inventory of papers—have gone on to take the emergence of the sociology of science in the United States as a case in point. Its distinctive interest as a specialty centers on its strongly self-exemplifying character: its own history and behavior exemplify sociological ideas and findings about the emergence and development of scientific specialties generally. Nor is this an occasion for surprise. Were the sociology of science not self-exemplifying, then either the general ideas and findings would have to be thought unsound or the field itself is nothing like the scientific specialty it is commonly supposed to be.

COGNITIVE AND SOCIAL IDENTITIES

Since the authors of the papers in this volume are themselves practicing sociologists of science, they understandably adopt perspectives drawn from their special discipline in reporting on its development and current condition in several European societies. With due regard for its socio-historical contexts, they focus, in varying degree, upon the *cognitive identity* of the specialty in the form of its intellectual orientations, conceptual schemes, paradigms, problematics, and tools for inquiry. And, in varying degree also, they focus correlatively upon its *social identity* in the form of its major institutional arrangements.[1] These arrangements include modes of recruitment to the field and procedures for training, education, and research, both individual and collaborative. They also include the basic patterns of communication, both informal and those established in journals given over to the subject in greater or lesser part. Of special importance for the development of the field are the cognitive and social contexts that limit or facilitate the emergence of "invisible colleges" of investigators engaged in mutually connected research, interchange, and not infrequent controversy.

It was Derek J. de Solla Price ([1961] 1975:85 ff., 1963, with Beaver, 1966) who, in a brilliant stroke of terminological recoinage, adopted and conceptually extended the seventeenth-century term "invisible college" which had been introduced by the twenty-year-old Robert Boyle to describe a small group of natural philosophers (scientists) that antedated the formation of what was to become the highly visible college of the Royal Society. Ironically enough, the term was misapplied by the eighteenth-century Thomas Birch (1756–57), then Secretary and historian of the Royal Society and, more in point, the editor of Boyle's works and the correspondence in which the term first appeared in print (Boyle, 1744, 1:20, 24). However new the term "invisible college" may have been to sociologists of science, it had long held (diverse) meaning for historians of science. For decades and down to the present moment, the historians have debated the question of the precise group to which Boyle had affixed the memorable label and of the historical connection of that group to the origins of the Royal Society. (For only a few examples, see Stimson, 1935; Merton, [1938] 1970:114–5; Purver, 1967, pt. 2, chap. 3; Hill, 1968; Rattansi, 1968; Hall and Hall, 1968; Webster, 1967, 1975.) Poised at an intersection of the history and the sociology of science, Price adopted the term to give focus to continuing inquiry into these social formations of scientists. As he has indicated and as Crane (1972), Mullins (1973b), Garfield, Malin, and Small (1977), and others have amply confirmed, invisible colleges do much to advance knowledge, both in the early days of a specialty and after it has become firmly institutionalized.

Invisible colleges can be construed sociologically as clusters of geographically dispersed scientists who engage in more frequent cognitive interaction with one another than they do with others in the larger community of scientists. At the outset, members of an emerging invisible college regard themselves as major reference individuals and regard themselves collectively as a reference group, whose opinions of their work matter deeply and whose standards of cognitive performance are taken as binding.[2] As the field of inquiry grows in numbers of investigators and differentiates cognitively, another structural adaptation of progressively pinpointed informal communication between specialized scientists seems to develop. This takes the form, as Jonathan Cole has suggested to me, of invisible colleges developing *within* the onetime invisible college, now grown amply visible through networks of publication. Subsets of people at work in the developing field of inquiry come to adopt differing sets of reference individuals and reference groups. Cognitive disagreements are reinforced by social conflict (Merton, 1973, chap. 3). All this makes for a social structure that corresponds more or less closely to the differentiating cognitive structure of the field. (For instructive contexts of processes such as these, see Mullins, 1973b.)

INSTITUTIONALIZATION OF THE SOCIOLOGY OF SCIENCE

The process of institutionalization of the sociology of science reported in this volume is captured, in its essentials, in a paper by Edward Shils

that is the most instructive qualitative analysis of the institutio
tion of learning known to me.[3] A meticulously constructed para
in that paper (Shils, 1970:763), with its salient notion of "den
teraction," sums up conceptually much of what is reported empirically
in this volume.

> By institutionalization of an intellectual activity I mean the
> relatively dense interaction of persons who perform that activity.
> The interaction has a structure: the more intense the interaction,
> the more its structure makes place for authority which makes deci-
> sions regarding assessment, admission, promotion, allocation. The
> high degree of institutionalization of an intellectual activity entails
> its teaching and administered organization. The organization
> regulates access through a scrutiny of qualification, provides for
> organized assessment of performance, and allocates facilities, op-
> portunities, and rewards for performance—for example, study,
> teaching, investigation, publications, appointment, and so forth.
> It also entails the organized support of the activity from outside
> the particular institution and the reception or use of the results of
> the activity beyond the boundaries of the institution. An intellec-
> tual activity need not be equally institutionalized in all these re-
> spects. [And in an essential cautionary note, Shils concludes that]
> It should be remembered that an intellectual activity can be car-
> ried on fruitfully with only a rudimentary degree of institution-
> alization.[4]

Although not expressly couched in those terms, the phenomena of
institutionalization diversely described in this volume can be conceived of in terms of an interplay between the developing cognitive
and the professional identities of the sociology of science. More often
than not, the accounts are responsive to questions such as these:

> In broad outline, what have been the antecedents, both in-
> tellectual and institutional, of the field of inquiry that has come to
> be known as the "sociology of science" or by some kindred term?
> What constitutes the current problematics of the field and
> which modes of investigation are being utilized to tackle the di-
> verse problems? Along with individual scholars at work in the
> field, which forms of research organization have been evolving?
> What, then and now, are the cognitive traditions, disciplinary

boundaries, structural contexts (social, educational, economic, and political) which affect the character of the developing sociology of science: its foci of research, its modes of education and training, its styles of inquiry, and the resultant directions of development it has taken in each society?

The papers address these questions in differing scope and detail. It is not my intent to summarize the individual papers for the authors do that admirably for themselves. Instead, I shall confine myself to a few observations on aspects of the developing sociology of science which, though not uniformly emphasized in the several papers, nevertheless leap to the eye when they are juxtaposed and collated.

In reflecting upon the internationalization of the sociology of science, I shall draw from time to time upon personal observation of that development and participation in it. The disciplined use of such ordinarily fugitive historical data based upon reports of participant-observers was introduced in the concept of "oral history" by the American historian Allan Nevins (Voigt, 1971) and has since been developed into a network of archives for contemporary history in every department of social life and culture.[5] In the history of science, for example, the Center for the History of Physics of the American Institute of Physics has created a major archive of oral and associated documentary materials. If only because historical data of this kind are fugitive and inaccessible from documents alone, I shall introduce what amount to snippets of oral history (since the information was elicited by interviews) into this short account of the parochialization and internationalization of the community of scholars at work in the sociology of science.

The Ecumenical Precursors

Like its parent discipline of sociology, the sociology of science is plainly polyphyletic, deriving from various ancestral lines of sociological thought. With some variation, the prime ancestors are identified as Saint-Simon, Comte, and, of course, Marx (and for some, Condorcet, claimed by Saint-Simon himself as his anticipator).[6] It is appropriate to refer to Marx in the "of-course mood" because few, if any, would contest his basic influence upon widespread ways of construing the interaction between society and scientific thought. Even Karl Popper

(1965:332), famously or notoriously (as one wishes) no lover of Marx's work, has made a point of acknowledging that influence:

> Everyone learned from Marx that the development even of ideas cannot be fully understood if the history of ideas is treated (although such a treatment may often have its great merits) without mentioning the conditions of their origin and the situation of their originators, among which conditions the economic aspect is highly significant.

Mindful of the strikingly various versions of Marx's thought that have materialized over the years, Popper concludes this passage by maintaining that although

> it is impossible to understand mental developments without understanding their economic background [itself not the weakest of claims by a dedicated anti-historicist], it is at least as impossible to understand economic developments without understanding the development of, for instance, scientific or religious ideas.

What should claim our further attention is that each of the three widely acknowledged precursors of the offspring sociology of science—Saint-Simon, Comte, and Marx—has also been described as the father of the parent discipline, sociology. Such ascriptions of paternity—a devilishly tricky notion when applied to the history of thought—hold a double interest for sociologists of science. Whatever the intent, these ascriptions serve the latent function of providing a traditional cognitive identity to a field. Clearly, a discipline held to be fathered by Comte differs in theoretical commitment from one held to be fathered by Marx. To that degree, as Alvin Gouldner (1958:ixn) has also noted, ascriptions of paternity are more than exercises in the intellectual history of disciplines. In the course of according honor to one or another remote ancestor, they function as emblematic statements, claiming legitimacy for a theoretical commitment rooted in the given intellectual tradition. The genealogy of ideas need not affect their validity and, as we are sufficiently warned by the genetic fallacy, it surely does not provide grounds for judging their validity. But that genealogy, as reconstructed by one or another set of exponents of a discipline, does introduce constraints on the modes of substantive theorizing considered legitimate or, simply because of provenance, quite unacceptable.

Beyond such symbolic legitimatizing function, as I have noted before (Merton, 1968:2n), the nomination of a Saint-Simon, Comte, or Marx as *the* father of both sociology and the sociology of science presupposes more than is usually intended. Even as the biological idiom is deployed symbolically, it comes to be taken literally. It imports unexamined assumptions about the ways in which new disciplines come into being. Allusions to *the* father introduce a heroic imagery which, in true Olympian style, allows for a kind of parthenogenesis. Collaborators in the conception of a discipline become superfluous, as do socio-historical conditions. In the further absence of clear criteria for having fathered or mothered[7] a science, ambiguity obtains and predilections, whatever their source (socio-historical, ideological, patriotic, or idiosyncratic), prevail in the continuingly symbolic ascription of parenthood.

The overlap of remote ancestors ascribed to both sociology and sociology of science may be connected with an observation by J. Cole and Zuckerman (1975) about types of scientific specialties. They distinguish between specialties that are derived from or are at least congruent with the theoretical traditions central to the encompassing discipline and the specialties, such as molecular biology or sociobiology, that are intellectual hybrids, deriving from two or more disciplines and spanning departments in the organization of science. Cole and Zuckerman hypothesize that the first type, central to the parent discipline both cognitively and organizationally, encounters less initial resistance from practitioners in the discipline than the hybrid type. Their analysis locates the sociology of science (at least in the United States) centrally rather than peripherally in the larger discipline. Confirming that reading of the situation is the circumstance we have been examining in which the same distant ancestors—Saint-Simon, or Comte, or Marx —are invoked both for the parent discipline and for its recent offspring.

Immediate Antecedents

The three or four remote ancestors claimed by sociologists of science today make up a reasonably ecumenical list. Not having done the needed comparative content analysis, I can only report impressions. Comte appears to be claimed relatively no more often by French sociologists than by others. And, of course, Marx is claimed not only by German sociologists and, as we should expect since he did after all live more than half his sixty-five years in London, by British ones, but also by American, Belgian, Dutch, French, Italian, and Scandinavian sociologists to say nothing of the obvious lines of filiation to scholars in the socialist countries. Indeed, Marx transcends more than national boundaries. He is claimed as an ancestral influence by many sociologists who can truly say: *nous ne sommes pas Marxistes*.

The list of later progenitors of the sociology of science is noticeably more parochial, tending to be drawn disproportionately from the sociologist's own national heritage. Some convergence and overlap occur, of course, as in the common reference to the intermediate figure of a grand master such as Max Weber. But, as will be seen in the following papers, scholars in each country where substantial work in the sociology of science is being done and some even in countries where the discipline is just getting under way have identified their own national complements of recent founders.

The contrast between the ecumenical character of the remote ancestors and the parochial character of the recent founders is only to be expected. Those few theoretical orientations of the relatively distant past that survive in the present have had ample time to diffuse through what is in principle and often in fact organized as a universalistic community of scientists, transcending national and other boundaries. Whatever the formidable obstacles to such diffusion—cultural, linguistic, organizational, ideological, or technological—these can be overcome in the course of the generations.

Moreover, the surviving master-sociologists of a century or more ago provided comprehensive intellectual frameworks with axes for locating problems that were only later identified as specific to the sociology of science or to other domains of inquiry. While preserving their recognizable cast, their intellectual traditions became differentiated and extended in the course of transmission over the years. Whatever the local origins of these distant but still influential forefathers, they can emerge as ecumenical symbols.

In the parochial case of the immediate antecedents who focused their ideas specifically on the sociology of science, the intellectual traditions were of course largely in the making. There was, in this early phase, only a thin scattering of interest among European and (as Cole and Zuckerman [1975] show) American sociologists in systematically investigating the complex interrelations between science and society. There was even less interest in analyzing the social and cultural structure of science in order to lay the groundwork for relating that structure to the growth of scientific knowledge. Papers on any of these matters appeared only sporadically. The absence of concerted research programs and, intimately related, the absence of programs for training sociologists in the newly developing art of the sociological investigation of science as a composite cognitive, cultural, and social phenomenon, meant that there was no sufficient basis, cognitive or social, for following up through research the occasional papers that had pointed the way. Lacking significant response to their forays into the study of science by peers (the "significant others") in the discipline, the occasional sociologists who did undertake work in the field made it only a part, and usually not a major or continuing part, of their research programs. Until at least the 1960s, and still in some countries, there were, in Europe and the United States, practically no interacting groups of research workers committed to a common, overlapping, or mutually relevant research agenda in the field. As a result, few indeed developed a self-image as a "sociologist of science." All this amounted to a design for discontinuity rather than continuity of inquiry. This early phase in the development of the discipline thus provides another self-exemplifying pattern for one of the problems in the sociology of science, now much in need of intensive study, the problem of identifying the conditions and processes making for continuities and for discontinuities in science (Merton 1968:8–27).

With no invisible colleges devoted to study of the subject within national societies, there was next to no interaction across national boundaries. Indeed, the scattering of self-taught and sporadic contributors to the subject could scarcely decide how to describe the field of inquiry. They were certain only about their uncertainty. They found it hard to demarcate the subject and its distinguishing problematics, concepts, methods, tools, and doctrines. The institutional and cognitive identity of the field was blurred. The cognitive ambiguities were (and, to a degree, in some places, still are) reflected in the variety of tags proposed for the ill-demarcated field. In Poland, for example, as Krauze, Kowalewski, and Podgórecki note in their chapter, it was variously described as *wiedza o wiedzy* (knowledge about knowledge), *wiedz o nauce* (knowledge about science), or, increasingly, *nauka o nauce* (science of science). In Germany, the generic terms *Soziologie des Wissens* or *Wissenssoziologie* tended to blanket out descriptive terms for the more specific field of inquiry although as early as the mid-1920s, Scheler (1924,[1926] 1960) and others were adopting terms such as *Soziologie der positiven Wissenschaft* and later, some were even referring to *Wissenschaftssoziologie* or *Wissenschaftsforschung*. And, to take just one other terminological reflection of the blurred cognitive identity of the emerging field of inquiry, English-writing students of the subject would often turn to such circumlocutions as "the study of the social aspects of science," "social relations of science," or "studies in science and society" and later, such terms as "social studies of science" or "science of science," with only a handful having the temerity, early on, to refer to "the sociology of science" as though it were an identifiable subject.

The lonely few in each country who, through their own intermittent work, had pointed the way to a sociology of science are only now in retrospect being identified as the immediate antecedents, pioneers, or founders of the now identifiable discipline. The national, parochially distinctive rather than ecumenical lists of founders appear to be less an expression of national chauvinism than a response to the various structural (localizing) constraints which, as we have seen, make for prime awareness of the singularly few "premature" sociologists of science within each national community.

The historical bases for identifying founders of the discipline differ appreciably among the several nations. In Poland, for example, the ingredients of an institutionalized and cognitively identifiable field of inquiry appeared early, as Krauze, Kowalewski, and Podgórecki indicate. Several Polish scholars, including major sociologists, tried to achieve a concerted focus of inquiry into the social and political contexts of science as early as the 1920s. The Michalski formulation of 1923 suggests that the *Nauka Polska* group was trying to develop a cognitive and organizational basis for a new discipline. Above all others, however, it was Florian Znaniecki, with his remarkably prescient research agenda formulated in the mid-1920s and Stanislaw Ossowski (occasionally with the founding mother, Maria Ossowska) who developed the idea of a "science of science" that included a "sociology of science." But, the record shows, little of these brave beginnings diffused beyond the borders of Poland, and the intellectual tradition was disrupted in Poland itself by the vicissitudes of war and political turmoil.

Another case in point is provided by Germany (as can be seen from the account by Klima and Viehoff in their chapter "The Sociology of Science in West Germany and Austria"). There, standing above all others, remains the magistral figure of Max Weber. His diverse writings—particularly the incomparable lecture "Wissenschaft als Beruf" ([1919] 1951)—can now be seen to imply, to those attuned to the implications of his ideas, a number of basic problems in what would develop as a sociology of science (Tenbruck, 1974). His brother, Alfred Weber (1920), wrote, in quite another vein, his influential paper differentiating the concepts of "civilization" and "culture," a paper which soon diffused beyond national borders, eventually getting even as far as the then infinitely remote domain of American sociology. Weber's paper went further than most in arguing for ongoing, progressive "accumulation" in the sphere of civilization, which includes science and technology, in contrast to processes of change in the sphere of value-laden culture. (For the critique of that position I know best, see Merton, 1936.) But the most germane and powerful intellectual current that might have led early to an ongoing sociology of science was of course *Wissenssoziologie*, best known through the work of Max Scheler and Karl Mannheim. The two important Scheler volumes (1921, [1926] 1960), which occasionally went beyond the prevailing interest in a general sociology of knowledge to a more specific interest in a sociology of science, proved to be premature for reasons I have considered elsewhere (Merton, 1973, chap. 1). They did not elicit a sufficient resonance among sociologists to make for continuing programs of *systematic research* in the field. As Klima and Viehoff observe, it was the rare precursor, such as Helmuth Plessner, who focused on problems central to the special field of inquiry.

Perhaps enough has been said to indicate how structural constraints upon the various national sociologies have made for a more nearly parochial than ecumenical identification of founders of the special discipline. As long as the field had an indistinct identity and remained uninstitutionalized, the scattered work and ideas developed by a very few scholars in one area were not easily identified and connected up with that being done by others elsewhere. With no substantial numbers at work in the field, there was, for example, an insufficient market for translations of specialized monographs. And since the field still lacked public definition, there were few institutional arrangements for more direct international communication among the comparatively minute numbers of sociologists of science in countries around the world. As a result of these temporal and social contexts, work focused on problems in the sociology of science, with a few conspicuous exceptions, remained local rather than becoming cosmopolitan.

Institutional Structure

It was not until the 1960s, when the specialty was becoming more widely identifiable (although still largely as unfulfilled promise rather than as accomplished fact), that dense interaction began among the sociologists of science of differing countries. It can be said that the first substantial occasion for such focused interaction came as late as 1966, at the sixth quadrennial Congress of the International Sociological Association held in Évian. Of course, there had been earlier intimations of things to come. The Fourth Congress, held in 1958 in Stresa, had been devoted primarily to the theme of the Sociology of Sociology, with papers by Raymond Aron (1959) and myself (Merton, 1973, chap. 3) at the plenary sessions moving into questions that seemed pertinent for the sociological analysis of other disciplines as well as sociology. The response of the sizable audience was something less than overwhelming: I seem to recall a few asthmatic coughs and wheezes commingled with a scattering of discreet applause. Some kind observers might have described the response as negligible.[8] I am myself inclined to describe it as altogether nil. (The social contexts of the 1960s brought the winds of change. A decade later, as we all have reason to know from the work of Gouldner [1970], Friedrichs [1970], Reynolds and Reynolds [1970], and Halmos [1970], the sociology of sociology—the theme of the Congress—became a flourishing intellectual enterprise.)

That opportunity lost, the next appeared in 1962 at the Fifth Congress of the ISA, this one held in Washington. It was then, and there, that the groundwork was laid for what would emerge as an international Research Group in the Sociology of Science. This was the group made up of fewer than a dozen hardy souls that finally materialized four years later at the Congress in Évian to develop a research agenda before an attentive audience not much larger than the workgroup. From the standpoint of organized interaction among the growing number of largely self-taught sociologists of science, this international session was clearly the watershed. By the time of the next Congress held in 1970 at Varna, the Research Group had provided for several designated sessions, with as large and participative an audience as that reported by any other Research Group, and with a greater number of papers submitted than could be accommodated within the time made available by the organizers of the Congress. Much the same pattern appeared at the 1974 Congress in Toronto.

Intellectual Interchange

It is within the past decade that the pace of both the institutional and intellectual development of the field has greatly quickened, internationally and within most national complements of sociologists. The evidence of such development in European nations can be found in the chapters that follow: evidence for the United States appears in the Cole-Zuckerman paper (1975) which examines an array of indicators of growth such as the numbers of declared sociologists of science, doctoral dissertations in the field, an exponential increase in the specialized literature, diverse measures of both growing cognitive consensus *and* differentiation of perspective, and indicators of what amounts to "the consolidation of a research front."

Although the data are lacking for a decisive cohort analysis, Stehr and Larson (1972) have found strong evidence among American sociologists of growing interest in the form of age-graded variations in commitment to the specialty: among benighted sociologists in their fifties and sixties, who had entered the discipline before the sociology of knowledge and, *a fortiori*, the sociology of science had become institutionalized specialties rather than fields of incidental interest, the sociology of knowledge-and-science ranked only 28th in a list of 33 specialties. The picture changes significantly with successively younger cohorts. Sociologists in their forties rank the field 26th; those in their thirties, 22nd; while the newest recruits to sociology, still in their twenties, rank it in 17th place, just at the midpoint among all the indicated specialties. This last is, for me, a surprisingly high rank for an old interest but new specialty (especially since the absolute differences between top rank and 17th are small). I know of no comparable data-sets for other national populations of sociologists. But should the implied trend prove to be general and should it continue, even at a somewhat declining rate, we shall soon have enough sociologists of science at work to make significant inroads on the increasingly differentiated problematics of the field.

Just as with national developments, institutional and intellectual development can be gauged for the international sociology of science. Both institutional and cognitive growth is indicated by the evident rise of international invisible colleges. Networks of communication are being variously extended and, to adopt the Mullins term, "thickened" (Mullins, 1972; Griffith and Mullins, 1972). There is, as Shils would put it, increasingly "dense interaction." Conferences no longer wait upon the quadrennial Congresses of the ISA. The Research Group in the Sociology of Science of the ISA, for example, met twice in the interval between the 1970 Congress in Varna and the 1974 Congress in Toronto. Papers presented at the first of these conferences, held in London, have been collected in a volume already in print (Whitley, 1974) and the second, held in Warsaw, provided occasion for interchange that helped shape the program at the Toronto Congress. Other international conferences and seminars in the field, all apart from the ISA, have lately been held at Vienna and Berlin.

Published international symposia, such as this volume, which reflect, reinforce, and extend networks of scholarly interaction in the field, have begun to appear in rapid sequence. This volume, for example, has been preceded by a collection of papers edited by Halmos as a *Sociological Review Monograph* (1972), the volume edited by Whitley (1974), and most recently, by a symposium edited by Nico Stehr and René König (1975) as a special issue of the *Kölner Zeitschrift für Soziologie und Sozialpsychologie* and another edited by Knorr, Strasser, and Zilian (1975). The rapid succession of these international symposia bears its own witness to the emergence of the sociology of science as a special discipline.

NOTES ON THE BEGINNINGS

These recent developments, both organizational and cognitive, differ remarkably from the condition of things during the period from, roughly, the 1930s through the 1950s—in short, the period before the sociology of science had acquired a cognitive and professional identity. As we have noted, with the temporary exception of Poland in that primeval time, no country had more than a very few sociologists who devoted themselves even intermittently to research on sociological aspects of science or of technology. A bit of oral history about my own experience in the United States at the time may complement the accounts in this volume of what was going on contemporaneously in the various European countries.

In the 1930s, a bare handful of American sociologists, partly out of temerity, partly out of their state of innocence about what they were getting into, dared to undertake research on social aspects and contexts of science or of technology. I recall one indicator of the sparsity of commitment to this pursuit. When S. Colum Gilfillan published his *Sociology of Invention* in 1935, he decided to dedicate the book to "fellow students of the social aspects of invention." Unlike the dedication to the volume now in hand, which cannot have the space to enumerate and identify "Our Colleagues in the Sociology of Science," Gilfillan did undertake to identify his "fellow students." He quickly exhausted the list of Americans by referring to just eight colleagues: L. J. Carr, William F. Ogburn, Z. C. Dickinson, Joseph Rossman, Waldemar Kaempffert, B. S. Sanders, C. P. Wright, and myself. Of the eight, just three were properly validated, card-carrying sociologists; the eminent Ogburn, the well-known Carr, and the graduate student, Merton. That Gilfillan should have thought to include a mere student in this public affirmation of an invisible college testifies, in the personal aspect of the episode, to his generosity of spirit. That he should have had to dip down to the level of such a novice in order to achieve an invisible college numbering as many as eight testifies, in the structural aspect of the episode, to the poverty of choice he found available to him. In either case, it seems that even the dedication of books can serve as indicators of change in the condition of scholarship and science, as many seventeenth- and eighteenth-century authors, engaged in writing their typically ornamented dedications, intuitively sensed.

There were, of course, other, chiefly European scientists and scholars intensively concerned in the early 1930s with questions of a sociological sort about science. The ones best known to us in the United States were the English physical and biological scientists, typically of the first rank in their own scientific disciplines and Marxist in their social outlook. They included Bernal, Blackett, J. B. S. Haldane, Hogben, Huxley, Levy, Soddy (as well as the science journalist, J. G. Crowther), and, to my mind then and since, ranking far above them all, the biochemist now universally known as the author of the monumental *Science and Civilization in China*, Joseph Needham.[9] But stimulating as their observations were, they were generally not of the—dare o.ie say it, even now?—theoretical kind that linked up systematically with doctrines in the wider discipline of sociology. Nor, typically, were their observations based on *systematic* empirical inquiry, historical or contemporary, quantitative or qualitative. Reinforcing all these seeming obstacles was the anxious snobbery of practitioners in a discipline, like sociology in those days, still much on trial and eager to establish its distinctive cognitive and professional identity. That unthinking snobbery was of course most marked among some of the young Turks of American sociology, like myself, persuaded that the discipline required development along lines that we would surely bring to it. In a word, the few aspiring American sociologists of science read the English scientists then writing about "science and society" and appreciated them[10] but did not perceive their work as providing prime models for developing a sociological understanding of science.

(Anticipating a bit, I can now bear witness to my distinct lack of prescience in seeing that all this would one day evolve into a field known as "science policy studies" and, in the form of a subspecialty in the social studies of science, another known as the "political sociology of science." Those great debates of the 1930s over the public policy that should govern science acquired new orders of magnitude and urgency after the technological catastrophes that closed out World War II. The new terms of reference began to be set out, appropriately enough, in the conscience-haunted *Bulletin of the Atomic Scientists*. By 1954, the principal issues of science policy found disciplined formulation in the classic *Science and Government* by Don K. Price [1954, also 1965]. Ever since, public bodies and private scholars have increasingly investigated and thought about the political aspects of science in terms of national and international policy. The lineaments of these inquiries have been variously sketched out by participants, observers, and participant-observers in the formation of science policy, as is attested by the comprehensive work of the head of the Science Policy Division of the Organization for Economic Cooperation and Development [OECD], Jean-Jacques Salomon [1968, 1973]; the sage among today's American advisers on science policy, Harvey Brooks [1968]; the theoretical sociologist and founder-editor of the international journal, *Minerva*, Edward A. Shils [1966]; with a list of all but the most recent

publications in the field amassed in the two-volume bibliography by
Lynton K. Caldwell [1968–69]. In turn, the state of the art in the polit-
ical sociology of science has been variously set forth and assessed by
Blume [1974], Blissett [1972], Haberer [1969], Ravetz [1971], Rose and
Rose [1969], Schooler [1971], and not a few others. But now, to return
to the more or less chronological account.)

Emergence of a Problematics

The few sociologists at work in the nascent field from the 1930s to
the 1950s centered their attention principally on the problems of linkages between the development of science and the environing society
and economy, with some attention to the value-context and other cultural contexts of science (such as religious belief-systems, the idea of
progress, etc.). There is little doubt, I believe, that this focus had its
ultimate origins in Marx and its later origins in Emile Durkheim and
Max Weber. (After all, it was Marx who had written scornfully about
those who treat the history of science as though it had fallen from the
skies.)

The evolving problematics of the evolving field was not without a
certain interest, but there were few scholars engaged in actual investigation. That this was the case in the various European communities of
sociologists is abundantly indicated in the chapters of this book; the
extent to which it was also the case in the United States can be illustrated, if not gauged, by the paucity of work on the particular problems identified in my own work during the 1930s:

—How did the institutionalization of science as a field of activity develop in seventeenth-century England in competition with other
fields of occupational interest?

—As exemplified in the same historical case-study, what are the modes
of interaction between science and other cultural and institutional
domains, such as the apparently contrasting ones of religion and
economy?

—What are the direct and indirect modes of linkage between science
and technology in this early modern period of their development?

—What direct and indirect influences, if any, did military and economic interests of the time have upon the selection of scientific problems for investigation?

In short, the substantive problems defined as fundamental focused on the interaction between aspects of cognitive developments in science and aspects of the environing social and cultural structure.

A Theoretical Gap

Since the usefulness of oral history resides in its providing fugitive materials otherwise lost to view, I report my own experience with an early transition in the theoretical sociology of science. (I rather suspect that this experience had its counterparts in the experience of others at the time.) With far less insight into what was developing in the field than hindsight now allows me to conclude was actually developing, I turned my attention toward the end of the 1930s, more intensively than ever before, to the sociology of knowledge. By 1945, I felt myself ready to examine the cognitive state of the field. The resulting conspectus was described as a "paradigm for the sociology of knowledge"—not, however, in what would become the Kuhnian senses of the word "paradigm"—designed to identify basic concepts, theoretical presuppositions and, above all, its problematics.

At the core of the paradigm was a focus on the interactions between the social structure and the cognitive structure of knowledge generally and of scientific knowledge as a specific, major case in point. The paradigm claimed to identify and to assess the major modes of thinking about the social and cultural bases of knowledge (ranging from such bases as "power structure" and "social class" to such social processes as "competition and conflict"). It attempted also to identify the problematic aspects of cognitive structure that would have to be systematically examined for the sociology of knowledge to develop a substantial basis in systematic inquiry. To use the language of that paradigm (Merton, [1945] 1973: 12–13), empirical inquiry would have to deal with such cognitive aspects as the "selection of problems (foci of attention), level of abstraction, presuppositions (what was taken as data and what as problematical), conceptual content, models of verification, objectives of intellectual activity" and, as though this ambitiously differentiated program of research were not enough, the list concludes with the all-encompassing "and so on."

Having compared the ambitious requirements of the paradigm with the work actually being done, it dawned on me that the sociology of knowledge—as well as that of the narrower field, the sociology of science—*was being severely impeded by the absence of a conceptual framework for thinking about the social and cultural structure of science itself.*

No matter how the environing culture and society affect the development of scientific knowledge and, to take the more familiar problem, no matter how scientific knowledge ultimately affects culture and society, these influences are mediated by the changing institutional and organizational structure of science itself. In order to investigate the character of those reciprocal influences between science and society and how they came about, it was therefore essential to enlarge my earlier effort to find a methodical way of thinking about science as institutionalized ethos (its normative aspect) and science as social organization (its patterns of interaction among scientists). Only then, would there be an adequate basis for instituting and investigating new problems of social and cognitive interactions in science.

As Nico Stehr has suggested to me, such a theoretically and empirically grounded formulation of the values, norms, and institutionalized arrangements internal to science becomes all the more important in light of the exponential growth of science since at least the seventeenth century. That growth provided for large-scale social structures mediating between science and society that to some extent allow science to become cognitively insulated from society. These cognitive and social structures provided contexts in which the development of scientific knowledge could become somewhat less dependent upon extra-scientific ideas. It then becomes a critical question, long deserving the thorough investigation it is only now beginning to receive (for example, in the work of Elkana and Holton), of the extent and modalities of interaction between scientific knowledge and other forms of belief, opinion, images of knowledge, and themata. There is reason to suppose, from the perspective set forth here, that the extent and kinds of such cognitive interactions would greatly vary among differing socio-historical contexts and at differing phases in the development of science. Along with such historical processes making for the relative autonomy of science is the correlative outcome that the large-scale organization of science brings with it a greatly enlarged dependence upon society for the resources needed to advance scientific knowledge. (For a methodical analysis of the interaction between social and intellectual influences "internal" and "external" to the institution of science, see Stephen Cole, 1965.)

It was along such lines that, during the later 1940s and intermittently in the next decade, I continued my work on problems of the normative structure of science and turned to processes involved in its social organization. Attention was first centered on the process of social and cognitive competition in what Michael Polanyi (1951, 1958; Shils, [1954] 1972) called "the scientific community." Starting in the middle 1950s, this plan of work led to further inquiry into patterns of competition among scientists, the reward structure of science as related to the assessed significance of contributions to scientific knowledge and, most recently, to inquiry into the institutionalized processes of such cognitive assessment (as exemplified by refereeing). (For a more detailed reading of these developments, see Storer, 1966, 1973; Hagstrom, 1965; Cole and Zuckerman, 1975; and for recent work on competition in science, see Hagstrom, 1974; Mulkay, 1972; Gaston, 1971, 1973; Cole and Cole, 1973.)

As we have seen, the sociology of science was gathering force as an identifiable specialty in the 1960s. It was just about then that there appeared a major new impetus to sociological interest in the problem of interaction between social and cognitive structures in science. That impetus came from ideas being advanced by Thomas S. Kuhn and Karl Popper in the collateral field of the philosophy of science, itself a discipline in course of transformation. As I shall try to indicate later in this essay, the intricate interaction between the sociology of science and the philosophy of science has left its indelible mark on both disciplines.

From such sources both endogenous and exogenous, there has lately developed in the sociology of science the growing concentration of sociological research on the emergence and operation of scientific specialties to which I referred at the outset of this essay. That work exemplifies as fully as any other current work the feasibility of empirically investigating the interplay between social formations of scientists and cognitive developments in a field of science. Significantly enough, this is a problem-set that has become part of the international research agenda, engaging the interest of sociologists of science in most countries having substantial programs of research in progress. This may be the prelude to diverse programs of empirical investigation, in place of continued energetic debate, promissory notes and pronouncements, of other patterns of interaction between social and cognitive structures in science.[11]

THE TRANSFER OF RESEARCH PROCEDURES

The Jourdainian Case of Content Analysis

Substantive problems such as these required the finding or devising of appropriate methods of investigation. For example, shifts in the foci of cognitive interest among the working scientists of the time were estimated through quantitative analysis of the content of papers in the only scientific journal published in seventeenth-century England, the *Philosophical Transactions* of the Royal Society (Merton, [1938] 1970). In this case, I was adopting a research procedure which Harold Lasswell (1938; and Leites, [1949] 1965) would eventually designate as "content analysis," no more aware that *that* was what I was doing than Molière's Monsieur Jourdain had been aware, before the moment of epiphany, that he had actually been speaking prose all his life.

This instance of systematic "content analysis" being adapted to a particular purpose in the specialty is another case of self-exemplifying uniformities in the sociology of science. It exemplifies the basic process of transfer of research procedures from one scientific specialty to another. Little is known about the vectors of such transfers between more or less established specialties and emerging ones, but cognitive and organizational facilitators and inhibitors of interspecialty transfers of theories, models, and concepts, as well as of research procedures, are being investigated. (In the case of the discovery of sexual recombination in bacteria which laid the foundations for the new specialty of bacterial genetics, see Zuckerman, 1974; Lederberg and Zuckerman, 1977.)

A snippet of oral history may serve to illustrate the unprogrammed, almost inadvertent way in which, for me, the procedure of content analysis came to be transferred from other sociological specialties to the proto-specialty of the sociology of science. It was in 1929, during my second year as an undergraduate at Temple University in Philadelphia, that I first stumbled onto the procedure. Then still so undeveloped a research technique as to be unchristened, it was not even taught in courses on sociological method. But, as it happened, George Eaton Simpson, a young instructor at Temple and my first teacher of sociology, was then at work on his doctoral dissertation, *The Negro in the Philadelphia Press* (Simpson, 1936). Substantively, the dissertation could be located within the specialty of "race relations" or "minority groups." Procedurally, since the raw data were the contents of newspapers, it can be located but only anachronistically within the sociology of mass communications, for that field was yet to be established as a specialty. But Simpson could adopt from that field a procedure, greatly developed in Willey's impressive monograph, *The Country Newspaper* (1926), for methodically scanning the contents of newspapers. As a student-apprentice, I was allowed to do some of the routine work: classifying, counting, measuring, and statistically summarizing the references to Negroes (not "Blacks," which in those days was considered a demeaning epithet imposed by white racists) over a span of decades in Philadelphia newspapers. The purpose, of course, was to gauge changes in public images of Negroes and public attitudes toward them.

When, in 1933, I began work on my own doctoral dissertation, it might not have become evident to me that I could adapt the same procedure to the purpose of gauging shifts in foci of scientific interest. But a second apprenticeship provided the bridging experience that made it inevitable. At Harvard, Pitirim A. Sorokin was doing the research for his massive *Social and Cultural Dynamics* (1937). His ambivalent attitude toward statistics notwithstanding, he saw no alternative to their systematic use for identifying long-term changes in social and cultural phenomena. Once again, I was set to work to compile quantitative indicators through content analysis, this time, owing to my announced interest in the social aspects of scientific knowledge, in the fields of science, technology, and medicine rather than that of racial attitudes and images. Along with qualitatively examining historical fluctuations in theories of atomism, evolution, abiogenesis, and so forth, I compiled numerical indicators of scientific development based upon such standard sources as Darmstädter's *Handbuch zur Geschichte der Naturwissenschaften und der Technik* and Garrison's *In-*

troduction to the History of Medicine. At the same time, I was working on my own study of science in seventeenth-century England and it soon became self-evident that the technique could be utilized for the quantitative analysis of shifts in the foci of scientific interest as registered in the *Philosophical Transactions*. By then, the transfer of the procedure of content analysis from the emerging specialty of mass-communications research to the proto-specialty of the sociology of science had been fully effected in the United States.

On the European scene, as I learned in the course of further work on the dissertation, essentially the same procedure had been in equally sporadic use. But it had not come into use through the same route as in the United States. Rather, it was being employed chiefly by an occasional practicing scientist and avocational historian of science, with a few bibliographers and statisticians thrown in for good measure. A small sampling must serve. As early as 1917, there was the professor of zoology, Francis J. Cole, of the University College (now University) of Reading in England, collaborating with the Museum Curator of the University, Nelly B. Eales, in a path-extending article, "The History of Comparative Anatomy: A Statistical Analysis of the Literature" (Cole and Eales, 1917). Building upon the foundation they laid was the Sandar's Reader in Bibliography at Cambridge and sometime Librarian of the Patent Office, E. Wyndham Hulme, in his *Statistical Bibliography in Relation to the Growth of Modern Civilization* (Hulme, 1923), a work that did not fulfill the great promise in its title. Further statistical analyses of lists of discoveries, inventions, and patents continued to appear in the 1920s: for examples, Weinberg (1925, 1926) and Rainoff (1929). However, the established scholars in the then discernible field of the history of science generally did not take kindly to numerical indicators of scientific development. And the sociology of science had yet to acquire an institutional as well as cognitive identity of its own. In the absence of a specialized journal, the small numbers of papers devoted to the subject were scattered amongst a variety of journals with little overlapping readership: for example, *Science Progress, Journal of the Royal Statistical Society, Isis, Staatsvetenskaplig Tidskrift*, and *Revue générale des sciences*. Widely dispersed, the papers and monographs failed to converge into an intellectual tradition involving the continual use and development of quantitative content analysis as a research tool in the historical sociology of science.[12]

The Jourdainian Case of Prosopography

Much like the tool of content analysis of scientific papers, lists of discoveries, inventions, and patents provided data for the tool of statistical analysis of collective biography. When I began to investigate the substantive question of shifts in the occupational interests of the English elite during the course of the seventeenth century, I turned at once to the quantitative analysis of some six thousand biographies in the *Dictionary of National Biography*. Once again, it seems, I was emulating Monsieur Jourdain. This time, with a lag of thirty years or so. For it was not until 1970 that I discovered from a paper by the Princeton historian, Lawrence Stone (1971:50–57), that I had been utilizing the research art of "historical prosopography" and, it was said, contributing to its development. In Stone's words, "prosopography is the investigation of the common background characteristics of a group of actors in history by means of a collective study of their lives" (1971:46). And, of course, that *had* been the sort of thing I was driven to in an effort to gauge shifts in occupational interest among the English elite of the seventeenth century.

In adopting that procedure, however, I had evidently known of the truly pioneering efforts by Francis Galton ([1869] 1952, 1872, 1874), Alphonse de Candolle ([1872–73] 1885), as well as the later work along these lines by Alfred Odin (1895) and Havelock Ellis ([1895] 1904). They had obviously engaged in the quantitative analysis of biographies of scientists and of questionnaires elicited from them. For the inference that I had known of their long-neglected work, there is the best of evidence: my book makes extensive reference to them all (Merton, [1938] 1970:131–36).[13]

In a recent article that is bound to revive interest in Candolle's work, the sociologically-minded Soviet historian of science, Mikulinsky (1974) has emphasized the neglect of Candolle's pioneering book of a century ago. There were, as Mikulinsky notes, a few approving responses. In 1872, Darwin wrote an appreciative letter upon being sent the book by Candolle; in 1893, the German botanist, Engler, described the book as "'very interesting and remarkable,' but restricted himself to just one quotation from it" (Mikulinsky 1974:224); in 1911, Wilhelm Ostwald, having just published his *Grosse Männer*, had Candolle's book translated into German and wrote a favorable introduction to it, focused in his mythopoeic fashion only upon its implications for a "science about geniuses" rather than on its central method and substance; in 1939, the Russian K. A. Timiryazev noted briefly in an article for the encyclopedia *Granat* that Candolle's book "'presents a curious [N.B.–rkm] attempt at determining statistically the natural and social conditions which favour or handicap the development of talents in science'"; and even the recent entry on Candolle in the *Dictionary of Scientific Biography* (1971, 3:42, quoted by Mikulinsky, p. 224) exhausts its discussion of the matter by noting that "Besides his interest in politics, Candolle was passionately devoted to the history of science and in 1873 [or 1872–rkm] published a remarkable book, *Histoire des sciences et des savants depuis deux siècles*. The book displays both the naturalist's objectivity and the jurist's clarity.'" As we shall see, Karl Pearson (1914–30) deals extensively with Candolle's book in his monumental *Life, Letters and Labours of Francis Galton*, since it relates intimately to Galton's own work along parallel lines. But if we are to judge from Mikulinsky's summary of the century of relative neglect, only a doctoral dissertation written in the mid-1930s (Merton, 1938) when the still nascent sociology of science was struggling for survival, actually drew upon the substance and method of Candolle's work, rather than merely according it a few sentences of (sometimes misplaced) praise.

No doubt there were other studies in direct continuity with Candolle's quantitative analysis of scientists and science that do not appear in Mikulinsky's roundup. It is hard to believe, for example, that no French scholars or that, especially after the German translation of the book in 1911, no German scholars followed in Candolle's footsteps. But even so, it is evident that no intellectual tradition of quantitative analysis had become established.

Unidentified both cognitively and institutionally, the pathway to the method of collective biography of scientists that was being opened up in the latter nineteenth century could not be assigned to any special domain of knowledge. (Recall only Timiryazev's description of Candolle's book as "curious," a judgment that could appear as late as 1939.) Rather than becoming an established tradition, the quantitative procedure remained free-floating in the ample interstitial spaces between disciplines, there to be picked up by the occasional odd scientist or scholar who happened to become interested in that sort of thing. Only the very few making active use of the method, the pioneers them-selves, entered into active communication, unconfined by disciplinary boundaries or by national ones. It may be that rates of direct interac-tion across linguistic and national boundaries are, relative to the num-bers at work on a problem-area, temporally bimodal: a high rate of communication between a handful of workers in the very early days before the subject or method shows signs of crystallizing into a con-tinuous intellectual tradition and high also when a relatively small in-visible college has come into continuing operation but before the sub-ject or method has attracted large numbers of workers and has become incorporated into the major research programs of the discipline.

The English pioneer in the art of scientific prosopography, Gal-ton, and the Swiss pioneer Candolle, provide a case in point of such prematurity. Influenced by the Belgian master of human statistics, Adolphe Quetelet, Galton had published his *Hereditary Genius* in 1869. In it, he applied his statistical imagination to questions of nature and nurture in the formation of genius, just as he applied it to the many other subjects he turned his agile mind to, ranging from standardiza-tion of the theory and practice of fingerprinting as a means of identify-ing criminals to his unique arithmetical analysis of the "efficacy of prayer." In that book, Galton studied eminent *men* in every depart-ment of social and cultural life: poets, painters, authors, musicians, divines, judges, statesmen and, most relevantly for our purposes, men of science. From his statistically arrayed biographies and genealogies, Galton concluded broadly and most egregiously that, with some dif-ferences among spheres of activity, heredity largely accounted for genius or great talent while environment had somewhat more to do with the sphere in which the talent found expression.

Candolle's monographic study, *Histoire des sciences et des savants depuis deux siècles*, first appeared late in 1872 (though his publishers, after the fashion of that guild, shrewdly arranged for it to be dated 1873, thus making it thoroughly up-to-date and ensuring reiterative confusion among later bibliographers). In it Candolle contrasted his own focus on the "influences extérieures" affecting the development of science by acting upon the most eminent scientists with what he re-garded as Galton's mistaken emphasis on the *origins* of eminent scien-tists and with his misplaced interpretation in terms of heredity. In his recent paper, Mikulinsky (1974) has argued that it was Candolle, not Galton, who took the lead in adopting statistical methods to analyze the development of science. Our task is not to try to adjudicate this century-old dispute about priority. Rather, we see it as another sign of the convergence and mutual reinforcement of interest, in those days, in developing the emerging art of prosopography in the study of science as a social and cultural phenomenon. The detailed interchange is not without interest.

Beginning the personal interaction between them, Candolle sent Galton (as he had Charles Darwin) one of the first copies of his book. This initiated a five-year-long correspondence in which they wrangled more or less politely about their respective claims to priority and about their contrasting but, in the event, somewhat converging ideas about the interplay of heredity and environment in the formation of outstanding scientists. From that correspondence, it appears that Galton was led by 1874 to expand his chapter on scientists in his *Hereditary Genius* into a new book, *English Men of Science*, both as rebuttal and extension of Candolle's intervening work. Friendly disputes by letter embroidered with genuine, not merely courteous, expressions of mutual admiration flowered into repeated efforts to meet, but these somehow never came off.

What did emerge from the correspondence, however, was the strong and shared sense that it was important to have what would eventually be described as "indicators" of scientific eminence. A sign of Galton's resonance to the notion of such an indicator is found in his first letter (27 December 1872) to Candolle (Pearson, 1914–30, 2:135). He begins with a polite sentence acknowledging receipt of the book which he had "read and re-read with care and with great instruction" during the preceding fortnight and then, from all the pages of that large book, he seizes first upon the invention of a "science indicator" for favorable methodological comment:

> Allow me to congratulate you upon the happy idea of accepting [i.e. of treating statistically] the nominations of the French Academy and similar bodies as reliable diplomas of scientific eminence, and on thus obtaining a solid basis for your reasoning.

Galton then proceeds to devote the rest of his twelve-hundred-word letter to specifying, in friendly but unsparingly firm language, principally the misunderstandings of his own work, then doubtful speculations, and finally a "serious statistical error" that he had encountered in Candolle's book. He concludes by commending Candolle on the "great service you have done in writing it" and, in accord with the ethos of international science, promises "to do what I can to make it known, as it ought to be, in England" (Pearson, 1914–30, 2:136). As we shall see, Galton redeemed this promise in most unusual fashion, seeing to it that Candolle's academic inquiry should bear upon a moot science policy.

Whether the post-Christmas–post-New Year's season provided unusual leisure or whether intense interest in the subject and in Galton's provocative letter prompted swift reply or whether opportunity-and-motivation intersected to make for prompt reply, we cannot say. But, in any case, Candolle does reply within the week (2 janvier 1873). His letter, written in French (as were all the rest he wrote in the comfortably bilingual correspondence that ensued), ran to twice the length of Galton's. In it, he responds seriatim to every one of Galton's observations and criticisms. Among these responses, we pause here during this excursion to those early days in the developing art of scientific prosopography only to note his revealing paragraph on the use of academic nominations and affiliations as indicators of scientific eminence. It provides a wonderfully apt synopsis of the constraints of the social structure of authority and esteem and of a personal code of civility (in the apt French idiom, *politesse*) that kept him, for four decades, from pursuing the statistical analysis of affiliations with honorific societies in the domain of science.[14] Quietly announcing his longtime priority of conception in devising these indicators, Candolle incidentally reveals the patterned diffidence in those infinitely remote days of a young (French) man of science vis-à-vis his widely esteemed father and the other established elders of science:

> L'idée de consulter les nominations par les Académies m'est venue il y a 40 ans! J'avais prié un de mes amis de prendre au sécretariat de l'Institut les listes des Associés étrangers et Correspondants de 1750 en 1789. Les noms modernes sont aisés à trouver ailleurs. J'avais redigé en 1833 un mémoire sur ces listes de Paris et sur celles de la Société Royale. Si je ne l'ai pas publié alors c'est qu'il me semblait un peu présomptueux chez un jeune homme de mesurer ainsi la valeur de savants illustres, parmi lesquels se trouvait son père et quelques hommes distingués à côté de lui. Une fois moi-même sur certaines listes, il me répugnait d'en parler. Enfin, à 66 ans, après une série de travaux spéciaux propres à justifier ma position, le courage m'est venu et j'ai pensé

pouvoir m'élever au dessus des considérations personnelles de toute nature.

Some of us today can take comfort in this indication that emancipation of the spirit can begin at age sixty-six.

Galton's reply—we are now into May 1873—says no more about the use of affiliations with national academies as a valuable indicator. But it does testify that, even a century ago, documented ideas in what amounts to the historical sociology of science could be drawn upon to affect the formation of public policy governing scientific education. Galton writes Candolle (Pearson 1913–30, 2:139):

> Your work has been read by many of my scientific friends here, and a passage in it prompted one of the most effective parts of by far the most effective speech,—that of Dr. Lyon Playfair,—in the recent Parliamentary debate upon Irish University Education. The debate, as perhaps you may have seen, was one of extreme importance to the future of science in Ireland, and the question was how far it should be submitted to or emancipated from Catholic control. Lyon Playfair quoted the effect of Calvinism in Geneva on science, during the time of its ascendancy in wholly suppressing it, which was shown by the immediate start by science as soon as the strict dogmatic influence began to wane.[15] He spoke with excellent effect and success, and I know that he derived at least that part of his argument from you, because I had myself directed his attention to your work previously as having a direct bearing on his then proposed speech.

The Galton-Candolle modes of quantitative analysis proceeded quite independently of parallel developments in the use of collective biography principally for the study of ancient history, and specifically the history of Rome. It is this strand of more or less statistical analysis that came to be known as "prosopography" while the other strand was innocently developing without any special tag to identify it. The term, and its associated concept of historical method, has recently come to the attention of a greater variety of modern historians and sociologists chiefly as a result, in the United States, of the informative paper by Lawrence Stone (1974) to which I have referred as my ticket of entry into knowledge about rather than acquaintance with prosopography and, in Europe, chiefly as a result of the papers by Nicolet (1970) and

Chastagnol (1970) in an issue of *Annales: Économies, Sociétés, Civilisations* which was partly devoted to *"Prosopographie et histoire sociale"* and *"La prosopographie, méthode de recherche."*

The useful word "prosopography" has been retrieved from the eighteenth century (Nicolet, 1970:1210, *n.* 3) in much the same fashion as we have seen Derek Price retrieving and extending the useful term "invisible college" from the seventeenth. That is to say, prosopography can be traced back to 1743 but the methods of inquiry associated with it, cannot. These have evolved slowly, becoming clearly identifiable, according to Stone (1971:48–57) only in the late 1920s and 1930s. Prosopography has virtually become a new methodological specialty in history, its methods adopted by large numbers of historians at work on just about every time and place for which the requisite source documents can be, however laboriously, assembled.

There is something of a cognitive affinity between the method of prosopography principally used by historians and the method of multivariate analysis of social survey data long employed and developed by sociologists. Indeed, Stone says as much in characterizing prosopography and its method.

> Prosopography is the investigation of the common background characteristics of a group of actors in history by means of a collective study of their lives. The method employed is to establish a universe to be studied, and then to ask a set of uniform questions—about birth and death, marriage and family, social origins and inherited economic position, place of residence, education, amount and source of personal wealth, occupation, religion, experience of office, and so on. The various types of information about the individuals in the universe are then juxtaposed and combined, and are examined for significant variables. (Stone 1970:46, cf. p. 57)

As the statistician William Kruskal reiteratively and usefully reminds us, retrospective studies of the kind often caught up in prosopography are misleading when they abstract common characteristics from an aggregate of units—eminent scientists, for example—without systematically comparing these with characteristics of complementary aggregates—anything but eminent scientists, for example. This warning that the logic of the control group must be exercised in prosopographic studies is no less in point for its being ancient in conception. One periodically needs to recall from one's student days the pertinence of the story told by Diogenes Laertius about Diogenes the Cynic who, when shown the votive tablets suspected by sailors who had escaped shipwreck "because they had made their vows," inquired "Where are the portraits of those who perished in spite of their vows?" This is a logic built into multivariate analysis in present-day sociological surveys.

The isomorphism between historical prosopography and sociological surveys was recognized, in effect if not in so many words, by Francis Galton and others who used the same kinds of analysis for both kinds of data. In his *English Men of Science*, for example, Galton collected statistical arrays of data from documentary and published sources and also generated new data of his own by use of questionnaires addressed to scientists. The enormous *social and cognitive distances in the academic organization of the disciplines* that separate a discipline such as ancient history from one such as sociology have long impeded the joint recognition of isomorphism in some of their methods of inquiry and have blocked reciprocally useful exchange. The journeyman sociologist, typically focused on his own studies of contemporary public opinion or class structure or family organization, as the case may be, would scarcely turn to any of the numerous volumes on the shelves of his university library bearing such titles as *Prosopographia Imperii Romani* (1893) or even the very recent *Prosopography of the Later Roman Empire: Volume 1 AD 260–395* (1971). It is less difficult, in these days of quantitative history and cliometry, to conceive of an ancient historian approaching his colleagues in sociology to be briefed on recently developed techniques of multivariate analysis that might be applied to his own prosopographic studies.

There is growing evidence, however, that the two strands in the developing tradition of prosopography are becoming intertwined in the historical sociology of science. An outstanding use of the prosopographical method in that field from the 1930s to the recent past is probably the "remarkable study," as I continue to describe it, by Nicholas Hans (1951). That monograph is based upon statistical analysis of the social origins, education, and subsequent careers of some 3,500 individuals (including 680 scientists) forming the British intellectual elite, principally during the eighteenth century, the data having been systematically assembled from what then seemed, for all its limitations, a seemingly inexhaustible mine of materials for historical sociology, the *Dictionary of National Biography*.

We have had to wait another quarter-century for a thoroughgoing analysis of prosopography as a "coherent and well-developed technique" suitable for the study of the historical development of science. In their paper, emblematically and programmatically entitled "Prosopography as a Research Tool in History of Science: The British Scientific Community 1700–1900," Steven Shapin and Arnold Thackray (1974) also provide a detailed "critical assessment of the kinds of biographical sources available" for the study of that scientific community. To my regret at losing an old prosopographical friend, Shapin and Thackray compellingly assert that the *DNB* will no longer do, at least as the exclusive source for collecting biographical information for those British individuals, over the centuries until our own, "who *published* science." They recognize the great value of that venerable and venerated compilation, but see a new thrust beyond its capabilities.

Shapin and Thackray document this thrust by providing a critical assessment of the various other kinds of prosopographical sources available for the study of the British scientific community in the eighteenth and nineteenth centuries. After noting that neither the *DNB* nor the *DSB* are sufficient published sources for collective biography in science, they go on to direct our attention to ancillary materials that extend and deepen those biographical dictionaries as indispensable sources. Beyond the published materials, of course, are the archival materials, much of these still to be plumbed.

With these beginnings of a fresh phase in the historical sociology of science, it seems safe to assume that the earlier discontinuities in the use of the prosopographical method will be followed by distinct continuity of inquiry, now that the newer generation of sociologically oriented historians of science have identified and partly realized the potentialities of the method. Clearly, what's past in prosopographical analysis is only prologue.

What is more, that past could have witnessed somewhat more advance had not certain disciplinary traditions about allowable procedures in the history of science put a stop to a planned merging of the historical and sociological prosopography of science. This episode of unfulfillment represents another self-exemplifying case in the sociology of science, this being one in which commitment to the central tradition in a particular discipline inhibits cognitive interplay with a proto-specialty just emerging in another discipline. And since the unfulfilled research program could have provided a prosopographic archive for inter-nation comparisons of scientific development over the years, the episode distinctly relates to one of the principal purposes of this volume.

Sociological and Historical Prosopography of Science: A Near Miss

Again, a bit of oral history must serve to describe an instructive episode in the recent historical sociology of science that never found publicly visible expression. The data are distributed in the files of the chief participants and in their joint and several memories. Without engaging in extensive documentary research and the associated interviews required for a tight-knit inquiry in oral history, I shall draw upon documents in hand and my own inevitably selective memory, occasionally aided by the humbling correctives of external evidence. And as further warning against the possibility that my memory *is* selective, I should report, at the outset, that I have often reflected upon (not, of course, brooded over!) this episode as one that might have afforded a unique opportunity to advance the historical sociology of science, one that was lost for sociologically identifiable reasons.

In short, the case we are about to examine in inordinately great detail (since the fugitive materials will otherwise be lost altogether) holds some intrinsic interest as a moment in the history of the historiography of science and also provides another self-exemplifying instance in the sociology of science. It exhibits the kind of discontinuity in the development of a discipline that we know as a "near-miss."

The case concerns the beginnings of the *Dictionary of Scientific Biography (DSB)*. Its first volume appearing in 1970 and its fourteenth (from Verrill to Zwelfer) in 1976, this long-needed and, in the event, brilliantly achieved resource for historians and sociologists of science is composed of nearly five thousand biographies of scientists from ancient times to the almost immediate present. (There are, by design, no articles on living scientists.)

The idea for what would eventuate as the *DSB* came to one of the Charles Scribners who have long presided over the distinguished publishing house bearing the family name. It is not surprising that this should have been so. After all, Charles Scribner's Sons had published, from 1928 to 1936, the twenty volumes of the *Dictionary of American Biography (DAB)* as well as the occasional supplementary volumes. The Charles Scribner who was running things in the 1960s (and still is) conceived of a comparable publication devoted entirely to the biography of scientists and perceived the *DAB* as a possible prototype.

The distinctly national *DAB* had distinctly multinational origins. As its editor made plain, plans for the *DAB* had greatly benefited from "studies of the great repertories of national biography published or in progress in other lands" (*Dictionary of American Biography* 1957, 1:viii). But above all other predecessors, the *DAB* was indebted in concept and design to "the British *Dictionary of National Biography* [*DNB*] (1885–1900) [which] aroused in the minds of many Americans a desire that their own country should have a biographical dictionary of similar fullness and if possible of similar quality, prepared with an amount of scholarly labor not to be expected in the case of any book of reference whose total costs must not exceed the expected revenue from sales" (*DAB* 1957, 1:vii). The essential lineage thus runs from *DNB* to *DAB* to *DSB*.

Just as the family tradition in publishing led Scribner to the idea of a biographical dictionary of scientists, so the family tradition in education led him to a scholar who might help convert that idea into reality. Our Charles Scribner was a loyal and active alumnus of Princeton University, like all the scions of the publishing house since the founding Charles Scribner was graduated in 1840 from what was then known as the College of New Jersey. (Only in 1896 did Princeton University become so designated.) Among the many indicators of this sustained academic loyalty, consider only this one: the Charles Scribner who presided over the publishing house for half a century (1879–1928) saw to it that the Princeton University Press should be elegantly housed just as his grandson (our man) in his turn agreed to serve as president of the Press. Constraints of family tradition and enduring academic relationships thus made it probable that, in looking for expert appraisal of his idea, Charles Scribner would turn to Princeton and, more specifically, to the founder of its Program in the History and Philosophy of Science, Charles C. Gillispie.

Gillispie was at once taken with the idea. He was confirmed in his opinion of its merit by fellow historians of science, at the outset principally Marshall Clagett, Thomas S. Kuhn, and Henry Guerlac. It was abundantly evident that, unlike the various national collections of biographies, a scholarly dictionary of scientists' biographies would have to be ecumenical rather than nationally parochial in scope.

In due course, it was decided to bring the idea to the attention of the American Council of Learned Societies (ACLS). Here again, one can detect the constraints of traditional precedent, established relationships, and, it should be added, reasonable judgment. For it had been the ACLS that, half a century before, had initiated and then supervised the making of the *Dictionary of American Biography* in happy collaboration with Charles Scribner's Sons as publishers. Indeed, it was symbolically apt that the historian Frederick J. Turner should have proposed having the Council undertake preparation of "a cyclopedia of American biography" at its first meeting, in 1920 (*DAB*, 1957, 1:vii).

It was nothing strange, therefore, that the ACLS should agree to sponsor the new *Dictionary of Scientific Biography*, an enterprise also endorsed by the (U.S.) History of Science Society, and that the ACLS should designate as its Editor in Chief, the scholar who had done much to develop the concept of the work, Charles C. Gillispie. Advising him was a board of nine distinguished historians of science who served as associate editors and a liaison committee with the ACLS composed of eight others.

As with other massive scholarly enterprises of this kind, it was of course essential that the Editor in Chief be broad-gauged in his scholarly competence, gifted with powers of reasonably detached judgment and able to mediate among the inevitably conflicting opinions about the thousand-and-one decisions that would have to be made. It would also be helpful for him to be much respected by his peers for his own scholarship. And so it was. (Or, to put it with appropriate scholarly caution, so it seemed to me then, as in retrospect it does now.)

From the beginning of his scholarly career to the time of his appointment as Editor in Chief, Gillispie had given, first promise, then evidence, of distinguished scholarship in the institutionally still youthful discipline of the history of science. (After all, at the time he became editor, the History of Science Society had just celebrated its forty-first birthday.) He had taken a good undergraduate degree at one of the outstanding colleges of liberal arts (Wesleyan University), had had a year of graduate work at the demanding Massachusetts Institute of Technology, and had taken his Ph.D. degree in the Harvard department of history.

From his stint as tutor and teaching Fellow at Harvard, Gillispie, not yet thirty, accepted an instructorship in history at Princeton and some years later, gingerly tried his hand at giving a course in the history of science. Evidently, the experiment prospered. Gillispie rose through the academic ranks at Princeton at a rate considered rapid by his age-cohort (though at tortoise speed when gauged by expectations generated since in the academic marketplace). By his early forties he was a full professor, and by his later forties, held a named chair of European history (to be followed, most recently, by an even more elevated chair). His scholarly publications included wide-ranging volumes such as *Genesis and Geology* (1951) and *The Edge of Objectivity: An Essay in the History of Scientific Ideas* (1960), which, though securely grounded in the history of science narrowly construed, were tinged with philosophical themes, together with other monographic publications that amply testified to his technical competence as gauged by the most demanding requirements of his guild. His scholarship and good judgment were institutionally recognized by his becoming president of the History of Science Society while still in his forties and his acumen in judging talent in the field by his having brought Thomas S. Kuhn to Princeton, soon after the appearance of *The Structure of Scientific Revolutions*.

This sociological pen portrait of status-sequences in the career of the chief editor of the *DSB* may be enough to indicate' grounds, beyond his authority of office, for assuming that his would be the last word on policies governing that scholarly enterprise even when his views clashed with those of a majority of his colleagues. That portrait may also help to explain how it was that a scholar like Gillispie, located at the center of his discipline but himself venturing into interpretative essays on the character of scientific thought, would be sufficiently confident of his powers of judgment to be willing to move toward its established cognitive periphery, and beyond. If he had been ready to traffic with philosophical problems and ideas in the 1950s, when it was scarcely typical for historians of science to do so, then he might be ready to amplify historical ideas and methods with sociological ones, even at a time when the cognitive and institutional identities of the sociology of science were still blurred and when the standing of that obscurely perceived discipline among historians of science was, shall we say, still insecure.

The evidence was soon forthcoming. Soon after he had been designated chairman of the editorial board to plan the *DSB*, Gillispie wrote to say that the plan called for a board of consulting editors—chiefly historians of science, of course, but including a few scholars and scientists from related fields. He then went on to describe his judgment that

> What we need is guidance in order that we may compile a work which will be of the *maximum use to what the sociology of science will come to be*. I need not rehearse the degree to which I share your views on the sociology of science as an imperative desideratum. Our own articles will not pretend to be sociology. Indeed, we conceive their primary job to be scientific—giving an accurate narrative of the development of the actual work of a Newton or a Lavoisier or whomever. At the same time, *I hope they will contain the items of information which sociologists of science will wish to have, or at least will guide them to it.*
>
> . . . There is one immediate thing I should like to ask: that you give your criticism of the enclosed draft of instructions to contributors. . . . I should be glad for your special attention to page 3, where we set down the items of personal information we want to include in every article. What else should we ask for? How else should we ask for it?—so that *our DSB would give you the kind of information you wish you had had in the DNB, or that future sociologists will seek in our work*. (Gillispie to Merton, 27 April 1965; italics inserted)

There could scarcely have been a more forthcoming invitation to interdisciplinary collaboration—and it was accepted at once. Gillispie had himself put me in mind of that experience in the 1930s when I was trying to work up a quantitative analysis of the magnificent *DNB* (*Dictionary of National Biography*). The principal obstacles to a full-fledged analysis had been the variability in the kinds of information included in the biographies. Short biographies, usually indicating the editors' judgments that their subjects were of comparatively little historical importance, were perforce thin and uninformative, often including little more than a few bare facts of existence, from birth to death. Even the long, detailed biographies did not always provide comparable (and needed) data. All this introduced great constraints, as Gillispie evidently realized, on the quantitative analysis of aggregates of biographies (what we now know as prosopography). But of course nothing could be done to remedy those defects for the *DNB*; no individual or small group of scholars could be counted on to dig up the vast amount of supplementary information required for systematic quantitative analysis.

But here, in the forthcoming *Dictionary of Scientific Biography*, was a wholly new opportunity to arrange for abundant comparable data needed for the historical sociology of science on a scale inconceivable before. Unlike the *DNB* which dealt with the elite in every department of culture and social life, the *DSB* would deal exclusively with scientists (the category being broadly construed), thus producing a deeper and wider array of pertinent biographical data than ever before available. And in contrast to the national boundaries adopted by the *DNB*, confined to English, Irish, Scottish, and Welsh elites, the *DSB* would attempt to be truly universalistic, including scientists from every culture and era.

Beyond that, the new technology of computers introduced wholly new possibilities. Obviously, the printed volumes of the *DSB* could not misuse the scarce space available by printing accounts of relatively inconsequential contributors to the development of science in as full detail as accounts of the most significant ones. And, of course, there was always the limiting condition of the amount of biographical information available about scientists in various times and of differing magnitudes of accomplishment. But the new technology of the computer coupled to the old concept of the social survey, with its comparability of data through use of settled-upon categories of data, could reduce these limitations to the irreducible minimum.

A schedule of standardized information could be developed by collaboration between historians and sociologists of science. The schedule for each scientist would be filled out, so far as possible, by the contributors to the *DSB* while they were engaged in collecting data for their biographical articles. Within the limits of available information, precisely the same kinds of data for each scientist would be recorded on computer tape, even though, in many instances, exigencies of space would require much of this information to be omitted from the *printed* volumes. Periodically, as the data were assembled for successive volumes of the *DSB* and the extended version of the sociological schedule was coded onto tape, trial quantitative analyses of the materials in hand could be conducted. Unanticipated flaws and gaps in the data could thus be detected in process and, while a standardized core of information would be retained for all biographies, appropriate changes could be periodically introduced to provide for increasingly adequate information about successive subsamples. In the end, along with the completion of the published *Dictionary of Scientific Biography*, there would emerge a computerized archive of biographical information ready for (prosopographical) analysis of a scale and depth never before achievable.

This, then, was the gist of the idea for creating an archive in the historical sociology of science to complement the forthcoming volumes in the history of science. It would translate into effect what had been only the barely expressed hope of a decade before.[16] Professor Gillispie's enthusiasm for the idea rivaled my own. He encouraged me to proceed with the preparation of a detailed schedule on an amplified scale specifying the information to be supplied by contributors to the *DSB* for the sociological archive if not necessarily for their own articles.

Accordingly, much of the academic year (1965–66) in the Columbia University graduate seminar in the sociology of science,[17] with Harriet Zuckerman as Research Associate and myself as instructor, was given over to the preparation, development, and trial runs of the schedule of sociologically relevant information. In the process, we discovered a large number of previously unconsidered difficulties that arise in attempting to provide comparable categories of information about scientists and proto-scientists over the millennia and in different cultures. Most of the difficulties, it turned out, could be resolved.

During the year's work, it also turned out, and not at all surprisingly for sociologists of science who have investigated the phenomenon of the independent multiple occurrence of the same idea, that others in the international community of historians of science were beginning to think along the same lines. Altogether unsurprisingly, in view of his long-standing interest in the quantitative study of science, one of these was Derek J. de Solla Price, together with his doctoral student and onetime collaborator, Donald deB. Beaver (Price and Beaver, 1966). As he neared completion of his Yale dissertation, "The American Scientific Community, 1800–1860: An Historical and Statistical Study," Beaver was led to inquire of Gillispie about possible access to the forthcoming *DSB* data for statistical analysis. Upon being informed that the needed propaedeutic work was under way, Beaver followed Gillispie's suggestion to meet with our seminar group and in April 1966 reported his own experience with problems in the statistical use of biographical data.

In the meantime, Gillispie's interest had taken deeper root, his initiatives outrunning the development of our work. Toward the end of the year (1965), he was prepared to present the idea to the History of Science Society, in his twin capacity as president of the Society (which had endorsed the *DSB*) and as Editor in Chief of the *DSB*.

> If you have a firm enough sense of feasibility, or a draft of any of the schedules, I should be awfully glad to take the whole prospect up in an informal way before the council of the Society. It is even possible, if we feel sure enough, that I might take the occasion of the annual dinner to devote the remarks I have to make as president to our mutual concerns. (Gillispie to Merton, 30 November 1965)

There could be no better indicator of the depth of Gillispie's commitment to the notion of a statistical archive for (what we now know as) prosopographical analysis. It was, he knew, a risky decision. Most historians of science at the time were not inclined to take kindly to the quantitative study of any aspect of their subject (nor, perhaps, are they now). They were not apt to be kindly disposed toward having the president of their learned Society advocate a research program of that kind. As it happened, the data-schedules were not ready, and the risky occasion for unveiling the idea had to be passed over.

The provisional schedules of information were drafted by March 1966 and made available to Gillespie. Soon afterward, he met with the committee of the American Council of Learned Societies (which, it will be remembered, was the sponsor of *DSB*) charged to oversee the enterprise. The committee was at best ambivalent, their "reactions drastically divided between enthusiasm and hostility." Understandably, Gillispie could not put the entire undertaking at risk in order to introduce an innovation that he (and only a few of his colleagues) found promising.

> I confess to feeling daunted by the experience of the resistance of which, it is true, you did forewarn me last summer. . . . Neither Tom Kuhn nor I are persuaded by the actual content of the criticisms, reservations, and objections advanced. What does deter

me is the fear that [these] . . . may be representative of the reception we would receive in the profession at large. I dare not jeopardize the DSB itself, to which of course I have prior commitments. I have a very real fear that I will jeopardize this if I push ahead without regard to what I have learned about one extreme in the range of response likely to be encountered. That the other extreme is enthusiastic does not really reassure me. This only emphasizes the divisiveness of the thing as a whole. (Gillispie to Merton, 15 April 1966)

The idea was evidently premature. It was not yet feasible to develop a full-scale computerized data bank as an integral part of the *DSB*. There followed a new round of discussion with Gillispie and consideration of an alternative plan in which the statistical archive would be based upon the actual (far from wholly standardized) content of the articles but without requesting contributors to the *DSB* to do the additional work required to ferret out information beyond that to be included in the printed articles. The *DSB* and the archive would develop along parallel lines rather than being interdigitated.

For a time, it appeared that the alternative plan might work out. The prospects seemed even brighter when, just a month after the session with the ACLS committee, Gillispie received a letter of inquiry from R. M. MacLeod, of the Unit for the Study of Science Policy at the University of Sussex. He reported having learned of the pending *DSB* from Dr. Robert Young at Cambridge and expressed an interest in the statistics of science during the nineteenth century. Like Derek Price and Donald Beaver, and like Harriet Zuckerman and myself, the Sussex Unit (with its director, Christopher Freeman, as the moving spirit, and its chairman, Asa Briggs, as sympathetic endorser) arrived at the idea of computerizing the *DSB* data for statistical analysis of the development of science. But after several months of correspondence, this possibility too came to nothing.

By May of 1967, Gillispie stoically summed up the stillborn idea in a memorandum addressed to the Board of Editorial Consultants to the *DSB*:

At one time we were considering the possibility of cooperation with Robert Merton's group in the sociology of science. I then hoped that we might be able to accompany the DSB with the constitution of a computerized information bank about the social and political aspects of the environment of science, drawing the requisite information from our biographers. Professor Merton and his group did draw up the draft of a questionnaire which might have been applied to this purpose. Discussing that project with colleagues, and particularly with the members of the ACLS committee, we were cautioned by colleagues whose judgment we respect, that it might jeopardize the realization of the DSB itself to undertake an additional project of such large dimensions and of so novel a sort. We have not thought it wise to press ahead in the face of that criticism. At the very least it seems prudent to concentrate for the time being on the production of our first volume. If it thereupon were feasible to collaborate with an independent but associated project in the sociology of science, I should be very glad. But this does not now form an active part of our planning.[18]

This case of a near-miss in the development of the historical sociology of science exemplifies two connected patterns of behavior that have been investigated over the years in the discipline itself.

1) It exemplifies the ways in which the social composition, cognitive orientation, and technological base of the field can make for the multiple independent appearance of the same idea (as with the Columbia group, the Yale group, and the Sussex group). These provided the contexts for a convergence of ideas that should not be taken as uniformly transparent. After all, when Leslie Stephen edited the first volumes of the *Dictionary of National Biography* in 1885 and Sidney Lee completed editing the final volumes in 1902–3, it was not self-evident that provision should be made for a thoroughgoing statistical analysis of its contents (although the editors did manage to put together some informative descriptive statistics on numbers of articles and the like). But given the social, cognitive, and technological prerequisites for hitting upon the idea of a data bank for the *DSB* in its time, the idea was bound to occur to a variety of people. A sufficient number of historically minded sociologists of science was by then on hand; a once discontinuous practice of quantitative analysis of collective biography had crystallized into a continuing tradition; and the technology of the computer allowed the realization of an otherwise unattainable idea.

2)   The case also exemplifies, in ways made familiar by Barber (1961), Stern (1941), and others (Merton, 1973:372 ff.), the complexities of resistance to new ideas in the community of scholars and scientists. To a degree, it represents an a fortiori instance of such resistance (which, in this accounting, is not a term of disparagement). For as we have seen in some detail, Professor Gillispie, the chief advocate of the idea among the historians of science, was admirably situated in the social structure of the discipline to have his strongly held judgments heard and given special weight. Central as he was to the discipline, endowed with the prime responsibility for day-to-day direction of the enterprise, esteemed for his scholarly judgment, and accepted by his advisory groups as *primus inter pares*, Professor Gillispie nevertheless could not persuade enough of his colleagues of the utility of the proposed archive and of the kinds of scholarly investigation it would make possible.

In retrospect, it seems to me that the conception was chancier than I was then prepared to believe. No doubt, many contributors would have balked at doing the hard work to dig up obscure data which limitations of space would not allow them to record in print. Perhaps, the anonymity of these contributions to the archive would have sapped motivation as well. Perhaps, more than I realized, historians of science would look askance at some of the wide array of questions incorporated in the schedule, see small point in them or find them altogether absurd from the perspective of their own specialized competence, and refuse to take any further part in the *DSB* itself, let alone in contributing to the suspect archive. Perhaps, too, it only now crosses one's mind, since few potential contributors to the *DSB* were themselves ancient historians familiar with the principles and tactics of prosopography, the discipline-encouraged doubts about quantifying any aspect of the history of science might have eroded their confidence in the larger enterprise. And so through a continuing list of possible obstacles, secondary effects and unanticipated consequences that might have put in question not only the computerized archive of prosopography but the parent *DSB* itself.

Yet, in reviewing the twin sources of prosopographical studies in the historical sociology of science today, I am saddened by what still appears to have been a missed opportunity. I rather suspect that Professor Gillispie is too. I hope that the scholars who put their controlling stamp of disapproval upon the idea would now prefer, as occasionally is the case with other august courts of final judgment, to reverse their earlier decision.

SPECIALTY-SPECIFIC RESEARCH PROCEDURES

The method of qualitative and quantitative content analysis as well as the related research procedures of historical prosopography entered the evolving sociology of science principally through two routes. In large part, they were invented and developed in other disciplines—disciplines as distant in the academic scheme of things as ancient history and mass communications research—and then applied, modified, and extended to provide tools for the empirical investigation of substantive problems in the new specialty. But as introduced long ago by Galton and Candolle, for example, some of these procedures were institutionally and cognitively rootless (which is far from saying that they were without foundation), not having been rooted in any other discipline before being adopted by the sociology of science.

Lately research procedures have been developed that are specific to the discipline of the sociology of science. They are specialty-specific procedures in a double sense: first, in their being connected to certain distinctive aspects of the cognitive and social structures of scientific knowledge and second, in having been invented as part of that discipline or of having first been put to use in it.

Citation Analysis: The Garfield Input

These subject-specific research procedures relate to a basic aspect of the social structure of science. This was identified some time ago (Merton, [1942] 1973:273–75) as the distinctive or seemingly paradoxical circumstance that, in science, the more freely the scientist gives his intellectual property away, the more securely it becomes his property. Science is public not private knowledge. Only when he has published his ideas and findings has the scientist made his scientific *contribution* and only when he has thus made it part of the public domain of science can he truly lay claim to it as his. For his claim resides only in the recognition accorded his work by peers in the social system of science through reference to his work. In those rare cases where it is judged to be of major cognitive significance, recognition takes the lofty form of the commemorative eponym, as with the Copernican system, Boyle's law, Darwinian evolution, or Planck's constant. Since recognition of the worth of one's work by qualified peers is, in science, the basic form of reward (all other rewards deriving from it) and since it can only be widely accorded within the social system of science when the attributed work is widely known, this provides institutionalized incentive for the open publication, without direct financial reward, of scientific work. Since recognition is the basic coin of the scientific realm, and since the cognitive structure of science makes for independent multiple discoveries, this social and cognitive complex gives rise to the concern of scientists to get there first and to establish their self-validating claim to priority of discovery. As the complex became institutionalized in science, it made for the growth of public knowledge and the eclipse of private tendencies, still identifiable as late as the seventeenth century, toward secrecy and private knowledge. The institutionalized system of open-communication-and-correlative-reward became normatively operative in modern science, and it was this that was described as the element of "communism" (or, as others later preferred to call it, "communalism") in the normative structure of science.[19]

The distinctive anomalous character of intellectual property becoming fully established in the domain of science only by being openly given away (published) is linked with the normative requirement for scientists making use of that property to acknowledge (publish) the source, past or contemporaneous. As was noted:

> The communal character of science is further reflected in the recognition by scientists of their dependence upon a cultural heritage to which they lay no differential claim. Newton's remark—"If I have seen further it is by standing on the shoulders of giants"—expresses at once a sense of indebtedness to the common heritage and a recognition of the essentially cooperative and [selectively] cumulative quality of scientific achievement. (Merton, [1942] 1973:274–75)

In retrospect, we can summarize that substantive analysis of the social structure of science as observing

1)   that the institutionalized pressure for public diffusion of one's scientific work "is being reinforced by the institutional goal of advancing the boundaries of knowledge and by the incentive of recognition which is, of course, contingent upon publication" (p. 274);

2)   that there is the correlative obligation, within the institutional structure of science, for the user of that freely published knowledge to make open reference to the sources to which he is indebted; not to do so is to incur the sanctions visited upon those judged guilty of stealing another's intellectual property (*i.e.* plagiary); and

3)   that the institutionalized reciprocity of incentives for conformity and sanctions for nonconformity were required for science to work as "part of the public domain . . . [through] the imperative for communication of findings."

Here, then, with the formidable advantage of hindsight (and its attendant risk of anachronism), we find described all the *substantive* characteristics of science required for the invention and application of a research tool that is largely specific to the history and sociology of science: the *tool of the citation index* and the correlative *method of citation analysis*. But if all the substantive ingredients for invention of that tool were being observed back in 1942, why was the citation index in science not then invented? Why was it clearly described only in the mid-1950s, designed and constructed in pilot form only in the early 1960s, and actually introduced as the *Science Citation Index* (for 1961) only in 1963?

The answer is, I believe, simple enough. "All" of the substantive ingredients for the invention were there—except for the essential ones. True, the theoretical model had pictured science as a system of open publication involving a reciprocity of role obligations on the part of scientists, supported by the incentive of peer recognition. In this role system, each practicing scientist was required to publish the method and results of his investigations just as each scientist making use of that work was required to acknowledge the source in the publication of his own investigations. That acknowledgment (citation and reference) was in turn the principal form in which peer recognition routinely occurred.

But it was one thing to have this sketchy substantive model of how the reciprocity of roles worked, and quite another thing to have the idea that this composite communication-and-reward system and some aspects of its cognitive output could be investigated by means of a citation index. Absent from this early thinking was the very notion of moving from substance to procedure. Absent was the wit to draw out from the substantive model the several operational implications needed to arrive at the invention. Absent was the specific idea of devising a method for *systematically* identifying the observable outputs of scientists who were obliged to specify the sources of the knowledge they drew upon, doing so freely and routinely as a result both of having internalized the norm and of having incentive since their work, in turn, might in due course receive the ultimate reward of peer recognition in the same way. (For if one's work is not being noticed and used by others in the system of science, doubts of its value are apt to arise.) Absent was the basic perception of what was so obvious as to remain unnoticed: that there had evolved, long ago, a device for publicly and routinely acknowledging such intellectual debts in the form of the reference and citation. The absence of these basic ideas precluded the further crucial insight that once citations were aggregated, sorted out, and systematically analyzed, they should in principle reflect cognitive as well as other linkages between scientists, as individuals and as members of latent as well as more visibly organized groups. These were the large and critical conceptual gaps that separated the substantive model from any notion of a citation index as a tool for such systematic, quantitative analysis. As I say, all the conceptual ingredients for the invention were there—except the essential ones.

Beyond these missing conceptual ingredients were technological ones. Absent from the early 1940s was computer technology. We know from the best of evidence that that technology was *not essential* to the idea of a citation index since the first prototypes of the *Science Citation Index* were compiled through the use of punched card equipment in the 1950s. But plainly, the advent of the computer, or its functional equivalent, would greatly facilitate the construction of a citation index on the needed comprehensive scale. And along with the technological capability of the computer for generating and processing large batches of citation data were the in-principle-Thorstein-Veblen-anticipated styles of thought that went along with the use of that technology, especially in working with complex models of linkages, both contemporaneous and genealogical.

In a word, that partly formed model of a communication-and-reward system was no case of a "missed opportunity" in the invention of the research tool now known as the *Science Citation Index*. Nor was it a "near-miss" of the kind that so often turns up in the history of science and technology. It was, instead, a total miss: a prime example of how easy it is *not* to see the seemingly direct implications of one's own ideas, when attention is focused on one problematic aspect—in this case, substantive ways of thinking about the social and communication structure of science—at the expense of another problematic aspect—in this case, systematic research *procedures* for systematically, not spottily, investigating that structure. It is a case that exemplifies the ways in which cognitive sets (in the psychological sense of disposition) and cognitive contexts keep one from noticing what one ostensibly sees. It is this sort of thing, of course, that the psychologists of perception have done so much to elucidate in general and Thomas Kuhn ([1962] 1970, chap. 6) has done so much to clarify for the history of science in particular. On the distinctly minor scale of importance, it is also the sort of thing caught up in that apothegm of Whitehead's (1917:127) which I like to quote in and out of season:

> But to come very near to a true theory, and to grasp its precise application, are two very different things, as the history of science teaches us. Everything of importance has been said before by somebody who did not discover it.

And, Whitehead might have added: by somebody who is usually persuaded in retrospect that it was a near miss even when it was in fact a total one.

This is not the place to review the history and the current condition of citation analysis as a specialty-specific research tool. There is a substantial and exponentially growing literature on the subject[20] since the mid-1950s when Eugene Garfield (1955) and, in an associated paper, Adair (1955) published their decisive papers on "citation indexes for science" and particularly since the early 1960s when Garfield established the Institute for Scientific Information. Since 1963, the ISI has been issuing the *Science Citation Index* (*SCI*), with a current data base of some twenty-seven hundred of the most frequently cited journals as sources in about a hundred scientific and technical fields, and since 1973, a rapidly expanding *Social Sciences Citation Index (SSCI)*.

For our limited purposes, we need make only a few observations on the emergence and development of the citation index as a specialized tool for sociological research.

First, that use came as an almost instant by-product rather than being the principal initiating purpose. The *SCI* was originally designed as an efficient tool for swift and wide-ranging bibliographical search in science. Indeed, an enterprise such as the *SCI* probably could not have found the substantial economic base it requires had it been thought of solely as a tool for the historical and sociological study of science. The small number of historians of science and the even smaller number of sociologists of science could not possibly have provided a sufficient market. And governmental grants on the needed scale would scarcely have been forthcoming to meet such expensive needs for those small and, in the minds of governmental beholders, rather unprepossessing disciplines. With the sort of irony that would have amused a Karl Marx, this one of the few research tools with primary (if not exclusive) utility for the history and sociology of science could only have come into being as a by-product rather than by design: in capitalist and socialist societies alike, market conditions still do not provide for a comprehensive citation index designed wholly to meet the needs of sociological and historical research.

Second, though the *SCI* was primarily designed for bibliographic retrieval, its potentialities as a tool for the sociology of science were recognized almost immediately after a pilot citation index was actually compiled by Garfield and his associates. As Garfield (1963:289) noted at the time,

> interest in using citation indexes for retrieval and dissemination is equaled, if not exceeded, by the interest in its use for sociological and historical research. Indeed, Newell stated: "Citation Indexing will generate a spate of empirical work on the sociology of science. . . . It is rather easy to predict, I think, that the publication and wide availability of an extensive citation index will have strong social consequences along the line of becoming a controlling variable for the advancement and employment of scientific person-

nel. . . ." Merton said: "I am persuaded that your materials should be a rich source for the sociologist of science. As it happens, I am now in the midst of working on a problem in the field which needs precisely the kind of evidence you are putting together in your Citation Index."

Third, just as Newell confidently predicted, another unplanned by-product of the *SCI* has been the practice, in some quarters, to make the numbers of citations to one's work "a controlling variable for [decisions on] the advancement and employment of scientific personnel." The use of citations as the determining or principal basis for assessing the performance and potentialities of scientists falls into the category of "promiscuous and careless use of quantitative citation data for . . . evaluation, including personnel and fellowship selection." That description, in the form of a forewarning, comes, significantly enough, from the most ardent advocate of his *Science Citation Index*—Eugene Garfield himself (1963:290). Just as careful quality control of citation data and recognition of their limitations are required for their effective use in sociological research (Cole and Cole, 1971; Menard, 1971, chap. 5), so there are severe constraints on their value in assessing the performance of research scientists. Citation-frequency provides only one piece of information among much more detailed information required for such appraisals (in about the same sense, as Gardner Lindzey has noted, as GRE [Graduate Record Examination] scores provide one among many pieces of information utilized to assess applicants for graduate schools). But to adopt the number of citations to a scientist's work as the exclusive, or even major, criterion simply represents conspicuous malpractice. As Garfield (1963:290) summed it up even before he published the *SCI*: "It is preposterous to conclude blindly that the most cited author deserves a Nobel prize." Plainly, like other research tools, the citation index in science lends itself to all manner of abuse, in the case of historical or sociological research as in the case of making science policy or career decisions.

Fourth, the universe of citations to scientific work is inescapably worldwide, reflecting the transnational character of scientific knowledge. It is obviously essential to the formation of a valid citation index that its sample of sources be fully representative of work published in the fields covered by the index. Continued monitoring and periodic intensive checkups are required to maintain a sample representative of the geographic provenience of sources within each discipline.

Fifth, research is required on the differences between the disciplines with respect to the kinds of publication sources that must be included in order to have a sample representative of what is going on in each discipline. The various sciences and humanities make differing use of journal articles, monographs, and books to report work at the research front. Using journals alone as sources may be altogether adequate for such disciplines as physics and molecular biology but quite lopsided for such disciplines as sociology and systematic biology, to say nothing of a field such as history.

Sixth and, in this abbreviated inventory, final, there is evident interaction between the continuing development of citation analysis as a research tool and the spectrum of substantive problems in the sociology of science that are being empirically investigated. The recent introduction of co-citation analysis by Small (1973; Small and Griffith, 1974), Griffith (et al., 1974), and Marshakova (1973) has opened up new possibilities of identifying emerging specialties, their changing boundaries, and invisible colleges (Garfield, Malin, and Small, 1977). If the substantive problematics of the sociology of science is to be investigated across the entire spectrum, other subject-specific tools of inquiry need to be developed. Else, as has not infrequently been the case in the development of a discipline, those problems best investigated by the most powerful methods available at the time will preempt attention at the expense of other, theoretically significant problems.

Parameters of Science: The Price Input

Still another type of quantitative analysis of scientific development had its own independent source in the work of Derek Price. As he has recently reported:

> Some twenty-five years ago I published a first little paper on exponential growth of scientific literature. It had been inspired by my baptism as an historian of science during which I had read through all the volumes of the *Philosophical Transactions of the*

Royal Society of London since its beginning in 1665. As reading progressed I had begun to wonder at the increasing weight of each annual installment and in the spirit of my recent prehistoric past as an experimental and theoretical physicist I posed myself the question which James Clerk Maxwell asked so often as a child, "What's the go of it? What's the *particular* go of it?"

. . . In those days as now my interest in philosophy of sciences was perhaps shallow and naive, my appetite for major discovery brash as any physicist's. Had I known that others had several times considered head-counts in science and had recorded regularity of growth, it would not much have diminished my sense of deep discovery. What appealed to me was the existence of a simple underlying principle that would produce such exponential growth, that in some sense knowledge had bred new knowledge at a constant rate. (Price, 1977)

Price, like many another after him, has been investigating the same parameter of the growth constant in science ever since. But, as we have seen to be the case with other early modes of inquiry into the development of science through the use of content analysis and prosopography, this one too did not begin as an immediately continuous research program, eagerly pursued by a subset of the scientific community. For a quarter of a century ago, there was no such community of sociologists of science ready to make use of Price's new perspectives and tools of inquiry, while, as we have also seen, the small numbers of historians of science were not generally receptive to the idea of quantitative investigation.

In the first flush of enthusiasm over his discovery, Price published his findings on the exponentiality of growth of scientific papers as well as growth in the number of journals, scientists, and "the sort of economic data about science and technology that could be gathered from the pioneering work of Bernal" (Price, 1977). He published, moreover, in a forum presumably dedicated to advancing ways of investigating the historical development of science: the *Archives Internationales d'Histoire des Sciences* (1951) and the *VI Congrès International d'Histoire des Sciences* (1951). Evidently, the historians were not then interested in that kind of thing.[21] As Price reports it: "the paper fell flat." Or, in less refreshing but more self-exemplifying idiom:

so far as can be gauged from the absence of citations to the paper in the period immediately following publication, scholars took no notice of it.

The deafening silence of colleagues in the history of science was scarcely calculated to reinforce Price's continued efforts along the same lines. Had he only known it, there was a small, dispersed but potentially receptive audience for his ideas among the sociologists of science, thinly distributed in Europe and the United States. But they were not then likely to be attending an international congress of historians of science or to be looking through the proceedings of that congress. The current social structure of the history and sociology of science together with associated cognitive outlooks and propensities were admirably designed to have Price's pioneering paper pass unnoticed.

In the absence of the rewarding response of recognition of his work by scholarly peers, in the absence of any intellectual tradition (known to him) which his own work could extend, and in the absence of any interaction with the one barely identifiable community of scholars who might have responded to his work, it is understandable that Price did not immediately continue with his work in the early 1950s. He did not publicly return to the subject until the end of the decade when he seized the occasion, in a series of public lectures at Yale University, to attract the notice of humanists and scientists to what he preferred to describe not as the History of Science, but by "the eccentric, broader term, Humanities of Science" (Price, [1961] 1975:xiii). As he has reminiscently described it: "I did not take up the matter again until it forced itself into my work as an historian of science, being needed to explain why science had progressed as it did in certain periods, and gradually to my mind suggesting more and more links between historical explanation and the field of sociology of science about which I was gradually becoming more aware" (Price, 1977). The lectures were published in the consequential book, *Science Since Babylon* (1961), soon followed by the even more consequential book, *Little Science, Big Science* (1963).

By then, as the citation-analysis I have not yet done will no doubt show (requiring me to amend this informal history if it does not),[22] there was a growing audience for Price's quantitative work, chiefly among the growing numbers entering the sociology of science in the 1960s. Gathering force ever since, that line of inquiry has been widely used, developed and, in accord with the normative structure of "organized skepticism," critically appraised (e.g., Gilbert and Woolgar,

1974) by investigators in converging sectors of the history and sociology of science. Not least in point is Price's work on "the demography of scientific research" which deals with the variety of inputs and outputs of science among the nations of the world, the units of analysis including national populations of scientists and scientific work disaggregated by disciplines, age, and so forth. Of particular interest here are Price's recent observations about the national differences and international agreements on foci of attention and research programs in the various branches of science. (Price, 1977)

Science Indicators

What we have seen to be the long, discontinuous, slowly aggregated effort to develop measures of one or another aspect of science as a social and cognitive enterprise has recently found another expression in a periodic publication entitled *Science Indicators*. The first, for 1972, constituted the fifth, and the second, for 1974, the seventh Annual Report of the National Science Board of the National Science Foundation, but *Science Indicators 1972* was the first to take the form of attempting

> to develop indicators of the state of the science enterprise in the United States. The ultimate goal of this effort is a set of indices which would reveal the strengths and weaknesses of U.S. science and technology, in terms of the capacity and performance of the enterprise in contributing to national objectives. If such indicators can be developed over the coming years, they should assist in improving the allocation and management of resources for science and technology, and in guiding the Nation's research and development along paths most rewarding for our society. (National Science Board, 1973:iii)

In a style not ordinarily conspicuous in reports addressed to the President of the United States, the Letter of Transmittal reiteratively emphasizes the backward state of the art of establishing science indicators:

> Because of present limitations in data and methodology, the indicators in this Report deal principally with resources—funds, manpower, and equipment—for research and development and the

areas to which the resources are directed. The Report presents relatively few measures of the outputs produced from these resources — the scientific advances and technological achievements, and their contributions to the progress and welfare of the Nation. The present paucity of such indices limits the conclusions which can be drawn concerning the quality and effectiveness of our scientific and technological effort.

The letter concludes with what amounts to a charter for a continuing research program: "The Report represents only an initial step toward a system of science indicators. The further development of such indicators is a matter of high priority for future reports in this series."

Understandably, there is nothing in *Science Indicators 1972* or *Science Indicators 1974* about the long prehistory of efforts to develop measures of the state of science although the reports recognize, by reference, the continuing work along these lines by the Science Policy Division of the OECD (Organization for Economic Cooperation and Development), particularly under the direction of Jean-Jacques Salomon. The reports bear witness to the need for examining the technical problems of constructing science indicators within broader historical and sociological contexts. Accordingly, at the request of the (U.S.) Social Science Research Council and under the joint auspices of the Council and the Center for Advanced Study in the Behavioral Sciences, a quintet then at work at the Center on the historical sociology of scientific knowledge arranged for a conference on the subject of science indicators in June 1974. The conference was attended by scholars in the history, politics, economics, philosophy, and sociology of science, and has had two identifiable outcomes. The one, a volume of papers[23] presented at the conference supplemented by others generated by the discussion which set out the history, problems, and contexts of developing indicators of the cognitive and institutional aspects of science, together with proposals for their further development. The other immediate outcome is a programmatic group of nine participants in the conference who have been constituted by the SSRC Center on Social Indicators to facilitate further research on the subset of *science* indicators.

I have been suggesting that the recent emergence of the sociology of science as an identifiable special discipline resulted from the coalescence of both social and cognitive developments. On the social side, was the deepening public concern with the character, condition, and consequences of science found in many societies around the world. On the cognitive side, was a degree of disenchantment with certain theoretical orientations in sociology and the convergence, both theoretical and methodological, of ideas, conceptual schemes, and actual inquiry focused on the workings and growth of science that had been developing in comparative isolation. In view of the enlarged public concern with the problematic aspects of science, the now rapid growth of the sociology of science, and the long prehistory of quantitative measures of science (which has here been barely touched upon), it does not seem too much to suppose that sustained work on the problem of devising suitable indicators of the various aspects of science will attract the interest of sociologists of science everywhere. All apart from considerations of the applicability of science indicators for science policy, such indicators, usually tacit though occasionally explicit, find their way into every perspective on science, whether it be historical, sociological, economic, political, or eclectically humanistic. In the end, these diverse perspectives, caught up in the social studies of science, are all variously needed to form the kind of science policy that can engage our respect. Although apt development of these perspectives will of course not induce a consensus of policy, it can clarify the implications of clashes over policy.

COGNITIVE CONTEXTS AND INTERSECTIONS

As we have seen, there have been times in the short history of the sociology of science when its practitioners have exhibited tendencies toward a double parochialism: confining their scholarly horizons within national boundaries and within disciplinary boundaries. This only goes to show that although scientific knowledge *can* be transnational, it need not be so under all historical conditions. As the discipline has slowly acquired a degree of cognitive and professional identity sufficient to provide a sense among its practitioners that it possesses autonomous claims to knowledge, it has become increasingly international and interdisciplinary in scope.

This is not the place for methodical detailed examination of the cognitive and social interactions of the sociology of science with other disciplines. Instead, I shall draw upon documentary records and oral history to sketch out a few selected aspects of that interaction that have not received widespread notice. Most specifically, it appears evident that the internationalization and advancement of the sociology of science have been influenced by concurrent developments in the history and philosophy of science. Before turning briefly to a few aspects of these developments in the historical present, we can gain needed perspective by glancing at a collateral moment in the historical past.

THE SARTONIAN PRESENCE

Only in the last decade or so can an ongoing, *substantial* interaction be said to have developed between the history and the sociology of science. The chief reason for this is almost embarrassingly evident; until recently, there *was* no discipline of the sociology of science. Too few were at work in the field to do much of what plainly had to be done. And the history of science, cultivated by more but not nearly enough workers in the vineyard, was not much better off. Yet more than half a century before, a scholar had expounded the ecumenical vision of a history of science that would transcend both national and disciplinary boundaries.

This far-reaching conception was put forward by George Sarton, a Belgian-born-and-educated scholar who, fleeing from the invasion of his country in 1915, continued his life and work in the United States to become the chief architect of the history of science there and throughout the world. We need not consider how he went about the complex task of building the discipline (on this, see Thackray and Merton, 1972, 1975). It is enough to note how he conceived of the discipline in the early part of the century before it had become significantly institutionalized.

When Sarton decided to devote his life to what he described in his journal as *"living* history, the passionate history of the physical and mathematical sciences" (May Sarton, 1959:64), the subject had no established place in the university scheme of things, either in his own Belgium or anywhere else. There were no established academic posts for teaching the subject and none outside the academy for scholarly work in the field. The history of science was a sideline for most of its exponents or a belated commitment for scholarly scientists in their twilight years.

Nevertheless, the youthful and energetic Sarton was prepared to take needed institutional initiatives. In 1912, at age twenty-eight, he made the bold decision to found the journal *Isis*, a "Revue consacrée à l'histoire de la science." (That was the same year in which his daughter, May, was born and ever since he delighted in referring to the two together, dedicating one of his books to "E.M.S. mother of those strange twins, May and Isis." On this and other aspects of her father's life as seen by a poet-observer, turn to May Sarton, 1959:69; 1962.) Sarton's vision, full of innocence and hope, of the unifying cognitive and moral roles of the history of science was set forth in a fifty-page pamphlet describing the *Isis*-to-be as "'at once the philosophical journal of the scientists and the scientific journal of the philosophers, the historical journal of the scientists and the scientific journal of the historians, the sociological journal of the scientists and the scientific journal of the sociologists'" (May Sarton, 1959:69). The daunting aspiration called not only for a philosophy, history, and sociology of science but also for a science of philosophy, history, and sociology, all to find suitable expression in this variously ecumenical journal. That aspiration, it might be said, was not diminished by the circumstance that, two years after its founding, *Isis* had acquired a world total of one hundred and twenty-five subscribers.

"Displaying that singleminded and disinterested opportunism which marks the actions of a man wholly convinced of his mission, Sarton rounded up a distinguished board" of scholars and scientists who were both of the first rank and of varied nationalities and disciplines (Thackray and Merton, 1972:478). The national, disciplinary, and accomplishment-recognizing composition of the board provides a succinct and unmistakable·indicator of Sarton's image of the history of science as ecumenical.

PARTIAL LIST OF MEMBERS
OF FOUNDING EDITORIAL BOARD, *ISIS*

—SIR THOMAS HEATH, the British historian of Greek astronomy and mathematics;

—SVANTE ARRHENIUS, the Swedish chemist (who had been awarded a Nobel Prize some ten years before);

—JACQUES LOEB, the German-born American pioneer in physical and chemical biology;

—WILHELM OSTWALD, the Latvian-born German chemist (who had been awarded a Nobel Prize three years before but, more pertinently, had recently published his *Grosse Männer* [*Great Men of Science*] and, as we have seen, had introduced the German translation of Candolle's *Histoire des sciences . . .*);

—SIR WILLIAM RAMSAY, the British chemist, still another Nobel laureate;

—DAVID EUGENE SMITH, the influential American historian of mathematics;

—HENRI POINCARÉ, the French mathematician and physicist (whose *not* having been awarded a Nobel Prize is widely regarded as prime evidence of the distinct fallibility of the judges sitting in Stockholm and, more in point, of whom Sarton had written in his journal that "I will become the pupil, if I prove worthy, of Henri Poincaré: the most intelligent man of our time"); and, of distinct interest to us here,

—ERNEST WAXWEILER, the Belgian sociologist and director of the Solvay Institute of Sociology; and most tellingly, for all of us who see him as a founding father of modern sociology,

—ÉMILE DURKHEIM.

For the young Sarton, plainly enough, history of science subsumed the history of the various sciences and required the interdisciplinary guidance of scientists, historians of philosophy, and sociologists drawn from a variety of national cultures. The mature Sarton retained his encyclopedic vision. He insisted upon an ecumenical history of science that would transcend the Western world to take account of the Islamic world as of China, India, and Japan. He also retained his sympathetic, humanistic interest in sociological perspectives on the history of science. At times, he could even write that "the history of science in

the main amounts to psycho-sociological investigation," and would cas-
ually refer to "my sociology of science" (Sarton, 1948:51; 1952:94, *n.*
87). But as Thackray and I were compelled to observe: "his scholarly
writings show little sense of what sociology and psychology were really
about, little awareness that their methods and assumptions might offer
fundamental challenges to his own progressivist faith" (1972:480).

With hindsight, we might describe Sarton's early sympathy for the
history of science in terms of "psycho-sociological investigation" as
"premature." It was certainly an idea not much appreciated by the few
then at work in the history of science. But in his maturity, Sarton became ambivalent toward a sociology that had largely lost its early Comtean, progressivist aspect. He could not bring himself to keep in close
touch with the work actually being done in sociology and psychology
and did not much like what he did see of it. But also, he could not
bring himself to abandon altogether his early conviction that because
"'sociology remained for a long time outside scientific investigation, . . . there are a great many social questions that have not yet
been *completely* explored'" (May Sarton, 1959:47).

Perhaps it was a renewed symbolic expression of that early commitment to sociology that led Sarton, in the early 1930s, to accept,
upon the recommendation of his valued Harvard colleague, the economic historian, E. F. Gay, a graduate student in the new department
of sociology as an apprentice in studying the history of, chiefly,
seventeenth-century science. I like to think, but cannot truly say, that
Sarton's decision enabled that graduate student to provide a sociometric and cognitive link between Sarton and the emerging field of the
sociology of science. (For more on the role of graduate students in
providing such linkages, see the later section of this study, "The Kuhnian Presence.")

Although, as his daughter notes, George Sarton was "a man of few
if any intimate friends except epistolary ones," I can testify that he
could greatly befriend his occasional graduate students, even one
drawn from a department of learning in which Sarton took no active
part. He would do so, that is, providing that the student did not
threaten Sarton's "disciplined routine" of scholarship nor require him
to abate "the fury with which he set himself to work" (May Sarton,
1962:103, 107). In any case, Sarton did allow me to spend more than
three years in his famed workshop, Widener 189. It was perhaps a
further expression of his early attachment to sociology that then led

him to serve on my doctoral committee and, immediately after I received the Ph.D. in 1936, to appoint me an Associate Editor of *Isis*, charged with seeing to it that sociological work bearing upon the history of science should not be neglected in the pages of that journal. That soon led to the editorial decision to introduce the subject of the sociology of knowledge into the pages of *Isis* by an article on the work of Scheler, Mannheim, Max Weber, Alexander von Schelting, and on the first history of the subject, Ernst Grünwald's *Das Problem der Soziologie des Wissens* (Merton, 1937).

Another possibly symbolic but, for me, decidedly practical act suggests that Sarton had not abandoned his early orientation to the sociological aspects of scientific development. Like other newly minted Ph.D.'s in those Depression years of the 1930s, I had just about accepted the fact that if my dissertation was to get into print, I should have to (yet obviously could not) subsidize its publication. But then Sarton intervened with the astonishing offer to publish *Science, Technology, and Society in Seventeenth-Century England* in the monograph series he had just established as a complement to *Isis*: entitled, naturally enough, *Osiris: Studies on the History and Philosophy of Science, and on the History of Learning and Culture*. I did not refuse the offer.

One last episode can be taken to exhibit Sarton's continuing though indirect relation to sociology which, in this case, took the form of repeated, even insistent kindness to a student from that field who had wandered into Sarton's own domain. About ten years after leaving Harvard, I sent a copy of a new book, *Social Theory and Social Structure*, to my mentor. So far as I can recall, this was with no thought that Sarton would regard the book as appropriate for review in *Isis*. For by then, in 1949, the press of other commitments had led me to resign the post as Associate Editor for Sociology, and no one had been appointed to take my place. Nevertheless, Sarton soon wrote me a card: "I would like to have it reviewed for *Isis* by somebody who could explain it to our readers in Isidic terms. Do you know such a person?" (Sarton, dated 4909.30, according to a pattern of his own invention). Nor, evidently, would Sarton be put off by a graceless (and, to me even now, inexplicable) lack of response. A month later, his research secretary, Frances Siegel, was reminding me that "A couple of weeks ago, Prof. Sarton wrote asking you to suggest a possible reviewer for your book.

The letter must have gone astray [it had not]: so I am asking again for a possible reviewer."

Now, as editor, Sarton was not given to the practice of asking authors to propose reviewers for their books. Nor was he simply indulging a former student. Rather, Sarton was at a loss to identify suitable reviewers. Since he wanted this book of sociology to be examined in "Isidic terms"—that is, in terms relevant to the history of science—this called for a reviewer of a kind that was in short supply, as my labored reply indicates:

> I do want to take up your kind suggestion of listing some possible reviewers. In a recent talk with Philipp Frank [Einstein's successor at Prague whose interest had turned to the philosophy of science], I learned that he has become increasingly interested in the sociology of science. Perhaps he might be interested in reviewing the book from this standpoint. That would mean, of course, that he would probably neglect the first two parts of the book, which deal with more narrowly technical problems of sociology. I therefore make the following additional suggestions. Perhaps Talcott Parsons might be interested in doing an analytical review of the book, if this should strike you as suitable for ISIS. If not, another possibility might be Bernard Barber who, as you probably know, is in the Department of Sociology at Smith College. On second thought, he might seem to be a case of nepotism-in-reverse since he was a protégé of mine. As a last suggestion, therefore, may I mention Professor Leland H. Jenks, Chairman of the Department of Sociology at Wellesley College, and now associated with the Research Center [at Harvard] in Entrepreneurial History. (Merton to Sarton, 4911:02)

Clearly, no great array of sociologists of science with an interest in theoretical sociology came to mind. (Quite irrelevantly to this point of Sarton's vicarious interest in the field, the book was reviewed in *Isis* by the sociologist, Charles H. Page.)

These episodes may be enough to suggest that, as editor and teacher, Sarton retained a mediated connection with the field of sociology, even though it had grown away from the Comtean tradition. It was, however, quite independently of quantitative tendencies in the sociology of the time, to which he gave scant notice, that Sarton invented forms of numerical analysis which, as we have seen, were to develop into prosopography and citation-analysis in the sociology of science. As early as the 1920s, he was employing what amounted to content analysis of his notes for the unique *Introduction to the History of Science* (Sarton, 1927–48), whose three volumes in five books numbering 4,243 pages take us from the ninth century B.C. to the end of the fourteenth century A.D. As early as 1923, in his annual report to his employer, the Carnegie Institution, he classified 1,248 scholars and scientists up to the end of the thirteenth century according to their cultural and disciplinary provenience. The cultural distribution he reported as follows:

362 – in the ancient Greek world and Eastern Christendom,
373 – in Western Christendom,
324 – in Israel and Islam, and
189 – in India, Central Asia, and the Far East.

He suggested that the ratios exhibited the extent of the scientific heritage of science deriving from outside the world of classical antiquity and went on to say, virtually in the language of science-indicators, that graphs arranged by time provide a picture "of the amount of scientific activity accomplished at different periods by different provinces of mankind" (Sarton, 1923:235–37, quoted by Thackray and Merton, 1972:491–93).

Two observations must be made about Sarton's early use of such science indicators. First, he chose not to make this earliest work part of the public knowledge of scholarship by publishing it in an appropriate journal of scholarship; the most appropriate one being, of course, *Isis*, the journal he had founded and still edited. (He did, however, publish such statistics there later on.) Instead, as has been noted, he reserved his statistical data and graph for a report to the Carnegie Institution, a document not apt to be avidly studied by his colleagues in the history of science and even less likely to be inspected by sociologists.

Sarton's bent for synoptic numbers and indicators, though unlike Galton's not at all obsessive, found expression in other forms of quantitative analysis. I hope not to misuse the dangerous asset of hindsight, that ever-present source of anachronism and adumbrationism, in suggesting that the Sartonian arithmetic independently and knowingly utilized quantitative content analysis and provided the rude beginnings for citation-analysis. Throughout his great *Introduction*, he would repeatedly assay the intellectual structure of a scientist's or scho. work by indicating the amount of space devoted to each of its constituent parts, before going on to more detailed qualitative analysis. In like fashion, he would quantify its citations to previous writings as one way of establishing its intellectual heritage. Having started this sort of thing in the 1920s and 1930s, Sarton could scarcely be expected to foresee that computerized citation indexes would become an important tool for the sociological analysis of contemporary scientific development. But it should be noted that a student of his in the 1930s, the one writing this paper, might have put together his subsequent awareness of Sarton's numerical use of citations and the ex-student's own substantive observations that the norms of science called for an open-communication-and-correlative-reward system to arrive at the notion of a systematic citation index. That student *might* thus have put 1 + 1 together to reach a clear result but, as the historical record indisputably shows, he did not.

In summary, although Sarton touched upon sociological aspects of science, invented simple numerical techniques for describing and analyzing selected aspects of science and, from the start of his life as a historian of science, had an ecumenical vision in which the history of science would provide for a sociological perspective, there has been no direct Sartonian presence in the slowly emerging sociology of science. His remains a continuing indirect influence, mediated by a few historians and sociologists of science.

INTERACTION OF THE HISTORY, PHILOSOPHY, AND SOCIOLOGY OF SCIENCE

Just as with the founding fathers who initiated and defended the intellectual legitimacy of the parent discipline, sociology, so with the early practitioners of the sociology of science (Merton, [1961] 1973:50–53). They found it necessary to demarcate their field from others if only to have a private sense, publicly expressed, of what they were up to. The cognitively and socially induced search for a public identity led them to delimit a jurisdiction distinctly their own.

As with the larger discipline in quest of cognitive and institutional legitimacy the effort to achieve a degree of autonomy involved isolation of the field from neighboring ones. We have only to remember, for example, Durkheim's taboo on the use of systematic psychology which, partly misunderstood, for so long left its stamp on the work stemming from the influential tradition he initiated in sociology. To a less but still discernible extent, the early days of an empirically oriented sociology of science involved a *de facto* (rather than doctrinal) differentiation and separation from the philosophy and history of science.

As the sociology of science began to be accorded legitimacy, the pressure for separatism declined. No longer seriously challenged as having a right to exist, the developing specialty linked up again with some of its siblings. New cognitive requirements stemming from the differentiation of the problematics of the specialties also made for linkages with related disciplines. And once the field was demarcated and recognized as a specialty, it was "there" for new recruits to enter. They, not having lived through the times in which the discipline was much on trial, felt no need to keep their distance from neighboring disciplines. Moreover, those disciplines were in turn being transformed in cognitive outlook so that *their* problematics were leading practitioners to a correlative, deepened interest in the sociological aspects of science.

The most recent years, then, have witnessed alternating currents of cognitive influence flowing to and from the neighboring disciplines of the philosophy, history, and sociology of science.[24]

THE POPPERIAN PRESENCE

The most marked philosophical influences upon the sociology of science during the past decade or so have evidently come from the work of two scholars: the grand master of the modern historical philosophy of science, Karl Popper, and the physicist turned historian-philosopher of science, Thomas S. Kuhn. Their ideas have diffused widely and, it appears, unevenly among the disciplines. One gains the impression that Popper's long-developing work has been more consequential than Kuhn's in the philosophy of science while Kuhn's work receives somewhat more attention in the history and sociology of science. That impression is roughly confirmed by an unpublished analysis of citations to their writings. In (forty-five journals of) philosophy, Popper is cited some two-and-a-half times as often as Kuhn while Kuhn is cited some one-and-a-half times as often as Popper in the ninety-nine journals of sociology and the seven journals in the history of science covered in the 1973 and 1974 *Social Science Citation Index* (Gieryn and Merton, 1975; nothing need be said here of further informative differences in the extent of attention accorded the work of these key figures by scholars in a dozen countries and some forty other disciplines).

As indicated earlier, I confine myself here to only a few general observations on the contexts within which Popper's and Kuhn's work has become relevant for the sociology of science and do not at all undertake to examine their fundamental doctrines in detail.

In the case of Popper, citation analyses confirm the impression that his influence on the discipline of sociology as a whole derives less from his writings centered on social and political philosophy than from his lifelong development of a distinctive philosophy of science. What is more, the analysis of citations to his various writings suggests that the sociology of science is becoming the principal gateway for Popperian philosophy to enter into the larger sociological discipline.

Of course, as Popper emphasizes throughout his autobiography (Popper, 1974, 1:3–181), there is no sharply defined boundary between his ideas in the philosophy of science and his ideas in political and social philosophy. He reports that, from his early twenties, he was developing his

> ideas about the *demarcation between scientific theories* (like Einstein's) and *pseudoscientific theories* (like Marx's, Freud's, and Adler's). It became clear to me that what made a theory, or a statement, scientific was its power to rule out, or exclude, the occurrence of some possible events—to prohibit, or forbid, the occurrence of these events: *the more a theory forbids, the more it tells us.* (Popper, 1974, 1:31)

This concern with "testability or falsifiability" as the criterion for demarcating science from pseudo-science differs from the concern then common among the positivists of the Vienna Circle with demarcating science from metaphysics. Popper's concern with the problem of demarcation continued to find expression in just about all his writings.

Still, differences of focus distinguish his methodological and technically philosophical writings—for example, his first book of enduring
importance, *Logik der Forschung*—from the books that set forth what
he describes as his "knowledge of political problems," *The Poverty of
Historicism* (1944) and *The Open Society and Its Enemies* (1945), the
latter of which, Popper tells us, "at first I had intended to call: 'False
Prophets: Plato—Hegel—Marx.'" Variously related to the Marxist view
of the interactions between science and society, as Ravetz (1971:311–
12) has noted, these early works have had an historically changing significance—not least, for the field of sociology.

When the *Logik der Forschung* appeared in the mid-1930s,[25] it
was, Popper writes, "surprisingly successful, far beyond Vienna." To
confirm his apparently contemporary as well as retrospective judgment
about the "success" of the book, Popper adopts what are in effect science indicators which take the form of the number and national provenience of reviews of the book and, as aftermath, of academic invi-
tations:

> There were more reviews, in more languages, than there were
> twenty-five years later of *The Logic of Scientific Discovery*, and
> fuller reviews even in English. As a consequence I received many
> letters from various countries in Europe and many invitations to
> lecture. (Popper, 1974, 1:85)

After a quick-and-ready search of the reviews of the *Logik der
Forschung* and of citations to it in the 1930s, I must conclude that the
early diffusion of the book apparently did not reach into the social sciences generally and into sociology specifically. That influence was delayed for some twenty-five years, until the publication of the expanded
English edition, *The Logic of Scientific Discovery* (1959). Nor, apparently, was its initial success in other circles sustained. By 1945, Popper
reports, his wife "pointed out to me that my *Logik der Forschung* had
long been unobtainable and by then was very nearly forgotten" (Popper, 1974, 1:118).

Before a more careful investigation of the matter has been concluded, we cannot much expand upon the strong impression that Popper's influence upon sociology has stemmed principally and increasingly from his developing philosophical ideas rather than from his
sociological and political ideas. There is poetic justice in this outcome.
Ater all, *The Poverty of Historicism* and its "truly unintended conse-

quence" *The Open Society* (which thus joins William Graham Sumner's *Folkways* [1908] and Charles Cooley's concept of "primary groups" in his *Social Organization* [(1909) 1956] as Shandean surprises to their authors) "did not represent my [Popper's] philosophical interests, for I was not primarily a political philosopher" (Popper, 1974, 1:118). Moreover, these were books directed against "the renewed influence of Marxism and the idea of large-scale 'planning' (or 'dirigism')" and though Popper meant the books as "a defense of freedom against totalitarian and authoritarian ideas, and as a warning against the dangers of historicist superstitions" (ibid., p. 91), they were taken by many a social scientist as intemperate attacks on central ideas of Marx which they regarded as fruitful and sound.

With the recent growth of the sociology of science, however, Popper's philosophical ideas of falsificationism, "World 3," and processes of scientific development are being adopted even by sociologists of science who see themselves as Marx-oriented if not as downright (= upright) Marxists. All this suggests that delayed cognitive influences wait upon appropriate cognitive and institutional developments in neighboring disciplines before they actually become operative. It is not so much that Popper's ideas have basically changed during the last decade that has given them currency in the sociology of science. Rather it is that the evolving problematics and research development of the discipline, together with growing numbers at work in it, have provided a new basis for Popper's old ideas to become salient.

THE KUHNIAN PRESENCE

If the early Popperian ideas were slow to elicit the attention of the handful of sociologists of science in the 1930s and 1940s preoccupied with trying to give the field its own cognitive identity, the ideas advanced by Thomas Kuhn in the 1960s, when the specialty was clearly on the ascendant, were identified as sociologically significant immediately upon the appearance of *The Structure of Scientific Revolutions* (Kuhn, [1962] 1970). Published in 1962, the book promptly received a major review in the April 1963 number of the *American Sociological Review*, the official journal of the American Sociological Association. In that review, Bernard Barber described the book as unquestionably "important." More in point of our interest here in the developing reciprocal interplay between the history and the sociology of science, Barber welcomed the book as another sign that

> the newer generation of historians of science has become more and more quasi-sociological. Increasingly, historians of science like C. C. Gillispie, T. S. Kuhn, Hunter Dupree, and David Joravsky produce works in the history of science which are so nearly oriented to the explicit theoretical concerns of the sociologist that only the least effort is required to show how they exemplify or develop those sociological concerns. A very good current example is this important book. Indeed, Kuhn himself points out that (p. 8) "many of my generalizations are about the sociology or social psychology of scientists." (Barber, 1963:298)

Barber then distills the quintessential Kuhnian conceptions and in effect presses for even closer theoretical linkage between the history and the sociology of science by explicating what he meant at the beginning of his review in describing Kuhn's work as "quasi-sociological":

> I meant that his sociological analysis of the process of scientific discovery was not as theoretically explicit as we might wish it, nor does it include some sociological factors that would improve his analysis by enlarging it. Kuhn is aware of these other factors, some of which he calls "external factors," but he has not dealt with them as directly and intensively as we should like. When we are given so much, of course, we should not ask for more. We can, instead, take it as a challenge to try and give it ourselves. (Barber, 1963:298–99)

This prompt appreciative recognition of Kuhn's book by one of the very few American veteran sociologists of science calls for more than casual notice. (For responses from the late 1960s onward, see Bohme, 1974.) That Bernard Barber, then forty-four, can be aptly described as a veteran (who had been at work in the largely untilled field for more than fifteen years), tells us something about the early development of the specialty. But more in point, the instant response to Kuhn's book by Barber and by his close associate in the sociology of science was no mere happenstance. It can be seen as deriving from the sociometric structure of an emerging invisible college of sociologists and historians of science. The case holds some intrinsic interest as another moment in the evolving sociology of science, one in which the sociology, history, and philosophy of science intersected. The case also holds some analytical interest as exemplifying one way in which ideas flow to and from related fields of inquiry through (sometimes publicly invisible) social networks of scientists and scholars.

To piece together the sociometric structure in which this early reception of Kuhn's book was embedded, we must return to Barber's review and note the quartet of sociologically-minded historians of science mentioned there. All four, it turns out, are of an age with Barber himself: Gillispie and Barber having been born in 1918, Dupree in 1921, Kuhn in 1922, and Joravsky, in 1925. And except for Joravsky, who prepared for his work on Russian science by graduate study at Columbia, the rest were all graduate students at Harvard in the late 1940s. After a stint in one or another military or governmental service in World War II, three of them received their Ph.D. degrees in 1949: Barber in sociology; Gillispie in history; and Kuhn in physics; with Dupree getting his degree in history three years later. In the Harvard of those days, these differences in departmental affiliation were no bar to their getting to know one another and to learn of their common interest in the history and sociology of science.

This sociometric configuration in the latter 1940s had followed a similar interdisciplinary configuration that emerged at Harvard in the 1930s. That grouping was a trio made up of Barber, I. B. Cohen, and myself. To describe us as a trio is only to say that we were interacting most intensively in puzzling over the possible connections of the sociology and the history of science. In the immediate milieu, however, were the mentors, each educating us after his own fashion: George Sarton, of course; and also the biochemist, historian of science, and Paretan biologist, L. J. Henderson (1970) who, in 1910, had given the first course in the history of science at Harvard College and, in 1924, had been the first president of the History of Science Society; and intermittently, owing principally to his deep interest in the role played by Puritanism in' seventeenth-century science, the former chemist, self-taught historian of science, and president of Harvard University, James B. Conant (Conant, 1942).

Having received his undergraduate degree at Harvard in physics in 1937, I. B. Cohen entered upon graduate study in the first independent program for a doctoral degree in the history of science to be established in the United States. (Until then, the occasional historians of science had been granted their degrees in departments of history and one or another of the sciences [Hiebert, 1975].) As it happened, Cohen was to take only ten years after his undergraduate degree to meet the extraordinary range of austere requirements — scientific, linguistic, historical, and philosophical — which Sarton thought essential to a satisfactory degree in the history of science (Sarton, 1930, 1931). Cohen thus became the second person (after Aydin Sayili) in the United States to receive a Ph.D. degree in the History of Science. Cohen was destined to become Sarton's successor at Harvard, the principal director of the subsequently flourishing department of the history of science and, together with Alexander Koyré, editor of the variorum edition of Newton's *Principia*, and leading Newtonian scholar (Cohen, 1971, 1974a, 1974b).

Four years older than Cohen, I was an instructor and tutor in sociology at the time that he was finding his way into Sarton's workshop in Widener 189. With no thought, of course, that a field such as the historical sociology of science might be in the offing — a *field* as distinct from such sporadic monographs as my own on seventeenth-century English science — Cohen, Barber (then my undergraduate tutee at Harvard), and I found ourselves exchanging ideas with only an occasional sense that disciplinary boundaries separated us. My own relationship with Cohen continued, though finding only intermittent expression, when I was at Columbia. In a word, cognitive and social interaction were mutually reinforcing. After his stint in the Navy, Barber returned to Harvard and became another sociometric link between the interdisciplinary trio of the 1930s and the growing group of young historians of science at Harvard in the 1940s.

All this provides part of the publicly invisible social and cognitive context for Barber's having been in an informed and strategic position to introduce Kuhn's book to the sociological guild as an "important book" by one of the "newer generation of historians of science [who have] become more and more quasi-sociological." I shall have a little more to report on my own interaction with Kuhn but, for the moment, I note only the possibility that, with the professionalization of science and learning, graduate students serve significant cognitive and sociometric functions, especially perhaps in the early days of a developing discipline. I know of no systematic investigation focused on the subject (but see Wright, 1954, for a cognate study of graduate students in sociology). In any case, it is of interest that, upon reading the

foregoing account, Warren Hagstrom was able to report another frag-
ment of oral history which provides a little more information about the
contexts in which sociologists were variously linked up with Kuhn's
major book. Hagstrom writes that he was led to

> recall my own graduate student days at Berkeley in the late 1950s
> and early 1960s where I, a student of a student of yours *i.e.* Hanan
> Selvin, took a seminar from Thomas Kuhn. . . . I had the privilege
> of reading *The Structure of Scientific Revolutions* in draft and
> gave Tom five pages of single-spaced comments on it. At that
> time, I was still heavily under the influence of University of Min-
> nesota logical positivism, and my comments were rather conserva-
> tive and not very sociological. I don't think they influenced Tom at
> all, and I'm not sure when, if ever, I asked the question attributed
> to me (in the 1962 edition, page 40).[26] . . . Ergo, graduate stu-
> dents often serve as sociometric links. (Hagstrom, private com-
> munication)

Intellectual Milieux and Sociocultural Contexts

Such interactions between teachers and their students, or between graduate students themselves, are only specific instances of the
diverse and still poorly understood ways in which interpersonal milieux
influence cognitive orientations and formation of specific ideas. The
effort to provide understanding of the intellectual development of individual scientists and scholars is of course often detectible in the ancient form of the biography and the newer forms of the autobiography
and life-history.[27] But as George Stigler has lately pointed out, in his
characteristically pointed and therefore penetrating fashion, next to
nothing is known, in any systematic way, about the kinds of biographical information required to interpret an individual's scientific work.[28]
Several of us currently struggling with just that problem can testify
that, in relative contrast to the analysis of aggregates of scientists and
their work, of the kind found in prosopography, nothing like a conceptual scheme for the biographical analysis of individual scientists has yet
evolved.[29]

Intellectual history also makes a place, albeit more often descriptive than explanatory, for the influence of milieux constituted by interacting individuals. However, systematic investigation of the proc-

esses of intellectual influences in intellectual microenvironments has scarcely begun. Mullins (1973b) has provided one approach in his study of the formation of "theories and theory groups in contemporary American sociology." And the studies of invisible colleges, to which I have made frequent reference, provide correlative ways of approaching the general problem. It now appears that next steps might include the mounting of *fine-grained inquiries* into the interactive composite of socio-structural, interpersonal, and cognitive influences upon individuals—and clusters of individuals—who, like Thomas Kuhn, have sparked basic cognitive developments in a field of inquiry.

The following sketch focuses on some not widely known interpersonal and sociocultural contexts of Kuhn's immensely consequential *Structure of Scientific Revolutions* rather than attempting to add to the good-sized and rapidly growing library of substantive appreciation and criticism of it. What I briefly examine here exemplifies the twin notions that (1) personal encounters and relationships which prove to be consequential for the cognitive development of individual scientists and scholars themselves result to a significant degree from their *self-selection of intellectual microenvironments* and (2) that such self-selection is in turn socially patterned by such contexts as institutional arrangements, selective processes and the reward system in the domains of science and scholarship.

From documentary sources and from the prefaces to *The Structure of Scientific Revolutions* and to Kuhn's forthcoming (and still untitled) volume of essays, we can reconstruct the sequence of his institutional affiliations and locate in that sociological chronology the appearance of some of his principal cognitive contributions. There is, of course, no mechanically uniform connection between such social existential contexts and the substance of the work Kuhn was doing in each of these contexts. A paradigm for the sociology of knowledge long ago suggested the untenability of the notion that cognitive developments directly "reflect" underlying social structures or the location of thinkers within those structures (Merton [1945] 1973:7–40). But the rejection of a "reflective" or "correspondence" doctrine is far from a rejection of any forms of significant interplay between sociocultural contexts and cognitive forms or substance. Thomas Kuhn himself recognizes the possible significance of that interplay in his instructive preface to *The Structure of Scientific Revolutions* when he notes that "the autobiographical fragments with which this preface opens will serve to acknowledge what I can recognize of my main debt both to the works of scholarship and to the institutions that have helped give form to my thought" (1962:xii–xiii). I take this statement of Kuhn's to be anything but just another perfunctory or ritualized nod in the direction of "friends and acquaintances" "whose suggestions and criticisms have at one time or another sustained and directed my intellectual development" (p. xiii). It is, rather, a thoughtful distillation of experience by a self-aware, sociologically-minded historian of science. As I have suggested, interpersonal networks and the social process of allocations of resources and rewards interact with cognitive developments in science and scholarship. A short case-study serves to examine ways in which those developing networks and social processes made for Kuhn's differential access to ideas and information that were selectively utilized in the evolution of his thought. Kuhn's own insightful reference to consequential "works of scholarship" *and* "institutions" is largely borne out in this limited examination of available evidence.

T. S. KUHN'S INSTITUTIONAL AFFILIATIONS
AND SELECTED COGNITIVE PRODUCTS
A Chronological Outline

1943   Harvard University, B.S.,
            summa cum laude in physics

1943–45   American-British Laboratory,
            Office of Scientific Research
            and Development, Research
            Associate

1945–48   National Research Council,
            predoctoral fellow

1946   Harvard University, A.M.

1948–51   Harvard Society of Fellows,
            Junior Fellow

1949   Harvard University, PH.D.

1951–56	Harvard University, instructor to assistant professor in General Education and the History of Science	
1951	Lowell Institute, Boston, Lowell Lecturer	"The Quest for Physical Theory," eight public lectures, Lowell Institute (March 1951)
1954–55	Guggenheim Fellow	
	Center for Advanced Study in the Behavioral Sciences, invitation to become Fellow perforce declined	
1956–64	University of California, Berkeley—successively assistant professor, associate professor, and professor of History of Science	*The Copernican Revolution: Planetary Astronomy in the Development of Western Thought* (1957)
1958–59	Center for Advanced Study in the Behavioral Sciences, Fellow	"Energy Conservation as an Example of Simultaneous Discovery" (1959)
1961–64	Director, Project on Sources for the History of Quantum Physics	
1964	*Dictionary of Scientific Biography*, member of Editorial Board	*The Structure of Scientific Revolutions* (1962; rev. 1970); "Historical Structure of Scientific Discovery" (1962)
1964–66	Social Science Research Council, member Board of Directors	
1964–68	Princeton University, professor of the History of Science	(with others) *Sources for History of Quantum Physics, Memoirs,*

1968–   Princeton University, Taylor
          Pyne Professor of the History of
          Science

1968–70   History of Science Society,
          President

1972–   Institute for Advanced Study,
          Member

American Philosophical
Society (1967)

"The History of Sci-
ence," *International
Encyclopedia of the
Social Sciences* (1968)

"Second Thoughts on
Paradigms" (1974)

"Tradition mathéma-
tique et tradition expé-
rimentale dans le
développement de la
physique," *Annales:
Économies, Sociétés,
Civilisations* (1975)

Untitled volume of
selected essays (forth-
coming)

Foreword to Ludwik
Fleck, *The Genesis and
Development of a Sci-
entific Fact* (forth-
coming)

To flesh out this chronological skeleton with the materials in hand
would require the scale of a monograph devoted to the subject. But it
may be enough to state some general impressions of what is laid out in
these bare bones and to examine a few in contextual detail. This may
serve to suggest how institutional affiliations made for those encounters
with people who in turn influenced access to ideas that were selectively
caught up and developed in Kuhn's evolving thought.

Inspecting the left-hand column, we find a variety of patterns, both generic and specific, that exhibit the interplay between role-performance, access to the opportunity-structure, and the workings of the reward system in the higher reaches of American universities and related institutions:

1) From the outset, presumably superior performance as an undergraduate is socially signalled by publicly identifiable symbols: the *summa* in a university of the first rank also carried with it election to the two honorary societies, Phi Beta Kappa and Sigma Xi. Other indicators registering a high quality of intellectual performance were incorporated in

2) an almost unbroken series of affiliations with elite academic and research institutions, and advancement within them. Subject to detailed investigation, one provisionally infers that this sequence of affiliations was aided by

3) an array of elite fellowships intermittently acquired over a span of some fifteen years. Fellowships appear as both reward for past performance and facilities for future performance, thus entering into what has been described as "the accumulation of advantage" in science and scholarship.

4) In due course there appears a series of extramural posts of discipline-wide or interdisciplinary scope such as membership on the Boards of the SSRC and the *DSB* and the presidency of the History of Science Society.

5) What remains tacit in this list is the array of relationships with other scientists and scholars that developed in the succession of these institutional affiliations, relationships that Kuhn suggests may have variously affected the development of his work.

Inspecting the right-column of the chronological outline, with its specimen list of Kuhn's writings, we can begin to detect

1) a pattern of continuity in the evolution of the Kuhnian paradigm from the early, unpublished Lowell Lectures to the most recent version of his basic essay on the two traditions in the history of physics,

2) an evolution involving the differentiation and progressive consolidation of sociological and philosophical orientations to the historical development of science.

3) What the specimen list of writings fails to exhibit adequately is the distinctly unhurried, even slow maturation of Kuhnian ideas in each phase of their development just as

4) it fails to exhibit the long intervals that often occurred between the actual formulation of ideas in writing and their being committed to public print, a pattern that stands out in sharp contrast to the frenetic programs of rapid publication that often obtain in the competitive world of science and some fields of scholarship.

5) Nor, of course, does this bare list of writings tell us anything about the significant interactions of Kuhn with reference individuals and reference groups in the various organizational contexts that might have influenced the evolution of the Kuhnian paradigm.

By examining a few cases of such interactions, albeit in far less detail than they deserve, we can identify some of the patterns of social and cognitive linkage.

Institutionalized Serendipity I:
The Case of the Harvard Society of Fellows

Reverting to the sketchy calendar of Kuhn's development as a scholar, we note that after a strong undergraduate degree in physics, followed by a two-year stint during World War II in the OSRD, the major center for weapons-related research and development that included many scientists of the first class, and three years as an NRC Fellow engaged in graduate work at Harvard, Kuhn was appointed a Junior Fellow in the Harvard Society of Fellows.

The Society of Fellows was conceived of and (at first anonymously) funded by the exiting president of Harvard, A. L. Lowell, and was established in 1933, the year in which James Bryant Conant assumed the presidency (Brinton, 1959). Leading to no academic degrees and for a time actually discouraging junior fellows from studying for a degree, the Society was a distinctly elite institution designed to bypass the narrow specialization that often went with graduate study. Its freedom from set rules and requirements provided instead for self-defined programs of study by the Fellows that would broaden their interests and competence beyond the traditional confines of their disciplines of origin or would facilitate the transition from one field of science or learning to another. The young men selected as Junior Fellows—not at all surprisingly for the time and the institution, no serious thought was given to young women—were drawn from a national pool of nominations by select members of university faculties around the country, with the lion's share coming from graduates judged to be the pick of the crop at Harvard itself. This altogether elite academic Society had no precedent in American universities although it has since witnessed emulous parallels.

By 1948, the year in which Kuhn began his three years as a Junior Fellow, the Society had developed a subculture in which self-education that drew widely on the then typically ample intellectual resources of the University had a thoroughly established pattern. Some autobiographical snippets in Kuhn's writings provide clues to immediate and delayed cognitive outcomes of working in that microenvironment. In his judgment, the institutionalized freedom provided by the Society greatly facilitated the "transition to a new field of study . . . that might [otherwise] not have been achieved" (Kuhn, [1962] 1970:vii).

The Society of Fellows was the first of the two serendipity-prone microenvironments in which Kuhn was to find himself, the other being, as we shall see, the Center for Advanced Study in the Behavioral Sciences. (His recent membership, as of 1972, in the Institute for Advanced Study may have provided a third.) These are work environments that encourage the sort of wide-ranging exploration of developing interests and interaction with scholars and scientists drawn from other disciplines that make for serendipity in the domain of learning. Since serendipity is the chance discovery of ideas or phenomena that were not expressly being sought, it typically involves turning aside from prior cognitive interests to new ones. In anticipatory fashion upon becoming a Junior Fellow, Kuhn elected to turn away for a time from work on his dissertation for the doctorate in physics to educate himself in the history of science (Kuhn, preface to the still untitled essays). And, as he had observed earlier, he spent much of his time "exploring fields without apparent relation to history of science but in which research now discloses problems like the ones history was bringing to my attention" (Kuhn, [1962] 1970:viii). In making this observation, Kuhn is reflectively finding for himself a pattern resembling one that has been described as the "self-exemplifying character" of the sociology of science (Merton, [1961] 1973:68–69, 352–56 passim).

From those same brief autobiographical reports, we can piece together a few of the serendipitous episodes, reflected in the development of Kuhn's thought, that were apparently facilitated by both the social microenvironment and the microculture which the Society of Fellows provided in those days. One episode has to do with Kuhn's coming upon the book which he describes, over-generously, as "an essay that anticipates many of my own ideas." Referring to that somewhat anticipative essay, Kuhn remarks that only through "the sort of random exploration that the Society of Fellows permits . . . could I have encountered Ludwik Fleck's almost unknown monograph, *Entstehung und Entwicklung einer wissenschaftlichen Tatsache* (Basel, 1935)" (Kuhn, [1962] 1970:viii–ix). Only now, in the foreword to the English translation of Fleck's monograph which Kuhn agreed to write only after strong urging by Thaddeus J. Trenn and myself as editors of that work,[30] does Kuhn report *how* he happened to come upon the monograph. It was, he tells us, through a footnoted citation improbably located in Hans Reichenbach's *Experience and Prediction* (1938:224n). The chance encounter was evidently of no little moment. Reinforced by interaction with a sociologist in the vari-textured microenvironment, that encounter sensitized Kuhn to sociological aspects of his developing ideas. As he says, "Together with a remark from another Junior Fellow, Francis X. Sutton, Fleck's work made me realize that those ideas might require to be set in the sociology of the scientific community" (Kuhn, [1962] 1970:ix). In this case, it appears, ideas reaped from scholarship in print and from personal interaction were mutually reinforcing. This is reminiscent of the finding, long established in the sociological study of communications, that "the joining of mass media and direct personal contact" contributes to the effective transmission of ideas (Lazarsfeld and Merton, 1948:116–18).

Kuhn reports another serendipitous moment in his preface to *The Structure of Scientific Revolutions* (p. viii): "A footnote encountered by chance led me to the experiments by which Jean Piaget had illuminated both the various worlds of the growing child and the process of transition from one to the next." This encounter also proved to be consequential. As Kuhn goes on to say in a note of his own, "Because they displayed concepts and processes that also emerge directly from the history of science, two sets of Piaget's investigations proved particularly important." As in the case of his coming upon a reference to Fleck, so with the case of Piaget. This time, I am pleased to learn from

Kuhn's foreword to our edition of Fleck's monograph, it was "A foot-note in R. K. Merton's *Science, Technology and Society in Seven-teenth-Century England* [which] led me to the work of the develop-mental psychologist Jean Piaget."

Kuhn's allusions to those consequential footnotes hold a double interest for sociologists of science. They remind us of what we are sometimes disposed to forget: a prime cognitive function of citations is to facilitate the transmission of knowledge by directing readers to sources in the literature that bear significantly upon matters being dealt with in the text. The Kuhn allusions also put us in mind of the use of citation analysis as a field-specific research tool for the sociology and history of science. Like all tools and technologies, citation analysis can of course be misused. As we have noted, it can be put in the service of purposes for which it is ill adapted or purposes which are themselves questionable.

Kuhn's retrospective account allows us to identify both uses and limitations of citation analysis for tracing the *fine-grained* social-and-cognitive interactions that have affected a piece of scientific or schol-arly work. A major limitation derives from the conventions governing scientific and scholarly publication which allow no place for detailed accounts of how the investigation "actually proceeded."[31] *By itself*, citation analysis cannot trace all the complex sources of cognitive influences upon a particular work since *explicit citations*, which are ordinarily the only kind entered into quantitative citation-analyses, do not adequately reflect the story. The inclusion of *tacit citations* — the kind that can be reconstructed from such textual evidence as epony-mous allusions, terminology bearing the stamp of the source of an idea or finding, and the like — can help round out the analysis. It would still, however, omit those cognitive influences which find no expression in citation, explicit or tacit. As we have seen in the case of Kuhn, prefaces and their functional equivalent in the form of acknowledgements tucked away in the footnotes of papers can supply further information. Even so, a fine-grained analysis would have to be supplemented by focused interviews with scientists reporting on contexts of what they have set in print. As Kuhn symptomatically concludes his paragraph on the Society of Fellows in the preface to *Scientific Revolutions*: "readers will find few references to either these works [such as Fleck's and Piaget's] or conversations [such as those with Sutton and Quine] below,

[although] I am indebted to them in more ways than I can now reconstruct or evaluate."

Harvard Influential: The Case of James B. Conant

In view of the significance of the Society of Fellows for Kuhn's
early development, it is symbolically appropriate that Conant should
have presided over Harvard at the time that the Society was instituted.
For Kuhn singles out Conant as the man

> who first introduced me to the history of science and thus initiated
> the transformation in my conception of the nature of scientific
> advance. Ever since that process began, he has been generous of
> his ideas, criticisms, and time—including the time required to
> read and suggest important changes in the draft of my manuscript.
> (Kuhn, [1962] 1970:xiii)

Those of us who attend to dedications as crisp indicators of cognitive
influences will find all this admirably summarized in the dedication to
The Structure of Scientific Revolutions:

To

JAMES B. CONANT

Who Started It

That this particular president of Harvard should have reached out
to Tom Kuhn in this way came as no great surprise to me. My startle-
response had come a decade or so before. It was then I discovered that
Conant would not allow his lofty office to cut him off from his emerging
scholarly interests or from others, of whatever status, cultivating a
similar interest. So it was that he took notice of a paper, "Puritanism,
Pietism, and Science," published by a graduate student—what's more,
a student in the department of sociology which, having been established only five years before, was generally regarded at Harvard with a
sceptical if not downright suspicious eye. The first I knew of all this
was having Conant ask me to lunch "so that we might on a strictly
non-academic and unofficial basis talk about the history of science."
And it was something of an encouragement to have him write me,
when my dissertation was published, that "Having read somewhat ex-

tensively in this period on a strictly amateur basis, I was delighted to find that my tentative conclusions were exactly those which your exhaustive work had determined" (Conant to Merton, 21 October 1938). Conant had no cause for his generous diffidence as a self-described amateur: witness his salient contribution to the literature entitled "The Advancement of Learning during the Puritan Commonwealth" (1942).

Conant's interest in the history and, derivatively, the sociology of science was not altogether fortuitous. He, too, was being responsive to the successive microenvironments at Harvard from the time of his being a student in the department of chemistry. Like L. J. Henderson some fifteen years before him, Conant had been

> a student in Chemistry 8, the course largely on "the historical development of chemical theory," which Theodore W. Richards taught. It was Richards's work which set the stage for Henderson and Sarton [and, one must add, Conant]. Thus, at Harvard, as elsewhere, the history of chemistry was godmother to the history of science. (Thackray and Merton, 1972:484n)

Nor do the historical networks of personal relations at Harvard involving Conant and subsequently, therefore, Kuhn, end there. By the year 1916, when Conant had completed his graduate work and Henderson had assured Sarton that funds had been assembled to bring him to Harvard, Theodore Richards was a scientist of world renown. He had worked indefatigably, together with cadres of students, to improve the chemical determination of atomic weights and had demonstrated the existence of isotopes for which, in 1915, he had received the Nobel Prize. In view of his historical interests, he was understandably one of the many influentials in science selected by Sarton to receive an eight-page letter designed to elicit formal endorsement of an Institute "'dedicated to the history of science'" (Thackray, 1975:448). In contrast to this peripheral connection, Conant had double occasion for a close and enduring relationship to Richards: he had become a colleague in the department of chemistry and later married Richards's only daughter.

Like others heading up major organizations, Conant was both a "local" and a "cosmopolitan influential."[32] As a local, he exerted influence within his organization, both in shaping its character and, as exemplified in the cases of Kuhn and myself, in relation to particular members of the organization. As a cosmopolitan, he exerted a considerable influence in the larger scientific community and in national and international public life. And once again, biographical details of this one influential figure illuminate the intricate crisscrossing of social networks that provided significant contexts for others, among them, Thomas Kuhn.

So it was that Conant's path crossed Kuhn's not only in Harvard yard but in the greater world outside. It will be remembered from Kuhn's sociological calendar that he spent the last two years of World War II as a research associate of the Office of Scientific Research and Development. Conant had had a hand in the founding of this organization which was the outcome of frequent meetings between President Roosevelt and a quartet of scientist-influentials: Karl T. Compton, then president of the Massachusetts Institute of Technology and perennial adviser to government on scientific matters; Frank B. Jewett who, at the turn of the century, had grown up as a research assistant to the first American Nobel laureate, A. A. Michelson, had become president of the Bell Laboratories in 1925, a member of President Roosevelt's Science Advisory Board in 1933, and president of the National Academy of Sciences in 1939; Vannevar Bush, the president of the Carnegie Institution (its charter prescribing that it "shall in the broadest and most liberal manner encourage investigation, research, and discovery," a mandate sufficiently broad to provide, as we have seen, for George Sarton's research program in the history of science); and by no means least, James B. Conant. It would have been difficult to assemble a small group more high and mighty in the national array of science-institutions. Representing much authority and great power, they were, during the war years, doers and shakers in shaping the national organization of American science. As Hunter Dupree (1957:370) observes, their "decisions taken together revolutionized the relation of the federal government to the other estates of science."

One of those decisions was to establish the OSRD which came into being in June 1941 through President Roosevelt's executive order. Its first director was Vannevar Bush and its deputy director, James Conant. Within such a social network, it was nothing strange that Kuhn should in due course find his way into the OSRD.[33]

After the war, Conant and Kuhn both resumed their lives at Harvard, Conant as president and Kuhn as graduate student in physics. Kuhn's excellence of performance continued to open up new opportunities in a process of cumulating advantage. After three years of graduate work, supported by a fellowship from the National Research Council, Kuhn had his important years in the Society of Fellows and then, in 1951, took up his first full-time teaching post. Again, this represented a critical intersection of Conant's and Kuhn's life-paths.

That teaching position was as instructor (and soon afterward, as assistant professor) in General Education and the History of Science—a program of instruction that had been personally initiated by Conant. To those of us who were not in Cambridge during the 1950s, that program is known through the *Harvard Case Histories in Experimental Science*, gathered together and edited in two volumes by Conant (1957), with L. K. Nash as associate editor. It is these further linkages of the Conant and Kuhn biographies which are expressed in Kuhn's further sentence in the preface to *The Structure* (xiii): "Leonard K. Nash, with whom for five years I taught the historically oriented course that Dr. Conant started, was an even more active collaborator during the years when my ideas first began to take shape, and he has been much missed during the later stages of their development."

Nash was another of those *summas* at Harvard collected by Conant to work with him in the *Case Histories* program.[34] Possessing the further merit of being trained as a chemist—he has been a professor of chemistry at Harvard for the past twenty years—Nash could the more easily enter into the program. The year before Kuhn came aboard, Nash had already published his significant case history on Dalton: *The Atomic-Molecular Theory* (1950). Apart from his linkage with Kuhn's work, Nash holds a special interest for sociologists of science as a result of his sociologically informed book, *The Nature of the Natural Sciences* (1963). Among its signal contributions is an understanding of normative ambivalence in science (p. 322 ff.) which I have had occasion to discuss elsewhere (Merton 1976, chap. 3).

Kuhn could not have known, of course, that in electing to come to Harvard, he would find himself in significant personal interaction with the variously influential scientist-scholar who happened to be president of the university. Nor could he have foreseen how greatly this association would affect his intellectual development and life-course. But from a sociological perspective (even without the practically useful but dubious theoretical advantage of hindsight), we can say that in choosing an elite university such as Harvard, the young Thomas Kuhn had enlarged the probability of his encountering *some* faculty members engaged in extending the frontiers of their fields as well as *some* first-class minds among the self-selected and institutionally selected student-peers who would stretch his mind in other ways. If we grant that fine-grained analysis of the individual case can provide a specimen of coarse-grained social uniformities, we can take Kuhn's experience to exemplify the *process of cumulative advantage*.[35] That process derives from a model along the following lines:

> Processes of individual self-selection and institutional social selection interact to affect successive probabilities of access to the opportunity-structure in a given field of activity. When the role-performance of the individual measures up to demanding institutional standards, and especially when it greatly exceeds them, this initiates a process of cumulative advantage in which the individual acquires successively enlarged opportunities to advance his work (and the rewards that go with it) even further. Since elite institutions have comparatively large resources for advancing work in their domains, talent that finds its way into those institutions has the heightened potential of acquiring differentially accumulating advantages. The systems of reward, allocation of resources, and social selection thus operate to create and maintain a class structure in science by providing a stratified distribution of chances among scientists for enlarging their role as investigators. Differentially accumulating advantages work in such a way that, in the words of Matthew, Mark, and Luke, unto every one that hath shall be given, and he shall have abundance: but from him that hath not shall be taken away even that which he hath.
>
> *Mutatis mutandis*, cumulative advantages accrue for organizations and institutions as they do for individuals, subject to countervailing forces that dampen exponential cumulation.

Structural Contexts in the Reward System:
The Guggenheim Fellowship

Kuhn's further movement through a succession of elite institutions for learning and research exemplifies other aspects of the cumulation of advantage that derives from outstanding role-performance. Only a few of these aspects can be examined in this schematic case-study of ways in which the reward system can indirectly influence the formation of consequential ideas developed by a scholar of the first class.

As may be recalled from the sociological calendar, Kuhn was awarded a Guggenheim Fellowship for the academic year 1954–55. It is symbolically fitting that the complement of Fellows that year should also have included the daughter of George Sarton, the poet May Sarton, as well as Kuhn's future colleague, Charles C. Gillispie, then already at Princeton where, after a period at Berkeley, Kuhn would join him a decade later. To obtain a Guggenheim is to have come through an intricate process of self-selection and social selection in the higher reaches of the academic reward system. Of the several hundred thousand scientists, scholars, and artists, only a self-selected few find it in themselves even to enter the rigorous competition for a Guggenheim: in the year of Kuhn's own application, 1,295 of them. And of the comparatively few who feel themselves called, fewer still find themselves chosen: in that same year, 243 of them or one in every five or so.[36]

As the figures show, the very act of applying for a Guggenheim put Kuhn in a fairly select group of young academics prepared to take the not entirely cost-free risk of losing out in the competition. His decision to apply also exemplifies the role of organizational contexts in the process of self-selection. To begin with, at Harvard Kuhn was in an academic subculture where it was commonplace for young (and not-so-young) faculty members to apply for Guggenheims (and other competitive grants and awards). Within that context, he would have had ample reason not to feel himself wanting in trained capacity. However much he might be inclined to discount his abilities, he could scarcely fail to note the many signals coming to him from the time he arrived at Harvard College fifteen years before. These signals uniformly conveyed the message that he was being assessed as a considerable talent indeed. In quick sequence, the signals had included a *summa* in the tough undergraduate competition in physics (followed by practically inevitable election to Phi Beta Kappa and Sigma Xi), the NRC fellowship, the altogether telling election to the Society of Fellows, the appointment as a junior faculty member in the program of instruction which the president of the university had himself originated and, perhaps most emblematic of all, his having been designated, in 1951, to deliver a series of public lectures at the Lowell Institute.

The full meaning of such signals is itself a function of the organizational contexts in which they are being emitted. In the secondary colleges and universities, young faculty members might understandably retain doubts about their ability to survive a national competition of talent in spite of strong positive signals from their local academic environment. But in the elite institutions, with their relatively high densities of talent owing to the intellectual traditions and resources that ordinarily attract academic talent, their counterparts would have greater cause to feel reassured by local recognition.

The elite institutions thus provide conjoint structural contexts for faculty and students to enter into national competitions for scarce rewards-and-resources such as a Guggenheim: first, a local tradition of doing so which is reinforced by a record of frequently successful outcomes over the years and second, an exacting competition of talent *within* the institution apt to create and validate self-images of intellectual worth among those coming through it. All this can be taken as structural context, not of course strict determinant, of the decision by a young faculty member at Harvard, such as Kuhn, to apply for a Guggenheim.

The episode of Kuhn's applying for a Guggenheim and, in the event, receiving it, exemplifies another kind of advantage provided by the elite universities to their young faculty members. These universities tend to have a disproportionate share of eminent scholars and scientists on their faculties who, through their national and, for that matter, international networks of personal ties, can provide *early visibility* for their promising young colleagues. By bearing witness to local talent, the eminent seniors extend the local reputations of the juniors, often in those circles which are apt to include a good share of the gatekeepers engaged in allocating rewards and resources. This is important for the young academics before they have become widely visible through their publications and especially so for those inclined to resist the pressure for early, frequent (and sometimes premature) publication. As we have seen, Kuhn was not given to free-and-easy publication that might allegedly help him make his mark in the academic world.[37] Had the criteria for a Guggenheim award been wholly confined to the record of publication, his prospects would probably have been dim. By the age of thirty-two, when he made his application, he had published few articles: principally, one with Van Vleck in physics on a simplified method of computing the cohesive energies of monovalent metals which appeared in *Physical Review* (1950:382–88) and the other, a historical piece on Boyle and structural chemistry in the seventeenth century which appeared in *Isis* (1952:12–36). (He had elected not to publish the eight Lowell lectures.) Furthermore, on the bare formal record, Kuhn might have come under suspicion for having left the highly regarded field of physics for what was regarded in some quarters as the dubious field of the history of science which, as everyone knew back then, was a preserve set aside for elderly scientists in their declining years.

But the appraisals of young candidates by former teachers and current colleagues in elite universities are seldom based only on publications; more often, and often primarily, they are based on the assessed quality of mind as encountered at close range. These status-judges might on occasion prefer their young colleagues to publish—and, as the data show, they generally do publish more, particularly in the high-ranking journals, than their counterparts in other universities and colleges[38]—but if some of those judged as being first-rate minds proved reluctant to publish until they were good and ready, that too was acceptable. The outstanding senior members in the elite universities are generally confident in their powers of discriminating judgment—their confidence having been confirmed by the responses of reference groups to their previous judgments. When they conclude that a student or young colleague is "absolutely first class," they do not need the further evidence of publications, then and there, to confirm their (sometimes arrogant) judgment based on first-hand observation. As a result, the younger scholars locally judged to be first among their peers—at Harvard, for example, by being designated Junior Fellows—might be least subject to structurally induced pressures to publish.

These local judgments readily become translated into cosmopolitan judgments. Strong recommendations by referees of great reputation carry weight on several interrelated counts. Having generally acquired that reputation through their scholarly or scientific work, the referees are assumed to know whereof they speak; having been on the faculty of the major universities, they are apt to have encountered cohorts of highly selected students and young academics and so to have evolved exacting criteria for judging academic horseflesh; being in the elite universities, with their tradition of having members enter into the national competitions for awards and grants, they have had frequent occasion to write recommendations and, in the process, to have acquired skill in doing so; having made a good many recommendations over the years, their "error rate" can be impressionistically (seldom is it rigorously) checked against the subsequent records of their prize candidates (records in any case sometimes facilitated by elements of the self-fulfilling prophecy contributing to them); knowing that they will be called upon to write more recommendations in the future to much the same granting organizations, they are the more motivated to retain credibility by giving discriminating and measured appraisals in universalistic terms rather than indulging in excessive praise that primarily reflects particularistic allegiances.

These structurally induced tendencies for according special weight to the judgments of eminent referees are not, of course, uniformly realized in practice. Status-judges are themselves being judged by other status-judges. Many a referee of lofty scholarly standing has had his recommendations systematically discounted, either because he repeatedly allows his personal and organizational allegiances to get the better of his judgment or because he has notoriously poor judgment in these matters to begin with. But in focusing, as we are, on structural contexts in academia rather than on the biography of this or that individual, we observe the described tendencies often entering into the ongoing process of cumulative advantage in gaining differential access to the opportunity structure.

Having access to cumulative opportunity for scholarly work is one thing; seizing that opportunity and putting it to effective use is quite another. The Guggenheim together with a sabbatical from Harvard gave Kuhn a year free from teaching obligations in which to write a monograph that would consolidate some of the ideas he had been evolving during his term as a Junior Fellow and, more immediately, in the series of lectures he had been giving since 1949 in a General Education science course at Harvard. That monograph—*The Copernican Revolution: Planetary Astronomy in the Development of Western Thought* (1957)—indicates its social and cognitive contexts in ways that have grown familiar to us in the preceding pages. Its dedication reads

To

L. K. NASH

For a Vehement Collaboration

giving us some flavor of the intensive interaction taking place in the development of the course, with its collateral *Harvard Case Histories in Experimental Science*, edited by Conant with Nash as associate editor. Kuhn's preface in *The Copernican Revolution* bears witness to Conant's role in putting Kuhn on the path he was now traveling.

> Work with him [by then, Ambassador James B. Conant] first persuaded me that historical study could yield a new sort of understanding of the structure and function of scientific research. Without my own Copernican revolution, which he fathered, neither this book nor my other essays in the history of science would have been written. (Kuhn, 1957:ix)

Not only does the book reflect these social interactions within the microenvironments at Harvard in which Kuhn had been working but it is propaedeutic to some of the ideas that would become central to *The Structure of Scientific Revolutions*, ideas that Kuhn had been intermittently brooding over for about a decade. He identifies the monograph as a composite of science history and intellectual history which may seem incongruous because it is an unusual kind of inquiry. But, he argues, rarity need not be identified with intrinsic incongruity.

> Scientific concepts are ideas, and as such they are the subject of intellectual history. They have seldom been treated that way, but only because few historians have had the technical training to deal with scientific source materials. (Kuhn, 1957:vii)

Kuhn characterizes the monograph as an outgrowth of the Conant-initiated course that was designed to advance the general rather than specialized education of students. He then happens to make passing use of the word "paradigm," not as a concept central to his argument but as one incidental to his explaining that since the students were not going on to further work in science, "the principal facts and theories that they learn function principally as paradigms rather than as intrinsically useful bits of information." In all this, there is still no publicly manifest sociological orientation to the development of science although, as we know, Kuhn had been intermittently musing over that aspect since his time of interactive self-study as a Junior Fellow. The Guggenheim year was evidently a watershed period in Kuhn's developing conceptions, not least in enabling him to crystallize some of his ideas in the monograph and to clear the decks for returning to philosophical and sociological as well as historical reflections on patterns of scientific development (cf. Kuhn, 1977, preface).

Visibility in the Reward System: The Foreclosed Year at the Center for Advanced Study in the Behavioral Sciences

By attending to another context of the Guggenheim award we are led to an aspect of reward- and allocation-systems that is commonly lost to view in the sociological analysis of social mobility (and, in the present case, associated cognitive mobility). The focus upon *competition between individuals*, severally and in aggregates, that obtains even in so seemingly structural a concept as Max Weber's notion of class-patterned life-chances, tends to exclude consideration of correlative types of competition. Such a focus of course has its demonstrated uses — provided that it does not develop into an exclusive focus. For as Kenneth Burke reminded us long ago and as I have been fond of repeating after him ever since: "A way of seeing is also a way of not seeing — a focus upon object A involves a neglect of object B" (Burke, 1935: 50 ff.; and in proselytizing reiteration, Merton, [1940] 1968: 252).

This case-study of the linkage between the reward system and cognitive development thus far indicates the ease with which a focus on competition between individuals obscures correlative forms of competition and leads to their neglect. For what is competition for access to the opportunity structure for individual scholars and scientists is, on each level of that structure, competition between the organizations designed to provide such access. Organizations, such as the Guggenheim Foundation, whose *raison d'être* is to identify talent and to facilitate its development, are structurally in competition with other organizations having the same reason for being. In short, we have to conceive of the reward system as involving not only the competition *of* talent but also the competition *for* talent.

In the case of Kuhn, the year 1954 provides an instructive instance of this inadvertent competition between elite institutions dedicated to the early identification and nurturing of talent.[39] Having just accepted the Guggenheim, Kuhn found himself confronted with an embarrassment of academic riches in the form of an unsolicited invitation to a fellowship-year at the newly instituted Center for Advanced Study in the Behavioral Sciences.

Had Kuhn been in a position to accept the Center fellowship, he would have been, at age thirty-two, among the six youngest Fellows in the first-year's cohort of 36, for this was an institution, like the Guggenheim, designed to facilitate the work and development of already accomplished scholars and scientists along with highly promising ones. Moreover, Kuhn would have been the only Fellow drawn from the field of the history of science or, for that matter, from any other field of historical study. (That situation would greatly change in later years, with substantial numbers of historians coming to the Center.) Not surprisingly for a Center established specifically for advancement of the behavioral sciences, its Fellows were recruited chiefly from the disciplines of psychology, sociology, anthropology, political science, and economics, with a sprinkling, that first year, of behavioral biologists. All this presents us with an engaging puzzle in this case-study of the workings of the reward system in relation to the cognitive development of a scientist-scholar whose work has proved to be greatly consequential for the history, philosophy, and sociology of science.

In its most concrete, historical form, the puzzle is this: how did it happen that Thomas Kuhn was invited to be among the very first cohort of fellows at the Center? In slightly more general, analytical form, the puzzle amounts to this: how did it come about that access to the opportunity presumably to be provided by the new Center was offered to a young, largely self-taught, and new-made historian of science; moreover, one who had elected to publish comparatively little and that in a field which was then regarded as at best peripheral to the behavioral disciplines? Or in a form reflecting a particular sociological orientation, the puzzle comes down to this: what social structures and processes led to a thus doubly marginal young scholar acquiring enough visibility to be identified in a national competition for valued opportunities in fields widely defined as alien to his own?

In examining the multiform question, we begin by noting the formal process of selection and recruitment adopted by the Center. Unlike the Guggenheim Fellowship, the Center used the procedure of nomination, not application, with nominees being assessed by national panels of five to seven senior scientists in each field. As Ralph W. Tyler, its first Director, reported soon after the Center got under way:

> There is no difficulty in getting consensus from the panel on senior nominees—that is, those over 45 years of age—who are usually full professors in universities. Also, for most of those who are in the age range 35 to 45 and are usually associate professors, a majority of the ratings are in agreement. These nominees have worked in the field long enough to have produced publications and to be generally known to their colleagues.
>
> The juniors, on the other hand—those under 35—have not been in the field very long. Few of them have published works that have become widely known. Before they can be judged intelligently, the panel needs to have more information about them. For this purpose, we build a dossier on each nominee who is not well known to a majority of the panel. The dossier includes a personal history, copies of his publications, and ratings and comments from colleagues who know him. If these indicate great promise, arrangements are made for interviews by panel members.
>
> Since about 2000 of the nominees are juniors, a major task of the past 2 years has been the building of dossiers that will provide adequate bases for panel judgments. (Tyler, 1956:406)

As might be expected, this process of nomination and review by a national panel was not fully institutionalized as the Center got under way. Especially for the first year's cohort of Fellows, which Kuhn was invited to join, nominations came chiefly from an external Advisory Committee[40] and from the first Board of Directors of the Center[41] and in particular from its Committee on Fellows who sifted and sorted these early nominations for approval by the Board.

As Tyler reported, the Center immediately confronted the considerable recruitment problem of finding ways to identify the most promising young prospects, since typically they would not yet have achieved a national public identity through their scientific publications. In this phase of their careers, the visibility of young scientists and scholars tends to derive from their location in the cosmopolitan social and cognitive networks in the academic world, cosmopolitan in the sense of transcending local institutions and disciplinary boundaries. In national networks, that location is typically mediated by the location of their sponsors in both local and cosmopolitan networks. Thus, in the case of Kuhn, it appears that his early visibility in the then seemingly alien fields of the behavioral sciences was considerably heightened by such institutional and interdisciplinary networks. Dangerous (though, for analytical purposes, inevitable) as counterfactual history may be, we can nevertheless surmise that the then almost impermeable institutional boundaries between the behavioral sciences on the one hand and (surely) physics and (largely) the history of science on the other, meant that, in the absence of unplanned inter-institutional and interdisciplinary social networks, a young historian such as Kuhn would not have been nominated for a fellowship in the first year of the Center. The chances are that nomination would have come only after he had acquired visibility for himself with the appearance in 1957 of his *Copernican Revolution* — and possibly, it would not have come until the appearance of his masterwork in 1962.

But as we have seen in sketching out some of the sociometric networks at Harvard with which Kuhn was linked, he had become abundantly visible to several sociologists of science early on. These networks, it should be emphasized, were both social and cognitive, transcending both the boundaries of universities and the disciplinary boundaries of the time. This sociometric linkage connected the Harvard group in the history of science with some of the behavioral scientists variously engaged in helping to institute the Center. One such cognitive and social link was provided in the person of Edward A. Shils. He had a longstanding interest in the sociology of knowledge — together with Louis Wirth, he had translated Mannheim's *Ideology and Utopia* in 1936 — and had spent some time at Harvard in his periodic collaboration with Talcott Parsons (as reflected in *Toward a General Theory of Action*, 1951, and *Working Papers in the Theory of Action*, 1953). And, as we have seen, Shils was in the advisory group of social scientists brought together to discuss ways of meeting the need for advanced training. The other cognitive and social link was myself. As I have reported, my linkage with the Harvard historians of science provided me with ample occasion to learn, directly and indirectly, of Kuhn's early promise — as indicated, for example, by the oral (not printed) publication of the Lowell Lectures, the unpublished work in progress, and the stringently limited publications in print.

It is essential for this reconstructed analysis of social and cognitive networks to specify the indicators that were taken as signs of great scholarly promise. For on occasion, network analyses convey the impression that social relationships alone account for indicated outcomes, all apart from the substance of what is being transmitted in these interactive relationships. But it seems to me plain that if the young Kuhn—we were all variously young back in those days—had not been instructing and impressing others in his local and extended networks by his work in progress, the cumulation of advantage in the form of enlarged access to the opportunity structure for further scholarly work would have come to a halt. His location at a node in those networks would have been of no great consequence. To reiterate the general point: access to the opportunity structure is one thing; what one does with that access by way of role performance is quite another.

Strategic location in the extended networks does however make for visibility. With their potential for direct communication which complements and reinforces the indirect communication through public print, the social networks did provide me with information about Kuhn which was not then and there accessible through his publications. I had been hearing for some time about the high regard in which he was held by what I took to be his tough-minded mentors at Harvard, in both physics and the history of science. That appraisal and my own were only confirmed by Kuhn's remarkable paper on Boyle and structural chemistry in the seventeenth century which appeared in *Isis* in 1952. That I had come upon the paper only exemplifies the interdisciplinary cognitive and social networks that were developing at the time. For though I had resigned as an associate editor of Sarton's journal *Isis* three years before, I had been sufficiently influenced by my historianmentor to keep in close touch with that journal and particularly with its papers on seventeenth-century science. As the subscription lists of *Isis* at the time would doubtless show, few sociologists regarded that journal as indispensable to their work. That by 1952 I should have been a subscriber, editor, and contributing author for almost two decades was, as we have seen, a function of my own local networks at Harvard as a graduate student. Unplanned inter-cohort linkages of this sort make one privy to information that is not yet public about oncoming recruits to the ranks and reinforce the attention paid to their published work.

It was the composite of such information—transmitted over the private channels of social and cognitive networks and transmitted over the public channels of print—that led me to the easily formed conclusion that the thirty-year-old Thomas Kuhn was ideally suited to the new Center. Clearly, he would benefit at this phase of his development by having opportunity for sustained interaction with behavioral scientists under the conditions planned for the Center. Those conditions included cohorts of Fellows selected for their scientific accomplishments or promise insulated from the responsibilities and distractions accumulating at their home institutions and simultaneously able to interact in self-selected fashion and to get on with their work in hand. And correlatively, Kuhn would benefit others in the Center microenvironment, with its avowed objective of linking up the behavioral sciences with other scientific and humanistic fields of investigation.

The wholly independent judgment to the same effect reached by Edward Shils did much to quiet doubts I might have had about my own judgment. I recognized that we shared a cognitive network in the sociology of knowledge (with special emphasis in my case on scientific knowledge) and that we were expressing, in such judgments, a preference for certain lines of sociological scholarship which, in our opinion, were being badly neglected.[42] Still, within that framework, Shils and I had come to independent judgments about the young Kuhn in the precise sense that we had not discussed our respective opinions of his promise. As vice-chairman of the group that had evolved the plan for the Center—Ralph Tyler, its first director, having served as chairman —and as a member of its first Board of Directors and, most particularly, as a member of its committee on the selection of Fellows, I could therefore only second Shils's strong recommendation of Kuhn. It came as a comfort but as no surprise that further inquiries by the Center's staff confirmed these judgments. In the end, there was full agreement among the committee on Fellows and the Director that here was a prime prospect for the Center having the further merit of being outside the narrowly conceived sphere of the behavioral sciences. And so the invitation was extended to Thomas Kuhn to help initiate the Center—only to uncover the inadvertent competition with the Guggenheim Fellowship awarded not long before.[43]

Apart from illustrating—I was about to write, illuminating—the competition *for* scarce talent as a complement to the competition *of* that talent, the episode highlights other aspects of the operation of allocative systems of rewards-and-resources in the domain of science and scholarship. Those network linkages that largely account for the early visibility of a young scholar also serve as an unplanned mecha-

nism for bridging the hazardous gap between universalism and particularism[44] in such allocative systems. The nomination and endorsement of that young scholar in the history of science did not, after all,
represent a case of particularism in the strict sense of simply reflecting
a common membership in the same solidary social systems. It was the
case, rather, that the social and cognitive networks provided otherwise
inaccessible information about the ongoing role performance of that
not yet widely identifiable young scholar, role performance primarily
gauged in terms of what constitutes "good science and good scholarship." True, it is a basic and familiar theoretical issue that those
standards, in turn, might be functions of social formations, but not an
issue requiring examination here. The more interesting implication at
the moment is that the relatively fine-grained analysis[45] possible in an
individual case-study can provide a corrective to the conclusions commonly and swiftly drawn from the coarse-grained analysis of aggregated statistics exhibiting skewed distributions in the allocation of resources and rewards. These instant conclusions assume rather than
demonstrate that such skewed distributions must reflect purely particularistic loyalties rather than differentials in visibility of demonstrated capability that come, during the early years of the academic's
career, with differences in institutional affiliation.

The case study does indicate, once again, the differential advantage in access to the opportunity structure for further accomplishment
that comes from locally visible role-performance within an elite institution, such as Harvard, where influential members of the faculty are
especially apt to be linked with other elite institutions. But once again,
it appears that that advantage, most marked and consequential in the
early years of an academic career, would presumably not have continued to accumulate had the opportunities thus afforded not been put
to effective use. To put it baldly, had Thomas Kuhn been a bust during
those early years of his committed and venturesome transfer from
physics to the history of science, he would scarcely have been invited
to a fellowship at a newly founded center dedicated to interdisciplinary
interaction in an effort to advance behavioral knowledge.

But, as we know, in the avid institutional competition to aid the
development of an identified talent, the Guggenheim was there first.
And once having accepted the Guggenheim Fellowship, Kuhn could
only decline the Center Fellowship. (It had not yet occurred to anyone, in that first year of the Center, that the two grants-in-aid might be

dovetailed.) In the course of his Guggenheim year, Kuhn wrote *The Copernican Revolution* although, still far from eager to rush into print, he did not have it published until 1957. By then he had left Harvard for a post at Berkeley where he was to begin an experimental program of teaching and research in the history of science. This move placed him in another elite university, then clearly in the ascendant, and, incidentally, in geographic proximity to the Center.

Institutionalized Serendipity II:
The Center for Advanced Study in the Behavioral Sciences

In the event, Kuhn did get to the Center, upon renewed invitation, in 1958–59. And it was in that serendipity-prone microenvironment that eleven years after "stumbling upon the concept of a scientific revolution" (Kuhn, 1977, preface), seven years after he had first publicly formulated some of his ideas on scientific development, five years after he had received the invitation from Charles Morris (of the University of Chicago) on behalf of his coeditors Rudolf Carnap (Chicago) and Philipp Frank (Harvard) and himself to contribute a volume to the *Encyclopedia of Unified Science* (which he elected to write on "The Structure of Scientific Revolutions"), and two to three years after he had cleared the decks by writing the propaedeutic *Copernican Revolution* – it was in the microenvironment provided by the Center that Kuhn scored one of the breakthroughs [46] in reaching toward a solution to the problem of modes of development of scientific knowledge.

It was at the Center, as Kuhn reports in the preface to his consequential "essay," that he was struck in truly serendipitous style by the special character and multiplicity of explicit disagreements over fundamentals between behavioral scientists which seemed to him quite unlike the disagreements that occur among physical and biological scientists. Reflecting upon this episode, Kuhn observes in a remarkably instructive passage that

> spending the year in a community composed predominantly of social scientists confronted me with unanticipated [N.B.] problems about the differences between such communities and those of the natural scientists among whom I had been trained. Particularly, I was struck by the number and extent of the overt disagreements between social scientists about the nature of legitimate

scientific problems and methods. Both history and acquaintance made me doubt that practitioners of the natural sciences possess firmer or more permanent answers to such questions than their colleagues in social science. Yet, somehow, the practice of astronomy, physics, chemistry, or biology normally fails to evoke the controversies over fundamentals that today often seem endemic among, say, psychologists or sociologists. Attempting to discover the source of that difference led me to recognize the role in scientific research of what I have since called "paradigms." These I take to be universally recognized scientific achievements that for a time provide model problems and solutions to a community of practitioners. Once that piece of my puzzle fell into place, a draft of this essay emerged rapidly. (Kuhn, 1962:ix–x)

This phase in Kuhn's slowly crystallizing thought provides an admirable example of serendipity of a kind described as "part of the Idea of the Center" by its second director, the historian O. Meredith Wilson (1968:9). Even in Kuhn's compactly summarizing paragraph, the episode corresponds in its every aspect to what I once identified as the constituents and form of "the serendipity pattern":[47] "the fairly common experience of observing an *unanticipated, anomalous, and strategic* datum which becomes the occasion for developing a new theory or for extending an existing theory." In elucidated form

> the datum is, first of all, unanticipated. A research directed toward the test of one hypothesis yields a fortuitous by-product, *an unexpected observation* which bears upon theories [better to say: ideas] not in question when the research was begun.

> Secondly, the observation is *anomalous, surprising*,[48] either because it seems inconsistent with prevailing theory or with other established facts. In either case, *the seeming inconsistency provokes curiosity*; it stimulates the investigator to "make sense of the datum," to fit it into a broader frame of knowledge. He explores further. He makes fresh observations. He draws inferences from the observations, *inferences depending largely, of course, upon his general theoretic orientation*. The more he is steeped in the data, the greater the likelihood that he will hit upon a fruitful direction of inquiry. In the fortunate circumstance that his new hunch proves justified, *the anomalous datum leads ultimately to a*

new or extended theory. The curiosity stimulated by the anomalous datum is *temporarily* appeased.

And thirdly, in noting that the unexpected fact must be strategic, i.e. that it must permit of implications which bear upon generalized theory, *we are, of course, referring rather to what the observer brings to the datum than to the datum itself. For it obviously requires a theoretically sensitized observer to detect the universal in the particular*. (Merton, [1948] 1968:158–9, italics added)[49]

As Kuhn reports in the preface to his forthcoming collection of essays, he had no great difficulty, soon after arriving at the Center, in drafting a chapter on the conception of revolutionary change in science, for that had long been gestating. It was the problem of finding a way of thinking about the interludes of normal science that gave him trouble because, it appears, that he had mistakenly taken normal science to require a consensus on the definitions of basic quasi-theoretical terms.

But it is not for me to tell, at second remove, of how Kuhn, halfway through his year at the Center, came to solve that problem by conceiving of quite another kind of consensus. That Kuhn himself does, with great clarity though all-too-briefly, in the preface to his collection of essays (1977) which includes the paper, "The Essential Tension: Tradition and Innovation in Scientific Research," (Kuhn, [1959] 1963), that introduced but did not greatly elucidate the primary term of "paradigm."

While at the Center, Kuhn of course continued to interact with a variety of colleagues-at-a-distance as well as beginning to interact with a self-selected few of his fellow Fellows.[50] One such interaction, as J. Cole and Zuckerman (1975:159) remind me in a passage I can conveniently quote at length, occurred when Kuhn sent me his·paper on the function of measurement in the development of physical science (which he had prepared for a conference at the Social Science Research Council on "the history of quantification in the sciences," initiated by Paul F. Lazarsfeld and reported by myself,[51] thus exemplifying still further ramifications of the social-cognitive networks that were then developing). In responding to my close reading of that paper, as Cole and Zuckerman report the immediate episode and its aftermath, Kuhn went on to write:

I am sending you . . . a much-revised draft of my first chapter on "Scientific Revolutions." If you have a chance to look at it, I shall be very grateful for your reactions. Meanwhile, or at least until you call me off, I shall continue to pester you with pieces in this vein as they become available.

Merton was deeply impressed by the manuscript. When Kuhn was ready to send *The Structure of Scientific Revolutions* to the University of Chicago Press, he wrote to Merton asking that he intercede with the Press if it proved reluctant to publish the volume independently of the Encyclopedia of Unified Science. Merton replied:

Of course, I'll be glad to write to the Chicago Press along the lines you suggest. After all, I've read the earlier draft and this alone is enough to justify a strong recommendation to the Press that they proceed as you would have them do.

Kuhn's apprehensions proved groundless. The Press agreed to publish as Kuhn requested and it appeared at the end of 1962. Merton wrote to Kuhn:

I have just this day received a copy of your new book. . . . Having read this version in its entirety, I must say that it is merely brilliant. More than any other historian of science I know, you combine a penetrating sense of scientists at work, of patterns of historical development, and of sociological processes in that development.

Kuhn replied:

I think you know how much your good opinion of the sort of work I have tried to do in the book means to me. . . . Of course I'll inscribe your copy. . . . I always hate that particular task, but it will be a small price to pay for the chance to talk the whole area over with you. (J. Cole and Zuckerman, 1975:159)

That chance was jointly seized and the conversation has been intermittently renewed during the nearly two decades since Kuhn's significant year at the Center—publicly, in such papers as his 1968 article, "The History of Science," in the *International Encyclopedia of the Social Sciences* and, more briefly, in my 1975 article, "Structural Analysis in Sociology"; privately, in occasional correspondence and fragmentary meetings.

An Anomaly of Acolytes

When *The Structure of Scientific Revolutions* appeared in 1962, then, it was only after some fifteen years of slowly developing thought. The pace of development greatly quickened toward the close of this period of gestation. Once the chapter on the concept of scientific revolutions had been written and the concept of paradigm had been formulated, the rest which amounted to the almost final version was soon drafted—in the year beginning with the summer of 1959 (Kuhn, 1977, preface).

In the first dozen years since its publication, the book has given rise to a library of appreciative applications and diversely critical commentary.[52] Without adding still another interpretation of the book here, one can note that both in it and in an important supplementary paper (Kuhn, 1970), Kuhn makes three major points that link up with this episodic account of moments in the developing sociology of science. In one, he joins Popper in a major concern with "the dynamic process by which scientific knowledge is acquired rather than . . . the logical structure of the products of scientific research." In the second observation, he sees as central to this kind of inquiry an understanding of "what problems [scientists] will undertake." And in the third major formulation which places his position at a far remove from that of many philosophers of science (not least, that of Imre Lakatos), Kuhn argues that "the explanation [of problem-choices] must, in the final analysis, be psychological or sociological. It must, that is, be a description of a value system, an ideology, together with an analysis of the institutions through which that system is transmitted and enforced" (Kuhn, 1970:1, 21).

In these central formulations, Kuhn reinstitutes a concern central to the sociology of science during its early days in the 1930s: an understanding of changing foci of scientific attention; more specifically, the question of how it is that scientists "find" some problems to be important enough to engage their sustained attention while others are ignored as simply uninteresting. Since some scientists work intensively on problems that others regard as uninteresting, the framework of analysis must also provide ways of accounting for such variability in self-selected foci of scientific attention.

As Zuckerman and I (1972:350–51) have remarked upon Kuhn's

basic formulations, in a fashion that some may describe as a reversal of roles between the historian and the sociologists of science,

> Kuhn seems to us too restrictive in saying that the sociological form of the answer to questions of this kind must ultimately be in terms of a value system and the institutions that transmit and enforce it. [Values, norms, and institutions are indeed basic elements in the behavior of scientists, as one of us has been known to maintain but] sociological interpretations of *extra-theoretical influences* upon the selection of problems for investigation in a science include more than its norms and institutional structure. They also include exogenous influences upon the foci of research adopted by scientists that come from the environing society, culture, economy, and polity, influences of a kind put so much in evidence these days in the heavily publicized form of changing priorities in the allocation of resources to the various sciences and to the problem areas within them as to become apparent even to the most cloistered of scientists. All apart from such exogenous influences, there is the question . . . of (the largely unintended) influences upon the foci of research that derive from the social structure as distinct from the normative structure of science, that is, that derive from the social composition and relations of scientists at work in the various disciplines.

That Kuhn and I are at one in the significance attached to the value system of science together with its institutions as a salient (which means, far from exclusive) context for cognitive decisions appears as fully in this limited critical commentary as in a variety of explicitly identified convergences.

The substance of Kuhn's work must, however, be distinguished from its occasional fate. Few cases better document the observation that the author of a book cannot be responsible for what others make of it. Kuhn's paradigm (in the pre-Kuhnian sense) about paradigms has been taken to mean all manner of things to all manner of people in all manner of scientific, philosophical, and ideological communities (Masterman, 1970:69; Watkins, 1975:92). Nor was this entirely unexpected. Paul Samuelson reports that

> When Thomas Kuhn published his *Structure of Scientific Revolutions* in 1962, I formed the impression that his treatment of the incommensurability of different paradigms did not do justice to

the degree to which one paradigm in the physical sciences often unambiguously "dominates" another.[53] (Dr. Kuhn has since made clear that he is of a similar opinion.) But, all such surmises aside, I knew that in the social sciences the Kuhn paradigm about paradigms would be rampantly misused. This prediction has, alas, been abundantly fulfilled. (Samuelson, 1973:65)

Along with the great number of scholars and scientists who have put the Kuhnian ideas to effective use are varieties of acolytes who have transmuted those ideas to accord with their own ideological dispositions. This is no doubt the sort of thing that gave rise to the ancient, and periodically reinvented, proverb: "God defend me from my friends; from my enemies, I can defend myself." Among those uninvited friends, two distinct though occasionally coalescing varieties have been among the more vociferous. The first of these kinds are the romantics eager to discredit science by denying any trace of objectivity to scientific knowledge. These manage to put to one side all of Kuhn's efforts to deal with the problem of demarcation between science and pseudoscience or the problem of the selective accumulation of scientific knowledge (on which I have commented more than once before; for example, Merton, 1968:13). In place of these continuing efforts, they substitute, and impute to Kuhn, an extreme subjectivism in which science is simply another form of opinion, no different in any significant respect, from other sets of opinions, just as they impute an extreme relativism, in which claims to scientific knowledge vary with none having any more warrant than the rest.

The second of the self-appointed acolytes come from the ranks of the declared political revolutionaries of one stripe or another, all alike however in perceiving the Kuhnian ideas as supporting their own. The semantical overtones of the word "revolution," it appears, are enough to have some of the self-styled political revolutionaries resonate sympathetically to the language, if not the concept, of scientific revolution.[54] When these revolutionaries are Marxist in ideology, we are presented with the anomalous combination of dedicated subjectivists and would-be Marxists trying to reconcile Marx's great emphasis upon the objectivity of social structures and of basic science with the subjectivist doctrine that scientific knowledge is, in the end, no more than another ideology.

On the ideological and political planes, we are presented with the engaging spectacle of declared anti-Establishmentarians adopting as the legitimatizing basis for their ideological claims the ideas, suitably transmuted, of a scholar who, as the amply available public record shows, had developed his ideas within the social and cognitive contexts of the most indisputably elite of American academic institutions.

All this inevitably calls to mind the case of Marx being driven to declare, as he surveyed the motley arrays of his disputatious disciples, that "all I know is, I am not a Marxist" (*je ne suis pas marxiste*). And as Kuhn surveys comparably variegated arrays of his acolytes, he must in turn be tempted to declare: "*je ne suis pas kuhniste.*"

It is perhaps symbolically apt that I should be concluding this schematic account of some social and cognitive contexts of Kuhn's masterwork at the same Center for Advanced Study where he wrote a first crucial chapter, and that I should be utilizing that copy of *The Structure of Scientific Revolutions*, now worn with use by successive cohorts of Fellows, which Thomas Kuhn presented to the Center in 1962.

CODA

These fragmentary notes of oral and documentary history can at last be brought to a close with a heavily personalized note on the recent past and proximate future of the sociology of science.

Nearly forty years ago, a paper addressed to the American Sociological Society (as it was then known) began by quoting a fateful observation once made by Max Weber in which he called attention to the chancy character of cultural values, not excluding the value set upon scientific truth. In Weber's incisive reminder: "The belief in the value of scientific truth is not derived from nature but is a product of particular cultures" ([1919] 1951:213). I then went on to add "and this belief is readily transmuted into doubt or disbelief" (Merton, [1937] 1973:254).

That latter judgment about the ultimately tenuous basis for the social support of science derived from a functional analysis of the utilitarian argument many scientists had adopted to justify the ways of science to society. For centuries, it has been argued that science deserves support because of the Promethean gifts it brings to mankind.

But this utilitarian case for science (or for any cultural activity) is a double-edged sword: if scientists claim credit for what are widely regarded as the beneficent consequences of science in advancing the health, convenience, and power of humankind, then they must also take discredit for what are widely regarded as its maleficent consequences in vastly enlarging the means of destruction and the various pollutions that derive from technological developments rooted in science. Nor does it remain easily possible to claim responsibility for the anticipated consequences of science while disowning responsibility for unanticipated consequences. Bent on advancing the cause of science, many scientists have assured the powers that were in their time that science deserves support because of its reliable technological, often military by-products. Even a limited roster of scientists expressly linking part of their scientific work to military applications would include the most illustrious names in the annals of science: for examples, Leonardo, Galileo, Descartes, Leibniz, Newton, several of the Bernoullis, Hooke, Boyle, Wallis, Halley, Euler, to move no closer to the amply documented present day. (For one version of the cognitive interaction between science and military technology, see Merton, [1938] 1970, chap. 9.) Not merely the utility but the truth of science was legitimatized by demonstrating the power of knowledge harnessed to tools of destruction. In Whewell's opinion, for example, "practical [military] applications of the doctrine of projectiles no doubt had a share in establishing the truth of Galileo's views" (Whewell, 1847, 2:39). Intermittently, some scientists—for example, Lavoisier and Cuvier—experienced crises of conscience as they observed the military by-products of advancing scientific knowledge.

Against this background of history and analysis, it was suggested that however legitimatized and institutionalized science may have become, its accepted place could be jeopardized by its actual or assumed dysfunctional consequences for the life and fate of human society. On that basis, and it must be confessed without that foreknowledge of the holocausts of Hiroshima and Nagasaki that is given only to the prophet, I had the temerity to suggest that a transformation in the public evaluation of science was in the offing for a variety of reasons and most particularly because "Science is held largely responsible for endowing these engines of human destruction which, it is said, may plunge our civilization into everlasting night and confusion" (Merton, [1938] 1973:262).

About a quarter-century ago, when I was accorded the privilege of writing the foreword to *Science and the Social Order* by Bernard Barber (1952), then the only student in my eighteen years of teaching willing to commit himself to work in the nascent and unestablished special field of inquiry, I seized the occasion to review the ample evidence for the neglect of the sociology of science by sociologists—though not altogether by practicing physical and life scientists—and went on to speculate about the reasons for such conspicuous neglect and the prospects for a marked change in that condition. The conclusion was that interest in the subject would greatly increase and that the discipline would greatly develop only when science itself came to be widely regarded as a social problem and as the powerful source of social problems.

The public imagery in the United States had long pictured science as the unquestionable fount of all things good: providing the true exemplar of authentic knowledge, the basis for the restoration of health and the prevention of disease, and, above all, as the ultimate source, through science-based technologies, of abundant creature-comforts and pleasant distractions. And the atomic bomb had demonstrated, beyond all measure, that knowledge really was power. But in the early 1950s, signs of change in this public image of science had begun to appear with increasing frequency, although apparently unnoticed by most American scientists themselves as they found their research publicly supported on a scale previously unknown. The construction of the atom bomb had validated, seemingly once and for all, the worth of scientific knowledge for the military and political powers that be. But, equally, the explosions over Hiroshima and Nagasaki had had the short-run incidental consequence and the long-run potential consequence of producing a growing disenchantment with science and its threatening implications among many, and most particularly, among the intellectuals publicly expressing their judgments in the United States and Europe.

As a quite minor by-product of this impending change of public attitudes toward science, it seemed to me, the condition of the sociology of science should change from one of long neglect to one of widespread cultivation.

Many people who had simply taken Science for granted, except when they occasionally marveled at the Wonders of Science, have become alarmed and dismayed by these demonstrations of human destructiveness. Science has become a "social problem," like war, or the perennial decline of the family, or the periodic event of economic depressions. Now, as we have noted, when something is widely defined as a social problem in modern Western society, it becomes a proper object for study. Particularly in American sociology, new special branches have developed in response to new sets of problems. (Merton, [1952] 1973:218)

By the 1960s and 1970s, public concern with science as the seeming source of social problems had become greatly enlarged, differentiated, and intensified. Developments in the social, political, economic, ecological, and technological contexts of science and in the scientific disciplines themselves led science to become increasingly problematical. Anti-science ideologies and movements emerged, in a mirrorlike reversal of popular image, ready to find science the unquestionable fount of all things evil: as laying false claim to objective knowledge that is in fact altogether subjective; reinforcing through its misplaced conceptual outlook the barren one-dimensionality of human consciousness; in its more material manifestations, polluting every aspect of the biological environment, destroying hundreds of animal species, producing the dangerous knowledge needed for genetic manipulation and genocide, advancing the new imperialism through the spread of science-derived technologies to the Third World and, as its ultimate display of malevolent power, creating the spectre of imminent destruction that haunts all mankind.

This truncated bill of particulars may be enough to suggest the respects in which science has been publicly declared to be a social problem continually generating other social problems. Understandably, the public indictment of science has engaged the interest of those variously involved in the scientific enterprise (Stehr, 1975:9–18). Students thinking about possible careers in science, individual scientists, the professional associations of scientists, and, not least, the public agencies and private foundations supporting science have all become the more deeply concerned with understanding the social dynamics of science and of its place in society.

That there has been change in the perceptions of science among the public at large in the United States (and presumably in other coun-

tries as well) is tentatively indicated by the scattered evidence provided in polls of public opinion that have been taken intermittently
over the last two decades. The poll data have several defects. An evident flaw is their being composed of discrete questions dealing with
attitudes toward one or another aspect of science and the scientific
enterprise. It is a commentary on the primitive state of the art as
applied to the domain of science that the long-known procedures of
devising reliable and valid *indexes* of attitudes, rather than relying on
responses to single unconnected questions, have not yet been adopted
in the study of public attitudes toward science. Another manifest limitation of the data is the absence of closely spaced time-series of observations on these matters based on repeated use of the same indicators
and indexes. Still another gap is the total absence of opinion surveys
focused on the variety of influentials most directly involved in affecting
the social position of science: with regard to the allocation of resources
in support of science, such policy makers as members of Congress,
executives in governmental agencies, and major staff-members in the
great private foundations; with regard to the public formulation of
attitudes toward science and images of it, such influentials as jour-
nalists, editorial writers, and the free-floating intellectuals who express
their own concerns in every form of the mass media of communication
and, to an unknown extent, may be influencing the policy makers in
the realm of science as well as self-selected segments of the general
population.

Though faulty in these and other respects, the data available on
the perceptions of science current among Americans (and perhaps also
among Europeans in countries where similar barometric readings have
been taken at several points in the last twenty years) are more inclusive
and thoroughgoing than the data available for any earlier time (Etzioni
and Nunn in Holton and Blanpied, 1976). And there is reason to suppose that the still primitive art of inventing science indicators in
greatly needed variety will be differentiated and advanced by newly
focused methodological work (see, for example, Elkana et al., 1977).
Such developments should contribute to macrosociological investigation of the social, political, and economic contexts of science and, in
turn, to the convergence of perspectives drawn from diverse disciplines in what have come to be organized as "social studies in science."[55]

NOTES

[1]   The notions of the twin cognitive and professional identities of a discipline are slightly developed by Thackray and Merton (1972).

[2]   For basic formulations of the notions of reference groups and reference individuals, see the most recent work by the originator of the concept "reference group" back in 1942, Hyman (1968, 1975) and Hyman and Singer (1968).

[3]   Nor am I alone in that kind of judgment; for example, see Cairns (1974:345–46, n. 21).

[4]   For congruent but not as compact analyses of institutionalization in the domain of science and learning see Daniels (1967), Riesman and Jencks (1968), Clark (1968), Ben-David (1971), Zuckerman and Merton (1971), Thackray and Merton (1972). On the general theory of institutionalization, the key contributions remain Parsons (1951) and Eisenstadt (1965).

[5]   Particularly in nonliterate cultures, all history is perforce "oral history," based upon traditions handed down through generations of storytellers, poet-singers, bards, and grand old men and women. Even in literate cultures, historians have occasionally drawn upon oral accounts by participants in recent historical events and by firsthand observers of them. Thus, John Aubrey (1898), author of *Brief Lives*, that delicious and informative chronicle of seventeenth-century Englishmen of varying consequence, reports of himself in the incredulous third person, "when a Boy, he did ever love to converse with old men, as Living Histories." But Allan Nevins converted the incidental and often undisciplined use of such oral testimony into a systematic and disciplined mode of inquiry, the procedures having since been substantially developed by his associates and successors.

[6]   Taking no pleasure in the vice of "adumbrationism"—the denigrating of new ideas by claiming to find them old through nimble reconstructions—I do not review here the evidence for regarding Francis Bacon as an even more remote ancestor of the sociology of science. For a serving up of the ingredients of a sociology of science which are scattered in the Baconian *oeuvre*, see Merton (1973:346–52). On adumbrationism generally, see Merton (1968, chap. 1).

[7]   Dead metaphors of gender have a way of coming alive in these days of articulate social movements of women. Historically, no woman has been described as the mother of a science. (Even Marie Curie is known as the mother of Irène Curie rather than as the mother of radio-activity.) Equally in point, when the parental nouns are converted into metaphorical verbs, they plainly have different connotations: to "father" a science connotes being its unique or principal begetter while to "mother" a science, should the metaphor ever be

instituted, would at first probably connote looking after the fledgling with tender loving care.

8   For a kinder allusion still, see Cairns (1974:338).

9   It meant much to me to have Needham remark, in a kind review of my dissertation, that it "exhibits a quantitative sense unusual in an historian." That Needham should have described the author of the book as an historian (even though he had done so little to merit that lofty designation) is not altogether strange. Sociologists were then a largely alien academic breed in England—suspect if not downright illegitimate within the precincts of Cambridge and Oxford, their strange doings largely confined to the London School of Economics. Although he delivered the Herbert Spencer Lecture in the mid-1930s, even so unorthodox a scientist as Needham, then Dunn Reader in Biochemistry at Cambridge, would seldom have encountered an academic sociologist in the flesh. He would have known historians of science for the best of reasons: he was one of them, his unexampled *History of Embryology* having appeared in 1935. A letter to George Sarton recently disinterred from the archives (Thackray and Merton, 1972:491) has Needham congratulating George Sarton on his *Introduction to the History of Science* as early as 1927. *Historians* of science had a familiar academic identity; *sociologists* of science had none.

10   A recently compiled bibliography by Mary Wilson Miles (1975) which has me publishing reviews of books by Huxley, Soddy, Hogben, and Bernal provides a reminder that at least this was so in my own case. It was plainly also the case for Bernard Barber. In his then comprehensive examination of the sociology of science, the first of its kind in the United States, roughly half of the books and articles on which he drew had been written by practicing scientists (Barber, 1952). As I noted in the foreword to that book, "the sociology of science has been nudged into being, not so much by sociologists as by physical and biological scientists who occupy their leisure hours by working on this subject."

11   The substantial body of work on specialties cited at the beginning of this study is being amplified by much work in progress, in press or recently published. The volume edited by Nico Stehr includes papers on the subject by Richard Whitley, D. A. MacKenzie and S. B. Barnes, D. O. Edge and M. Mulkay, among others. Another such inquiry in the interaction of social and cognitive structures has been mounted by a colleague in the Columbia University Program in the Sociology of Science, Stephen Cole (1975).

12   For historical accounts of the developing use of content analysis in fields other than the sociology of science, see Stone et al. (1966) and Riley and Stoll (1968), which include excellent bibliographies.

13   It may be of interest to examine this episode as an example of the absence of direct intellectual influence in situations where most of us would take such influence as prima facie evidence. The dean of historians of science, George Sarton, was a teacher of mine and, indeed, allowed me to work for three years in his famed office in the Widener Library at Harvard. At the time, another

teacher of mine, P. A. Sorokin, and I collaborated on a study of the course of Arabian intellectual development from 700 to 1300, based upon the arithmetical analysis of collective biographies. It was in accord with Sarton's character rather than with scholarly obligation that he never mentioned his much earlier forays into quantitative and graphic analysis of such biographical materials when he enthusiastically decided that this little paper (Sorokin and Merton, 1935), based on data drawn from his own monumental *Introduction to the History of Science*, should appear in *Isis*, the journal he had founded and continued to edit. The early invisibility of Sarton's pioneering in the art of collective biography (prosopography) is described by Thackray and Merton (1972:491–93).

[14]   Thus also providing a prime case of what has been described as "post-mature discoveries or contributions in science": those which the evidence indicates could have been made and developed substantially sooner than they were if only their cognitive ingredients (the constituent questions, concepts, procedures, theoretical frameworks and images of knowledge) were required for the outcome. On this version of counterfactual history, see Zuckerman (1974).

[15]   This careful formulation of part of Candolle's interpretation is accurate so far as it goes. But, as I reported in describing his book as the "one study which has most carefully and circumstantially treated the association of certain religious affiliations with interest and accomplishment in science" (Merton, [1938] 1970:134) and as Mikulinsky (1974:226, 240–41) rightly notes, Candolle found a close positive association between moderated Protestantism and the growth of modern science. See also Candolle's letter to Galton of 2 January 1873 to this same effect (Pearson, 1914–30, 2:137).

[16]   In 1957, then still unaware of the tradition of prosopography in the history of ancient Rome, I emitted a clarion call for the wider use of collective biography, the call being somewhat muffled by being buried in one of those long footnotes and postnotes (like this one) attended to only by other scholars who themselves suffer from addiction to them. The call to arms went as follows: "Studies in historical sociology have only begun to quarry the rich ore available in comprehensive collections of biography and other historical evidence. Although statistical analyses of such materials cannot stand in place of detailed qualitative analyses of the historical evidence, they afford a *systematic* basis for new findings and, often, for correction of received assumptions. At least, this has been my own experience in undertaking statistical analyses of some 6,000 biographies (in the *DNB*) of those who comprised the elite of seventeenth-century England; of the lists of important discoveries and inventions listed in Darmstädter's *Handbuch zur Geschichte der Naturwissenschaften und der Technik*; and of 2,000 articles published in the *Philosophical Transactions* during the last third of the seventeenth century. (Cf. Merton, *Science, Technology and Society in Seventeenth-Century England*, 1938, Chapters II–III.) The most extensive use of such statistical analyses is found in P. A. Sorokin, *Social and Cultural Dynamics* (New York: American Book Co., 1937). Of course, the preparation of statistical summaries of this kind has its hazards; routinized compilations unrestrained by knowledge of the historical contexts of the data

can lead to unfounded conclusions. For a discussion of some of these hazards, see P. A. Sorokin and R. K. Merton, 'The course of Arabian intellectual development: a study in method,' *Isis*, 1935, 22, 516–524; Merton, *op. cit.*, 367 ff., 398 ff., and for a more thorough review of the problems of procedure, Bernard Berelson, *Content Analysis* (Glencoe: The Free Press, 1951). Numerous recent studies of the social origins of business elites in the historical past have utilized materials of this sort; see the studies by William Miller, C. W. Mills, and Suzanne Keller, instructively summarized by Bernard Barber, *Social Stratification* (New York: Harcourt, Brace & Co., 1957)." This footnote within a note is from Merton ([1949, 1957] 1968:653n–54n).

[17]   The hardworking members of that seminar were Marshall Childs, Linda Christiansen, Jonathan Cole, Stephen Cole, R. G. A. Dolby (a student of Gillispie's and Kuhn's at Princeton), Sarajane Heidt, Coit Johnson, David Landau, Patricia Nash, Jeffrey G. Reitz, Dean B. Savage, Daniel Sullivan (for a time), Lenore J. Weitzman and, as a post-doctoral student, Esther Wey. From the minutes of discussion of the seminar reports, it appears evident that wide-ranging questions of cognitive contexts had been explored in the course of formulating the schedule of sociologically relevant information.

[18]   Since the schedule of information prepared a decade ago is still in hand, it can be used to facilitate a prosopographical analysis once the final volume of the *DSB* has appeared. That analysis will of course be limited by absence of the data which were not included in the *published* biographies, this being precisely the sort of limitation, holding for the analyses of other biographical dictionaries, that the proposed innovation was designed to reduce to a minimum.

[19]   For further elucidation of this basic attribute of the social structure of science which in effect amounts to an exchange of information for recognition, see Barber, 1952, chap. 4; Storer, 1966:76–136; Hagstrom, 1965 passim; Price, 1977; Mulkay, 1972, chap. 3.

[20]   A varied abundance of studies utilizing the always dangerous and often useful tool of citation analysis have come along since that analysis by Gross and Gross (1927) of citations appearing in the *Journal of the American Chemical Society*, now considered a classic in library and information science. A brief bibliography is provided in *Social Science Citation Index: 1974 Annual, Guide and Journal Lists* (Philadelphia: Institute for Scientific Information, 1974), pp. 69–74. Some indication of the mushroom growth of citation analysis, which includes its own complement of toadstools, is provided by the extensive bibliographies on it and related quantitative procedures now (1975) in progress. These include bibliographies being prepared by Henry Small and Francis Narin. A critical bibliography of the range of science indicators is being prepared by Arnold Thackray on behalf of the Science Indicators working committee established by the (U.S.) Social Science Research Council.

[21]   There are ample signs of change. Now that quantitative modes of inquiry have increasingly found their way into the work of English, French, and American historians (Tilly, 1974; Fogel, 1975)—consider only the comparative studies by intellectual descendants of Marc Bloch, cliometricians, and histori-

cal demographers—these methods may find more favor among historians of science. A straw in the historical wind is the symposium devoted to Quantitative Methods in the History of Science arranged by Roger Hahn and held in August 1976 at the Center for History of Science and Technology at the University of California (Berkeley).

22   Upon reading this essay, Jonathan Cole and Harriet Zuckerman have reminded me that this citation analysis need not be left entirely to the future. Quantitative evidence already exists testifying that Price's modes of quantification have become of major interest to sociologists of science since the mid-1960s. In the rank-ordered lists, compiled by Cole and Zuckerman (1975: 152), of authors in the journal literature of the sociology of science from 1950 to 1973, Price's work was not among the twenty or so most often cited works during the decade 1950–59. By 1960–64, his work ranked only 22nd, whereas from 1965 to 1973, his work has been the second most often cited in the nine sociology and science journals used as data-sources.

23   The volume is entitled *Toward a Metric of Science: The Advent of Science Indicators* (1977). It is edited by the quintet initiating the conference— Yehuda Elkana, Joshua Lederberg, Robert K. Merton, Arnold Thackray, and Harriet Zuckerman—and contains papers by Stephen Cole, Jonathan Cole, and Lorraine Dietrich; O. D. Duncan; Yaron Ezrahi; Eugene Garfield, Morton Malin, and Henry Small; Zvi Griliches; Gerald Holton; William Kruskal; Derek J. de Solla Price; John Ziman; and the editors.

24   To refer to these demarcated fields of inquiry is not to reify the boundaries between them. It is only to take account of the cognitive and behavioral differences between the practitioners at work in the several disciplines: their differences in announced self-images, formulations of objectives, problematics, choices of journals in which to publish, primary reference individuals and reference groups, and so forth.

25   As we have seen to be the case with Candolle's *Histoire des sciences*, which was being read by Darwin and Galton in the last months of 1872, although the book bears the imprint of 1873, so, it seems, with Popper's early classical book. Lakatos notes somewhere, with less than keen approval, that Popper invariably insists on pointing out that although the *Logik der Forschung* bears the imprint of 1935, it was actually printed in 1934, and was "typed on foolscap typing paper" in 1933. This report of the dates of composition, printing, and publication may be intended merely to put the public chronological record straight. But the reiterated emphasis suggests a deeper concern with establishing the earliest moment at which the book came into being, a type of concern shared by the most exalted of scientists over the centuries.

26   The allusion is to Kuhn's question about the rules which he identifies as implied in "normal-scientific traditions": "What can we say are the main categories into which these rules fall?" Kuhn goes on to say that "I owe this question to W. O. Hagstrom, whose work in the sociology of science sometimes overlaps my own" (Kuhn, [1962] 1970: 40).

27 For an informed, informing, and altogether unpretentious examination of the biography as evidence, see John A. Garraty, *The Nature of Biography* (1957). An early book on the distinctive character of the autobiography is the "critical and comparative study" by A. R. Burr (1909) which has been deepened and extended in some respects by A. M. Clark, in his *Autobiography: Its Genesis and Phases* (1935). Aron Halberstam is well along on a dissertation in the Department of Sociology at Columbia University, drawing out the sociological implications of the autobiography as form and substance. J. Olney examines autobiography as metaphor in his analytical monograph, *Metaphors of Self: The Meaning of Autobiography* (1973). John Dollard pioneered in his classic work, *Criteria for the Life History* (1935), this being supplemented by G. W. Allport's basic analysis of "the use of personal documents in psychological science" (1942) and Louis Gottschalk's parallel study of "the use of personal documents in history." Unparalleled in other disciplines is the series devoted to the *History of Psychology in Autobiography* (1930–74), now in its sixth volume, the first four volumes having been edited by Clark Murchison, the fifth by E. G. Boring and Gardner Lindzey, and the sixth by Lindzey alone. (I am indebted to Dr. Lindzey for putting me on to several of the preceding monographs on autobiography.)

28 Many of the perceptively critical observations in George Stigler's paper (1975) have a conceptual character that is distinctively his own and thus advance our understanding of the limitations and scientific uses of scientific biography well beyond the boundaries of preceding discussions. Stigler has come upon the art of prosopography and reports that he has found "relatively few interesting applications of this technique to the history of science." It is safe to suppose that this condition will soon be changed.

29 This refers to an ongoing collaborative effort to investigate the biography of a scientific discovery, recombination in bacteria, which provided the foundations for bacterial genetics. A chief architect in that discovery, Joshua Lederberg, is in the research role of retrospective participant-observer, with two sociologists of science, Harriet Zuckerman and myself, attempting to provide theoretical guides to the retrieval of evidence—documentary sources, historical published materials, independently confirmed memories, and retrospections—and the historian of science, Yehuda Elkana, providing further context in terms of his notion of "images of science." For a preliminary report, see Zuckerman (1974) and for a fuller report, Lederberg and Zuckerman (1977).

30 It is symbolically appropriate that Thomas Kuhn should introduce the English-language edition of Fleck's monograph; after all, it was he who had introduced the original edition to Trenn and myself—as to countless others.

31 See chap. 1 of Merton (1968) on the failure of the public record to record the actual course of scientific inquiry, a failure noted long ago by Bacon —"never any knowledge was delivered in the same order it was invented"—and Leibniz—"I wish that authors would give us the history of their discoveries and the steps by which they have arrived at them." It has been periodically rediscovered by other observers of the mores of science such as Mach, A. A. Moles,

Agnes Arber, and Peter Medawar. On the institutionalization of the scientific paper which places a taboo on such instructive disclosures, see Zuckerman and Merton, 1971:68–76.

[32] On the concepts of local and cosmopolitan influentials, see chap. 12 of Merton (1968); for their application to academia, see Gouldner (1957–58) and Glaser (1964) for their application to scientists. For the notion that leaders of major organizations are functionally required to be both locals and cosmopolitans, see Merton ([1970] 1976:86), and for the designation of L. J. Henderson as a "cosmopolitan local," see Barber (1970:32). This is the same Henderson, of course, who was continuously influential at Harvard in many moments entering my account: as early (1911) teacher of the history of science, local patron of Sarton, a founding father of the Society of Fellows and *primus inter pares* among its Senior Fellows, compelling expositor of Pareto's work (in sociology, not economics) in his unexampled slender monograph *(Pareto's General Sociology: A Physiologist's Interpretation)* and in his uniquely constituted seminar (which in its first year included among its members, H. A. Murray and Talcott Parsons, then on the Harvard faculty, Charles P. Curtis, Jr., then of the Harvard Corporation, Kingsley Davis and myself, then graduate students, and George Homans, then an undergraduate). Adding to the variety was the hardheaded and tumultuous essayist, folklorist, and American historian, Bernard de Voto, who made periodic use of Pareto's orientation during his later occupancy of Easy Chair in *Harper's Magazine*.

[33] Coming as it did just before the United States entered as a combatant in World War II, the OSRD was designed "'to serve as a center for mobilization of the scientific personnel and resources of the Nation in order to assure maximum utilization of such personnel and resources in developing and applying the results of scientific research to defense purposes'" (Dupree, 1957:371). This was of course not the first time in history that science had been mobilized for military purposes but the OSRD became one of the first—perhaps the very first—to have its programs in basic research transferred and institutionalized in a permanent organization that would support basic research without known potentials of relevance for the military. While the war was still on, Roosevelt "set in motion the investigation leading to the report, *Science, The Endless Frontier*, with its suggestion of a National Research Foundation" which was eventually established in 1950 (Dupree, 1957:375).

[34] Of the eight case studies gathered up in the Harvard volumes, four were by Conant, two by Nash, one by Duane Roller, and the last by Duane Roller and Duane H. D. Roller. Conant's introduction still holds interest, not least for its formulation of the connections between concepts and observations.

[35] Appearing briefly and without elucidation in my 1942 paper on the normative structure of science (Merton, 1973:273), the notion of the accumulation of advantage in systems of social stratification (which links up with the concepts of the self-fulfilling prophecy and the Matthew effect) lay dormant in the sociology of science until it was reactivated a quarter-century later in "The Matthew Effect in Science" ([1968] 1973:esp. 457–8). After an empirical investigation of the Matthew Effect by Stephen Cole (1970) and the over-

view of stratification in American science by Harriet Zuckerman (1970), cumulative advantage has been examined in a series of studies: Zuckerman and Merton (1972:325); Cole and Cole (1973:237–47 passim); Allison and Stewart (1974), a comment on the Allison-Stewart paper by Michael A. Faia (1975) and their reply (1975:829–31); Zuckerman and Cole (1975:99–101); Zuckerman (1977, chaps. 3, 8); J. Cole (1977). Derek Price links up my earlier exposition of the Matthew Effect with various inequalities in the distributions of people, institutions, and fields (Price, 1965:235–36). In the third Paley Lecture at the New York Hospital-Cornell Medical Center (September 30, 1975), I have indicated countervailing mechanisms that dampen the increasing concentration of resources, rewards, and scientific productivity, "The Matthew Effect in Science II: Problems of Cumulative Advantage."

[36]   Of the 243 recipients, 216 were members of university and college faculties, the rest being divided among 27 unaffiliated writers, artists, poets, and composers, and 10 researchers affiliated with nonacademic organizations. The familiar steep stratification of American academia (Zuckerman, 1970; Cole and Cole, 1973) appears once again, this time in the skewed distribution of Guggenheim Fellowships. Among the approximately 2,000 American universities and colleges, only a small fraction were represented by any applicants at all. Although the data on the distribution of applications are not available for the year 1954, data for later years indicate that it is almost as skewed as the distribution of awards. The 216 academic fellowships were distributed among 68 universities and colleges, with two-thirds of them concentrated in the 22 ranking universities (as gauged, for the 1950s, by the Kenniston-Berelson ratings of institutional quality, see Berelson, 1960:124–29).

	Number Percentage of Fellowships		Av. # per institution
Top 12 universities	93	43%	7.8
Next 10 universities	44	20	4.4
Remaining 46 universities and colleges	79	37	1.7

(It is of mildly coincidental interest that one of the Guggenheim Fellows in 1954 should have been Hayward Kenniston who three years later would do the national survey supplying the ratings I have just put to use.)

[37]   Kuhn's reluctance to publish until he was convinced that he knew whereof he wrote—witness his decision not to publish his Lowell Lectures of 1951—and the considerable impact of what he did publish locate him as a "perfectionist" in the classification developed by Cole and Cole, 1973:91–93. This pattern is quite distinct from those of the "mass producers," who publish much but inconsequentially; the "prolific" scientists who publish in abundance with their work being much used; and the relatively "silent" scientists whose infrequent publications are little used by others in the field. Kuhn's early pattern of severely limited publication and affiliation with top-ranked universities is consistent with the Coles's general finding for physicists that it is primarily the

assessed *quality* of a scientist's work rather than its mere quantity that is associated with the rank of the departments with which they are affiliated.

[38]   Berelson (1960:127) does not stratify faculty members by age but does find, for the year 1958, that the "top universities, with less than 10% of the total faculty . . . account for almost 40% of the authors in the leading learned journals."

[39]   On this aspect of processes of evaluation in the sciences and humanities, dealing with the competition between organizations committed to the objective of searching out talent as early as possible in order to further their development, see " 'Recognition' and 'Excellence': Instructive Ambiguities," in Merton, [1960] 1973:419–38.

[40]   For the purpose of secondary, network analysis, it is useful to list the names and institutional affiliations of the individuals variously instrumental in establishing the Center. The Advisory Committee, appointed in the early days to help formulate plans for the Center consisted of Carl Hovland (Psychology, Yale), Paul F. Lazarsfeld (Sociology, Columbia), Robert Merton (Sociology, Columbia), Henry A. Murray (Psychology, Harvard), Edward A. Shils (Committee on Social Thought, Chicago), Herbert A. Simon (Organizational Analysis, Carnegie Institute of Technology), and Joseph Spengler (Economics, Duke).

[41]   The first Board of Directors of the Center consisted of Paul Buck (historian and recently Provost, Harvard), F. F. Hill (Provost, Cornell), Clark Kerr (Chancellor, University of California), Robert K. Merton (sociologist, Columbia), Robert Sears (psychologist, Stanford), Frank Stanton (President, Columbia Broadcasting System, who began his research on mass communications in taking his doctorate in psychology at Ohio State), serving as chairman, Ralph W. Tyler (formerly Dean of the Division of Social Sciences, University of Chicago), serving as President of the Center and its Executive Director, Alan T. Waterman (Director of the National Science Foundation), and Theodore Yntema (economist and vice-president of the Ford Motor Company). The Board's Committee on Fellowships consisted of Buck, Merton, and Sears.

[42]   Shils was describing the sociological study "of science and scientific institutions" as an undeveloped area in the state of American sociology as it was practiced in 1948 just as two years later, in my foreword to Bernard Barber's *Science and the Social Order*, I was puzzling over the reasons for this condition of continued neglect.

[43]   This case of organizational competition takes on added point in light of the following formulation, by a member of the Planning Group for the Center, of its essential character: It is, he wrote, "A *Guggenheim with feedback.*" The Guggenheim fellowships make "no provision for systematic feedback. It is here that the Center, with its insistence upon creating a community of scholars, fills the gap by providing the conditions for both obtaining and giving feedback. At what I have called the middling-old level of professional and perhaps chronological age, it is this feedback that permits the testing of reality, and at once provides training and facilitates creative effort. It is the opportunity to communicate that can make of collections of pedants communities of scholars

and from contrivers of esoteric (if not autistic) theories creators of public and fruitful theories."

44   It is Talcott Parsons, of course, who has done most to introduce and explicate the sociological concepts of universalism and particularism, from his magisterial *The Structure of Social Action* (1937) onward.

45   Only *"relatively"* fine-grained" for it is evident that I have confined this sketchy analysis to certain social contexts of Kuhn's cognitive development which resulted in part from his self-selecting choices among socially structured alternatives. But I have made no effort to analyze those consequential choices in detail: for examples, the decision to go to Harvard rather than, say, Temple University or Clemson College; the decision to study physics followed by the risky and, for our purposes, highly consequential decision to shift to the history of science; the successive decisions to be a candidate for a National Research Council fellowship, for membership in the Harvard Society of Fellows, for a Guggenheim Fellowship and to decline the invitation from the Center for Advanced Study in the Behavioral Sciences. Analysis of these socially patterned and consequential choices would require formidable data of a kind not available to me (although data of that kind are being assembled in that other case to which I have referred, the study of the role of Joshua Lederberg in the beginnings of bacterial genetics). Still, even this sketch, focused on social contexts rather than on the dynamics of individual choices, may serve as a relatively fine-grained supplement to such aggregative investigations as those by Lowell Hargens and Warren Hagstrom (1967) on "sponsored and contest mobility of American academic scientists" and Diana Crane (1970) on the mobility of faculty members.

46   I rarely use the term "breakthrough" but it invariably brings to mind the jesting observation by the economist and polymath Kenneth Boulding intended to capture the intellectual excitement of the first year of the Center's existence: Fellows would greet one another not with a "Good morning," "Hi," or even "Grüss Gott," but with a simple "Any breakthroughs today?"

47   Evidence to the contrary not yet found, I harbor the belief that the term-cum-concept, "serendipity," was ushered into the domain of the social sciences in the 1945 paper, "Sociological Theory" (Merton, 1968:150). In properly self-exemplifying fashion, I had stumbled upon the odd-looking, uniquely apt coinage by Horace Walpole while browsing in the incomparable *Oxford English Dictionary (OED)*, a kind of peripatetic activity to which a good many of us are addicted. An unpublished monograph by Elinor Barber and myself entitled *The Travels and Adventures of Serendipity: A Study in Historical Semantics and the Sociology of Science* deals with the social and cultural contexts of the coinage of serendipity in the eighteenth century; the climate of relevant opinion in which it first saw print in the nineteenth century; the patterned responses to the neologism when first encountered; the diverse social circles of litterateurs, physical and social scientists, engineers, lexicographers, and historians in which it diffused; the changes of meaning it has undergone in the course of diffusion, and the ideological uses to which it has been variously put.

[48]   In these days of renewed interest in Peirce's ideas, the note appended to the 1948 text at this point may bear repetition: "Charles Sanders Peirce had long before noticed the strategic role of the 'surprising fact' in his account of what he called 'abduction,' that is, the initiation and entertaining of a hypothesis as a step in inference. See his *Collected Papers*, VI, 522–28."

[49]   The added italics are intended to direct attention to the then current conviction in many quarters that facts presuppose theory—in more recent idiom, that "facts are theory-laden." The reiterated "of courses" in these passages—that, of course, inferences depend largely upon one's theoretical orientation; that, of course, the unexpected fact refers to what the observer brings to the datum—are intended to signal these views as being commonplace at the time. (On the "of-course mood" in exposition, see Merton, 1965: 149n, and as further indexed.)

[50]   To illustrate the possibilities of fine-grained network analyses of social and cognitive contexts, I note just a few of the many making up the 1958–59 cohort of Fellows: E. A. Shils, W. V. O. Quine, K. Pribram, K. D. Naegele, G. A. Miller, M. Janowitz, R. Jakobson, G. C. Homans, J. Greenberg, C. Geertz, M. Fortes, R. Firth, C. Dubois, L. Benson, D. Bell, F. Barron, M. Argyle, and D. Aaron. More detailed investigation would identify the significant reference individuals for Kuhn in that cohort.

[51]   The account of the conference appears in Merton, 1960: 1–5; the principal papers were eventually published in *Isis*, Kuhn's own paper being locatable in *Isis* 1961: 161–90 and being republished in Kuhn, 1977.

[52]   For the most comprehensive and, in some of its essays, penetrating examination of Kuhn's ideas, see the creatively edited volume: Imre Lakatos and Alan Musgrave (1970); for a strong criticism of Kuhn *and* Lakatos, see Joseph Agassi (1971).

[53]   That Paul Samuelson should maintain that Kuhn did not adequately recognize the dominance of one paradigm in at least the physical sciences while Imre Lakatos indicted Kuhn for holding, in 1962, that "major fields of science are, and must be, always dominated by one single supreme paradigm" (Lakatos, 1971: 177) emphatically indicates that the book could lend itself to diametrically opposed interpretations by minds of a very high order, versed in the ways of science.

[54]   For an analysis of the concept of "scientific revolution," see Stephen Toulmin (1970, 1: 98–130)—though, through a familiar typographical error he appears to rob Robert to pay Thomas; and on "the 18th-century origins of the concept of scientific revolution," see I. Bernard Cohen (1976: 257n) who observes in "the reaction to Kuhn's thesis of social dynamics of scientific change" that "the secondary literature on the philosophy and history of science has become saturated with books and articles using the world 'revolution' in almost every possible context, and dealing with almost every aspect of scientific revolutions, save one: there has been no adequate study of what the particular uses of this word and concept may have been in successive past ages." See also Klein, "Einstein on scientific revolutions" (1975). For an account of the ideas

and terminology of "revolution" generally, see Perez Zagorin (1976) and the literature cited there.

[55] It is perhaps prognostic that an international organization formed in 1975 —the Society for Social Studies of Science (the 4S)—draws its members from such disciplines as anthropology, economics, history, information science, philosophy, political science, psychology, research administration, science policy studies, and sociology.

NOTE: The National Science Foundation provided support for this study by grants to the Columbia University Program in the Sociology of Science and the Program on Science, Technology, and Society at the Center for Advanced Study in the Behavioral Sciences. I am indebted for helpful criticism to colleagues at Columbia and the Center (Jonathan R. Cole, Stephen Cole, Yehuda Elkana, Joshua Lederberg, Arnold Thackray, and Harriet Zuckerman) and to colleagues-at-a-distance (Bennett Berger, Eugene Garfield, Charles C. Gillispie, Warren Hagstrom, William Kruskal, Morton Malin, Nicholas C. Mullins, Rodney Stark and Nico Stehr). The errors of fact and judgment that remain are indisputably my own.

References

ADAIR, WILLIAM C.
  1955 "Citation Indexes for Scientific Literature?" *American Documentation* 6:31–32.
ALLISON, PAUL D., AND JOHN A. STEWART
  1974 "Productivity Differences among Scientists: Evidence for Accumulative Advantage." *American Sociological Review* 39:596–606.
ALLPORT, GORDON
  1942 *The Uses of Personal Documents in Psychological Science*. New York: Social Science Research Council, Bulletin No. 49.
ARON, RAYMOND
  1959 "Société moderne et sociologie." *Transactions of the Fourth World Congress of Sociology*. London: International Sociological Association 1:1–19.
AUBREY, JOHN
  1898 *Brief Lives*. Oxford: Clarendon Press.

BARBER, BERNARD
  1951 *Social Stratification*. New York: Harcourt Brace Jovanovich.
  1952 *Science and the Social Order*. New York: Free Press.
  1961 "Resistance by Scientists to Scientific Discovery." *Science* 134:596–602.

1963 "Review: T. S. Kuhn, *The Structure of Scientific Revolutions.*" *American Sociological Review* 28 (April):298–99.

BEAVER, DONALD DEB.
1966 "The American Scientific Community, 1800–1860: An Historical and Statistical Study." Ph.D. dissertation, Yale University.

BEN-DAVID, JOSEPH
1971 *The Scientist's Role in Society: A Comparative Study.* Englewood Cliffs, N.J.: Prentice-Hall.

BEN-DAVID, JOSEPH, AND RANDALL COLLINS
1966 "Social Factors in the Origins of a New Science: The Case of Psychology." *American Sociological Review* 31:451–65.

BERELSON, BERNARD
1951 *Content Analysis.* New York: Free Press.
1960 *Graduate Education in the United States.* New York: McGraw-Hill Book Co.

BIRCH, THOMAS
1756–57 *The History of the Royal Society.* 4 vols. London: A. Millar.

BLISSETT, MARLAN
1972 *Politics in Science.* Boston: Little Brown.

BLUME, STUART S.
1974 *Toward a Political Sociology of Science.* New York: Free Press.

BÖHME, GERNOT
1974 "Die Soziale Bedeutung kognitiver Strukturen (I. Typen der Kuhn-Rezeption in der Wissenschaftssoziologie)." *Soziale Welt* 25:188–208.

BORING, EDWIN G., AND GARDNER LINDZEY (EDS.)
1966–67 *A History of Psychology in Autobiography*, vols. 4 and 5. New York: Appleton-Century-Crofts.

BOYLE, ROBERT
1744 *Works.* 5 vols. Edited, with the Life of the Author, by Thomas Birch. London.

BRINTON, CRANE (ED.)
1959 *The Society of Fellows.* Cambridge, Mass.: Harvard University Press.

BROOKS, HARVEY
1968 *The Government of Science.* Cambridge, Mass.: M.I.T. Press.

BURKE, KENNETH
1935 *Permanence and Change.* New York: New Republic.

BURR, A. R.
1909 *The Autobiography: A Critical and Comparative Study.* Boston: Houghton Mifflin.

CAIRNS, ALAN C.
1974 "National Influences on the Study of Politics." *Queen's Quarterly*, 81(3):333–47.

CALDWELL, LYNTON K.
1968–69 *Science, Technology and Public Policy: A Selected and Annotated Bibliography*. 2 vols. Bloomington: Indiana University Press.

CANDOLLE, ALPHONSE DE
[1872–73] 1885 *Histoire des sciences et des savants depuis deux siècles*. Geneva-Basel: H. Georg.

CHASTAGNOL, ANDRÉ
1970 "La prosopographie, méthode de recherche sur l'histoire du Bas-Empire." *Annales: Économies, Sociétés, Civilisations*, 25ᵉ année, no. 5: 1229–35.

CLARK, ARTHUR MELVILLE
1935 *Autobiography: Its Genesis and Phases*. Edinburgh: Oliver.

CLARK, TERRY
1968 "Institutionalization of Innovations in Higher Education: Four Models." *Administrative Science Quarterly* 13: 1–25.

COHEN, I. BERNARD
1971 *Introduction to Newton's 'Principia'*. Cambridge, Mass.: Harvard University Press.
1974a "History and the Philosopher of Science." In Frederick Suppe (ed.), *The Structure of Scientific Theories*, pp. 308–73. Urbana, Ill.: University of Illinois Press.
1974b "Newton's Theory vs. Kepler's Theory and Galileo's Theory." In Yehuda Elkana (ed.), *The Interaction Between Science and Philosophy*, pp. 299–338. Atlantic Highlands, N.J.: Humanities Press.
1976 "The Eighteenth-Century Origins of the Concept of Scientific Revolution." *Journal of the History of Ideas* 37: 257–88.

COLE, F. J., AND N. B. EALES
1917 "The History of Comparative Anatomy: A Statistical Analysis of the Literature." *Science Progress* 11: 578–96.

COLE, JONATHAN R., AND STEPHEN COLE
1971 "Measuring the Quality of Sociological Research." *American Sociologist* 6: 23–29.
1973 *Social Stratification in Science*. Chicago: University of Chicago Press.

COLE, JONATHAN R., AND HARRIET ZUCKERMAN
1975 "The Emergence of a Scientific Specialty: The Self-Exemplifying Case of the Sociology of Science." In Lewis A. Coser (ed.), *The Idea of Social Structure*, pp. 139–74. New York: Harcourt Brace Jovanovich.

COLE, STEPHEN
1965 "In Defense of the Sociology of Science." *The GSSS Journal*, pp. 30–38. Columbia University Graduate Sociological Society.
1970 "Professional Standing and the Reception of Scientific Discoveries." *American Sociological Review* 76: 286–306.
1975 "The Growth of Scientific Knowledge: Theories of Deviance as a

Case Study." In Lewis A. Coser (ed.), *The Idea of Social Structure*, pp. 175–220. New York: Harcourt Brace Jovanovich.

CONANT, JAMES BRYANT

1942 "The Advancement of Learning during the Puritan Commonwealth." *Proceedings*, Massachusetts Historical Society, vol. 66:3–21.

1957 *Harvard Case Studies in Experimental Science*. 2 vols. Cambridge, Mass.: Harvard University Press.

COOLEY, CHARLES H.

[1909] 1956 *Social Organization*. New York: Free Press.

CRANE, DIANA

1969 "Social Structure in a Group of Scientists: A Test of the 'Invisible College' Hypothesis." *American Sociological Review* 34:335–52.

1970 "The Academic Marketplace Revisited: A Study of Faculty Mobility Using the Cartter Ratings." *American Journal of Sociology* 75:953–64.

1972 *Invisible Colleges*. Chicago: University of Chicago Press.

DANIELS, GEORGE H.

1967 "The Process of Professionalization in American Science: The Emergent Period, 1820–60." *Isis* 58:151–66.

DARMSTÄDTER, LUDWIG

1908 *Handbuch zur Geschichte der Naturwissenschaften und der Technik*. Berlin: J. Springer.

DICTIONARY OF AMERICAN BIOGRAPHY

1957 Allen Johnson (ed.). New York: Charles Scribner's Sons. 11 vols.

DOLLARD, JOHN

1935 *Criteria for the Life History: With Analyses of Six Notable Documents*. New Haven: Yale University Press.

DOVRING, KARIN

1954 "Quantitative Semantics in 18th-Century Sweden." *Public Opinion Quarterly*, 18(4):389–94.

DUPREE, A. HUNTER

1957 *Science in the Federal Government: A History of Policies and Activities to 1940*. Cambridge, Mass.: Harvard University Press.

EDGE, D. O., AND M. J. MULKAY

1974 "Case Studies of Scientific Specialties." Preprint of paper in *Kölner Zeitschrift für Soziologie und Sozialpsychologie*, Spring 1975.

1976 *Astronomy Transformed: The Emergence of Radio Astronomy in Britain*. New York & London: Wiley-Interscience.

EISENSTADT, SHMUEL N.

1965 *Essays on Comparative Institutions*. New York: Wiley.

ELKANA, YEHUDA

1973a "The Problem of Knowledge in Historical Perspectives." *Proceedings of the Second Hellenistic Humanistic Symposium*, pp. 191–247. Athens.

1973b *The Discovery of the Conservation of Energy.* Cambridge, Mass.: Harvard University Press.

1974a "Euler and Kant: Scientific and Metaphysical Problems." In R. S. Cohen and M. W. Wartofsky (eds.), *Methodological and Historical Essays in the Natural and Social Sciences*, pp. 277–305. Dordrecht, Netherlands: D. Reidel.

1974b "Boltzmann's Scientific Research Programme and the Alternatives to it." In Elkana (ed.), *The Interaction between Science and Philosophy*, pp. 243–79. Atlantic Highlands, N.J.: Humanities Press.

ELKANA, YEHUDA; JOSHUA LEDERBERG; ROBERT K. MERTON; ARNOLD THACKRAY; AND HARRIET ZUCKERMAN (EDS.)

1977 *Toward a Metric of Science: The Advent of Science Indicators.* New York: Wiley-Interscience.

ELLIS, HAVELOCK

[1895] 1904 *A Study of British Genius.* London: Hurst and Blackett.

ETZIONI, AMITAI, AND CLYDE NUNN

1976 "A Public Appreciation of Science in Contemporary America." In Gerald Holton and W. Blanpied (eds.), *Science and Its Public: The Changing Relationship.* Dordrecht and Boston: D. Reidel.

FAIA, MICHAEL A.

1975 "Productivity among Scientists: A Replication and Elaboration (Comment on Allison and Stewart)." *American Sociological Review* 40:825–31.

FISHER, CHARLES S.

1966 "The Death of a Mathematical Theory: A Study in the Sociology of Knowledge." *Archive for the History of Exact Sciences* 3:137–59.

FLECK, LUDWIK

[1935] forthcoming *The Genesis and Development of a Scientific Fact.* Edited with commentary and analysis by Thaddeus J. Trenn and Robert K. Merton, with Foreword by Thomas Kuhn, and Biographical Sketch of Fleck by Mark Kac. Chicago: University of Chicago Press.

FOGEL, ROBERT WILLIAM

1975 "The Limits of Quantitative Methods in History." *The American Historical Review* 80:329–50.

FRIEDRICHS, ROBERT W.

1970 *A Sociology of Sociology.* New York: Free Press.

GALTON, FRANCIS

[1869] 1952 *Hereditary Genius: An Inquiry into its Laws and Consequences.* New York: Horizon Press.

1872 "On the Causes which Operate to Create Scientific Men." *Fortnightly Review* 13, N.S., 345–510.

1874 *English Men of Science: Their Nature and Nurture.* London: Macmillan.

GARFIELD, EUGENE
  1955 "Citation Indexes for Science." *Science*, vol. 122, no. 3159:108–11.
  1963 "Citation Indexes in Sociological and Historical Research." *American Documentation*, vol. 14, no. 4:289–91.
GARFIELD, EUGENE; MORTON MALIN; AND HENRY SMALL
  1977 "Citation Data as Science Indicators." In Y. Elkana; J. Lederberg; R. K. Merton; A. Thackray; and H. Zuckerman (eds.), *Toward a Metric of Science: The Advent of Science Indicators*. New York: Wiley-Interscience.
GARRATY, JOHN A.
  1957 *The Nature of Biography*. New York: A. A. Knopf.
GARVEY, WILLIAM D., AND BELVER C. GRIFFITH
  1964 "Scientific Information Exchange in Psychology." *Science* 146:1955–59.
  1966 "Studies of Social Innovations in Scientific Communication in Psychology." *American Psychologist* 21:1019–36.
GASTON, JERRY
  1971 "Secretiveness and Competition for Priority of Discovery in Physics." *Minerva* 9:472–92.
  1971 *Originality and Competition in Science*. Chicago: University of Chicago Press.
GIERYN, THOMAS F., AND ROBERT K. MERTON
  1975 "Citations as Indicators of Local and Cosmopolitan Influentials in Science: A Research Memorandum." Unpublished.
GILBERT, G. NIGEL, AND STEVE WOOLGAR
  1974 "The Quantitative Study of Science: An Examination of the Literature." *Science Studies* 4:279–94.
GILFILLAN, S. COLUM
  1935 *The Sociology of Invention*. Chicago: Follett Publishing Co.
GILLISPIE, CHARLES COULSTON
  1951 *Genesis and Geology: A Study in the Relations of Scientific Thought, Natural Theology and Social Opinion in Great Britain, 1790–1850*. Cambridge, Mass.: Harvard University Press.
  1960 *The Edge of Objectivity: An Essay in the History of Scientific Ideas*. Princeton: Princeton University Press.
GILLISPIE, CHARLES COULSTON (Editor in Chief)
  1971– *Dictionary of Scientific Biography*. New York: Charles Scribner's Sons.
GLASER, BARNEY G.
  1964 *Organizational Scientists*. Indianapolis: Bobbs-Merrill.
GOTTSCHALK, LOUIS
  1945 *The Use of Personal Documents in History, Anthropology, and Sociology*. New York: Social Science Research Council.
GOULDNER, ALVIN W.
  1957–58 "Cosmopolitans and Locals: Toward an Analysis of Latent Social

Roles: I and II." *Administrative Science Quarterly* 2:281–306, 444–80.

1958 "Introduction" to Émile Durkheim, *Socialism and Saint Simon* [*Le Socialisme*], edited by A. W. Gouldner, pp. v–xxix. Antioch, Ohio: Antioch Press.

1970 *The Coming Crisis of Western Sociology*. New York: Basic Books.

GRIFFITH, BELVER C., AND A. J. MILLER

1970 "Networks of Informal Communication among Scientifically Productive Scientists." In Carnot E. Nelson and Donald K. Pollock (eds.), *Communication Among Scientists and Engineers*. Lexington, Mass.: D. C. Heath.

GRIFFITH, BELVER C., AND NICHOLAS C. MULLINS

1972 "Coherent Social Groups in Scientific Change." *Science* vol. 177, no. 4053:959–64.

GRIFFITH, B. C.; H. SMALL; J. A. STONEHILL; AND S. DEY

1974 "The Structure of Scientific Literatures II: Toward a Macro- and Microstructure for Science." *Science Studies* 4:339–65.

GROSS, T. L. K., AND E. M. GROSS

1927 "College Libraries and Chemical Education." *Science* 66:385–89.

HABERER, JOSEPH

1969 *Politics and the Community of Science*. New York: Van Nostrand Reinhold Co.

HAGSTROM, WARREN

1965 *The Scientific Community*. New York: Basic Books.

1974 "Competition in Science." *American Sociological Review* 39:1–18.

HALL, A. RUPERT, AND MARIE BOAS HALL

1968 "The Intellectual Origins of the Royal Society–London and Oxford." *Notes and Records of the Royal Society of London*, vol. 23, no. 2:157–68.

HALMOS, PAUL (ED.)

1970 *The Sociology of Sociology*. The Sociological Review Monograph, no. 16.

1972 *The Sociology of Science*. The Sociological Review Monograph, no. 18.

HANS, NICHOLAS

1951 *New Trends in Education in the Eighteenth Century*. London: Routledge and Kegan Paul.

HARGENS, LOWELL, AND WARREN HAGSTROM

1967 "Sponsored and Contest Mobility of American Academic Scientists." *Sociology of Education* 40:24–38.

HENDERSON, L. J.

1970 *On The Social System: Selected Writings*. Edited and with an introduction by Bernard Barber. Chicago: University of Chicago Press.

HIEBERT, ERWIN N.
1975   "Citation for the Award of the 1974 Sarton Medal." *Isis* 66:478–81.
HILL, CHRISTOPHER
1968   "The Intellectual Origins of the Royal Society–London or Oxford?"
       Notes and Records of the Royal Society of London, vol. 23, no.
       2:144–56.
HULME, E. WYNDHAM
1923   *Statistical Bibliography in Relation to the Growth of Modern Civili-
       zation.* Cambridge: Cambridge University Press.
HYMAN, HERBERT H.
1968   "Reference Groups." In David Sills (ed.), *International Encyclopedia
       of the Social Sciences*, vol. 13, pp. 353–61. New York: Macmillan and
       Free Press.
1975   "Reference Individuals and Reference Idols." In Lewis A. Coser
       (ed.), *The Idea of Social Structure*. New York: Harcourt Brace
       Jovanovich.
HYMAN, HERBERT H., AND ELEANOR SINGER
1968   *Readings in Reference Group Theory and Research*. New York: Free
       Press.

KLEIN, MARTIN J.
1975   "Einstein on Scientific Revolutions." *Vistas in Astronomy* 17:113–
       20.
KNORR, KARIN D.; HERMANN STRASSER; AND HANS G. ZILIAN (EDS.)
1975   *Determinants and Controls of Scientific Development*. Dordrecht,
       Holland: D. Reidel.
KRÖBER, GÜNTER; HUBERT LAITKO; AND HELMUT STEINER (EDS.)
1974   *Wissenschaft und Forschung in Sozialismus*. Berlin: Akademie-
       Verlag.
KUHN, THOMAS S.
1957   *The Copernican Revolution: Planetary Astronomy in the Develop-
       ment of Western Thought*. Cambridge, Mass.: Harvard University
       Press.
1959   "Energy Conservation as an Example of Simultaneous Discovery." In
       Marshall Clagett (ed.), *Critical Problems in the History of Science*.
       Madison: University of Wisconsin Press.
1962   "Historical Structure of Scientific Discovery." *Science* 136:760–64.
[1962] 1970 *The Structure of Scientific Revolutions*. Chicago: University of
       Chicago Press.
1968   "The History of Science." In David L. Sills (ed.), *International En-
       cyclopedia of the Social Sciences*, vol. 14, pp. 74–83. New York:
       Macmillan and Free Press.
1970   "Logic of Discovery or Psychology of Research?" In Imre Lakatos
       and Alan Musgrave (eds.), *Criticism and the Growth of Knowledge*,
       pp. 1–23. Cambridge: Cambridge University Press.
1974   "Second Thoughts on Paradigms." In F. Suppe (ed.), *The Structure*

of Scientific Theories, pp. 459–82. Urbana: University of Illinois Press, 1974.

1975 "Tradition mathématique et tradition expérimentale dans le développment de la physique." *Annales: Économies, Sociétés, Civilisations*, September–October, 5:975–98.

1977 Untitled essays. Chicago: University of Chicago Press.

forthcoming Foreword to Ludwik Fleck, *The Genesis and Development of a Scientific Fact*, edited by Thaddeus J. Trenn and Robert K. Merton. Chicago: University of Chicago Press.

LASSWELL, HAROLD D.

1938 "A Provisional Classification of Symbol Data." *Psychiatry* 1:197–204.

LASSWELL, HAROLD D., AND NATHAN LEITES

[1949] 1965 *Language of Politics: Studies in Quantitative Semantics*. Cambridge, Mass.: MIT Press.

LAW, JOHN

1973 "The Development of Specialties in Science: the Case of X-ray Protein Crystallography." *Science Studies* 3:275–303.

LAZARSFELD, PAUL F., AND ROBERT K. MERTON

1948 "Mass Communication, Popular Taste, and Organized Social Action." In Lyman Bryson (ed.), *Communication of Ideas*, pp. 95–118. New York: Harper and Row.

LEDERBERG, JOSHUA AND HARRIET ZUCKERMAN

1977 "From Schizomycetes to Bacterial Sexuality: A Case Study of Discontinuity in Science." Mimeo.

LINDZEY, GARDNER (ED.)

1974 *A History of Psychology in Autobiography*, vol. 6. Englewood Cliffs, N.J.: Prentice-Hall.

MARSHAKOVA, I. V.

1973 "System of Document Connections Based on References." *Nauchno-Teknicheskaia Informatsiia* 2:3–8.

MASTERMAN, MARGARET

1970 "The Nature of a Paradigm." In Imre Lakatos and Alan Musgrave (eds.), *Criticism and the Growth of Knowledge*, pp. 59–89. Cambridge: Cambridge University Press.

MENARD, HENRY W.

1971 *Science: Growth and Change*. Cambridge, Mass.: Harvard University Press.

MERTON, ROBERT K.

1936 "Civilization and Culture." *Sociology and Social Research* 21:103–13.

1937 "The Sociology of Knowledge." *Isis* 27:493–503.

[1938] 1970 *Science, Technology, and Society in Seventeenth-Century England*. New York: Harper and Row; Howard Fertig.

[1949, 1957] 1968 *Social Theory and Social Structure*. New York: Free Press.

1960 "The History of Quantification in the Sciences." *Items*, Social Science Research Council, vol. 14 (March): 1–5.

1965 *On the Shoulders of Giants: A Shandean Postscript*. New York: Harcourt Brace Jovanovich.

1973 *The Sociology of Science: Theoretical and Empirical Investigations*. Norman W. Storer (ed.). Chicago: University of Chicago Press.

1975 "The Matthew Effect in Science II: Problems of Cumulative Advantage." The 3d Paley Lecture. The New York Hospital-Cornell Medical Center (September).

1976 *Sociological Ambivalence and Other Essays*. New York: Free Press.

MERTON, ROBERT K., AND ELINOR BARBER

1955 "The Travels and Adventures of Serendipity: A Study in Historical Semantics and the Sociology of Science." Unpublished monograph.

MIKULINSKY, S. R.

1974 "Alphonse de Candolle's *Histoire des Sciences et des Savants depuis Deux Siècles* and its Historic Significance." *Organon* 10:233–43.

MILES, MARY WILSON

1975 "Bibliography." In Lewis A. Coser (ed.), *The Idea of Social Structure*. New York: Harcourt Brace Jovanovich.

MULKAY, M. J.

1972 *The Social Process of Innovation*. London: Macmillan.

MULKAY, M. J., AND D. O. EDGE

1974 "Cognitive, Technical and Social Factors in the Growth of Radio Astronomy." *Social Science Information* 13:25–61.

MULKAY, M. J.; G. N. GILBERT; AND S. WOOLGAR

1975 "Problem Areas and Research Networks in Science." *Sociology* 9:187–204.

MULLINS, NICHOLAS C.

1968 "The Distribution of Social and Cultural Properties in Informal Communication Networks among Biological Scientists." *American Sociological Review* 33:786–97.

1972 "The Development of a Scientific Specialty: The Phage Group and the Origin of Molecular Biology." *Minerva* 10:51–82.

1973a "The Development of Specialties in Social Science: The Case of Ethnomethodology." *Science Studies* 3:245–73.

1973b *Theories and Theory Groups in Contemporary American Sociology*. New York: Harper and Row.

NATIONAL SCIENCE BOARD

1973 *Science Indicators 1972*. Washington, D.C.: U.S. Government Printing Office.

1975 *Science Indicators 1974*. Washington, D.C.: U.S. Government Printing Office.

NASH, LEONARD K.
1963   *The Nature of the Natural Sciences*. Boston: Little Brown.
NEEDHAM, JOSEPH
1954–74   *Science and Civilisation in China*. 5 vols. Cambridge: Cambridge
University Press.
NICOLET, C.
1970   "Prosopographie et histoire sociale: Rome et l'Italie à l'époque républicaine." *Annales: Économies, Sociétés, Civilisations*, 25ᵉ année, no.
5:1209–28.

ODIN, ALFRED
1895   *Genèse des grands hommes*. 2 vols. Paris: Librairie Universitaire.
OLNEY, JAMES
1972   *Metaphors of Self: The Meaning of Autobiography*. Princeton:
Princeton University Press.

PARSONS, TALCOTT
1937   *The Structure of Social Action*. New York: McGraw-Hill.
1951   *The Social System*. New York: Free Press.
PARSONS, TALCOTT; ROBERT F. BALES; AND EDWARD A. SHILS
1953   *Working Papers in the Theory of Action*. New York: Free Press.
PARSONS, TALCOTT, AND EDWARD A. SHILS (EDS.)
1951   *Toward a General Theory of Action*. Cambridge, Mass.: Harvard
University Press.
PEARSON, KARL
1914–30   *The Life, Letters and Labours of Francis Galton*, vols. 1–3b.
Cambridge: Cambridge University Press.
PEIRCE, CHARLES SANDERS
1931–35   *Collected Papers*. Cambridge, Mass.: Harvard University Press.
POLANYI, MICHAEL
1951   *The Logic of Liberty*, pp. 49–67. Chicago: University of Chicago
Press.
1958   *Personal Knowledge*. Chicago: University of Chicago Press.
POPPER, KARL R.
1934–35   *Logik der Forschung*. Vienna: Julius Springer.
[1944] 1957   *The Poverty of Historicism*. London: Routledge and Kegan
Paul.
1945   *The Open Society and Its Enemies*. 2 vols. London: George Routledge and Sons.
1960   *The Logic of Scientific Discovery*. Enlarged translation of 1934–35.
London: Hutchinson and Co.
1963   *Conjectures and Refutations: The Growth of Scientific Knowledge*.
New York: Basic Books.
1974   "Autobiography." In Paul A. Schilpp, *The Philosophy of Karl Popper*. 2 vols.; vol. 1, pp. 3–181. La Salle, Ill.: Open Court Publishing
Co.

PRICE, DEREK J. DE SOLLA
  1951 "Quantitative Measures of the Development of Science." *Archives Internationales d'Histoire des Sciences* 14:85–93, and *Actes du VI Congrès International d'Histoire des Sciences*, pp. 413–21. Paris: Hermann and Çie.
  [1961] 1975 *Science Since Babylon*. Enlarged edition. New Haven: Yale University Press.
  1963 *Little Science, Big Science*. New York: Columbia University Press.
  1965 "The Scientific Foundations of Science Policy." *Nature* 206 (April 15):233–38.
  1977 "Toward a Model for Science Indicators." In Y. Elkana; J. Lederberg; R. K. Merton; A. Thackray; and H. Zuckerman (eds.), *Toward a Metric of Science: The Advent of Science Indicators*. New York: Wiley-Interscience.
PRICE, DEREK J. DE SOLLA, AND DONALD DEB. BEAVER
  1966 "Collaboration in an Invisible College." *American Psychologist* 21:1011–18.
PRICE, DON K.
  1954 *Government and Science*. Cambridge, Mass.: Harvard University Press.
  1965 *The Scientific Estate*. Cambridge, Mass.: Harvard University Press.
PURVER, MARGERY
  1967 *The Royal Society: Concept and Creation*. Cambridge, Mass.: M.I.T. Press.

RAINOFF, T. J.
  1929 "Wave-like Fluctuations of Creative Productivity in the Development of West-European Physics." *Isis* 12:287–319.
RATTANSI, P. M.
  1968 "The Intellectual Origins of the Royal Society." *Notes and Records of the Royal Society of London*, vol. 23, no. 2:129–42.
RAVETZ, JEROME R.
  1971 *Scientific Knowledge and Its Social Problems*. Oxford: Clarendon Press.
REICHENBACH, HANS
  1938 *Experience and Prediction: An Analysis of the Foundations and the Structure of Knowledge*. Chicago: University of Chicago Press.
REYNOLDS, LARRY T., AND JANICE M. REYNOLDS (EDS.)
  1970 *Sociology of Sociology: Analysis & Criticism of the Thought, Research, & Ethical Folkways of Sociology & Its Practitioners*. New York: McKay.
RICHARDS, DICKINSON W.
  1953 "Homeostasis versus Hyperexis: or Saint George and the Dragon." *Scientific Monthly* 77:289–95.
RIESMAN, DAVID, AND CHRISTOPHER JENCKS
  1968 *The Academic Revolution*. New York: Doubleday.

RILEY, MATILDA WHITE, AND CLARICE S. STOLL
1968 "Content Analysis." In *International Encyclopedia of the Social Sciences*, vol. 3, pp. 371–77. New York: Macmillan and Free Press.
ROSE, HILARY, AND STEVEN ROSE
1969 *Science and Society*. London: Allen Lane. The Penguin Press.

SALOMON, JEAN-JACQUES
1973 *Science and Politics*. Cambridge, Mass.: M.I.T. Press.
SALOMON, JEAN-JACQUES (ED.)
1968 *Problems of Science Policy*. Paris: OECD.
SAMUELSON, PAUL A.
1973 "Reply on Marxian Matters." *Journal of Economic Literature* 11:64–68.
SARTON, GEORGE
1923 "Report." In *Carnegie Institution of Washington Yearbook*, vol. 22, pp. 335–37.
1927–48 *Introduction to the History of Science*. 3 vols. in 5 parts. Baltimore: Williams and Wilkins Co.
1930 "The Teaching of the History of Science." *Isis* 30:272–97.
1931 *The History of Science and the New Humanism*. New York: Henry Holt.
1948 *The Life of Science*. New York: Henry Schuman.
1952 *Horus: A Guide to the History of Science*. Waltham, Mass.: Chronica Botanica Co.
SARTON, MAY
1959 *I Knew a Phoenix: Sketches for an Autobiography*. New York: W. W. Norton.
1962 "An Informal Portrait of George Sarton." *Texas Quarterly* (Autumn):101–12.
SCHELER, MAX
[1926] 1960 *Die Wissensformen und die Gesellschaft*. 2d ed. Bern und München: Francke Verlag.
SCHELER, MAX (ED.)
1924 *Versuche zu einer Soziologie des Wissens*. München und Leipzig: Duncker & Humblot.
SCHOOLER, JR., DEAN
1971 *Science, Scientists, and Public Policy*. New York: Free Press.
SHAPIN, STEVEN, AND ARNOLD THACKRAY
1974 "Prosopography as a Research Tool in History of Science: The British Scientific Community 1700–1900." *History of Science* 12:1–28.
SHILS, EDWARD
[1954] 1972 "Scientific Community: Thoughts After Hamburg." In Shils, *The Intellectuals and the Powers: Selected Papers*, pp. 204–12. Chicago: University of Chicago Press.
1970 "Tradition, Ecology, and Institution in the History of Sociology." *Daedalus*, vol. 99, no. 4:760–825.

SHILS, EDWARD (ED.)
1966 *Criteria for Scientific Development: Public Policy and National Goals*. Cambridge, Mass.: M.I.T. Press.
SIMPSON, GEORGE EATON
1936 *The Negro in the Philadelphia Press*. Philadelphia: University of Pennsylvania Press.
SMALL, HENRY
1973 "Co-citation in the Scientific Literature: A New Measure of the Relationship between Two Documents." *Journal of the American Society of Information Science* 24:265–69.
SMALL, HENRY, AND BELVER C. GRIFFITH
1974 "The Structure of Scientific Literatures I: Identifying and Graphing Specialties." *Science Studies* 4:17–40.
SOROKIN, PITIRIM A.
1937 *Social and Cultural Dynamics*. New York: American Book Co.
SOROKIN, PITIRIM A., AND ROBERT K. MERTON
1935 "The Course of Arabian Intellectual Development, 700–1300: A Study in Method." *Isis* 22:516–24.
STARR, LOUIS M.
1971 "Oral History: Problems and Prospect." In Melvin J. Voigt (ed.), *Advances in Librarianship*, vol. 2, pp. 275–304. New York: Seminar Press.
STEHR, NICO
1975 "Zur Soziologie der Wissenschaftssoziologie." Introduction to Nico Stehr and René König (eds.), *Wissenschaftssoziologie: Studien und Materialien. Kölner Zeitschrift für Soziologie und Sozialpsychologie*, vol. 18.
STEHR, NICO, AND LYLE E. LARSON
1972 "The Rise and Decline of Areas of Specialization." *American Sociologist* 7 (August):3, 5–6.
STEPHEN, LESLIE, AND SIDNEY LEE (EDS.)
1885–1901 *Dictionary of National Biography*. 63 vols. London: Smith, Elder Co.
STERN, BERNHARD J.
1941 *Society and Medical Progress*. Princeton: Princeton University Press.
STIGLER, GEORGE J.
1975 "The Scientific Uses of Scientific Biography, with Special Reference to J. S. Mill." In John M. Robson (ed.), *Papers of the Mill Centenary Conference*, pp. 55–66. Toronto: University of Toronto Press.
STIMSON, DOROTHY
1935 "Comenius and the Invisible College." *Isis* 23:373–88.
STONE, LAWRENCE
1971 "Prosopography." *Daedalus* (Proceedings of the American Academy of Arts and Sciences), vol. 100, no. 1:46–79.
STONE, PHILIP; D. C. DUNPHY; M. S. SMITH; AND D. M. OGILVIE

1966 *The General Inquirer: A Computer Approach to Content Analysis.*
      Cambridge, Mass.: M.I.T. Press.
STORER, NORMAN W.
1966 *The Social System of Science.* New York: Holt, Rinehart and
      Winston.
1973 "Introduction and Prefatory Notes." In R. K. Merton, *The Sociology
      of Science,* pp. xi–xxxi, 3–6, 139–41, 223–27, 281–85, 415–18.
      Chicago: University of Chicago Press.
SUMNER, WILLIAM GRAHAM
1908 *Folkways.* Boston: Ginn and Co.

TENBRUCK, FRIEDRICH H.
1974 " 'Science as a Vocation' – Revisited." In Ernst Forsthoff and
      Reinhard Hörstel (eds.), *Standorte im Zeitstrom: Festschrift für Ar-
      nold Gehlen.* Berlin: Athenäum Verlag.
THACKRAY, ARNOLD W.
1975 "Five Phases of Prehistory [of the History of Science Society], De-
      picted from Diverse Documents." *Isis* 66:445–53.
THACKRAY, ARNOLD, AND ROBERT K. MERTON
1972 "On Discipline Building: The Paradoxes of George Sarton." *Isis*
      63:473–95.
1975 "George Sarton." In *Dictionary of Scientific Biography,* vol. 12, pp.
      107–14. New York: Charles Scribner's Sons.
TILLY, CHARLES
1973 "Computers in Historical Analysis." *Computers in the Humanities*
      7:323–35.
TOULMIN, STEPHEN
1970 *Human Understanding. Vol. 1: The Collective Use and Evolution of
      Concepts.* Princeton: Princeton University Press.
TYLER, RALPH W.
1956 "Study Center for Behavioral Scientists." *Science* 123:405–8.

VOIGT, MELVIN J. (ED.)
1971 "Oral History: Problems and Prospects." In *Advances in Librarian-
      ship,* vol. 2, pp. 275–304. New York: Seminar Press.

WATKINS, J. W. N.
1975 "Metaphysics and the Advancement of Science." *British Journal for
      the Philosophy of Science* 26:91–121.
WEBER, ALFRED
1920 "Prinzipielles zur Kultursoziologie: Gesellschaftsprozess, Civilisa-
      tionsprozess und Kulturbewegung." *Archiv für Sozialwissenschaft
      und Sozialpolitik* 47:1–49.

WEBER, MAX
  [1919] 1951 *Gesammelte Aufsätze zur Wissenschaftslehre.* 2d ed.
    Tübingen: J. C. B. Mohr.
    1949 *The Methodology of the Social Sciences.* Translated and edited by
    E. A. Shils and H. A. Finch. New York: Free Press.
WEBSTER, CHARLES
    1967 "The Origins of the Royal Society." *History of Science* 6:106–28.
    1975 *The Great Instauration: Science, Medicine, and Reform, 1626–1660.*
    London: Duckworth.
WEINBERG, BORIS
    1925 "Sur les lois d'évolution de la pensée humaine." *Revue générale des
    sciences* 36:565–69.
    1926 "Les lois d'évolution des découvertes de l'humanité." *Revue générale
    des sciences* 37:43–47.
WEINSTOCK, MELVIN
    1971 "Citation Indexes." In *Encyclopedia of Library and Information Sci-
    ence,* vol. 5, pp. 16–40. New York: Marcel Dekker, Inc.
WHEWELL, WILLIAM
    1847 *History of the Inductive Sciences,* 3 vols. New edition, revised and
    continued. London: John W. Parker.
WHITEHEAD, A. N.
    1917 *The Organisation of Thought.* London: Williams and Norgate.
WHITLEY, RICHARD D. (ED.)
    1974 *Social Processes of Scientific Development.* London: Routledge and
    Kegan Paul.
WILLEY, MALCOLM K.
    1926 *The Country Newspaper.* Chapel Hill, N.C.: University of North
    Carolina Press.
WILSON, O. MEREDITH
    1968 *Center for Advanced Study in the Behavioral Sciences.* Stanford:
    Center for Advanced Study.
WRIGHT, CHARLES R.
    1954 The Effect of Training in Social Research on the Development of
    Professional Attitudes. Ph.D. dissertation, Columbia University.

ZAGORIN, PEREZ
    1976 "Prolegomena to the Comparative History of Revolution in Early
    Modern Europe." *Comparative Studies in Society and History*
    18:151–74.
ZUCKERMAN, HARRIET
    1970 "Stratification in American Science." *Sociological Inquiry* 40:235–
    57.
    1974 "Cognitive and Social Processes in Scientific Discovery: Recombina-
    tion in Bacteria as a Prototypal Case." Paper presented at the annual
    meeting of the American Sociological Association, Montreal, Canada.

1977 *Scientific Elite: Nobel Laureates in the United States*. New York: Free Press.

ZUCKERMAN, HARRIET, AND JONATHAN R. COLE

1975 "Women in American Science." *Minerva* 13:82–102.

ZUCKERMAN, HARRIET, AND ROBERT K. MERTON

1971 "Patterns of Evaluation in Science: Institutionalisation, Structure, and Functions of the Referee System." *Minerva* 9:66–100.

1972 "Age, Aging, and Age Structure in Science." In Matilda W. Riley et al. (eds.), *A Sociology of Age Stratification*, pp. 292–356. New York: Russell Sage Foundation.

Part Two

THE SOCIOLOGY OF SCIENCE IN

West Germany

and Austria

Rolf Klima and Ludger Viehoff

SOCIOLOGY OF SCIENCE, as a separate academic specialty dealing with science as a social institution in its social context, is a relatively recent development in West Germany and Austria. It would be wrong, however, to assume that before its emergence as a specialty there has been no "sociology of science" in the German speaking countries. On the contrary, one may justly state that the changing relations of science and society constituted a subject matter of major concern for the classical tradition of German sociology since it found first full expression in the writings of Karl Marx and Max Weber.

This early interest in the connections between science and society is less surprising than it may appear, if one considers the historical and intellectual context in which that tradition emerged. The issue of primary concern to both Marx and Weber, the genesis and development of modern industrial capitalism, had special immediacy for Germans. Up to the large-scale introduction of capitalism in the nineteenth century, Germany had been, in Birnbaum's words (1953:126 f.):

> a curious amalgam of rational-legal and traditionalist political or-
> ganization. Industrial capitalism with its intrinsically dynamic
> qualities, had severely disruptive effects on German society. This

rendered capitalism a particular problem to German social thinkers; by contrast with England, where a more gradual development allowed figures like Adam Smith and David Ricardo to treat
capitalist economic processes as more "natural." It is against this
background that we can understand the concern of both Marx and
Weber with capitalism not as a limited, economic system, but with
its effects on society as a whole—on familial structure, political
authority, personality organization and on cultural phenomena
like science and art.

In much the same way, as against the feudal background, industrial capitalism did not appear as "natural" but as the result of a unique
historical development, modern empirical science, for German social
thinkers, was anything but a natural phenomenon. In England and
France, the advancement of science had been supported by a wealthy
and powerful middle and upper-middle class that shared the values of
science, and considered science an effective means for the solution
of all kinds of practical problems. Science in Germany, in contrast,
grew up as part of a socially insulated university system cultivating the
idea of a nonutilitarian "pure" knowledge which did not have to prove
its value for any practical purpose. The German university had originally been based on, and remained for a long time under the influence
of, a romantic and speculative educational philosophy which considered empirical science important, but certainly not the most important
segment of human knowledge. By about 1870, however, the results of
rapid scientific growth, in connection with the economic and political
developments that set Germany on the course of industrialization, had
led to a situation in which the immediate relevance of scientific research to technological, economic, and social progress could no longer
be ignored. These changes not only caused serious problems for the
traditional ideology of the German university but also called for a redefinition of the functions and the place of science in German society
in general (cf. Ben-David, 1971:126 f.). This is the background against
which we can understand the special concern of German theorists with
science as a particular "type of knowledge," distinguished, for example, from "philosophical-metaphysical knowledge" (cf. Scheler, [1926]
1960:15 ff.) and its "inner connection" with industrial capitalism as a
particular type of society.

Any attempt to outline briefly the different accounts of this peculiar connection of science and modern capitalism, as they appear in the writings of such men as Marx, Engels, M. Weber, A. Weber, Sombart, Mannheim, and Scheler would be inadequate. One point must be emphasized. When these classical pioneers of sociology, in particular Marx and M. Weber, wrote about the social relations of science, their focus of interest was always on understanding the characteristics of modern society as a whole rather than the "investigation of science as a particular sort of behavior which can be studied as an independent part of society" (cf. Storer, 1966:6). In the writings both of sociologists of culture and of Marxist sociologists, this wider approach to the sociological study of science continued to some degree in West Germany and Austria after the Second World War, as we shall try to show in this chapter. Recently, in two papers on M. Weber's famous lecture on "Science as a Vocation," Tenbruck (1974a, 1974b) has urged the need to reconsider Weber's insights into the origins and effects of science in society as these may afford us new clues also to the "multifarious questions about the meaning (or value) of science" with which we are faced today (see also Tenbruck, 1969a, 1969b).

The major interest of postwar sociologists of science in West Germany and Austria, as in the United States, has not been in the "comparative historical sociology of science in civilizational perspective" (cf. Nelson, 1974) as established by the classical tradition. Rather, the interest has been in the more restricted analysis of the institutions of science in their social context, the organization of research science policy, and science planning. The main bridge between the wider prewar perspective in the sociology of science and the narrower, more specialized postwar perspective was Helmuth Plessner's work. In this respect, his role in the German sociology of science is comparable to that of Merton in the United States (see Ben-David, 1970:12).

Plessner's (1924) essay began as a classical exercise in the sociology of knowledge. Under the influence of M. Weber and Scheler, he discussed the historical origins and the inner, meaningful connection of the modern scientific type of knowledge and the peculiar qualities of modern democratic-capitalist society. But this discussion soon proceeded to an analysis of the working conditions in the modern "research enterprise." The second part of this essay was an attempt to analyze, in sociological terms, the organizational features which explained the scientific productivity of the German university in the nineteenth and twentieth centuries. Following this essay, Plessner developed plans to undertake a larger empirical study of the German university system and its academic staff. These plans were interrupted when, in 1933, the Nazis took over the country and expelled Plessner, as they did many others, from his academic position, forcing him to emigrate to the Netherlands. While professor of sociology at the University of Groningen, he began to collect materials for a study of the Dutch universities. The materials were destroyed by military events during the Second World War, but he did not lose interest in the subject. Immediately after his appointment to the chair in sociology at the University of Göttingen in 1951, he started "to realize, after all, the old plan" (see Plessner, 1956a). The result of this work was the three volumes *Untersuchungen zur Lage der deutschen Hochschullehrer* (Plessner, 1956) which have remained, up to the present, the most comprehensive empirical study of the German universities and the German academic profession ever conducted. They established the sociology of science as a specialized branch of sociology in postwar Germany.

The development of the sociology of science has not been directed by developments in sociological theory but, rather, by the changing problems and needs of science and society in the German-speaking countries as they have actually developed in history. Therefore, we shall not organize the review in the following sections around abstract concepts derived from any available theoretical framework. In order to relate the development of the field to the historical background against which this development must be understood, we shall divide the main part of this review into three categories that have been the focus of most of the work in the field before and, particularly, after the Second World War: 1) the university as the central institution of the German language science system,   2) the organization of research and the role of the research worker, analyzed in terms of "labor" and "enterprise," and   3) the changing interrelationships of science and society in general. The final two sections will discuss recent developments in the sociological theory of science and current and conceivable future scholarly activities.

THE GERMAN UNIVERSITY
AS A SCIENTIFIC INSTITUTION

The literature on development and organizational structure of the German university system, including the Austrian universities (see Fischer and Strasser, 1973), is enormous. There are relatively few genuinely sociological studies on the subject, and even fewer based on systematic empirical or historical research (cf. Nitsch, 1967:9). We shall discuss this sociological literature (empirical and other) as it relates to the understanding of the German university as a scientific institution. Most of these studies have been conducted not as part of a systematic sociology of science but as contributions to the general discussion about "crisis" and necessary "reform" of the German system of higher education, a discussion which is almost as old as the German university itself.

The Classical German University

The eventual success of the German university as an organization of scientific research and training cannot be attributed to the philosophical ideas of W. v. Humboldt and his collaborators at the beginning of the nineteenth century (cf. Ben-David, 1971:117 ff.) upon which this university had been established. Nevertheless, the German university to the present considers itself the inheritor of the classical, Humboldtian "idea of university." Therefore anyone writing about the German university cannot avoid this tradition and the question of how to preserve it under changing historical circumstances.

The sociological.analysis of "idea and *gestalt* of the German university" (Schelsky, 1963) begins with Plessner's (1924) essay. Most of the variables important for the sociology of the classical German university are mentioned: the "combination of educational institution and research institution," the idea of the "educational relevance of science," "academic freedom" of students and professors, the seminar style of academic teaching and, last but not least, the definition of the two central academic roles, the *Ordinarius* (or full professor) and the *Privatdozent* ("private lecturer").

Plessner (1924:417) explains the institutional junction of teaching and research within the German university as a result of the socioeconomic situation of the German intellectuals in the eighteenth and nineteenth centuries: "Germany has been compelled to this close concatenation of research and teaching by the traditional poverty of her intellectually productive classes." Compared with England and France, Germany had been a relatively poor and backward country. It lacked the wealthy and politically independent middle and upper classes which in those countries supported science and intellectual life in general. Therefore, in Germany, only the state, represented by the numerous absolutist kingdoms and principalities, was able to create the conditions necessary for the growth of science. This happened by the transformation of the old, medieval universities into research universities in which the development of science found a new institutional basis. From the point of view of the sociology of science, the Humboldtian reform is important primarily because it made this transformation possible.

This transformation, however, was in no way *intended* by the reform. As a matter of fact, Humboldt planned anything but a scientific research university. On the contrary, he intended to exclude empirical and experimental research from the new type of university which he devised. It was not a scientistic movement led by scientists but, rather, the educational movement (*Bildungsbewegung*) of German philosophical idealism led by philosophers and humanists that brought about the establishment of the Humboldtian university (see Tenbruck, 1961). The purpose of the reform advocated by the protagonists of this movement (besides Humboldt himself, particularly Schelling, Fichte, Schleiermacher) was not to create an organization of scientific research and training, but rather to establish a national institution of higher education aiming at the moral improvement of its students by means of philosophical self-reflection. The "pure science" which according to these philosophers had to be the medium of that moral education did not mean the study of empirically observable natural phenomena but a speculative philosophy aiming at the creation of a comprehensive and closed system of "absolute" knowledge to be deduced from some a priori given and introspectively conceivable principles or "ideas."

The organizational principles of the new university, devised in order to implement the educational aims of philosophical idealism, have been analyzed from a sociological point of view by König ([1935] 1970), Rosenstock-Huessey (1958), Schelsky (1960, 1963:48 ff., 79 ff.), and Nitsch et al. (1965:18 ff.) They emphasize that one of the main goals of the Humboldtian university was to furnish the institutional framework for a kind of informal "sociality of scholars," thus creating for each member of the academic community (professors as well as students!) an intellectual atmosphere which was to support him in his individual striving for moral self-perfection through independent, "solitary" search for philosophical truth. Most other organizational features specific to the Humboldtian university derive from this basic principle. Thus, the original meaning of the idea of "unity of research and teaching" must be interpreted within this context. It referred to the inner unity of philosophical truth-seeking as an academic way of life, comprising both research, conceived as a speculative search for absolute knowledge, and teaching (conceived as a "Socratic dialogue" between older and younger truth-seekers) as inseparable, or even essentially identical constituents. The affinity of this new conception of academic education to ideas that had prevailed in ancient Greek schools of philosophy is obvious.

As König ([1935] 1970), Habermas (1957, 1963a, 1969), Tenbruck (1961), Nitsch et al. (1965), and others have pointed out in their analyses of the social-historical background of the educational movement of German idealism, the original goal of the reformers had been a definitely political one. They hoped to create, by educating a philosophically and morally enlightened elite, the preconditions for the development of a liberated society imbued with the spirit of philosophical reason. Under the special circumstances prevailing in Germany during the crucial years preceding the establishment of the new German university, such hopes seemed not totally unfounded. The defeat by Napoleon had weakened the military-aristocratic ruling class in Germany, especially in Prussia where the reform began, and had made the idea widely acceptable that only a state that represented the moral and spiritual aims pursued by the educational movement of German idealism would be able to overcome the traditional political backwardness and impotence of the Germans. As König (1970) writes, it was the "tragedy of the German university" that this idea of *Kulturstaat* could not assert itself against the reality of the autocratic police state that was restored in Prussia and the rest of Germany immediately after the liberation from the Napoleonic occupation. As the presumption of "preestablished harmony between the state and the university" (Ben-David, 1971) proved untenable, the universities found themselves under increasing pressure to defend their privilege of internal academic freedom granted to them during the struggle against Napoleon. They defended themselves by stressing their noninvolvement in politics and the value neutrality of the "pure science" which they cultivated. As a result, the "German idea of university" actually lost its original moral and practical dimension and degenerated into a mere ideology that helped to justify the elite position of the German universities and their increasing isolation from the rest of society.

Structural Change and Crisis
of the German University

Ben-David analyzed in some detail the structural preconditions of the transformation of the Humboldtian "philosophical university" into a scientific "research university" between 1825 and 1900. This transformation resulted from preconditions—"the capability of the German system to change itself according to the needs and potentialities of scientific inquiry in spite of the wrong ideas (from the point of view of empirical science) of the University's founders" (Ben-David, 1971:118)—that were situated in the extraordinary "opportunities for innovation" which derived from the interaction of two factors: 1) the great freedom of the individual scientist to use his university position for the pursuit of his own research interests, and 2) the competitive nature of the German university system as a whole, based on "the existence of the lively demand of universities for successful researchers." These opportunities for innovation led toward the emergence of the university research laboratories or "institutes" as centers of regular training and careers in scientific research (see Ben-David, 1971:123; cf. also Ben-David, 1960, 1965, 1968–69; Ben-David and Zloczower, 1962; Zloczower, 1966).

German sociologists of science who have studied this process usually focus their analyses on its consequences for the social structure of the university, in particular for the quantitative development, the composition and internal stratification, and the patterns of recruitment of the academic personnel. Pioneering work in this field has been done by Eulenburg (1904, 1908) whom one may consider as Germany's first empirical sociologist of science. Among the studies conducted after World War II, C. v. Ferber's important statistical analysis of the "development of the teaching staff of the German universities 1864–1954" has to be mentioned first. It was published in 1956 as volume III of the *Untersuchungen* edited by Plessner. It was followed by Busch's (1959, 1963) sociological study on the history of the private lectureship to which recently Bock (1972) has added his structural history of the assistantship.

Ferber's (1956) study is based on the biographical data of practically all (about twenty-three thousand) university teachers who have worked at German universities and other institutions of university status from 1864 through 1954. The main part of the analysis describes the rapid expansion and increasing differentiation of the university staff during the late nineteenth and early twentieth centuries, reflecting the transformation of teaching and research in the universities into a large-scale organized enterprise.

Ferber's data also reveal the "deflationary policy" (cf. Ben-David, 1971:129) adopted by the universities in the face of the expanding opportunities. The expanding demand for teaching and research staff was met not by a corresponding increase of the number of "chairs" but by a disproportionate increase of the number of dependent positions within the so-called institutes which were attached to the individual chairs. The ratio of the number of professors to the other academic ranks dropped from over 50 percent in 1864 to less than 20 percent in 1953. As a result, there arose a growing gap in power and status between the professorial elite and the other scientists working in the university. Officially, however, the university remained a corporation of professors (*Ordinarien-Universität*) because the institutes and their personnel, in particular the so-called assistants, were not regarded as part of the academic corporation but, rather, as quasi-private properties of the professors.

The resulting hierarchical arrangement of the university structure was still aggravated by a considerable modification of the position of the *Privatdozent*, as Busch (1959, 1963) shows. Originally, the private lectureship had been a "free" academic profession (cf. Kempski, 1953–54); the *Privatdozenten*, those who after having contributed an original piece of independent research had obtained the so-called *Habilitation*, had the right to lecture at the university. They were not incumbents of a chair and did not receive regular salaries, but received only attendance fees from the students who visited their lectures. As an "estate" of independent scholars, who were supposed to compete as teachers and as researchers with the established professors and who constituted a freely accessible reservoir of competent and highly motivated scientists for the recruitment of new professors, the *Privatdozentur* was considered as perhaps the most important safeguard to ensure the university's efficacy as a scientific institution.

The *Privatdozenten* could remain independent only as long as *1)* research in their respective fields continued to be an activity that could be done in private and with private facilities and *2)* they had enough private resources to survive until eventual appointment to a chair, because usually they could not subsist on their students' attendance fees. When research required increasingly large-scale laboratory facilities, as in the experimental sciences, and competition intensified as a result of the increasing resistance of the professorial elite to the establishment of new chairs, the academic career became increasingly risky. More and more *Privatdozenten* were compelled to take over assistant positions within the institutes subordinate to the established chairs.

For Bock (1972), the *Assistant* is the "problematic central figure" of the German university because the assistantship has been the German university's main instrument for coping with the problem of transforming itself into a large-scale, bureaucratic organization of teaching and research without endangering the highly privileged status of the professorial oligarchy that dominated it. In order to uphold the fiction that the university remained a corporation of free and equal scholars, in spite of its increasingly hierarchical structure, the assistant's role had to be defined in such a way as to legitimize his lack of academic standing within the university organization. Notwithstanding the clearly professional character of the teaching and research activities by which the assistants contributed to the goals of the university, their role was officially defined as that of scientific "apprentices," who were not yet fully qualified and who had to work under the direction of the professor-masters in order to prepare themselves for a scientific career.

The breakdown of the fiction that the university is a corporation of free and equal scholars in connection with the new political activism of the students and part of the assistants during the last few years signaled the end of the old, hierarchical *Ordinarien-Universität*. Today, the

West German university system is experiencing a radical reorganization, the outcome of which is difficult to predict. The necessity of such drastic reform was made clear by the empirical studies on the internal situation of the West German universities conducted when the conviction was still unbroken that the German university was basically healthy. These studies, particularly Asemissen et al. (1956), Busch (1956), based on results of the three Plessner volumes (e.g., Plessner, 1958; v. Krockow, 1958a, 1958b, 1958c), and Anger (1960), showed that the resistance of the professorial oligarchy to any modernization and democratization of the university organization had resulted in frustration of younger university scientists. That frustration had not only impaired the human relations within the universities, but also the efficiency of teaching and research and the legitimacy of their internal order.

What about the chances of reforming this university system? Scheler (1921), Habermas (1957, 1966a, 1967, 1969), Plessner (1959), Krockow (1959, 1963), Dahrendorf (1962, 1965), Schelsky (1963, 1967, 1969), Hofmann (1969), Lepsius (1969), and others who have discussed this question have pointed out that the permanent "crisis" of the German university system is, in the last analysis, a consequence of its long-lasting inability to adapt itself by extension and diversification of its functions to the growing demand of the society for practical, useful research and science-based professional education. The most visible symptoms of the maladjustments include the collapse of the traditional system of academic self-government during the 1960s, the intensified and increasingly politicized group conflicts within the university (including the so-called students' rebellion), the continued "emigration" of scientific research from the university into other institutions (especially into governmental and industrial research institutes) and the growing political pressure on federal and state governments to assume direct responsibility for the reorganization of the university system. There are other less visible symptoms. One need not agree with Schelsky (1969) who assumes that these developments spell the end of the German university as a center of scientific activity. It may regain strength if it is able to restore the balance between its research and teaching functions and the needs of society and thus to renew its internal and external legitimacy, as Lepsius (1969) suggests (cf. Ben-David, 1971:168). In order to attain this goal, however, the university must relate its research function more effectively to its training function and this, indeed, may not be possible without a deliberate limitation of its research tasks to what is actually required by the needs of higher education (see Bock, 1972:225 f.). In this case, the major research functions of the university will have to be assumed by other organizations, and the university will probably lose its position as the social unit representing the scientific community in the German-speaking countries to a more complex and specialized system of scientific institutions. As a matter of fact, East Germany, by having adopted the academy system of the USSR, has already demonstrated one possible policy that might be chosen for the reorganization of national science systems in West Germany.

SCIENCE AS "LABOR" AND "ENTERPRISE": THE ORGANIZATION OF RESEARCH

The emergence of the bureaucratic and hierarchic research institute in the German university during the last decades of the nineteenth century established a new type of social structure in the realm of science which resembled, at least on the face of it, the existing large-scale organizations of modern capitalist industrial society. This suggested an interpretation of this new organization of research in terms of a comparison with the social structures of modern bureaucracy and, in particular, of the capitalist enterprise itself. In 1890, the historian Mommsen (1905) coined the concept of "big science" (*Grosswissenschaft*). In 1905, Harnack (1911), who in 1911 became the first president of the newly established *Kaiser Wilhelm Gesellschaft*, wrote about the "large-scale enterprise of science." Within the sociology of science this view led to the development of what might be called the "industrial sociology approach" to the sociology of research. This approach was applied in the studies by Eulenburg (1904, 1908), elaborated by Weber in his lecture on "Science as a Vocation" ([1919] 1946) and in some paragraphs of his *Wirtschaft und Gesellschaft* (1964:723, 1048), and by Plessner in his essay of 1924. After World War II, concepts of industrial sociology, though usually in a modified form, were applied to the working conditions of organized research, particularly in Plessner's *Untersuchungen* (1956), in the studies conducted by H. P. Bahrdt and his collaborators (cf. Bahrdt, Krauch, and Rittel, 1960; Bahrdt, 1964a, 1964c, 1966a, 1966b, 1966c, 1971:154–86; Reimann, 1961; Rittel, 1966; Krauch, 1970a; Vogel, 1970; Wilhelm and Wille, 1971; Engelhardt and Hoffmann, 1974), and in studies by Baumgarten (1963); Baier (1962); Hetzler and Rausch (1962); Schelsky (1963:186–203); Nitsch et al. (1965:39–101); Klages (1967); Kaupp (1969); Hetzler (1970); Hartmann (1971), and Klingemann (1974).

Central categories of this "industrial-sociology approach" are the concepts of *Arbeit* ("labor") and *Betrieb* ("enterprise" or "plant"). These concepts were chosen to characterize the specifically new quality of organized research in the empirical, experimental sciences as distinguished from the former, preindustrial state of science, in particular the speculative "science" of philosophical idealism that originally had been the basis of the German university. Compared with a type of knowledge that was essentially a matter of charismatic inspiration, of introspective reflection or of philosophical speculation, and as such, inseparably connected with the individual personality of the knowing subject, modern empirical research is labor insofar as this is a methodical, learnable, and rationally controllable way of producing new knowledge. That is, modern empirical research is an activity which, on principle, everybody who has acquired the necessary skills is able to perform so that the individual researchers become interchangeable (see Plessner, 1924:413, 416). Similarly, the characterization of the new research institutes as "plants" or as "state-capitalist enterprises" (M. Weber) intended to emphasize that research in these institutes was different. It was no longer a "solitary and free" truth-seeking by independent scholars, "charged with the presentation of an original and presumably complete and closed view of a whole scientific discipline" (Ben-David, 1971:117), but rather the deliberately planned and organized specific cooperation of specialized "research workers" in dependent positions. Each research worker was competent only for a relatively small sector of a constantly changing and differentiating research field. The intention to destroy all romantic illusions about the survival of preindustrial and precapitalist social relationships in science (and in the German university) becomes especially clear when Max Weber ([1919] 1946) states that the situation of the institute assistant is determined by the "separation of the worker from the means of production," making him as dependent on his "director" as a factory worker or any other proletarian.

For Weber, the bureaucratization of science, including the monocratic domination of personally responsible institute directors-entrepreneurs, is enforced by technical rationality and is thus part of the universal process of rationalization. After 1945, this assumption has been the starting point for an intensive and controversial discussion of working conditions in science which has focused on two questions: 1) Is the bureaucratic and hierarchic organization of research which has become typical for the German science system really "technically necessary" and therefore inevitable? 2) Is modern research really "labor" in the strict sense of the word and can one really speak of an increasing "proletarization" of the scientists?

Helmut Schelsky (1963:186–203) has been the most prominent advocate of the hypothesis that the bureaucratization and hierarchization of the research organization are necessary consequences of the growing dependence on large-scale laboratory facilities and of the increasing "division of labor" in science. The specialization and "technicization of science" (cf. Baier, 1962), Schelsky (1963:196) suggests, require "functional differentiation, work plans and regulations, authority and work discipline. The leading scholar necessarily becomes organizer and manager of the work of his collaborators." However, as Nitsch et al. (1965:46 f.) have argued, Schelsky ignores the point that the bureaucratic and hierarchic structure of the German science system is a result not so much of "technical necessities" but, rather, of the peculiar historical circumstances which enabled the professorial elite of the German university to exploit the growth of research and teaching for enhancing their own status and power vis-à-vis the other researchers in the university.

Closer analyses of the problems of research organization have unanimously led to the result that too rigidly bureaucratic and hierarchic structures are in most cases detrimental to cooperative research, in particular because such structures usually hamper horizontal communication among researchers (see, e.g., Bahrdt et al., 1960, sec. 1, and Reimann, 1961) and their individual creativity (see Dreitzel and Wilhelm, 1966; Matussek, 1966a, 1966b). Therefore, as Baumgarten (1963) and especially Bahrdt (passim) argue, the bureaucratic and hierarchic organization of many German research institutions must be interpreted not as a consequence of the "industrialization" and "rationalization" of the "research enterprise" but, rather, as a symptom of its incomplete rationalization. Unlike industrial mass-production, scientific research usually cannot be coordinated simply by "leadership" but only by the "independent and free cooperation of scientific specialists" (Nitsch, 1967:24). Of course, such cooperation that is stabilized neither by institutionalized authority nor by bureaucratic regulation can lead to considerable interpersonal tension among researchers, as Claessens (1962) has shown in his study of a social-scientific research team.

According to Rittel (1966) and Krauch (1970a) it would be wrong, however, to deny that activities do exist in scientific research which may be rationalized by means of hierarchic direction and planning. The choice of a hierarchic or of a teamlike form of coordination should be made contingent on the research problem that has to be solved. A similar position has been adopted by Hartmann (1971) in his study of organizational problems of social research, and by Klages and Hetzler (1966). In his book *Rationalität und Spontaneität*, Klages (1967) argues that the question whether research can be rationally planned and controlled cannot be answered adequately as long as one conceives research either as completely irrational, spontaneous "creation" *or* as completely rational and controllable "labor." Each concrete research process includes elements both of creation and labor, of spontaneity and rationality. Klages therefore tries to distinguish different types of research according to the degree of rationality and irrationality that each contains. He concludes that the extent to which a research process can be rationally controlled depends on whether the research goal and/or the "tracing area" can be specified in advance or not. If the research goal or the tracing area are more or less undefined (which is usually the case in so-called basic research) the research organization must be flexible enough to let the researchers react spontaneously to possible serendipity. In his study of a sample of nonacademic research institutes Hetzler (1970) tried to demonstrate empirically this interdependence of research task and degree of bureaucratization and external control of the research process (see also Klages and Hetzler, 1966; Hetzler, 1966).

As the analogy between research institute and industrial enter-

prise has turned out to be only partially convincing, it is also questionable whether the change of the working conditions and the
socioeconomic situation of scientists can simply be interpreted as a
process of proletarization. It is true that during the last decade the
conditions of work for scientists have become more like those of other
employees than they had been in previous times. The average scientific worker of today—be he university assistant (see Kaupp, 1969;
Vogel, 1970; Wilhelm and Wille, 1971), professional scientist in private
industry (see Kurucz, Ochs, and Wanczek, 1972) or researcher in one
of the large-scale laboratories of "big science" (see Engelhardt and
Hoffmann, 1974)—is in a much less privileged and independent position than the "scholar" of the nineteenth century. Since the emergence
of organized research, the individual scientist has lost much of his former autonomy, his job has become more insecure, and he has been
integrated into more or less hierarchic structures. As a result, scientists
began to organize themselves in existing trade unions or to develop
other forms of collective interest representation. But, as the cited empirical studies also show, there are other aspects of scientific work
which make it difficult to speak of a proletarization of the scientist.
Even if he is in a subordinate position, he is still a member of an
academically trained elite. In addition, because of the specific requirements of innovative, creative work, the scientist still enjoys many
privileges which most other occupational groups of our society do not
possess. For example, a scientist has relatively great freedom in determining the objectives and organization of his own work. If the
"natural-scientific intelligentsia" does not develop a "class consciousness" as part of the working class, Engelhardt and Hoffmann (1974)
conclude that it is because of conditions of privilege and freedom.

There can be observed an increasing resistance of the lower
academic ranks against too steeply hierarchic organizational structures
in scientific research. But this should not be interpreted as a symptom
of the increasing proletarization of the scientific worker. It reflects,
instead, the increasing *professionalization* of research in West Germany. It appears that the professional scientist is no longer ready to
accept traditional bureaucratic structures which have long proved to be
dysfunctional to the needs of modern cooperative research.

SCIENCE AND SOCIETY

The rise of the social sciences in Germany, during the second half of the nineteenth century, occurred without the background of a scientistic movement based on broad social and political support (cf. Ben-David, 1971:127) and within a university originally based on an essentially ascientific educational philosophy. This fact has shaped sociological thinking about the relationship between science and society, as it developed in Germany in several ways. First, the close interdependence of modern "scientific" science and technology on one side and of modern industrial capitalism on the other side has been a focus of interest of German sociology from its outset. The historical forces which led to the rise of empirical science and science-based technology and to the rise of a liberal, increasingly equalitarian industrial society almost necessarily appeared as identical or, at least, as closely related, when seen against the background of a "German idea of university" which identified the moral purposes of a nonutilitarian, speculative "philosophical science" with the interests of an idealized but traditionally organized *Kulturstaat*. Thus, for Marx, M. Weber, and Sombart, but also for Scheler and Plessner, the development of science, technology, and industrial capitalism constituted an indissoluble whole, originated and governed by the same basic principles. This was long before the notion of modern society as a "scientific society" became a commonplace for sociologists of science (cf., e.g., Sombart, [1902] 1928). Important historical studies along these lines have been conducted by Borkenau (1932, 1934) who, using a Marxist approach, claimed that the mechanical world view of the seventeenth century derived from the rationalization of labor in the era of manufacture in the sixteenth and seventeenth centuries. Grossmann (1935) sharply criticized Borkenau's hypothesis, arguing that the mechanical philosophy was much more inspired by the observations of the working of actual machines and mechanisms.

Second, the rise of social science in universities affected thinking about science and society through the often ambivalent, if not explicitly critical or even pessimistic, attitudes of German sociologists toward scientism and scientific-technological "civilization" (which, in Germany, is distinguished from humanistic and artistic "culture"). As members of an academic cultural elite which was not part of a liberal middle class of independent people or of a scientistic socialist movement (cf. Ben-David, 1971:134 ff.), they did not share the belief that science and technology would necessarily lead to human self-liberation and unlimited progress but, rather, tended to interpret science-based technological growth as a self-generating, uncontrollable process which eventually might lead to the destruction of basic cultural values. This view has been elaborated in particular by "sociologists of culture" such as A. Weber and Freyer (see, e.g., A. Weber, 1920; Freyer, 1955; Freyer, Papalekas, and Weippert, 1965) and by "philosophical anthropologists" such as Scheler and Gehlen (see Scheler, [1926] 1960; Gehlen, 1957, 1961, 1965).

Third, while there has been much concern about the possibly destructive effects of scientific-technological growth on humanistic culture and, recently, an increasing interest in science policy and science planning as a means to harness science to societal purposes, there have been very few sociological studies raising questions of how to safeguard scientific values and the scientific community against pressures exerted by the surrounding society. At first sight, the lack of interest in this problem is surprising if one thinks of the concrete experiences with hostility against science which German sociologists and German scientists had the opportunity to observe under the Nazi rule. It is all the more strange if one remembers how intensely in the United States and in Britain these historical events stimulated sociological thinking about the relations between science and society (see, e.g., Merton, 1968:591–615). Yet the neglect of these questions becomes understandable within the context of a tradition which, if it appreciated empirical science at all, appreciated it only because of the instrumental utility of scientific knowledge. It never really accepted the basic values of science and scientism. There are some studies dealing with the specific difficulties of establishing the role of the empirical social scientist against the resistance of an antiscientific, ideologically minded cultural elite of humanists and intellectuals (see Scheuch, 1965; Klima, 1969, 1972).

The Debate on "Technocracy"

The continuity of the pessimistic attitude of the German sociology of culture toward the social effects of science and technology is best represented by Schelsky's analysis of the "scientific civilization." With his essay *Der Mensch in der wissenschaftlichen Zivilisation* (1961) he opened a theoretical, and often highly speculative, controversy which became known in German sociology as the "debate on technocracy" (cf. Stück, 1969; Koch and Senghaas, eds., 1970). Resuming ideas already propounded by Freyer and Gehlen, Schelsky states that modern society is exhibiting a constantly increasing tendency to treat all kinds of problems, including those of a social and political nature, as "technological" problems, each possessing only one optimal solution (the "one best way") which can be found through scientific methods. Because the solution of a technological problem following the "one best way" does not require any further legitimation, the traditional political institutions, devised to ensure the creation of a legitimate and therefore commonly acceptable political will, gradually lose their function. Thus, Schelsky concludes, a new type of social order, the "technical state," emerges. It replaces democracy (or any other form of the "rule of men over men") by "technocracy" which, for Schelsky, means that the impersonal "rule" of the logic of technological necessities determines the course of scientific civilization. It is not the "rule of the technicians," whose growing influence is merely a symptom of the first.

This negative utopia of a technical society has many critics. One line of criticism, represented by Bahrdt (1961b) and Krauch (1961, 1964, 1966:232–49 and 299–313, 1970a), maintains that the reality of modern society contradicts the description which Schelsky has given it. It is true that scientists, as technological experts and political advisors, are increasingly being involved in political decisions. These decisions, however, cannot be found in a purely technological way because they always depend on certain basic interests and value orientations which, in a pluralistic society, continue to be subject to political controversy between conflicting groups. In addition, the idea of the "one best way" is a mere myth. Even from a strictly technological point of view, most practical problems have not only one but several optimal solutions among which a political choice has to be made. Thus, instead of mystifying the political decisions of modern bureaucracy as the results of an alleged "technological necessity," one should devise new institutional arrangements able to secure a democratic control over the growing influence of the experts on public affairs (cf. also Eckert, 1971).

A second line of argumentation against Schelsky, based on a neomarxist position, is presented in the writings of Habermas (1963b, 1966b, 1968a, 1968b, 1968c, 1968d: 9–16) and Offe (1968, 1972). They contradict Bahrdt and Krauch and, thus, agree with Schelsky insofar as they, too, assume that the problem of technocracy cannot be reduced to the problem of the growing political influence of scientific experts. They hold that the political, economic, and social stability of modern, "late capitalist" societies has become dependent upon scientific-technological progress, both as the basis of permanent economic growth and, as far as the social sciences are concerned, as the basis for the development of a perfect system of social control. The extent of dependence is so great that, indeed, policy making may appear as being nothing but a response to objective "technological necessities." Schelsky ignores the point that under present conditions the development of science and technology is not really an autonomous process, but is still directed by societal interests which, in a capitalist society, means by the interests of the private owners of the means of production. It is not the alleged immanent logic of scientific-technological progress that determines the development of the social system. It is the immanent logic of the capitalist mode of production which dictates the direction and pace of scientific-technological growth, thus leading to a growing discrepancy between the factual utilization of science and technology and the real needs of the human race. According to Habermas, scientism and positivism, by restricting the legitimate goals of science to the production of experimentally controllable and therefore technically exploitable knowledge, have the ideological function of preventing scientists from reflecting upon the basic irrationality of this whole process and their own role in it.

Science and Policy

It was, in particular, the emergence of the new role of the scientist as political advisor which led, since the middle of the 1960s, to the development of a more empirically oriented discussion of the relations between science, state, and society. This discussion had been enhanced by several papers on "the new interdependence of science and policy" by Bahrdt (1961a, 1963, 1964b, 1966c; all reprinted in Bahrdt, 1971). In these papers, Bahrdt emphasizes that "interdependence" really meant mutual, not unilateral, dependence. Thus, he argued, although the increasing influence of the state as the most important financier and consumer of scientific research surely shapes science and its organization in many ways, this does not necessarily imply a loss of autonomy and influence on the part of the scientists. On the contrary, because of the growing dependence of public administrations on scientific information, scientists themselves may gain considerable ascendancy over the political decisions of these administrations.

Friedrich (1970) conducted an empirical study based on interviews of a sample of about a hundred higher civil servants from various federal ministries to test this assumption. It appears that in most cases, the political intentions of the administration, and not those of the science advisor, determine which use is made of the scientific knowledge furnished by him. The advisor has little opportunity to intervene, even if the administration totally disregards his suggestions. The only field in which science advisors can exert direct influence upon the political decisions of the government, according to Friedrich, is the field of science policy. In science policy, the science advisor, instead of being concerned with the application of his scientific knowledge to political and other nonscientific questions, functions mainly as interpreter of the internal needs and developments of science (cf. Kaplan, 1964:871 ff.).

The reactions of the scientific community to a developing national science policy have been analyzed in greater detail by Weingart (1970a) in a study on the emergence of a "science lobby" in the United States. Based largely on secondary sources, he describes the changes which the American scientific community has undergone as a consequence of the reorientation of American science policy which had been guided by laissez-faire principles, by and large accepting the philosophy that science would develop best without interference from the outside. Under such conditions, potential conflicts between the interests of the government and scientific norms and values could be avoided, and the representation of the interests of the scientific community, through small groups of "scientific statesmen" co-opted into the executive in accordance with their intrascientific reputation, seemed appropriate.

When the government started to use science policy as an instrument for attaining extrascientific goals, in particular economic goals, and began to interfere with the self-regulatory system of the scientific community, the community was forced to state its own political priorities and to want a more effective representation of these priorities vis-à-vis the politicians. As a consequence, scientific associations established lobbies in Washington to exert influence both upon the legislature and the executive. Finally, a new type of scientific interest representation emerged, the "associational interest group."

In this connection it may be noted that Weingart's book is not the only study by a West German sociologist dealing with the development of the American science system. Krauch, Kunz, and Rittel (1966), Krauch (1970b), and Rödel (1972) report on various aspects of science policy, science organization, and the military-industrial-scientific complex in the United States. One of the reasons for such studies is the assumption that the scientifically and technologically most advanced capitalist society of today may anticipate some developments to be expected in West German society.

Both in the United States and in West Germany, one of the problems which was created by the growing support for science and the emergence of national science policies was the increasing need for the public to understand what was happening in science and science policy in order to keep the making of science policy under public control. Empirical studies conducted in West Germany showed that the degree of interest of laymen in science-policy issues depended on the degree of their general political interest, and their interest in science policy was generally greater than expected. These studies also revealed a discrepancy between the priorities for science policy accepted by the government and those requested by politically interested laymen. Interested laymen were in striking agreement with the priorities recommended by science-policy experts (see Krauch and Schreiber, 1966; Krauch, Feger, and Opgenoorth, 1970; Krauch, 1970b; Feger, Krauch, and Feindl, 1971; Krauch and Volkmann, 1972).

The divergence of the official science policy from public needs, as perceived both by laymen and by experts, may partly be caused by the influence of industrial, military and other pressure groups as Krauch (1970b) suggests. In accordance with other authors (e.g., Lohmar, 1968, 1973; Lörincz, 1971; Böhme, 1973), Krauch concludes that public control of the national science policy can be guaranteed only if permanent communication exists between the government, science, and the public that provides knowledge of the decision-making processes in science policy.

Sociologists of science who adopt a Marxist approach tend to deny the possibility of a rational science policy guided by the interests of the population as long as the economic system of capitalism has not been overthrown. Their studies of science policy in West Germany (Rilling, 1969, 1970a, 1970b, 1970c; Hirsch, 1971, 1975; Schuon, 1971, 1972; Neuendorff, 1973) and in the United States (Rödel, 1972) try to demonstrate that in science policy the government acts mainly as an agent of the economic interests of the capitalists. They argue that the increasing support for science by the state is part of a more general tendency, reflecting the new function of the state within the system of modern "monopolistic capitalism," to guarantee continuous economic growth by providing private industry with the infrastructural innovations which the capitalist economy needs to maintain and to increase its profitability. Thus, the science policy of a modern capitalist state aims, directly or indirectly, to create technological knowledge which can profitably be exploited by private industry, in particular by the powerful monopolies. The empirical evidence to support this hypothesis is mainly of two kinds. First, the studies try to show that the bulk of financial support for science by the state is given to research areas of immediate relevance to technological utilization in industrial production which leads to a disproportionate growth of these fields (e.g., the physical sciences) while other fields which do not produce results of immediate profitability (e.g., biological and social sciences) are neglected although their social importance may be much higher. Second, these writers (especially Hirsch, 1971) refer to facts which indicate a direct influence of private, monopolistic industry on the formulation of national science policies and on the distribution of public subsidies for research among the various branches of science.

The assumption, among Marxist sociologists of science, of the growing influence of economic interests upon scientific research has led to a critique of the traditional value-system of the scientific community. Tomberg (1971) argues that the idea of the "autonomy of science" was justified only as long as it served to defend the freedom of scientific research against clerical and governmental suppression. Today, it is merely a bourgeois ideology concealing the factual restrictions imposed upon the free exercise of scientific inquiry by the prevailing mode of production.

There can be no doubt that in the last two or three decades in West Germany, as in other countries, the relations between science, the state, and the economy have become much more intimate and direct than in previous times. It seems questionable, however, whether the unequal growth rates of different research fields can be explained as a simple function of the unequal distribution of financial support and facilities among these areas, as some of the authors quoted tend to assume. The complexity of the interrelations of economic and political variables and scientific development can be learned from empirical studies on the development of science policy and scientific growth in Germany conducted by Pfetsch. In his analyses of the determinants of the growth of scientific organizations in Germany before World War I, he studied the development of a number of scientific organizations (research institutes, academies, learned societies, etc.) distributed among various research fields and the diverse federal states of the Reich. He identified the following factors as responsible for this development: state of scientific knowledge in the field; political organization of the society; cultural background; process of industrialization; population growth (see Pfetsch, 1970, 1971, 1974). In a correlative study on the institutionalization of subdisciplines of medical science in Germany until 1914, Pfetsch (1973) shows that innovation in science is determined by a complicated interplay of social and cognitive conditions internal to the scientific community and of external socioeconomic and political conditions. He demonstrates that this interplay can be described as a system of feedback processes. The institutionalization of a new research field stimulates the growth of scientific knowledge, and the emergence of new scientific ideas enforces the creation of new institutions. Of course, the development of new knowledge is not a sufficient condition for institutional innovation. Generally, there must be also some material support by the surrounding society, but it can be shown that scientific growth is not simply determined by changing socioeconomic needs. (On the importance of new, "exploitable" knowledge as a necessary condition for the institutionalization of new disciplines by science policy, see Daele and Weingart, 1975.)

We began this section by noting how sociological thinking about the interrelations of science and society in Germany has been shaped by the peculiarities of the German intellectual tradition. We conclude this section by indicating that for some years an increasing convergence can be observed in conceptualization and method of the work done in this field by West German sociologists and comparable work conducted in other countries. This surely is primarily a result of the similarity between the problems of the scientific-technological revolution and the emergence of national science policies in these countries.

NEW THEORETICAL PERSPECTIVES

The bulk of the work in the sociology of science we have discussed has been conducted in response to certain problematic or even critical aspects of the German science system and its interrelations with the surrounding society as they have actually developed in Germany from early nineteenth century up to the present. However speculative and abstract much of this work has been, it has paid little attention to the construction of a unifying conceptual framework for the sociology of science. Only recently have some new approaches to the development of such a conceptual scheme been suggested. As yet, none has been applied successfully in empirical research or even accepted as a general framework for the whole of the sociology of science.

Most of these approaches are attempts to apply general theoretical models of sociology or the other social sciences to the sociological study of science. Krysmanski was one of the first who made such an attempt with his unorthodox application of Parsons's theory of the social system to the analysis of the scientist's role in society (Krysmanski, 1966, 1967). Luhmann (1968) in a paper on the "self-regulation of science" applied his own particular version of general functionalist systems theory to explain the functioning of science as an autonomous system of social action. His main hypothesis is that the professional "reputation" which is ascribed to researchers and scientific organizations serves as a "generalized medium of orientation" for the selection and evaluation of scientific contributions and the allocation of rewards and resources. Without using reputation as a criterion for selection, the self-regulatory system of science could not function because the information-processing capacity of the system would be overloaded by the task of objectively evaluating the truth content of all contributed scientific information as actually required by the scientific norms (for a critique of this theory, see Weingart, 1970b). More recently, Münch (1974) has tried to combine elements from Luhmann's and Parsons's systems theory with Popper's "evolutionary epistemology" and thus to develop a general approach to the analysis of the evolution of the social system of science.

Scherhorn (1969) made an interesting attempt to extend the theory of economic markets to the analysis of competition in science or, as he calls it, in "scientific markets." In a scientific market, scientists come forward as suppliers and demanders of scientific information which contribute to the solution of theoretical problems of the demanders. This conception explicates the so-called exchange-theory of social control in science. In contrast to former formulations of the theory, Scherhorn gives a clear and simple account of *what* is being exchanged among scientists (namely problem solutions for recognition) and, in particular, *why* the exchange exists. It exists because the scientist is not only a producer of new data and concepts who wants to be rewarded for his achievements, but is also a demander and consumer of new data and concepts produced by other scientists which are usable by him as the basis for further exploration and in exchange for which he is ready to provide the reward of recognition.

Finally, under the influence of recent developments in the philosophy and history of science (in particular T. S. Kuhn's theory of "normal science" and "scientific revolutions") and stimulated by the writings of some British sociologists of science (e.g., Barnes and Dolby, King, Martins, Whitley), there have also been some attempts to outline first elements of what has been called a "cognitive approach" to the sociological study of science. As Nowotny (1973) notes in her discussion of the feasibility of such an approach, these attempts, though differing in many respects, share the emphasis on cognitive processes and information-processing aspects in the production and change of scientific ideas rather than on institutionalized behavior and the rejection of the conventional linear-cumulative growth model of scientific development (see also Nowotny, 1975). Böhme, van den Daele, and Krohn (1972, 1973), for example, suggest an interpretation of the history of scientific ideas in terms of Darwin's biological model of evolution. They try to specify a set of criteria which determine the survival value of scientific theories. The chances of a scientific idea to survive are higher the more it contributes to the survival of the scientific community which produced it. In such a way, the authors hope to establish a systematic relationship between the factual development of science and the social environment wherein it takes place. The weaknesses of this "evolutionary model" have already been pointed out by Nowotny (1973:285–86). A position similar to that of Böhme, van den Daele, and Krohn has been adopted by Weingart (1974b:45 f.) in a paper on a sociological theory of scientific change which concludes, from Kuhn's historical account of "revolutions" in the development of science and the "historicity" of scientific theories and methods, "that changes in the cognitive structures [of science need] to be explained partly in terms of social factors." Recently, Böhme (1974a), by analyzing a historical controversy about "rules of experimentation" in psychology, tried to demonstrate that the "elements of a disciplinary matrix" can justly be viewed as social norms which constitute a "scientific community" as suggested by Kuhn. In a comment on that article, Klima (1974b) argued that neither Böhme's interpretation of the historical case in question nor the underlying Kuhnian model of the scientific community can be considered convincing. In reply, Böhme (1974b) outlined a new model of the scientific community to be based partly on the Parsonsian theory of action (see also Böhme, 1974c).

Klima attempted to develop a cognitive approach to the sociological study of science. He applied the existing psychological and social-psychological theories of "cognitive consistency" and, more generally, the cognitive models of human behavior being developed in psychology, information theory, and so forth, to the analysis of the cognitive behavior of scientists in different social settings (Klima, 1974a). This approach presupposes that scientific thought, insofar as it is part of Popper's (1972) "World 2" of subjective events, can be explained by the same basic programming rules as ordinary thought. However, in contrast to views of a Kuhnian "sociology of scientific knowledge," this approach does *not* imply the rejection of the idea of objective knowledge and of a rational epistemology. As a matter of fact, a systematic neglect of the objective dimension of scientific knowledge (in Popper's sense) resulting from the rejection of epistemological realism in favor of epistemological instrumentalism and conventionalism seems to be one of the main features of the new, so-called cognitive sociology of science (besides the works already quoted see, for example, Böhme, 1974c; Dubiel, 1974; Daele and Krohn, 1975). No wonder, then, that this epistemological instrumentalism (which views scientific theories as mere instruments of calculation, not as descriptions of reality) has lead to ideas about the feasibility of the political planning (or "finalization") of the development of the *contents* of science that do not differ very much from the arguments used in support of the State control of science by Marxist instrumentalists like J. Bernal during the British debate on science-planning in the Thirties (see Böhme, Daele, and Krohn, 1973; Daele and Krohn, 1975; Daele and Weingart, 1975). Thus, a critical discussion of the epistemological assumptions underlying this (and any other) approach to the sociological study of science appears to be one of the main tasks of the future (cf. Radnitzky, 1974).

Up to the 1960s the only group continuously interested in the social aspects of science was the group led by Plessner and, later, by Bahrdt at the Sociological Seminar of the University of Göttingen. By about 1962, on Schelsky's initiative, another group (Klages, Hetzler) was established at the *Sozialforschungsstelle* in Dortmund. It later moved to the Institute of Social Science of the Technical University of Berlin. In 1964, the *Studiengruppe für Systemforschung* (Krauch), a nonacademic research unit investigating problems of science policy and research management was founded at Heidelberg. This slow growth of the field during the first two decades following World War II reflects the lack of public and governmental concern for science and science policy during this so-called period of reconstruction of the West German and Austrian economies. The situation changed drastically by the end of the 1960s when something like a "boom" in the founding of new institutes and research groups devoted to the social-scientific study of science set in (see Fig. 1). Today there are about thirty academic and nonacademic research units in the Federal Republic of Germany and Austria doing research in the sociology of science (Klima and Viehoff, 1974; Baitsch et al., 1973:3–46).

   This trend toward increasing institutionalization and professionalization is also reflected by the growing number of universities in which the sociology of science is taught (see Baitsch et al., 1973:47–75). At the Faculty of Sociology of the University of Bielefeld, which offers sociology students a full-course program in science planning, a first chair exclusively devoted to the sociology of science has been established. This is also the first West German university to establish an interdisciplinary center for science studies (the *Forschungsschwerpunkt Wissenschaftsforschung* of the University of Bielefeld), compris-

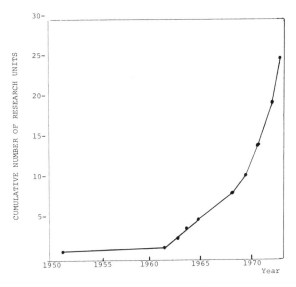

1: Cumulative number of new research units per year in
the sociology of science in West Germany and Austria
1951–1972. N = 27.
(*Compiled from a questionnaire survey by R. Klima & L.
Viehoff, March 1973, and from H. Baitsch et al., 1973,
Appendix 1, pp. 3–46.*)

ing several chairs from different faculties. Other indicators of the increasingly professional and institutionalized nature of research in the
sociology of science are the founding (in 1974) of a section for the
sociology of science within the German Sociological Society, the publication of readers and textbooks in the sociology of science (Weingart,
1972, 1974a, 1975; Spiegel-Rösing, 1973; Bühl, 1974), and the increasing space devoted to the field in German sociological journals.

It would be incorrect, however, to consider the sociology of science in West Germany and Austria as simply a subdiscipline of sociology. Although a majority are sociologists, there are political scientists,
social psychologists, economists, historians, philosophers, and
specialists from various natural sciences working in the field. Many
sociologists of science even prefer the terms "*Wissenschaftsforschung*"
("science studies") or "*Wissenschaftswissenschaft*" ("science of science") to the term "*Wissenschaftssoziologie*" ("sociology of science")
because they want to emphasize the interdisciplinary character of the
field.

In a questionnaire survey that we conducted in February and March, 1973, twenty-eight West German and Austrian organizations doing research in the sociology of science or, as one may also say, in the "social science of science" were asked to report on their current activities. The results of this survey have been published (Klima and Viehoff, 1974) so we can be brief in summarizing them here.

Studies on the organization of research, on the institutional conditions of scientific innovation, on the interdependence of the development of research technology and organizational structures in research, and on the university as a scientific institution are being conducted by groups at the University of Cologne (Alemann, Scheuch), the Technical University of Berlin (Klages, Hetzler, Schienstock), the University of Bielefeld (Rammert, Weingart), the *Wissenschaftszentrum Berlin* (Köhler), and the Institute for Advanced Studies at Vienna (Fischer, Strasser). At the Free University of Berlin (Lepenies), the University of Heidelberg (Pfetsch, Gizycki), the University of Ulm (Spiegel-Rösing, Baitsch, Fliedner), the *Institut für Sozialwissenschaftliche Forschung* at Munich (Altmann, Düll, Schmidt), and the Institute for Advanced Studies at Vienna (Knorr, Zilian), groups are conducting historical, and comparative or case studies of processes of institutionalization in science, such as the rise and decline of scientific disciplines, societal and political factors determining the growth of specialties, and the role of scientific institutions in scientific development. The interrelations of cognitive and social or of internal and external factors in the development of science and the conditions for the establishment of shared scientific standards are a focus of interest of groups located at the *Max-Planck Institut zur Erforschung der Lebensbedingungen der wissenschaftlichtechnischen Welt* at Starnberg (Böhme, Daele, Krohn, Schäfer) and at the University of Bielefeld (Klima, Schneider, Viehoff, Weingart). Finally, there are groups interested mainly in socioeconomic conditions and effects of scientific and technological growth, in science planning and science policy, and in comparative studies of scientific development, science organization, and science policy in different economic-political systems (in particular the two Germanys). Some of these groups are at the University of Frankfurt (Hirsch, Wetzel, Rolshausen and others), at the already mentioned Max Planck Institute at Starnberg (Neuendorff, Rödel), at the *Bundesinstitut für Gesellschaft und Wissenschaft* at Erlangen (Burrichter and his team; cf. Lades and Burrichter, eds., 1970), and at the *Institut für angewandte Soziologie* at Vienna (Kreutz, Hindler, Glaser).

Of course, there are many overlappings of the research interests of these groups, and we have no doubt neglected the activities of a great number of individuals not affiliated with one of the more or less institutionalized research units which were our informants in the survey.

We asked some questions regarding the future development of the sociology of science in the two countries. We asked our expert informants 1) what, in their opinion, were the likely types of problems to be studied in the next decade, 2) which problems they intended to investigate in the future, and 3) what they considered the most important and urgent problems of the sociology of science that remain to be solved. Although the answers varied considerably, some tentative conclusions may be drawn.

Most answers to the first question indicated that because of the growing demand by science administrators and politicians for advice from the sociology of science, more attention will be given to practical problems of science organization, science planning, and science policy. The answers to the other two questions suggest that the West German and Austrian sociologists of science will in fact react to this demand in much the same way as their colleagues in other countries when confronted with a similar situation (cf. Ben-David, 1970:14 f.). Finding themselves in a seller's market, they can afford to refrain from making hasty contributions to practical problems, and instead of doing what happens to be demanded by political and industrial clients, they can treat the problems of their field in an increasingly professional manner. This means that they will tie the sociology of science more closely and systematically to sociological theory and research in general. This trend is already recognizable in the current work in the sociology of science discussed in the section entitled "New Theoretical Perspectives." Depending on the future development of sociology as a whole, it is even conceivable that the spirit of the work done by the classical pioneers of a wider sociology of science in civilizational perspective will be renewed, and its substance recollected, as demanded in Tenbruck's (1974) recent reconsideration of M. Weber's "Science as a Vocation."

REFERENCES

ANGER, HANS
  1960 *Probleme der deutschen Universität: Bericht über eine Erhebung
        unter Professoren und Dozenten* [Problems of the German univer-
        sity: report on a survey of university teachers]. Tübingen: J. C. B.
        Mohr.
ASEMISSEN, ILSE; RENATE FRENZEL; DIETRICH GOLDSCHMIDT; CHRISTIAN
GRAF VON KROCKOW; AND HELMUTH PLESSNER
  1956 "Nachwuchsfragen im Spiegel einer Erhebung 1953–1955" [Ques-
        tions of recruitment mirrored in a survey 1953–1955]. In *Studies on
        the Position of Teachers in German Higher Education.* Göttingen:
        Vandenhoeck und Ruprecht.

BAHRDT, HANS PAUL
  1961a "Schamanen der modernen Gesellschaft? Das Verhältnis der Wis-
         senschaftler zur Politik" [Modern society's shamans? The relationship
         of scientists to public policy]. *Atomzeitalter* 4:75–79.
  1961b "Helmut Schelskys technischer Staat. Zweifel an 'nachideologischen
         Geschichtsmodellen'" [Helmut Schelsky's technical state: doubts
         about "post ideological models of history"]. *Atomzeitalter* 9:195–
         200.
  1963   "Forschung und Staat" [Research and state]. *Atomzeitalter* 4:84–89.
  1964a "Soziologische Probleme der Forschungsverwaltung" [Sociological
         problems of research administration]. *Atomzeitalter* 2:45–51.
  1964b "Die wissenschaftspolitische Entscheidung" [The scientific public
         policy decision]. *Atomzeitalter* 6:159–65.
  1964c "Moderne Forschungsorganisation–moderne Universität" [Modern
         research organization–modern university]. In Bahrdt, Hund, *et al.*
  1966a "Historischer Wandel der Arbeitsteilung in der Wissenschaft" [His-
         torical alteration in the division of labor in science]. In Krauch, Kunz,
         and Rittel (eds.), 1966:26–39.
  1966b "Soziologische Reflexionen über Forschungsinstitutionen neuen
         Typs in den USA" [Sociological reflections about new research in-
         stitutions in the USA]. In Krauch, Kunz, and Rittel (eds.), 1966:71–
         93.
  1966c "Der Status des Wissenschaftlers in der modernen Gesellschaft"
         [The status of the scientist in modern society] *Atomzeitalter*
         10:289–94.
  1971   *Wissenschaftssoziologie–ad hoc Beiträge zur Wissenschaftssoziolo-
         gie und Wissenschaftspolitik aus den letzten zehn Jahren* [Sociology
         of science–ad hoc contributions to the sociology of science and sci-

ence policy-making during the last ten years]. Düsseldorf: Bertelsmann Universitätsverlag.

BAHRDT, HANS PAUL; FR. HUND; W. RICHTER; W. TRILLHAAS; AND R. WIT-
TRAM

1964 *Die Universität. Kritische Selbstbetrachtungen* [The university: critical self-reflections]. Göttingen: Vandenhoeck und Ruprecht.

BAHRDT, HANS PAUL; HELMUT KRAUCH; AND HORST RITTEL

1960 "Die wissenschaftliche Arbeit in Gruppen" [Scientific work in
groups]. *Kölner Zeitschrift für Soziologie und Sozialpsychologie* 12
(no. 1):1–40.

BAIER, HORST

1962 "Dokumentation—ein Schritt zur Technisierung der Wissenschaft"
[Documentation—a step toward making science technological].
Soziale Welt 13:209–27.

BAITSCH, HELMUT; THEODOR M. FLIEDNER; JOACHIM B. KREUTZKAM; AND
INA SPIEGEL-RÖSING

1973 *Memorandum zur Förderung der Wissenschaftsforschung in der
Bundesrepublik Deutschland* [Memorandum on advancing science
research in the Federal Republic of Germany]. Essen: Stifteverband
für die Deutsche Wissenschaft.

BAUMGARTEN, EDUARD

1963 *Zustand und Zukunft der deutschen Universität* [Condition and future of the German university]. Tübingen: J. C. B. Mohr.

BEN-DAVID, JOSEPH

1960 "Scientific Productivity and Academic Organization in Nineteenth-
Century Medicine." *American Sociological Review* 25 (December):828–43.

1965 "The Scientific Role: Conditions of its Establishment in Europe."
Minerva 4:15–54.

1968/1969 "The University and the Growth of Science in Germany and the
United States." *Minerva* 7 (Autumn/Winter):1–35.

1970 "Introduction." *International Social Science Journal* 22 (no. 1):7–27.

1971 *The Scientist's Role in Society. A Comparative Study*. Englewood
Cliffs, N.J.: Prentice-Hall.

BEN-DAVID, JOSEPH, AND AVRAHAM ZLOCZOWER

1962 "The Idea of the University and the Academic Market Place." *European Journal of Sociology* 2:303–14.

BIRNBAUM, NORMAN

1953 "Conflicting Interpretations of the Rise of Capitalism: Marx and
Weber." *British Journal of Sociology* 4 (June):125–40.

BOCK, KLAUS DIETER

1972 *Strukturgeschichte der Assistentur. Personalgefüge, Wert- und Ziel-
vorstellungen in der deutschen Universität des 19. und 20. Jahrhun-
derts* [Structural history of the assistantship: personnel structure and
values and goals espoused in the German university of the 19th and
20th centuries]. Düsseldorf: Bertelsmann Universitätsverlag.

BÖHME, GERNOT

1973 "Über das Verhältnis des Wissenschaftlers zur Wissenschaftspolitik" [On the relationship between the scientist and scientific policy-making]. In Pohrt (ed.), pp. 175–92.

1974a "Die Bedeutung von Experimentalregeln für die Wissenschaft" [The significance of rules of experimentation for science]. *Zeitschrift für Soziologie* 3 (January): 5–17.

1974b "Ein handlungstheoretisches Konzept der Scientific Community" [A 'theory of action' approach to the scientific community]. *Zeitschrift für Soziologie* 3 (January): 106–9.

1974c "Die soziale Bedeutung kognitiver Strukturen. Ein handlungstheoretisches Konzept der Scientific Community" [The social meaning of cognitive structures. A theory of action model of the scientific community]. *Soziale Welt* 25 (no. 2): 188–208.

1974d "Die Bedeutung praktischer Argumente für die Entwicklung der Wissenschaft" [The relevance of practical arguments for the development of science]. *Philosophia Naturalis* 15 (no. 1): 133–51.

BÖHME, GERNOT; WOLFGANG VAN DEN DAELE; AND WOLFGANG KROHN

1972 "Alternative in der Wissenschaft" [Alternatives in science]. *Zeitschrift für Soziologie* 1 (October): 302–16.

1973 "Die Finalisierung der Wissenschaft" [The finalizing of science]. *Zeitschrift für Soziologie* 2 (April): 128–44.

BORKENAU, FRANZ

1932 "Zur Soziologie des mechanistischen Weltbildes" [On the sociology of the mechanistic world view]. *Zeitschrift für Sozialforschung* 1:311–35.

1934 *Der Übergang vom feudalen zum bürgerlichen Weltbild. Studien zur Geschichte der Philosophie der Manufakturperiode* [The transition from the feudal to the bourgeois world view: studies of the history of the philosophy of the manufacturing period]. Paris: Librairie Félix Alcan.

BUCHHOLZ, ARNOLD

1968 *Die Große Transformation* [The great transformation]. Stuttgart: Deutsche Verlags-Anstalt.

1971 "Die relative Selbständigkeit der wissenschaftlich-technischen Entwicklung" [The relative independence of scientific-technological development]. *Futurum* 1:52–62.

1972 "Wissenschaftlich-technische Revolution und Wettbewerb der Systeme" [Scientific-technological revolution and competition of systems]. *Osteuropa* 5:329–90.

BÜHL, WALTER L.

1974 *Einführung in die Wissenschaftssoziologie* [Introduction to the sociology of science]. München: Verlag C. H. Beck.

BUSCH, ALEXANDER

1956 *Stellenplan und Lehrkörperstruktur der Universitäten und*

Hochschulen in der Bundesrepublik und in Berlin (West) 1953/54
[The faculty social structure of universities and colleges in the Federal Republic and in Berlin, 1953–54]. Helmut Plessner (ed.), *Untersuchungen zur Lage der deutschen Hochschullehrer*, vol. 2. Göttingen: Vandenhoeck und Ruprecht.

1959   *Die Geschichte der Privatdozentur. Eine soziologische Studie zur
       großbetrieblichen Entwicklung der deutschen Universitäten* [The his-
       tory of the privatdozentur: a sociological study of the development of
       German universities as large-scale enterprises]. Stuttgart: Ferdinand
       Enke Verlag.

1963   "The Vicissitudes of the Privatdozent: Breakdown and Adaptation in
       the Recruitment of the German University Teacher." *Minerva* 1
       (Spring):319–41.

CLAESSENS, DIETRICH
1962   "Forschungsteam und Persönlichkeitsstruktur." [Research team and
       personality structure]. *Kölner Zeitschrift für Soziologie und
       Sozialpsychologie* 14:487–503.

DAELE, WOLFGANG VAN DEN, AND WOLFGANG KROHN
1975   "Theorie und Strategie: zur Steuerbarkeit wissenschaftlicher Ent-
       wicklung" [Theory and strategy: on the manageability of scientific
       development]. In Weingart (ed.), 1975:213–54.

DAELE, WOLFGANG VAN DEN, AND PETER WEINGART
1975   "Resistenz und Rezeptivität der Wissenschaft: Zu den Entstehungs-
       bedingungen neuer Disziplinen durch wissenschaftspolitische
       Steuerung" [Resistance and receptivity of science: on the emergence
       of new disciplines through science policy]. *Zeitschrift für Soziologie*
       4 (April):146–64.

DAHRENDORF, RALF
1962   "Starre und Offenheit der deutschen Universität: die Chancen der
       Reform" [Rigidity and flexibility in the German university: the
       chances for reform]. *European Journal of Sociology* 3:263–93.

1965   "Die Fakultäten und ihre Reform" [The faculties and their reform]. In
       Hess et al., 1965:17–30.

DREITZEL, HANS P., AND JÜRGEN WILHELM
1966   "Das Problem der 'Kreativität' in der Wissenschaft. Ein Beitrag zur
       Wissenschaftssoziologie" [The problem of creativity in science: a con-
       tribution to the sociology of science]. *Kölner Zeitschrift für
       Soziologie und Sozialpsychologie* 18, 1:62–83.

DUBIEL, HELMUT
1974   "Dialektische Wissenschaftskritik und interdisziplinäre Sozial-
       forschung. Theorie- und Organisationsstruktur des Frankfurter In-
       stituts für Sozialforschung (1930 ff.)" [Dialectical criticism of science
       and interdisciplinary social research. Theoretical and organizational

structure of the Frankfurt Institute for Social Research (1930 ff.)].
Kölner Zeitschrift für Soziologie und Sozialpsychologie 26 (no.
2):237–66.

ECKERT, ROLAND
   1971 *Wissenschaft und Demokratie. Plädoyer für eine verantwortliche
          Wissenschaft* [Science and democracy: a plea for a responsible sci-
          ence]. Tübingen: J. C. B. Mohr.
ENGELHARDT, MICHAEL VON, AND RAINER W. HOFFMANN
   1974 *Wissenschaftlich-technische Intelligenz im Forschungsgrossbetrieb.
          Eine empirische Untersuchung über Arbeit, Beruf und Bewußtsein*
          [Scientific-Technological intelligence in the large-scale research en-
          terprise: an empirical study of work, occupation and consciousness].
          Frankfurt: Deutsche Verlags-Anstalt.
EULENBURG, FRANZ
   1904 *Die Frequenz der deutschen Universitäten von ihrer Gründung bis
          zur Gegenwart* [The frequency of German universities from their
          founding to the present]. Leipzig: B. G. Teubner.
   1908 *Der "akademische Nachwuchs". Eine Untersuchung über die Lage
          und die Aufgaben der Extraordinarien und Privatdozenten*
          [Academic aspirants: a study of the situation and the tasks of the "Ex-
          traordinarien" and "Privatdozenten"]. Leipzig und Berlin: B. G.
          Teubner.

FEGER, HUBERT; HELMUT KRAUCH; AND ULRICH FEINDL
   1971 "Forschungsplanung II: Der Einfluß von Öffentlichkeitsmeinungen
          und Gruppendiskussion auf Präferenzurteile über Forschungs-
          schwerpunkte" [Research planning II: the influence of public opinion
          and group discussion on preferences for research priorities].
          Zeitschrift für Sozialpsychologie 1:187–97.
FERBER, CHRISTIAN VON
   1956 *Die Entwicklung des Lehrkörpers der deutschen Universitäten und
          Hochschulen 1864–1954* [The development of the faculty of German
          universities and colleges, 1864–1954]. In Plessner (ed.).
FISCHER, MARINA, AND HERMANN STRASSER
   1973 *Selbstbestimmung und Fremdbestimmung der österreichischen Uni-
          versitäten* [Internal and external decision-making of Austrian univer-
          sities]. Wien: Institut für höhere Studien.
FREYER, HANS
   1955 *Theorie des gegenwartigen Zeitalters* [Theory of the present era].
          Stuttgart: Deutsche Verlags-Anstalt.
FREYER, HANS; JOHANNES PAPALEKAS; AND GEORG WEIPPERT (EDS.)
   1965 *Technik im technischen Zeitalter. Stellungnahmen zur geschicht-
          lichen Situation* [Technique in the technological era: evaluations of
          the historical situation]. Düsseldorf: Schilling.

FRIEDRICH, HANNES
  1970   *Staatliche Verwaltung und Wissenschaft* [Public administration and science]. Frankfurt: Deutsche Verlags-Anstalt.

GEHLEN, ARNOLD
  1957   *Die Seele im technischen Zeitalter. Sozialpsychologische Probleme in der industriellen Gesellschaft* [The soul in the technological era: social-psychological problems in industrial society]. Hamburg: Rowohlt.
  1961   "Die Technik in der Sichtweise der Anthropologie" ["Technique" in anthropological perspective]. In A. Gehlen, *Anthropologische Forschung*, pp. 83–103. Hamburg: Rowohlt.
  1965   "Anthropologische Ansicht der Technik" [The anthropological view of "technique"]. In Freyer, Papalekas, and Weippert (eds.), 1965.

GROSSMANN, HENRYK
  1935   "Die gesellschaftlichen Grundlagen der mechanistischen Philosophie und die Manufaktur" [The societal bases of mechanistic philosophy and manufacturing]. *Zeitschrift für Sozialforschung* 4 (no. 2): 161–231.

HABERMAS, JÜRGEN
  1957   "Das chronische Leiden der Hochschulreform" [The chronic malaise of reform in higher education]. *Merkur* 11: 265–84.
  1963a "Vom sozialen Wandel akademischer Bildung" [On social alterations in academic training]. *Merkur* 17: 412–27. (Reprinted in Leibfried [ed.], 1967: 10–24.)
  1963b "Analytische Wissenschaftstheorie und Dialektik" [Analytical philosophy of science and dialectics]. In M. Horkheimer (ed.), *Zeugnisse. Festschrift für Theodor W. Adorno* [Testimonials: Festschrift for T. W. Adorno], pp. 473–501. Frankfurt: Deutsche Verlags-Anstalt.
  1966a "Zwangsjacke für die Studienreform" [Straitjacket for curricula reform]. *Der Monat* 18 (November): 7–13. (Reprinted in Leibfried [ed.], 1967: 86–93.)
  1966b "Verwissenschaftlichte Politik in demokratischer Gesellschaft" [Scientific public policy in democratic society]. In Krauch, Kunz, and Rittel (eds.), 1966: 130–44.
  1967   "Universität in der Demokratie—Demokratisierung der Universität" [University in democracy—democratizing the university]. *Merkur* 21: 416–33.
  1968a *Technik und Wissenschaft als "Ideologie"* [Technique and science as "ideology"]. Frankfurt: Suhrkamp.
  1968b "Praktische Folgen des wissenschaftlich-technischen Fortschritts" [Practical consequences of scientific-technological progress]. In H.

Maus (ed.), *Gesellschaft, Recht and Politik* [Society, law and public policy]. Neuwied and Berlin: Hermann Luchterhand Verlag.

1968c *Erkenntnis und Interesse* [Knowledge and human interest]. Frankfurt: Suhrkamp.

1968d *Antworten auf Herbert Marcuse* [Replies to Herbert Marcuse]. J. Habermas (ed.), Frankfurt: Suhrkamp.

1969 *Protestbewegung und Hochschulreform* [The protest movement and reform in higher education]. Frankfurt: Suhrkamp.

HARNACK, ADOLF VON

1911 "Vom Großbetrieb der Wissenschaft" [On the bureaucracy of science]. In A. v. Harnack, *Aus Wissenschaft und Leben*, vol. 1. [From science and life, vol. 1], pp. 10 ff. Giessen: A. Töpelmann.

HARTMANN, HEINZ

1971 *Organisation der Sozialforschung* [Organization of social research]. Opladen: Westdeutscher Verlag.

HESS, GERHARD; RALF DAHRENDORF; PETER MENKE-GLÜCKERT; AND JOACHIM RITTER

1965 *Strukturprobleme unserer wissenschaftlichen Hochschulen* [Structural problems of our institutions of higher education]. Köln und Opladen: Westdeutscher Verlag.

HETZLER, HANS WILHELM

1966 *Entwicklungstendenzen in der Forschung. Werkstattgespräche* [Developmental tendencies in research: proceedings of a workshop]. H. W. Hetzler (ed.). Dortmund: Sozialforschungsstelle an der Universität Münster.

1970 *Soziale Strukturen der organisierten Forschung. Trägerschaft und Organisation ausseruniversitärer Forschungseinrichtunger* [Social structures of organized research: sponsorship and organization in non-university research institutions]. Düsseldorf: Bertelsmann Universitätsverlag.

HETZLER, HANS WILHELM, AND RENATE RAUSCH

1962 "Integrationsprobleme der industriellen Forschung" [Problems of integration in industrial research]. *Soziale Welt* 13 (no. 3/4):228–38.

HIRSCH, JOACHIM

1971 *Wissenschaftlich-technischer Fortschritt und politisches System. Organisation und Grundlagen administrativer Wissenschaftsförderung* [Scientific-technological progress and the political system: the organization and basis of administrative encouragement of science]. Frankfurt: Suhrkamp.

1975 "Ökonomische Verwertungsinteressen und Lenkung der Forschung" [Economic interests and the direction of research]. In Weingart (ed.), 1975, pp. 194–212.

HOFMANN, WERNER

1969 *Universität, Ideologie, Gesellschaft. Beiträge zur Wissenschaftssoziologie* [University, ideology and society: contributions to the sociology of science]. Frankfurt: Suhrkamp.

KAPLAN, NORMAN
1964 "Sociology of Science." In R. E. Faris (ed.), *Handbook of Modern Sociology*, pp. 852–81. Chicago: Rand McNally.

KAUPP, PETER
1969 *Der Hochschulassistent und seine Probleme. Ergebnisse einer Umfrage zur sozialen, wirtschaftlichen und beruflichen Situation der wissenschaftlichen Assistenten an der Johannes Gutenberg-Universität Mainz* [The "assistant" in higher education and his problems: results of a survey of the social, economic, and occupational position of the scientific assistants at the Johannes Gutenberg University, Mainz]. Stuttgart: Ferdinand Enke Verlag.

KEMPSKI, JÜRGEN VON
1953/1954 "Wissenschaft als freier Beruf [Science as an independent profession]. *Kölner Zeitschrift für Soziologie und Sozialpsychologie* 6:423–34.

KLAGES, HELMUT
1967 *Rationalität und Spontaneitat. Innovationswege der modernen Grossforschung* [Rationality and spontaneity: innovative paths in modern big science]. Gütersloh: C. Bertelsmann Verlag.

KLAGES, HELMUT, AND HANS WILHELM HETZLER
1966 "Entwicklungswege der Forschungsorganisation [Avenues of development of research organizations]. *Humanismus und Technik* 10:18–26.

KLIMA, ROLF
1969 "Einige Widersprüche im Rollen-Set des Soziologen" [Some contradictions in the role-set of the sociologist]. In B. Schäfers (ed.), *Thesen zur Kritik der Soziologie* [Theses in the critique of sociology], pp. 80–95. Frankfurt: Suhrkamp.
1972 "Theoretical pluralism, methodological dissension, and the role of the sociologist: The West German Case." *Social Science Information* 11 (no. 3/4):69–108.
1974a "Scientific knowledge and social control in science: the application of a cognitive theory of behaviour to the study of scientific behaviour." In R. D. Whitley (ed.), *Social Processes of Scientific Development*, pp. 96–122. London and Boston: Routledge and Kegan Paul.
1974b "Sind Experimentalregeln 'soziale Verbindlichkeiten'?" [Are rules of experimentation social norms?]. *Zeitschrift für Soziologie* 3 (January):103–6.

KLIMA, ROLF, AND LUDGER VIEHOFF
1974 "Inventory of organizations and individuals doing research in the sociology of science in the Federal Republic of Germany and in Austria." *Social Science Information* 13 (no. 1).

KLINGEMANN, HARALD
1974 "Ein Beitrag zur Methode der Messung individueller wissenschaftlicher Leistung: dargestellt am Beispiel der Kernfor-

schungsanlage Jülich" [Toward constructing a method of measuring individual scientific achievement: exemplified at the Juelich nuclear research plant]. *Zeitschrift für Soziologie* 3 (October):356–74.

KOCH, CLAUS, AND DIETER SENGHAAS (EDS.)

1970   *Texte zur Technokratiediskussion* [Texts for the debate on technocracy]. Frankfurt: Deutsche Verlags-Anstalt.

KÖNIG, RENE

1970   *Vom Wesen der deutschen Universität* [On the essence of the German university]. Darmstadt: Wissenschaftliche Buchgesellschaft. (First printing 1935, Berlin: Die Runde.)

KRAUCH, HELMUT

1961   "Wider den technischen Staat" [Against the technical state]. *Atomzeitalter* (no. 6):201–3.

1964   "Glanz und Elend der Expertokratie" [Splendor and misery of "expertocracy"]. *Atomzeitalter* (no. 6):171–75.

1966   *Beiträge zum Verhältnis von Wissenschaft und Politik* [Contributions to the relationship between science and public policy]. In Krauch (ed.), Heidelberg: Studiengruppe für Systemforschung.

1970a   *Die organisierte Forschung* [Organized research]. Neuwied und Berlin: Hermann Luchterhand Verlag.

1970b   *Prioritäten in der Forschungspolitik* [Priorities for public policy on research]. München: Carl Hanser Verlag.

KRAUCH, HELMUT; HUBERT FEGER; AND WERNER OPGENOORTH

1970   "Forschungsplanung I: Verwirklichungschancen und Förderungswürdigkeit von Forschungsschwerpunkten im Urteil von Fachleuten und Studenten" [Research planning I: experts' and students' judgements of the probability of realization and value of research priorities]. *Zeitschrift für Sozialpsychologie* 1:155–66.

KRAUCH, HELMUT; WERNER KUNZ; AND HORST RITTEL (EDS.)

1966   *Forschungsplanung. Eine Studie über Ziele und Strukturen amerikanischer Forschungsinstitute* [Research planning: a study of the goals and structure of American research institutes]. München und Wien: R. Oldenbourg Verlag.

KRAUCH, HELMUT, AND KLAUS SCHREIBER

1966   "Forschung und technischer Fortschritt im Bewußtsein der Öffentlichkeit. Ergebnisse einer Repräsentativbefragung" [Public perception of research and technological progress: results of a representative survey]. *Soziale Welt* 17 (no. 4):289–315.

KRAUCH, HELMUT, AND W. VOLKMANN

1972   "Die Diskrepanz zwischen der staatlichen und der öffentlichen Präferenzordnung der wichtigsten Forschungs- und Entwicklungsaufgaben in der BRD" [The discrepancy between the official administrative and public views of the top priorities for research and development tasks in the FRG]. In Paschen and Krauch (eds.), 1972:21 ff.

KROCKOW, CHRISTIAN GRAF VON

1958a "Zur Situation der Luxuswissenschaften" [On the situation of the luxury sciences]. *Deutsche Universitätszeitung* 13:589–93.

1958b "Soziologische Aspekte der Klinischen Medizin" [Sociological aspects of clinical medicine]. *Deutsche Universitätszeitung* 13:650–58.

1958c "Zwischen Wissenschaft und Praxis. Studien über die Lage des akademischen Nachwuchses" [Between science and practice: studies on the position of aspiring academics]. *Schweizer Monatschefte* (no. 8).

1959 "Fiktionen der heutigen Universitätsverfassung" [Myths of present university constitutions]. In *Soziologie und moderne Gesellschaft.* Verhandlungen des 14. Deutschen Soziologentages. Stuttgart: Ferdinand Enke Verlag.

1963 "Möglichkeiten und Unmöglichkeiten einer Reform. Dargelegt am Beispiel der deutschen Hochschulen" [Possibilities and impossibilities of reform: illustrated by the example of German higher education]. *Atomzeitalter* (no. 6).

KRYSMANSKI, HANS JÜRGEN

1966 "Wissenschaft als Aussenseitertun" [Science as marginality]. *Jahrbuch für Sozialwissenschaft* 17:247–70.

1967 *Soziales System und Wissenschaft* [Social system and science]. Gütersloh: C. Bertelsmann Verlag.

KURUCZ, JENÖ; PETER OCHS; AND KARL PETER WANCZEK

1972 *Das Selbstverständnis von Naturwissenschaftlern in der Industrie: Ergebnisse einer Befragung promovierter Industriechemiker* [The self-image of natural scientists in industry: results of a survey of industrial chemists with Ph.D.'s]. Weinheim (Bergstrasse): Verlag Chemie.

LADES, HANS, AND CLEMENS BURRICHTER (EDS.)

1970 *Produktivkraft Wissenschaft. Sozialistische Sozialwissenschaft in der DDR* [Science as a productive force: Socialist social science in the GDR]. Hamburg: Drei Mohren Verlag.

LEIBFRIED, STEPHAN (ED.)

1967 *Wider die Untertanenfabrik. Handbuch zur Demokratisierung der Hochschule* [Against the oppression factory: Handbook on the democratizing of higher education]. Köln: Pahl-Rugenstein Verlag.

LEPSIUS, M. RAINER

1969 "Die Autonomie der Universität in der Krise" [The autonomy of the university in the crisis]. In G. Schulz (ed.), *Was wird aus der Universität? Standpunkte zur Hochschulreform* [What will become of the university? Opinions on reform in higher education]. Tübingen: Rainer Wunderlich Verlag Hermann Leins.

LOHMAR, ULRICH

1968 *Wissenschaftsforderung und Politik-Beratung. Kooperationsfelder* von *Politik und Wissenschaft in der Bundesrepublik Deutschland* [Promoting science and public policy advising: areas of cooperation between public policy and science in the FRG]. Gütersloh: C. Bertelsmann Verlag.

1973 *Wissenschaftspolitik und Demokratisierung. Ziele, Analysen, Perspektiven* [Scientific public policy and democratization: goals, analyses, and perspectives]. Düsseldorf: Bertelsmann Universitätsverlag.

LÖRINCZ, LAJOS

1971 *Die staatliche Lenkung der wissenschaftlichen Forschung* [Government direction of scientific research]. Düsseldorf: Bertelsmann Universitätsverlag.

LUHMANN, NIKLAS

1968 "Selbststeuerung der Wissenschaft" [Self-direction of science]. *Jahrbuch für Sozialwissenschaft* 19 (no. 2):147–70.

MATUSSEK, PAUL

1966a "Antikreative Tendenzen in der Wissenschaft" [Anticreative tendencies in science]. In Krauch (ed.), 1966:92–102.

1966b "Faktor Persönlichkeit in der Wissenschaftsplanung" [The personality factor in research planning]. In Krauch, Kunz, and Rittel (eds.), 1966:94–109. (trans. in R. A. Tybout [ed.], *Economics of Research and Development*. Columbus: Ohio State University Press, 1965.)

MERTON, ROBERT K.

1968 *Social Theory and Social Structure*. Enl. ed. New York: The Free Press.

MIKAT, PAUL, AND HELMUT SCHELSKY

1967 *Grundzüge einer neuen Universität. Zur Planung einer Hochschulgründung in Ostwestfalen* [Outlines of a new university: plans for the founding of a new university in East Westphalia]. Gütersloh: C. Bertelsmann Verlag.

MOMMSEN, THEODOR

1905 "Akademie-Rede, Berlin 1890" [Academic address, Berlin, 1890]. In O. Hirschfeld, *Reden und Aufsätze von Theodor Mommsen*. Berlin.

MÜNCH, RICHARD

1974 "Evolutionäre Strukturmerkmale komplexer sozialer Systeme am Beispiel des Wissenschaftssystems [Evolutionary structural properties of complex social systems exemplified by the social system of science]. *Kölner Zeitschrift für Soziologie und Sozialpsychologie* 26 (no. 4):681–714.

NELSON, BENJAMIN

1974 "On the shoulders of the giants of the comparative historical sociology of 'science'—in civilizational perspective." In R. D. Whitley (ed.), *Social Processes of Scientific Development*, pp. 13–20. London and Boston: Routledge and Kegan Paul.

NEUENDORFF, HARTMUT
1973 "Die Programme des BMBW zur Förderung der 'technologischen' Forschung und Entwicklung" [The programs of the federal education and science ministry for the promotion of technological research and development]. In Pohrt (ed.), pp. 144–71.

NITSCH, WOLFGANG
1967 Hochschule. Soziologische Materialien [Institutions of higher education: sociological materials]. Heidelberg: Quelle and Meyer.

NITSCH, WOLFGANG; UTA GERHARDT; CLAUS OFFE; AND ULRICH PREUSS
1965 Hochschule in der Demokratie. Kritische Beiträge zur Erbschaft und Reform der deutschen Universität [The university in democracy: critical contributions on the heritage and reform of the German university]. Berlin and Neuwied: Hermann Luchterhand Verlag.

NOWOTNY, HELGA
1973 "On the Feasibility of a Cognitive Approach to the Study of Science." Zeitschrift für Soziologie 2 (July): 282–96.
1975 "Controversies in Science: Remarks on the Different Modes of Production of Knowledge and their Use." Zeitschrift für Soziologie 4 (January): 34–45.

OFFE, CLAUS
1968 "Technik und Eindimensionalität. Eine Version der Technokratiethese" [Technique and one-dimensionality: one version of the technocracy thesis]. In Habermas, 1968d: 73–88.
1972 Strukturprobleme des kapitalistischen Staates [Structural problems of the capitalistic state]. Frankfurt: Suhrkamp.

PASCHEN, HERBERT, AND HELMUT KRAUCH (EDS.)
1972 Methoden und Probleme der Forschungs- und Entwicklungsplanung [Methods and problems of research and development planning]. München und Wien: R. Oldenbourg Verlag.

PFETSCH, FRANK
1970 "Scientific Organisation and Science Policy in Imperial Germany 1879–1914: The Foundation of the Imperial Institute of Physics and Technology." Minerva 8: 4–48.
1971 "Determinanten des Wachstums wissenschaftlicher Organisationen in Deutschland" [Determinants of the growth of scientific organizations in Germany]. Kölner Zeitschrift für Soziologie und Sozialpsychologie 23 (no. 4): 704–26.
1973 "Die Institutionalisierung medizinischer Fachgebiete im deutschen Wissenschaftssystem" [The institutionalization of medical specialties in the German system of science]. In Pfetsch and Zloczower, 1973: 9–90.
1974 Zur Entwicklung der Wissenschaftspolitik in Deutschland 1750–1914 [On the development of science public policy in Germany 1750–1914]. Berlin and München: Duncker und Humblot.

PFETŠCH, FRANK, AND AVRAHAM ZLOCZOWER
    1973   *Innovation und Widerstände in der Wissenschaft. Beiträge zur Ge-
            schichte der deutschen Medizin* [Innovation and resistance in science:
            contributions to the history of German medicine]. Düsseldorf: Ber-
            telsmann Universitätsverlag.
PLESSNER, HELMUTH
    1924   "Zur Soziologie der modernen Forschung und ihrer Organisation in
            der deutschen Universität" [On the sociology of modern research and
            its organization in the German University]. In M. Scheler (ed.), *Ver-
            suche zu einer Soziologie des Wissens*, pp. 407–25. München und
            Leipzig: Duncker und Humblot.
    1956   *Untersuchungen zur Lage der deutschen Hochschullehrer* [Research
            on the position of teachers in German higher education]. Plessner
            (ed.), 3 vols. Göttingen: Vandenhoeck und Ruprecht.
    1956a   "Vorwort" [Preface]. In Asemissen et al., 1956:9–18.
    1958   "Zur Lage der Geisteswissenschaften in der industriellen Ge-
            sellschaft" [On the place of the humanities in industrial society].
            Schweizer Monatshefte 38:647 ff.
    1959   *Möglichkeiten der Hochschulreform* [Possibilities for reform in
            higher education]. Bad Homburg: Forschungsrat des Landes Hessen.
POHRT, WOLFGANG (ED.)
    1973   *Wissenschaftspolitik—von wem, für wen, wie? Prioritäten in der
            Forschungsplanung* [Public policy for science—by whom, for whom,
            how? Priorities in research planning]. München: Carl Hanser Verlag.
POPPER, KARL R.
    1972   *Objective Knowledge. An Evolutionary Approach*. Oxford: Claren-
            don Press.

RADNITZKY, GERARD
    1974   "Was kann die Wissenschaftsforschung zur theoretischen Grund-
            legung der Wissenschaftspolitik beitragen?" [On the possible contri-
            bution of science studies to the theoretical foundation of science
            policy]. *Kölner Zeitschrift für Soziologie und Sozialpsychologie* 26
            (no. 4):801–18.
REIMANN, HORST
    1961   "Soziologische Aspekte der Verwendung von Kernkraft. Das Or-
            ganisationssystem eines Forschungsreaktors" [Sociological aspects of
            the application of nuclear energy: the organizational system of a re-
            search reactor]. *Kölner Zeitschrift für Soziologie und Sozial-
            psychologie* 13:217–26.
RILLING, RAINER
    1969   "Kriegsforschung und Wissenschaftspolitik in der BRD, 1" [War re-
            search and science policy in the FRG, 1]. *Blätter für deutsche und
            internationale Politik* (no. 12):1272–93.
    1970a   "Kriegsforschung und Wissenschaftspolitik in der BRD, 2" [War re-

search and science policy in the FRG, 2]. *Blätter für deutsche und internationale Politik* (no. 1):52–68.

1970b "Die Forschungspolitik der BRD" [Public policy on research in the FRG]. In A. W. Weinberg, *Probleme der Großforschung*, pp. 275–318. Frankfurt: Suhrkamp.

1970c *Kriegsforschung und Vernichtungswissenschaft in der BRD* [War research and "destruction" science in the FRG]. Köln: Pahl-Rugenstein Verlag.

RITTEL, HORST

1966 "Hierarchie oder Team? Betrachtungen zu Kooperationsformen in Forschung und Entwicklung" [Hierarchy or team? Reflections on forms of cooperation in research and development]. In Krauch, Kunz, and Rittel (eds.), 1966:40–70. (trans. in R. A. Tybout [ed.], *Economics of Research and Development*. Columbus: Ohio State University Press, 1965.)

RÖDEL, ULRICH

1972 *Forschungsprioritäten und technologische Entwicklung. Studien über Determinanten der Forschung und Schwerpunkte der Technologiepolitik* [Research priorities and technological development: studies on the determinants of research and priorities of technological policy]. Frankfurt: Suhrkamp.

ROSENSTOCK-HUESSY, EUGEN

1958 "Das Geheimnis der Universität" [The secret of the university]. In E. Rosenstock-Huessy, *Das Geheimnis der Universität. Wider den Verfall von Zeitsinn und Sprachkraft. Aufsätze und Reden aus den Jahren 1950 bis 1957*, pp. 17–34. Stuttgart: W. Kohlhammer Verlag.

SCHELER, MAX

1921 "Universität und Volkschochschule" [University and adult education]. In L. v. Wiese (ed.), *Soziologie des Volksbildungswesens* [Sociology of adult education]. München und Leipzig.

1960 *Die Wissensformen und die Gesellschaft* [Types of knowledge and
[1926] society]. 2d ed. Bern und München: Francke Verlag.

SCHELSKY, HELMUT

1960 *Einsamkeit und Freiheit. Zur sozialen Idee der deutschen Universität* [Loneliness and freedom: on the social idea of the German university]. Münster i.W.: Verlag Aschendorff.

1961 *Der Mensch in der wissenschaftlichen Zivilisation* [The human being in scientific civilization]. Köln und Opladen: Westdeutscher Verlag. (Reprinted in H. Schelsky, *Auf der Suche nach Wirklichkeit*, pp. 439 ff., Düsseldorf und Köln: Diederichs, 1965.)

1963 *Einsamkeit und Freiheit. Zur Idee und Gestalt der deutschen Universität und ihrer Reformen* [Loneliness and freedom: on the idea and form of the German university and its reforms]. Reinbek bei Hamburg: Rowohlt.

1967   "Berufsbild und Berufswirklichkeit des Professors" [The professor's occupational ideal and reality]. In Mikat and Schelsky, 1967:21–34.

1969   *Abschied von der Hochschulpolitik oder Die Universität im Faden-kreuz des Versagens* [Departure from higher education policy or the university in the crosspressures of failure]. Bielefeld: Bertelmann Universitätsverlag.

SCHERHORN, GERHARD
1969   "Der Wettbewerb in der Erfahrungswissenschaft: Ein Beitrag zur allgemeinen Theorie des Marktes" [Competition in empirical science: a contribution to the general theory of the market]. *Hamburger Jahrbuch für Wirtschafts- und Gesellschaftspolitik* 14:63–86.

SCHEUCH, ERWIN K.
1965   "Sozialer Wandel und Sozialforschung. Über die Beziehungen zwischen Gesellschaft und empirischer Sozialforschung" [Social change and social research: On the relations between society and empirical social research]. *Kölner Zeitschrift für Soziologie und Sozial-psychologie* 17 (no. 1):1–48.

SCHOLZ, HERBERT (ED.)
1969   *Die Rolle der Wissenschaft in der modernen Gesellschaft* [The role of science in modern society]. Berlin und München: Duncker und Humblot.

SCHUON, KARL THEODOR
1971   "Wissenschaft und Politik in der spatkapitalistischen Klassen-gesellschaft" [Science and public policy in the class society of late capitalism]. *Das Argument* 13:323–93.

1972   *Wissenschaft, Politik und wissenschaftliche Politik* [Science, policy, and scientific policy]. Köln: Pahl-Rugenstein Verlag.

SOMBART, WERNER
1928   *Der moderne Kapitalismus* [Modern capitalism]. München und Leipzig: Duncker und Humblot.

SPIEGEL-RÖSING, INA S.
1973   *Wissenschaftsentwicklung und Wissenschaftssteuerung. Einführung und Material zur Wissenschaftsforschung* [Development and direction of science: introduction to and material for research on science]. Frankfurt: Athenäum Verlag.

STORER, NORMAN W.
1966   *The Social System of Science*. New York: Holt, Rinehart and Winston.

STÜCK, HEINER
1969   "Wissenschaftssoziologische Kritik an deutschen Technokratie-Theorien" [Critique of German theories of technocracy from the perspective of the sociology of science]. *Futurum* 3:366–94.

TENBRUCK, FRIEDRICH H.
1961   "Bildung, Gesellschaft, Wissenschaft" [Education, society, science]. In D. Oberdörfer (ed.), *Wissenschaftliche Politik. Eine Einführung*

in Grundfragen ihrer Tradition und Theorie, pp. 365–420. Freiburg i. Br: Rombach.

1969a   "Regulative Funktionen der Wissenschaft in der pluralistischen Gesellschaft" [Regulative functions of science in pluralistic society]. In Scholz (ed.), 1969.

1969b   "Die Funktion der Wissenschaft" [The functions of science]. In G. Schulz (ed.), *Was wird aus der Universität? Standpunkte zur Hochschulreform*, pp. 55–76. Tübingen: Rainer Wunderlich Verlag Hermann Leins.

1974a   "'Science as a Vocation'—Revisited." In E. Forsthoff and R. Hörstel (eds.), *Standorte im Zeitstrom. Festschrift für Arnold Gehlen zum 70. Geburtstag am 29, Januar 1974*, pp. 351–64. Frankfurt: Athenäum Verlag.

1974b   "Max Weber and the Sociology of Science: A Case Reopened." *Zeitschrift für Soziologie* 3 (June): 312–20.

TOMBERG, FRIEDRICH

1971   "Was heißt bürgerliche Wissenschaft?" [What does bourgeois science mean?] *Das Argument* 13 (no. 6/7): 461–75.

VOGEL, ULRIKE

1970   *Wissenschaftliche Hilfskräfte. Eine Analyse der Lage wissenschaftlicher Hilfskräfte an Universitäten der Bundesrepublik, untersucht am Beispiel der Universität Göttingen* [Scientific assistance: an analysis of the position of laboratory personnel in the universities of the federal republic, as illustrated by the example of the University of Göttingen]. Stuttgart: Ferdinand Enke Verlag.

WEBER, ALFRED

1920   "Prinzipielles zur Kultursoziologie: Gesellschaftsprozess, Zivilisationsprozess und Kulturbewegung" [Principles of the sociology of culture (or cultural sociology): societal process, civilizational process and cultural movement]. *Archiv für Sozialwissenschaft und Sozialpolitik* 47: 1–49.

WEBER, MAX

1946   "Science as a Vocation." In H. H. Gerth and C. W. Mills (eds.), *From Max Weber: Essays in Sociology*, pp. 129–56. New York: Oxford University Press.

1964   *Wirtschaft und Gesellschaft. Grundriss der verstehenden Soziologie* [1922] [Economy and society]. Köln und Berlin: Kiepenheuer und Witsch.

WEINGART, PETER

1970a   *Die amerikanische Wissenschaftslobby. Zum sozialen und politischen Wandel des Wissenschaftssystems im Prozeß der Forschungsplanung* [The American science lobby: social and political change in the science system through the process of research planning]. Düsseldorf: Bertelsmann Universitätsverlag.

1970b   "Selbststeuerung der Wissenschaft und staatliche Wissenschaftspolitik" [Self-direction of science and governmental science policy]. *Kölner Zeitschrift für Soziologie und Sozialpsychologie* 22 (no. 3):567–92.

1972   *Wissenschaftssoziologie 1: Wissenschaftliche Entwicklung als sozialer Prozeß* [Sociology of science 1: scientific development as a social process]. Weingart (ed.). Frankfurt: Athenäum Fischer Taschenbuch Verlag.

1974a   *Wissenschaftssoziologie 2: Determinanten wissenschaftlicher Entwicklung* [Sociology of science 2: determinants of scientific progress]. Weingart (ed.). Frankfurt: Athenäum Fischer Taschenbuch Verlag.

1974b   "On a sociological theory of scientific change." In R. D. Whitley (ed.), *Social Processes of Scientific Development*, pp. 45–68. London and Boston: Routledge and Kegan Paul.

1975   *Wissenschaftsforschung: Eine Vorlesungsreihe mit Beiträgen von Ben-David, Hirsch, Kambartel, Lakatos, Radnitzky u.a.* [Science studies: a series of lectures with contributions by Ben-David, Hirsch, Kambartel, Lakatos, Radnitzky, and others]. Weingart (ed.). Frankfurt: Campus Verlag.

WILHELM, JÜRGEN, AND GERD WILLE

1971   "Arbeitssituation und Berufsprobleme junger Wissenschaftler an Universitätsinstituten. Ergebnisse einer Untersuchung an den Universitäten Hamburg und Göttingen" [Working conditions and occupational problems of young scientists at university institutions: results of a study at the Universities of Hamburg and Göttingen]. Research report. Mimeographed. Göttingen: Seminar für die Wissenschaft von der Politik der Universität Göttingen.

ZLOCZOWER, AVRAHAM

1966   *Career Opportunities and the Growth of Scientific Discovery in 19th Century Germany.* Jerusalem: The Hebrew University, the Eliezer Kaplan School of Economics and Social Sciences.

THE SOCIOLOGY OF SCIENCE IN

Poland

Tadeusz Krauze, Zdislaw Kowalewski, and Adam Podgórecki

THE DEVELOPMENT of the sociology of science in Poland is itself, to use Robert K. Merton's term, a self-exemplifying case study in scientific progress, exhibiting such interesting features as prematurity, language barriers in the diffusion of ideas, and discontinuity due to political upheavals. Such a study, however, cannot be undertaken within the confines of this chapter, which is limited to a descriptive survey of research trends in pre– and post–World War II Poland.

The section on pre–World War II Poland will deal with such indicators of the emergence of self-conscious activity as specialized publications and the appearance of a separate group devoted to the study of science; it will also summarize the contributions of the most important prewar thinkers, Florian Znaniecki and Stanislaw Ossowski. The discussion of the postwar period will concentrate on new directions of research, new publications, recruitment and career lines, and the effect of governmental policy on the structure of research organizations and themes of research.

THE PRE–WORLD WAR II PERIOD

Precursors of the Sociology of Science

The self-conscious study of science in Poland began largely through the efforts of the Mianowski Foundation, which was established in 1881 by academicians of the Central School of Warsaw to help support scientific activity. One of its major accomplishments was the publication of a series of volumes called the *Guide for Autodidacts* (1897–1939). Each volume, devoted to a separate branch of science, presented an authoritative description of the historical development of the discipline and the current state of knowledge in the field. Particularly after World War I, that is, after Poland regained her independence, these volumes helped to define the teaching programs in schools of higher education.

Even more important than this series was the launching of the journal *Nauka Polska* [Polish science] in 1918 by the Mianowski Foundation with the explicit purpose of reporting the needs, present state, and organization of science in Poland. Appearing in the form of annual volumes under the editorship of Stanislaw Michalski, it reflected the growing awareness, in editorial statements and the selection of articles, that the unification of various points of view on the "problem of science" might result in a new scientific discipline. What this discipline was to be called remained ambiguous. It was variously referred to as "knowledge about knowledge" (*wiedza o wiedzy*), "knowledge about science" (*wiedza o nauce*), and "science of science" (*nauka o nauce*), in a groping for terminology that reflected the early stages of disciplinary development, when a new body of knowledge seeks an identity.

As early as 1923, an unsigned editorial in *Nauka Polska*, probably by Michalski, self-consciously announced the emergence, and needed encouragement, of a new field called "knowledge about science," finding in that framework a place for the sociology of science. Because it is a pivotal statement, the editorial is quoted here extensively.

> Contributions contained in the published volumes of *Nauka Polska* have brought into full relief a complex of problems pertain-

ing to science as a social phenomenon; a separate division of the *knowledge about science* [all italics in original] has been delineated. Science, like other products of culture such as art and religion, is an object of research.

The appearance of a separate "knowledge about science" stems to some extent from the needs of life. Stimuli of a practical nature, such as reflections on the present needs of science and the implied need for its planned support, and on the relationship of science to other areas of culture and social life, require further deliberation upon creative scientific activity and the conditions of its development. Wherever some activity has been undertaken, the need to establish its own theoretical foundation eventually makes itself felt; hence the need for *research on science*. Thus the articles in *Nauka Polska*, though largely devoted to the needs of the separate sciences or to the organization of science, also include contributions devoted to problems of a theoretical nature, problems pertaining, for example, to the so-called *sociology of science*.

The statements made above provide a guideline for the program and direction of the journal. Its main task is to draw society's attention to the topical, but insufficiently popular, problem of science; for this purpose it is desirable to isolate this problem from other related problems and to investigate it separately, from both the theoretical and practical points of view. (*Nauka Polska* 4:vii)

By 1928, what Michalski called "knowledge about science" (*wiedza o nauce*) had become *naukoznawstwo*. The first part of this hybrid term derives from *nauka*, or academic discipline. The equivalent German concept is *Wissenschaft*. The second component, *znawstwo*, refers to "expertise," "practical knowledge," or "expertness." We may translate *naukoznawstwo* roughly as "science of science."

Since its beginnings in Poland, the science of science has been a broader intellectual enterprise than the sociology of science. Even now, sociologists of science find it easier to obtain sponsorship and to publish under the science of science rubric. The pressure of the name may have forced certain disciplinary alliances, preventing a full institutionalization of the sociology of science in Poland.

Publications and Organizations, 1918–1933

From its inception in 1918, *Nauka Polska* featured articles exhibiting a broad range of interests and themes which, if not specifically developed, had sociological dimensions. Among the superior examples are those on the internationality of science and the national character of the contributors (Gawrónski, 1923; Minkiewicz, 1918; Kochanowski, 1918; Dobrowolski, 1934); the traits of scientific investigators (Kotarbiński, 1929; Bujak, 1929); science and the "forms of social life" (Rybicki, 1929). Many autobiographies of prominent scientists appeared, well written but unanalytical in nature. Most important, the journal published Znaniecki's excellent, and never-translated early essay on "The Subject Matter and Tasks of the Science of Knowledge" (1925), several articles by Ossowski, and many contributions of the Science of Science Circle.

The Science of Science Circle

By 1928, activity and interest in this new field were apparently sufficient to produce a separate scientific group (again associated with the Mianowski Foundation) devoted to the discussion of problems in the science of science. About forty meetings took place in the decade between 1928 and 1939, generally well attended by distinguished representatives of the Polish intellectual elite. The average number of discussants was seven, and the discussions, at least in their published form, were erudite, often contributing new and sometimes startling perspectives. The meetings were usually chaired by Jan Lukasiewicz, the originator of multivalued logic, whose early (1915) article on creative elements in science is considered an exceptional and lucid essay (cf. Ossowski, 1923; Ajdukiewicz, 1957).

Nauka Polska played a major role in publicizing the work of this group. Not only did a large number of the presentations appear in the journal; the summaries of the discussions were themselves extensive and precise, identifying statements made by each contributor.

Organon

In 1936, the consolidation of the "science of science movement" (cf. Osińska, 1969) led to the publication of a new journal, *Organon*, also launched with the financial assistance of the Mianowski Foundation, and with Stanislaw Michalski, editor of *Nauka Polska*, as its editor in chief. Representing the effort of the Science of Science Circle to diffuse its influence to an international audience, *Organon* included contributions in the languages of the international congresses as well as translations from *Nauka Polska*. The lead article in its first issue was an English translation of "The Science of Science," by Ossowska and Ossowski (1935), the pivotal essay in which the authors outlined the dimensions and program of the new field.

Although *Organon* did not include quantitative empirical research, it did undertake a questionnaire survey of the international scientific elite on the subject of exchange of scientific information, international congresses, and the like, and reported the open-ended responses in great detail. The results, however, were not summarized, and the material remains unanalyzed. Several autobiographies of scientists were also published, apparently to illustrate various types of scientific creativity.

Only two volumes of the journal had appeared before the Second World War interrupted an important phase in the development of Polish sociology of science.

Major Theoretical Contributions

Florian Znaniecki, known for his collaboration with W. I. Thomas on *The Polish Peasant in Europe and America*, contributed throughout his life to the sociology of knowledge. Although *The Social Role of the Man of Knowledge* (1940) is his most prominent work in this area, Znaniecki produced a major theoretical statement as early as 1925. "The Subject Matter and Tasks of the Science of Knowledge" outlined a program of concrete investigations which regrettably have not been pursued. The central ideas in this long (seventy-eight-page) article are of more than historical interest; since it has never been published in English, this summary includes extensive quotations from the work.

Znaniecki begins with the observation that, while the theory of knowledge can be traced back to Heraclitus, its modern developments contain so many new ideas that it relates to classical theory as modern natural science does to natural philosophy. The modern theory of knowledge, "possessing its own empirical properties and amenable to empirical investigation, acquires the traits of positive, comparative, generalizing, and empirical science. Thus it distinguishes itself from epistemology, logic, and the strictly descriptive history of science."

If the theory of knowledge is to acquire its own point of view and method, Znaniecki maintains, it will have to break away from the disciplines in which its problematics emerged, that is, epistemology, logic, history, psychology, and sociology. His own perspective, he states, will be "humanistic"—a sociological perspective that takes into account the varying meanings of phenomena as they occurred to the investigated subjects, without intrusion of the researcher's own criteria of truth. "As a researcher, the theorist of knowledge has no right to ponder whether the phenomena presented to him as knowledge are really knowledge in terms of the ideal of knowledge which he considers decisive."

A theory of cognitive phenomena, like any scientific theory, must first analyze and classify, then provide a causal explanation of phenomena, Znaniecki states. He begins his own formulation with two fundamental concepts: "cognitive values" and "cognitive activities." "Every phenomenon to which somebody ever ascribes the characteristic of truthfulness . . . is called a cognitive value." Cognitive activities are primarily "thought activities" of observing, defining, reasoning. "Cognitive values are the objects of cognitive activities as their materials, tools or products; every change in cognitive values has its source in cognitive activities."

The development of human knowledge "presents itself as a creative cumulation of cognitive values and the emergence of new cognitive activities." Since this process involves both continuity and innovation, Znaniecki introduces several principles of an empirical character. The first principle is that of "developmental continuity of knowledge"; the second is the principle of "freedom and unpredictability" in this development, since Znaniecki maintains that creative development, insofar as it is creative, cannot be causally explained. He also posits a third principle, the "irreversibility of the developmental ordering of knowledge," which he suggests should be empirically investigated.

The principle of "developmental continuity" approaches each new cognitive activity as a logical and genetic continuation of antecedent cognitive activities. The new activity may be either a formal modification of the earlier activity, or a new thought function. Thus, for example, Znaniecki sees the problem of the dependence of culture on racial composition as a modification, or development, of the older mind-body problem, in this case applied to a collectivity rather than to individuals.

Newtonian theory provides an even clearer illustration of the functional differentiation of cognitive activities as they create new components. Though a major theoretical advance, Newtonian theory was logically and genetically a continuation of older theories of Kepler, Galileo, and Huygens. However, this genetic connection does not imply either historical continuity or an immanent rational order in the development of knowledge. "On the contrary, the actual cognitive development shows characteristics of irrationality and unpredictability in the emergence of new developmental lines." Thus there may be continuity in the development of knowledge, but there is no objective necessity that a *particular* activity, and not some other, will be realized. This, in essence, is what Znaniecki means by "freedom and unpredictability" in the development of knowledge.

There are two ways in which the actual development of cognitive activities may run counter to what assumptions of historical probability or purposiveness might dictate. In the first instance, we find disruptions of developmental lines of thought, or discontinuities in "progress." Examples are the heliocentric hypothesis of Aristarchus of Samos which, dormant for centuries, had to be created anew by Copernicus; the Cartesian theory of the vortex; and Leibniz's *characteristica universalis*. Conversely, new cognitive activities do not always appear as continuous extensions of an older theoretical tradition but break away from it, finding new continuities with the past, or using new departure points taken from outside the areas in which they are being developed.

Newtonian theory can be used to illustrate the principle of freedom and unpredictability as well as that of continuity. As a creation dependent on the synthesis of older theories, Newtonian physics could not have existed without its predecessors. However, given the work of Galileo, Kepler, and Huygens, there was no inherent necessity that Newton should develop their ideas, or pursue them in one particular way. The theories could have remained altogether neglected, or could have been developed in terms of other problematics.

The strategy of the theory of knowledge is to decompose the complex process of scientific creativity into simpler processes to which the principle of causality can be applied, a decomposition leading to two complementary types of substantive problems. The first type seeks to determine the dependence of cognitive creativity on its conditions, although the creative act itself cannot be explained in these terms. The second type of problem deals with questions pertaining to the occurrence of a given cognitive activity in a particular place and time, regardless of its conditions and results. "The empirical theory of knowledge is reducible to taking into account, investigating, and determining those factors in cognitive activity which stress the partial limitation of free and spontaneous creativity—that is, the limitation not resulting from norms imposed by logic and methodology, but by real conditions."

Cognitive activities create cognitive values, but these depend on the conditions within which cognitive activity takes place. As the available means of, or limitations on, development, such conditions may be intellectual, methodological, or technical: they are the prior concepts, tools, methods without which these cognitive values could not have been realized.

In language that reminds one of verbal descriptions of the principles of multivariate analysis, Znaniecki writes: "If we determine that a certain class of cognitive activities produces values of a certain class if and only if they are connected with certain conditions, then, assuming the activities to be constant, we conclude that between conditions and values of the appropriate class there exists a permanent relationship." He suggests that such an approach can be applied to several kinds of special problems dealing with the modes of dependence of cognitive values on prior conditions: *a*) the dependence of the development of specific areas of knowledge on factors which introduce previously unavailable data into the scope of research; *b*) the dependence of scientific results on technical tools; *c*) the dependence of research results on cognitive values used as tools, especially heuristic concepts and methodological principles; and *d*) the dependence of the results of cognitive activities on symbols used to denote the cognitive values and their objects.

The second type of problem in the theory of knowledge, and the one which he considers the most important, deals with the causal explanation of the occurrence of particular cognitive activities, "cognitive situations," and "cognitive tendencies," terms which he carefully defines.

In discussing the causal explanation of particular cognitive activities and events, Znaniecki is careful to specify what such explanation does not mean. It does not refer to the historical explanation of the genesis of any particular activity, or its source in previous activity. "There are problems in the creative development of cognitive thought which are outside the realm of causal explanation." The problem of concern to the theorist of knowledge is the time and place of the appearance, or "actualization," of an activity studied not in its own right, but as a point of departure for other interests in other times and places.

Most important, the sociologist's interest in such an occurrence, as distinct from a concern about the historically unique event, lies in seeing it as a type of phenomenon that should occur in other times and places.

> We are not interested in a specific activity, but in an entire class of activities more or less creative within a certain range of possibilities. Therefore we shall attempt to explain not only an individual fact of fulfillment, by some individual in a certain society, of a certain activity A1, but any fact of fulfillment, by anyone, anywhere, of an activity of class A, be it A1, A2 or A3.

The causal analysis of the occurrence of particular cognitive activities deals with the following problems: *a*) the influence of knowledge on other areas of human activity; *b*) the education of individuals, particularly scientists, in theoretical thinking; *c*) the social determination of creativity, for example, of the creative individual; *d*) the intellectual life of social groups; and *e*) the determination of innate intellectual dispositions, such as the cognitive character of the individual, nation, and race or species. Znaniecki devotes thirty pages of his text to an analysis of these five problems.

These excerpts can provide only an approximate, oversimplified, and highly selective description of a few major ideas in Znaniecki's essay. They do indicate, however, that his primary concern was with what we may describe as *cognitive structures*; in no sense was his "science of knowledge," then, confined to a sociology of scientists.

Yet in his later writings, Znaniecki changed the direction of his scholarly work without fully exploring the possibilities of these early ideas. Extensive studies described Polish scientists and Polish academic life (1936) and analyzed what he regarded as the incompatibility of the roles of teacher and researcher. Several of these essays adumbrate the ideas of *The Social Role of the Man of Knowledge* (1940).

A third interest related to the sociology of science was in social planning and the future role of science. However, Znaniecki's *The People of Today and the Civilization of Tomorrow* (1935), and his several papers on the subject published after World War II, have not influenced thinking on socioeconomic planning in Poland, despite the primacy of this research area. Undoubtedly Znaniecki's idealistic leanings could not be reconciled with the Marxist framework.

Ossowski's interest in the sociology of science can be traced to his early paper "The Historical Function of Science" (1923). Erudite and characterized by an ability to relate seemingly disparate areas of knowledge, the paper addressed several major intellectual problems of its time, notably the antagonistic movements of romanticism and utilitarianism, which were reflected, respectively, in Bergsonian and rationalistic views of scientific activity. In contrast to the prevailing interpretations of Polish Romanticism as being antithetical to science, Ossowski linked it to such conceptual explosions as multivalued logic and Einsteinian theory, maintaining that the Romantic movement was an inspiration to imagination and originality.

In the following years Ossowski developed his concept of the "science of science." His presentation on the "Problematics of the Science of Science," given at a meeting of the Science of Science Circle, is instructive. The summary which appeared in *Nauka Polska* (Ossowski, 1929) is translated here.

> The speaker presented a schematic table of science of science problems and their interrelationship. The problems enumerated in the table can be grouped into three categories containing: *1*) problems of epistemology and methodology: what is science? what are its criteria, methods, classification? *2*) how do scientific contributions come into being? (psychological and, in part, sociological problems); *3*) sociological problems: what is the influence of science on social life and of society on science?
>
> Consideration of science of science themes should logically begin by defining the fundamental concepts: the criteria of "scientificity," "scientific work," etc. In the problems of the second category one can start either with the investigation of scientific con-

tributions considered to be eminent, or with the characterization of types of scientists. Here a number of interesting problems arise: *a*) the motives for choosing a specific scientific specialty; *b*) the extrascientific dispositions of scientists; *c*) whether similarities between various types of scientists are stronger than those between each of these types and other types of creative workers; *d*) motives for scientific work (including motives toward scientific work in general, as well as motives for work at specific stages); *e*) "revelations" in scientific work: whether scientific creativity in the grand style can exist without them, etc. Among historical problems of particular interest would be the investigation of how in the course of history the concepts of science, scientific value, and the scientist have changed.

During the discussion, which attempted to expand the list of science of science topics, it was suggested that apart from individual creativity and social factors, science itself determines to a certain extent its subsequent shaping, as technology similarly conditions its own development. One can look there for the internal laws of development. With respect to the typology of scientists, it was pointed out that there is a need to analyze the type of eminent scientist who can work creatively in almost any area, as well as the types of artists who are successful in diverse fields of art.

The 1929 presentation was further developed in "The Science of Science," the classic paper Ossowski wrote with his wife Maria (Ossowska and Ossowski, 1935) systematizing the problems in this area. Creating a fivefold classification of problems concerning science, they divided the field into the following cognitive sectors: the philosophy, history, psychology, and sociology of science, and, "in close contact with sociological problems," a subfield treating questions of a "practical and organizing character." The sociology of science would examine science primarily in terms of its relationship to other sectors of society and products of culture, incorporating the German *Wissenssoziologie* and the problematics delineated by Znaniecki. In the area of practical problems, the Ossowskis included the organization of science, social and state policy regarding science, the organization of higher education and research, "protection of scientific workers," and the like. Their observation that practical needs had spurred the genesis of the science of science itself provides a clue to the importance of science of science in postwar Poland and to its program of research. Reprinted in *Minerva* in 1963, the essay has also appeared in several anthologies.

"Humanities and Social Ideology" (1937) analyzed the ways in which the social position of the investigator influences the results of his research. Ossowski stressed the effects on research of theoretical postulates which are programmatically linked to the ideology of an organized group.

Ossowski's magnum opus, *On The Peculiarities of the Social Sciences* (1962), surveyed the entire area of the social sciences, their relationships and cognitive distinctions characterizing the schools in social science, the types of sects as distinguished from schools, and so forth. Apart from a twenty-page English summary which appears in volume 4 of his collected works (1967), the book has never been translated.

Volume 6 (1970) of Ossowski's collected works contains many ephemeral writings in the sociology of science, including reviews of books of important authors (Bertrand Russell, H. G. Wells, George Sarton, Bogdan Suchodolski, Alfred North Whitehead, J. B. S. Haldane, Julian Huxley, Florian Znaniecki), as well as essays documenting his battles for freedom of scientific expression.

POLISH SOCIOLOGY OF SCIENCE AFTER WORLD WAR II

The Reemergence of the Science of Science, 1945–1950

During the Second World War there was a complete cessation of organized activity in the Polish sociology of science. As early as 1945, however, the practical tasks of reorganization of scientific life spurred the publication of a new journal, *Zycie Nauki* [*The Life of Science*]. Sponsored by the Ministry of Education, the journal recruited many contributors from the cadre of young scientific workers in the Jagiellonian University in Cracow, and emphasized problems relating to the expanded educational opportunities which the establishment of several new universities had created, as well as problems in planning the content and organization of higher education.

The contributors to *Zycie Nauki* were members of a new "Science of Science" circle which had emerged after the war. The circle planned to establish a sociology of science section which, among other things, would undertake empirical sociological research in science and technology.

Both the circle and the periodical were cut short, however, because of repercussions stemming from the publication, toward the end of 1948, of material about the Lysenko affair (see Choynowski, 1966). Choynowski, who was editor of *Zycie Nauki*, resigned soon afterwards; the Science of Science circle lost its support; and *Zycie Nauki* was moved from Cracow to Warsaw. It was later split into two publications, *Nauka Polska* [*Polish Science*] and *Zycie Szkoly Wyzszej* [*Life of the Schools of Higher Education*].

In 1947 the old *Nauka Polska* appeared once more with its twenty-fifth volume. This issue documented the human and material devastation of Polish science during the war and described the prospects for development of several scientific disciplines; one article projected the reorganization of scientific life in Poland. Three reports also discussed the activities of the three "Science of Science" circles which were active at the Universities of Warsaw, Cracow, and Poznan. The journal, however, was a casualty of the political transformations of the early postwar era. It is interesting that in 1953, when the newly created Polish Academy of Sciences issued a publication to succeed *Zycie Nauki* it used the name of this old and eminent journal, *Nauka Polska*.

In its early issues the new *Nauka Polska* contained many articles on science planning and policy, often by scientists who were also organizational and ideological leaders; it has rarely featured material with a sociologically relevant empirical base. Empirical work, however, is published in the journals of several centers engaged in science of science research.

The years 1950 to 1963 can be characterized as a period of stagnation in terms of substantive published work. Although there was much quantitative growth in writing about science in the first two postwar decades, these contributions generally carried a strong Marxist-Leninist ideological component and as a rule did not contain empirical findings. However, they present a vast untapped source of materials for the sociologist of ideas.

For a historical summary of science policy of the period 1944–52, see Hubner (1974). Bukowski (1971) provides a concise account of the state of Polish sociology of science through 1970, and Chaskielewicz (1968) has briefly enumerated the organization, centers of research, and major works in Polish science of science.

The Organization of Polish Education and Research

The political reorganization of education and research in the years after 1950 was geared to realigning these efforts with the needs of the Socialist state. On the one hand, the concept and function of the university were reformulated and its structure and recruitment base modified. On the other hand, a new organizational base for scientific and research activity was created in 1951 with the establishment of the Polish Academy of Sciences, which, as of 1972, maintained twenty-eight institutes and twenty-nine research centers (Trzebiatowski, 1972).

Thus, the links between science and social policy are multiple and deliberate, products of a self-conscious ideological stance that is based on the Socialist conception of science as an agent of societal transformation. The continuing importance of these links is reflected in a recent address by Edward Gierek (1974:15), the first secretary of the Polish United Workers' Party, to the Second Congress of Polish Science: "Socialism evolved as a result of the combination of science with the revolutionary working class movement. In science it finds its support; to science it refers; to science it links its vision of social development."

The organizational structure of science reflects its importance to the State and the Party. In both the Polish Academy of Science and the universities, elites overlap. In the Polish Academy of Sciences, 22 percent of its 357 Polish members in 1971 belonged to the Party or other political parties (Filipiak, Filasiewicz, and Zakrzewski, n.d.:17). In his study of the formal structure of the university as a social system, Szczepański (1963:302) found that the "representatives of the sociopolitical organizations constitute one of the three distinct but intersecting vertical structures fulfilling different functions." (The other two categories are for scientific and administrative workers.)

At present the organization of Polish science consists of three basic components: The Polish Academy of Sciences; the universities and other schools of higher education (engineering schools, medical schools, etc.); and the research institutes directed by various ministries. The various learned societies (including the Polish Sociological Association) are a fourth, less formal, base of scientific activity (Kubin, 1971; Rolbiecki, 1972).

The University System

Universities in Poland are highly differentiated with respect to size, number of Ph.D. degrees awarded, number of scientific workers per student, and so forth. By 1971 there were eighty-five schools of higher learning in Poland with a total of 31,236 academic teachers (Szarras, 1975). Until recently, about 90 percent of the Ph.D. theses in Poland were completed at the universities, but there has been a constant and significant shift to the Academy as a degree-granting agency for both Ph.D. and the habilitation degree, a postdoctoral degree.

The key principle of university organization is national central planning—of recruitment, of curriculum, and of the opportunity structure—in line with the idea of the "socialist university." As Szczepański (1963) has developed this theme, planned recruitment and placement are meshed with the "needs of the economy, as determined through economic plans, plans for cultural development, and plans for social development" as envisioned by the central political leadership. The division of work between the universities and other educational and research agencies, such as the Academy, is also planned by the state.

Recruitment to the universities is determined by competitive examinations. In line with the State effort to change the social composition of the educated group, sons and daughters of manual workers receive additional points in the examinations. Moreover, education is standardized, carried out according to uniform curricula and sequences of study to ensure effective incorporation of graduates into the national plan.

Finally, ideological education is achieved through the teaching of Marxist philosophy, sociology, and economics, both formally and through saturation of other subjects with Marxist tenets.

THE SPONSORSHIP OF SCIENCE OF SCIENCE

Today the university's traditional hegemony in shaping higher education has been challenged on several fronts, perhaps most importantly by the Polish Academy of Sciences, which has become a degree-granting agency, and is also a prime sponsor of research. The implications of agency-based sponsorship for science of science research are doubly significant because this area does not exist as a formal program in the universities. Its activities are governed largely by research centers of the Ministry of Science, Higher Education, and Technology, and the Polish Academy of Sciences.

One major research center operates under the aegis of the Ministry's Institute of Science Policy and Higher Education. Over the past two decades, it has conducted a large number of empirical studies related to the major policy concerns of the Institute—the problems entailed in the reorganization and expansion of the educational system and in its processes of recruitment. Published results of concrete empirical investigation appear in the journal *Zycie Szkoly Wyzszej* [*Life of the Schools of Higher Education*].

The Polish Academy of Sciences has supported three major research centers engaged in the study of the science of science: the Research Center on the History of Science and Technology, the Committee of the Science of Science, and the Research Center of Praxiology. (For details on sections, staff, and publications of these organizations, see the *Polish Research Guide*, 1974.)

The Research Center of the History of Science and Technology is the oldest of these centers, providing a link between the abortive postwar science of science efforts and the establishment of the Committee of the Science of Science in 1963. Partly because of the firm organizational support provided by the Research Center, the links between the history of science and the sociology of science are fruitful and numerous. The results of research are published in the *Kwartalnik Historii Nauki i Techniki* [*The Quarterly Journal of the History of Science and Technology*], issued since 1956 by the Center. Most of these studies—of particular scientific creators, discoveries, inventions, and academic institutions—are written within the Marxist framework of historical analysis, emphasizing class structure and social conditions. Thus, to a greater extent than comparable work in Western European or American history of science, Polish historical research stresses substructural factors in development.

The Center is headed by Bogdan Suchodolski, editor of the monumental *History of Polish Science*. In addition to the *Kwartalnik Historii Nauki i Techniki*, the Center issues *Organon*, an annual publication with contributions in English, French, and Russian, devoted mainly to the history of science.

Research in the science of science has proliferated since 1963, when the Polish Academy of Sciences established the Committee of the Science of Science, with Ignacy Malecki as its first chairman. As defined by Malecki (1965), the subject matter of the science of science is scientific activity and science as a body of knowledge. These two broad objects of investigation can be approached from the viewpoints of several disciplines, including philosophy, history, psychology, sociology, and economics.

In 1964 the committee organized a symposium on factors affecting the effectiveness of scientific research, and a year later began to publish the quarterly *Zagadnienia Naukoznawstwa* [*Problems of the Science of Science*]. Since 1970, the committee has issued an annual English-language issue of *Problems of the Science of Science*.

The third major base is the Academy's Research Center of Praxiology. Praxiology, the philosophical study of efficient action, was founded by Tadeusz Kotarbiński, a longtime student of science, who outlined the problems of the science of science in 1965. A prominent analyst of the conceptual problems entailed in the notion of efficiency, he attempts to relate philosophical interests to empirical investigation and policy orientations. He has also attempted to classify sciences from the point of view of policy, distinguishing them in terms of a multidimensional typology of scientific research. The first dimension is based on the amount of resources required for conducting research (expensive versus inexpensive research). The second classified applications of research are: directly useful research, directed basic research, undirected basic research, and undirected research which is not of a basic character. The third dimension distinguishes research of an ideological and of a nonideological nature.

The Research Center of Praxiology is now conducting a long-term, large-scale research project on the "Organization of Scientific Activity in the Area of Research and Development." In 1972, almost one hundred workers were involved in the project, and a further expansion was planned.

Other problems in the philosophy of science with implications for the sociology of science have been explored by Amsterdamski (1968, 1971, 1973). Amsterdamski criticized the Kuhnian paradigm for neglecting small "revolutions" in micro structures that are part of "normal" science, thus blurring the notion of scientific revolution.

As a multidisciplinary area, the science of science still lacks a formal base in the universities. Rather, specialists from the several relevant areas are recruited to work on specific problems in the universities. However, there have been many projections of the development of the science of science. Zieleniewski (1973), for example, has attempted a forecast of the science of science up to the year 1990. He presents data on the number of people who report the science of science as their passive, active, or central area of interest. Zieleniewski expects that expansion of this type of instruction will culminate in the establishment of a Ph.D. program in the science of science between 1981 and 1990.

Research at the universities is governed by the interests of the individual professors. A number of doctoral and habilitation dissertations which, from their summaries in the annual annotated listing of Ph.D. and habilitation theses *Katalog*, seems to be in the area of science of science, remain unpublished. (The dissertations seem to be based on empirical data in higher proportion than the publications of mature scholars; see the continuous publication, *Katalog*, [1974].)

Both formally and informally, Poland is to a large extent a center of East European research in the science of science. This is partly due to the strong tradition connected with the name of Ossowski, and partly to the publication of *Zagadnienia Naukoznawstwa* and other periodicals. Moreover, since the mid-sixties, Polish specialists in the science of science have organized a number of international conferences and symposia devoted to various problems in the science of science.

RESEARCH IN THE SOCIOLOGY OF SCIENCE SINCE 1963

The following themes in science of science research have been singled out as having the greatest direct bearing on the sociology of science. They cover the organization of research, the nature of the scientific career, and the scientific-technological revolution.

The Organization of Science

The several postwar reorganizations of scientific and educational enterprise have raised questions about the optimal social conditions for developing scientific knowledge. Thus, studies focusing on the new research centers and the comparative effectiveness of groups working within them have become an important area of empirical research.

By far the most comprehensive project, headed by Professor M. Mazur and sponsored by the Academy of Sciences as its Problem No. 32, is entitled "Conditions of Contemporary Scientific Activity in the Area of Research and Development." Although two volumes resulting from the study have appeared in mimeographed form, it is much too early to assess the contribution of the entire project.

Three studies summarized here illustrate research on the organization of science at the microlevel.

Matejko (1966) has attempted to determine the structural conditions of scientific creativity. His survey, carried out in 1964–65, was based on interviews with all members of fourteen selected productive research groups in the natural and social sciences. Its main conclusions were:

1) The more diverse tasks a given research center has, the more difficult it is for its members to concentrate on creative (as distinguished from administrative, routine, etc.) work.

2) The higher the degree of institutionalization in the research center, the greater the probability of bureaucratic structure and its possible dysfunctions.

3) The more careful the selection of the research center's members, the higher the probability of smooth, harmonious relations within the center.

4) The higher the degree of creative involvement of the research center's members in the common work, the more it tends to be one-sided.

5) The higher the creative involvement of the members of the research center, the more important the professional—and not the institutional—reference group becomes.

6) The more dynamic the research center is, the more flexible its internal structure must be, in order to coordinate the work of its members for the general good.

7) The tendency to impose a centralized organization upon the research center is greater when the leader has an authoritarian personality.

8) The efficient guidance of the research center is strongly connected with the skillful interweaving of stimulation and coordination—the former being considered more important.

9) The research center's creative development depends largely on decentralized organization.

10) The conflicts generated in the research centers are primarily about the assessment of academic standards at these centers.

Policy recommendations were linked to specific theoretical and empirical statements. To take one example, for the second finding, the following countermeasures were suggested: to make the organizational arrangements more flexible; to make parts of the center more independent of the headquarters; to increase, if necessary, the auxiliary elements of the center's operation; to stress personal relationships inside the research center.

Mlicka (1969) conducted a study of Warsaw research centers to determine the range of conditions that shaped the outcome of creative scientific work. On the basis of in-depth interviews, Mlicka concluded that 1) incentives were more effective than restrictions; 2) there was a wide discrepancy between the theoretically postulated and observed characteristics of scientific leaders (heads of scientific centers); 3) when postulated center requirements were compared with actual demands, organizational requirements were often neglected in a way that was dysfunctional to the center as a whole.

In 1968–69, Podgórecki (1972) compared academic standards at the University of Warsaw and the Polish Academy of Sciences. The sample consisted of all scientific workers who had lost their positions in 1961 and in 1967 at the University and at the twelve institutes of the Academy. The most frequent reason for dismissal was the failure to complete the Ph.D. or the habilitation thesis within the prescribed period.

Personal data on the dismissed workers were examined and all were interviewed. The findings were these: scientists who lost their positions at the institutes of the Academy tended to find work (usually in a lower position) in other institutes, whereas scientists dismissed from the University tended to leave the field of science altogether. At the Academy, more often than at the University, reasons outside the scope of science influenced the initial employment of the scientists. Scientists who had lost their jobs at the University, more often than those who had left the Academy, saw teaching as their main function. Before their dismissal, the university scientists carried a heavier load of duties than did their counterparts at the Academy. Several dismissals from the University, however, merely reflected the "brain flow" from the University to the Academy.

Problems pertaining to the organization of science in Poland are the prime subject matter of several periodicals. The *Review of the Polish Academy of Sciences* and *Nauka Polska* specialize in organizational problems of the Academy; *Zycie Szkoly Wyzszej* discusses these problems in their relation to the schools of higher education in Poland.

The Scientific Career

The characteristics and roles of scientists, as well as the nature of the scientific career, have been studied from university recruitment on. For university recruitment in science, "Olympics" are organized for high schools, and only the winners are permitted to compete at the higher level. Much of the future scientific elite, especially in mathematics and physics, is recognized early by means of these "Olympics."

Wiśniewski (1968) has found that grades on the University entrance examinations are a good predictor of whether students will pass the first year of study. (About 15 percent of first-year students fail.) Grades in the first year of study also correlate highly with entrance examination grades, but show a weaker correlation with grades in the high school examinations.

Cichomski (1972, 1974) has studied the careers of scientists in engineering sciences. One of his projects examines the relationship of dissertation quality to the degree of integration of a Ph.D. student with the members of his scientific team, and to the prestige of his sponsor. Conclusions from his data are that chances for success are strongly connected with the high position of the sponsor, independently of the level of integration with the team, and that strong integration with the team is an obstacle to success when the team is directed by a sponsor with a relatively lower scientific position.

Nowakowska (1973) has developed a theoretical model of a scientific career distinguishing over thirty types of events important in the scientific career: various kinds of publication, scientific positions, awards and prizes, consultantships, honorary memberships in scientific organizations, and so on. Each event in the career is evaluated along dimensions which can be interpreted as representing scientific prestige, and social power within an academic context. One event, "habilitation," was unique in the sense that it arbitrarily received the same value on both dimensions.

The author assumes that scientific prestige is cumulative: at any moment it is equal to the sum of prestige of the events which occurred previously. Social power is cumulative only with respect to those events which have a lasting effect. The above two concepts permit one to define the "normal" career in which the numerical indicators of prestige and power are close to each other; the "overcareer," in which social power exceeds prestige; and the "undercareer," in which social power is not as great as scientific prestige.

Nowakowska proposes a number of hypotheses to explain, for example, the difference between self-evaluation and evaluation of the same career by other scientists. For example, a scientist's colleagues will evaluate his career in the same terms as he does; that is, they will concur that a career is an "overcareer" or an "undercareer," in accord with the scientist's self-evaluation. In either case, however, they will amplify that evaluation, perceiving the career as more of an overcareer or an undercareer than the scientist himself does.

Another hypothesis is that a scientist's satisfaction with his own work (as measured by psychometric tools) will be negatively correlated with the absolute value of the difference between his scores on the dimensions of social power and scientific prestige.

The two types of career lines are further explained in terms of such additional variables as ability, motivation for success, and fear of failure.

Szarras's (1975) comprehensive survey of Polish academicians combines historical description of the training, structure and "dynamics" of academic employment from 1918 to 1972 with a variety of international comparisons and internal analyses of the collectivity of scientists—their age composition, the structure of employment, degrees awarded, and so forth. The study also describes incentives for scientific development at various stages of the academic career (e.g., fellowships, sponsored leaves, and visits to other institutions), and analyzes the distribution of scientific productivity along the lines set down by Lotka and Price.

The Scientific Technological Revolution

Although the concept of the scientific-technological revolution is by no means clearly defined, it is useful for surveying much of the literature of the sociology of science in Socialist countries. Encompassing the broad implications of the development of science-based technology for the structure and culture of societies, the concept provides a point of entry into the study of macrosocial changes resulting from planned industrialization, modernization of agriculture, changes in style of life, and so on. It also expresses the Marxist notion of the integrative character of social science when put to the use of societal transformation.

The concept of the technological revolution has been widely used in journalistic and popular literature in Poland; its more technical aspects are investigated in a special research unit of the Academy headed by Eugeniusz Olszewski. The processes of the scientific-technological revolution have been considered on a world scale (e.g., information exchange in science) and on a single country level. Olszewski (1971:565–70) has developed the concepts of "threshold of implementation," characterizing the capability of a country to implement foreign technological achievements; and of "threshold of leadership" or "advancement," which describes a country's ability to create and realize its own technological conceptions.

At present, Olszewski (1974:25) is refining a "model of the scientific and technological revolution in a medium-size socialist state."

Zacher (1974:68), working along the same lines, distinguishes four spheres, or subsystems, in which the processes of the scientific and technological revolution manifest themselves: "science, technology, economy, and man (society)." Societal guidance or "steering" involves choices among possible lines of development in each of these subsystems so that the processes of revolution produce optimal results.

Thus, analysis of the scientific and technological revolution is seen as contingent upon the goals of the future socialist society. Dulski and Kozminski (1974: 130) specify societal goals in the three major spheres of motivation, social structure, and culture. In the sphere of motivation, the goals include self-actualization through work and active involvement in both the work milieu and in social-economic policy. In the sphere of social structure, the goals are the quantitative growth of groups engaged in "research industry" and "education industry": egalitarian access to knowledge and information; conflict resolution through knowledge; and egalitarian access to participation in management. Finally, in the sphere of culture, the goals stress the primacy of the values of self-actualization, active re-creation, and the diffusion of the sociological and economic imagination. Policy concerns, then, suggest increasing state sponsorship of the sectors engaged in scientific research.

SINCE ITS BEGINNINGS, sociology of science in Poland has been a subsidiary part of the interdisciplinary field of the science of science. In this essay, the historical development of the science of science was implicitly divided into five periods, with major emphasis on those contributions employing distinctly sociological concepts or methods.

The roots of the science of science are found in the writings produced before 1918, mainly by philosophers (e.g., Lukasiewicz and Kotarbiński). The second period, which extends from 1918 to 1939, was of central importance to the development of the science of science in Poland. Organizationally it is marked by the establishment of *Nauka Polska* (1918), which gave cohesiveness and direction to the previously dispersed work in the area, the science of science circle (1928), and the publication of *Organon* (1936). Between 1928 and 1939 the concept of a science of science ("*naukoznawstwo*") also gained currency among Polish intellectuals.

Two major intellectual achievements of this period are the essays of Znaniecki (1925) and Ossowska and Ossowski (1935), with their programs for the science of knowledge and the science of science. Other studies carried out over these years were mostly programmatic and theoretical in character. Most of the empirical research that did take place remained unpublished or was destroyed during the Second World War.

The resumption of the academic activity, after World War II, marks the third period, which can be dated approximately from 1945 to 1950. Studies following the prewar themes were resumed, but pressures from a number of directions led to cessation of this work by 1950. The efforts to reconstruct science and education along Marxist-Leninist lines clashed with the liberal traditions implicit in the prewar studies.

In 1951, the Polish Academy of Sciences was created and this institution radically changed the organization and orientation of Polish science. Increasingly, attention was focused on the organizational problems and the ideological concerns of science. No empirical sociological studies were carried out during this time. Although the years 1950 to 1963 (the fourth period under discussion) saw the publication of a considerable body of work on the problems of scientific organization, planning, ideology, and personnel, very little of this work was sociological in character.

The political changes of the late 1950s and early 1960s led to a revival of research in the science of science from 1963 on. At first, the principal focus of attention was on the effectiveness of research in pure science and technology. By the late 1960s, however, a number of other themes had also emerged, for example, the conditions influencing scientific creativity, scientific careers, and recruitment to science, the debate on the scientific-technological revolution, and the role of social science in social development (cf. Kowalewski, 1971). Much of this work was carried out in the newly established units of the Polish Academy of Sciences, for example, the Research Center on Praxiology.

The journal *Zagadnienia Naukoznawstwa*, issued by the Committee on Science of Science since 1965, has been the principal forum for science of science studies. Although research in the sociology of science has, for the most part, remained nonempirical, a small but significant number of empirical studies have been carried out or are in progress.

The institutionalization of the sociology of science in Polish universities is still in its beginnings. There are no formal courses of instruction in the sociology of science at the universities, and there are no strong intellectual or organizational leaders involved in the development of the sociology of science as a specialty. The specialty remains an informal and fragmented network of scholars that is pulled in different directions by its links to longer established and stronger groups in its neighboring disciplines and in sociology itself, particularly the sociology of education, formal organizations, and occupations.

Because the sociology of science remains within the penumbra of the science of science, its links with this field remain stronger than its links to sociology. Thus Polish sociologists of science do not publish in sociological journals. This situation has had important consequences for the social and cognitive structure of the sociology of science. The foci of attention are derived largely from the policy orientation of the science of science, hence the concern with applications—scientific organization, science policy, and science planning. This cognitive focus has tended to lead to neglect of other types of problems in the sociology of science, for example, communication patterns, specialty development, and reward systems and competition. Karl Marx's fundamental insights into the relationship between superstructure and substructure have not been systematically developed in an empirical sociology of scientific knowledge in contemporary society.

However, there are some indications that within the next decade the existing intellectual and organizational trends in the sociology of science in Poland will result in a more differentiated and autonomous specialty and in a broader distribution of cognitive concerns.

REFERENCES

AJDUKIEWICZ, KAZIMIERZ
  1957 "On Freedom of Science." *Review of the Polish Academy of Sciences* 2 (January–June): 1–19.
AMSTERDAMSKI, STEFAN
  1968 "Poslowie. Historia nauki a filozofia nauki" [Afterword. History of science and philosophy of science]. In Thomas S. Kuhn *Struktura rewolucji naukowych*, pp. 189–206. Warsaw: Państwowe Wydawnictwo Naukowe.

1971   "Nauka współczesna a wartości" [Contemporary science and values].
       Zagadnienia Naukoznawstwa 7:59–73.
1973   "Science as Object of Philosophical Reflection." *Organon* 9:35–70.

BUJAK, FRANCISZEK
1929   "Dzialacz i badacz" [The activist and the investigator]. *Nauka Polska*
       11:11–23.
BUKOWSKI, JERZY
1971   "Naukoznawstwo w Polsce. Rozwój, osiagniecia, stan na przelomie lat
       1969/70" [The science of science in Poland: development, achieve-
       ments, status in 1969/70]. *Zagadnienia Naukoznawstwa* 7:177–86.

CHASKIELEWICZ, STEFAN
1968   "Information Concerning the Organization of Polish Research in the
       Field of the Science of Science." *Zagadnienia Naukoznawstwa*
       4:56–58.
CHOYNOWSKI, MIECZYSŁAW
1966   "O zakresie i znaczeniu naukoznawstwa oraz o krakowskim konwer-
       satorium naukoznawczym z lat 1945–50" [On the scope and im-
       portance of the science of science, and the science of science circle in
       Cracow during 1945–50]. *Nauka Polska* 4:129–38.
CICHOMSKI, BOGDAN
1972   "Doktoraty w naukach technicznych. Style kierowania rozwojem
       naukowym" [Doctoral degrees in the technical sciences. Styles of
       guiding the development of science]. In Adam Podgórecki (ed.), *Soc-
       jotechnika. Style dzialania*, pp. 289–302. Warsaw: Ksiazka i Wiedza.
1974   *Spoleczne uwarunkowania rozwoju mlodej kadry naukowej uczelni
       technicznych w Polsce* [Social influences in the development of young
       scientific personnel of engineering schools in Poland]. Warsaw: In-
       stytut Polityki Naukowej i Szkolnictwa Wyzszego.

DOBROWOLSKI, KAZIMIERZ
1934   "Cechy narodowe w twórczości naukowej" [National traits in scien-
       tific creativity]. *Nauka Polska* 19:411–15.
DULSKI, STEFAN, AND ANDRZEJ K. KOŹMIŃSKI
1974   "Realizacja celów socjalizmu w warunkach rewolucji naukowo-
       technicznej" [Realization of the goals of socialism under the condi-
       tions of the scientific-technological revolution]. In *Rewolucja
       naukowo-techniczna jako czynnik rozwoju*, pp. 114–35. Warsaw:
       Państwowe Wydawnictwo Naukowe.

FILIPIAK, BOLESLAW; ALEKSANDER FILASIEWICZ; AND EUGENIUSZ
ZAKRZEWSKI
n.d.   *Polska Akademia Nauk w liczbach 1966–1975* [The Polish academy of
       sciences in statistics, 1966–1975]. Warsaw: Polska Akademia Nauk.

GAWROŃSKI, ANDRZEJ
  1923   "Nauka narodowa czy miedzynarodowa" [Science: national or international]. *Nauka Polska* 4:36–44.
GIEREK, EDWARD
  1974   "Science, the Instrument of Socialist Development in Poland." In *Second Congress of Polish Science*, June 26–29, 1973, pp. 7–16. Principal Texts. Wroclaw: Ossolineum.

HUBNER, PIOTR
  1974   "Instytucjonalne formy organizacji ekspertów w polityce naukowej państwa polskiego 1944–1952" [Institutional forms for the organization of experts in science policy in Poland 1944–1952]. *Prakseologia* 49:173–93.

KATALOG
  1974   Katalog rozpraw doktorskich i habilitacyjnych, 1972 [Catalog of doctoral and habilitation dissertations, 1972]. Warsaw: Ministerstwo Nauki, Szkolnictwa Wyzszego i Techniki.
KOCHANOWSKI, JAN K.
  1919   "Kilka słów w sprawie nauki narodowej" [A few remarks about national science]. *Nauka Polska* 1:503–14.
KOTARBIŃSKI, TADEUSZ
  1929   "O zdolnościach cechujacych badacza" [On the abilities of the researcher]. *Nauka Polska* 11:1–10.
  1965   "Przeglad problemów nauk o nauce" [Survey of the problems of the science of science] *Zagadnienia Naukoznawstwa* 1 (2–3):3–25.
KOWALEWSKI, ZDISŁAW
  1971   *Nauki spoleczne a rozwój spoleczny* [Social sciences and social development]. Warsaw: Instytut Wydawniczy Pax.
KUBIN, JERZY
  1971   "O upowszchnianiu nauki" [On the dissemination of scientific knowledge]. In Tadeusz Cieślak and Jerzy Kubin (eds.), *Upowszechnianie nauki i zainteresowanie nauka*, pp. 27–46. Wroclaw: Zaklad Narodowy imienia Ossolińskich.

ŁUKASIEWICZ, JAN
  [1912] 1970   "Creative Elements in Science." In Jan Łukasiewicz, *Selected Works*, pp. 1–15. Amsterdam and London: North Holland Publishing Company; Warsaw: PWN-Polish Scientific Publishers.

MALECKI, IGNACY
  1965   "Od redakcji" [From the editors]. *Zagadnienia Naukoznawstwa* 1:3–4.
MATEJKO, ALEKSANDER
  1966   *System spoleczny zespolu naukowego* [The social system of research

teams in basic science]. Warsaw: Państwowe Wydawnictwo Naukowe.

MINKIEWICZ, ROMUALD
1918   "O polska twórczość Naukowa" [On Polish scientific creativity]. *Nauka Polska* 1:503–14.

MLICKA, W.
1969   "Bodźce i antybodźce pracy w katedrze" [Stimuli and counter-stimuli for work in a university department]. In Aleksander Matejko (ed.), *System społeczny katedry*. Warsaw: Państwowe Wydawnictwo Naukowe.

NOWAKOWSKA, MARIA
1973   "Model kariery naukowej" [A model of a scientific career]. *Zagadnienia Naukoznawstwa* 9:503–20.

OLSZEWSKI, EUGENIUSZ
1971   "Badania nad wdrazaniem postepu technicznego przez kraje nie bedace jego inicjatorami" [Research on implementation of technological progress by countries which are not its initiators]. *Kwartalnik Historii Nauki i Techniki* 16:565–70.
1974   "O badaniach nad zagadnieniami rewolucji naukowo-technicznej" [On research into problems of the scientific and technological revolution]. In Eugeniusz Olszewski and Lech Zacher (eds.), *Studia nad zagadnieniami rewolucji naukowo-technicznej*, pp. 7–26. Wroclaw: Zaklad Narodowy imienia Ossolińskich.

OSIŃSKA, WANDA
1969   "Les débuts de recherches systématiques sur la scienciologie dans le milieu varsovien au tournant des XIXe et XXe siècles" [The beginnings of systematic research on the science of science in the Warsaw milieu at the turn of the nineteenth and twentieth centuries]. *Organon* 6:279–96.

OSSAWSKA, MARIA, AND STANISLAW OSSOWSKI
1935   "Nauka o nauce" [The science of science]. *Nauka Polska* 20:1–12.

OSSOWSKI, STANISLAW
1923   "Funkcja dziejowa nauki" [The historical function of science]. *Nauka Polska* 4:8–35.
1929   "Problematyka naukoznawcza" [The problematics of the science of science]. *Nauka Polska* 13:167.
1937   "Nauki humanistyczne a ideologia spoleczna" [The humanities and social ideology]. *Nauka Polska* 22:1–24.
1962   *O osobliwościach nauk spolecznych* [On the peculiarities of the social sciences]. Warsaw: Państwowe Wydawnictwo Naukowe.
1967   *O nauce. Dziela. Tom IV* [On science. Works. Vol. IV]. Warsaw: Państwowe Wydawnictwo Naukowe.
1970   *Publicystyka. Recenzje. Dziela. Tom VI* [Articles and discussions. Re-

views. Works. Vol. VI]. Warsaw: Państwowe Wydawnictwo Naukowe.

PODGÓRECKI, ADAM
   1972   "Style oddzialywania na nauke" [Styles of exercising influence on science]. In Adam Podgórecki (ed.), *Socjotechnika. Style dzialania*, pp. 257–88. Warsaw: Ksiazka i Wiedza.
POLISH RESEARCH GUIDE
   1974   *Polish Research Guide*. Warsaw: PWN-Polish Scientific Publishers.

ROLBIECKI, WALDEMAR
   1972   *Towarzystwa naukowe w Polsce* [Scientific associations in Poland]. Warsaw: Wiedza Powszechna.
RYBICKI, PAWEŁ
   1929   "Nauka a formy zycia spolecznego" [Science and the forms of social life]. *Nauka Polska* 11:26–64.

SZARRAS, HENRYK
   1975   *Ksztalcenie kadr naukowych w szkolnictwie wyzszym* [Education of the academic staff in Polish universities]. Warsaw: Państwowe Wydawnictwo Naukowe.
SZCZEPAŃSKI, JAN
   1963   *Socjologiczne zagadnienia wyzszego wyksztalcenia* [The sociological problems of higher education]. Warsaw: Państwowe Wydawnictwo Naukowe.
   [1964] 1974   "Socjalistyczna koncepcja universytetu" [The socialist concept of the university]. In Jan Szczepański, *Odmiany czasu teraźniejczego*, pp. 399–410. Warsaw: Ksiazka i Wiedza.

TRZEBIATOWSKI, WŁODZIMIERZ
   1972   "W dwudziestolecie Polskiej Akademii Nauk" [On the twentieth anniversary of the Polish Academy of Sciences]. *Kultura i Spoleczeństwo* 16:3–9.

WIŚNIEWSKI, WIESLAW
   1968   "Wartość prognostyczna egzaminu wstepnego" [The predictive value of entrance examinations]. *Dydaktyka Szkoly Wyzszej* 1:35–76.

ZACHER, LECH
   1974   "Sterowanie procesami rewolucji naukowo-technicznej" [Control over the processes of the scientific and technological revolution]. In Eugeniusz Olszewski and Lech Zacher (eds.), *Studia nad zagadnieniami rewolucji naukowo-technicznej*, pp. 33–70. Wroclaw: Zaklad Narodowy imienia Ossolińskich.
ZIELENIEWSKI, JAN
   1973   "Wstepna prognoza rozwoju naukoznawstwa do roku 1980 i 1990" [A

preliminary prognosis of the development of the science of science to 1980 and 1990]. *Zagadnienia Naukoznawstwa* 9:309–27.

ZNANIECKI, FLORIAN

1925   "Przedmiot i zadania nauki o wiedzy" [The subject matter and tasks of the science of knowledge]. *Nauka Polska* 5:1–78.

1935   *Ludzie teraźniejsi a cywilizacja przyszłości* [People of today and the civilization of tomorrow]. Lwów and Warsaw: Ksiaźnica-Atlas.

1936   "Uczeni polscy a zycie polskie" [Polish scientists and Polish life]. *Droga*, no. 2–3:101–16 and no. 4:255–71.

1940   *The Social Role of the Man of Knowledge*. New York: Columbia University Press.

THE SOCIOLOGY OF SCIENCE IN

Britain

M. J. Mulkay

IT IS NOT EASY to formulate intellectual criteria that unambiguously separate contributions to be covered in a review of the sociology of science and contributions belonging to such neighboring fields as the philosophy and the history of science. I have attempted to solve this problem pragmatically by including in the References all discussions of the social relations of science which have, to my knowledge, been published in British journals of sociology. In addition, I have included all publications on this topic by professional British sociologists, wherever they have been published.[1] This procedure misses certain writings which, in terms of content, overlap considerably with the sociological literature; for example, the writings of Bernal (1939), Crowther (1967), and Polanyi (1958). I have decided that the work of these authors should not be considered here because it forms an intellectual tradition separate from that of the professional sociologists, because it is already widely known, and because it would reduce the space available for a discussion of the more recent and less well known sociological work. Similarly, I have not discussed Ravetz's (1971) recent book, partly because he is not a sociologist, but also because there is insufficient space to examine his complex and wide-ranging argument. I have, however, included some work by nonsociologists, such as that by Cardwell

([1957] 1972), where this work has been greatly influenced by sociological thought or where it takes up themes central to the sociological literature. Three further limitations on the content of this essay should be noted: first, it deals only with published work, second, it is concerned exclusively with the natural sciences,[2] and third, it is intended to be informative rather than critical.

Research in Britain into the sociology of science began to gather momentum during the late 1960s. Whereas only four of the items included in the References were published between 1950 and 1960,[3] thirteen were published between 1961 and 1968, and forty-eight between 1969 and early 1973. This growth in the rate of research has been accompanied by the formation of five "science studies" units in British universities during the second half of the sixties.[4] Many of the members of the units have been drawn from various natural science disciplines. These units have not been entirely responsible for the increase in research output, and a large number of contributions have come from members of groups with no special interest in the sociology of science.

In view of the recent emergence of the field, the creation of several independent research/teaching units, and the diversity of intellectual background among participants, the literature is surprisingly coherent. Two broad but distinct areas of investigation are clearly evident. I have, accordingly, divided the following discussion into two main sections. One section is devoted to studies primarily of scientists in industry and government and one to studies of science and scientists in universities. This division, although it corresponds roughly to that between "applied science" and "pure science," is based not on a distinction between two kinds of science but between two types of social setting in which scientific research occurs.

SCIENTISTS IN INDUSTRY AND GOVERNMENT

The first substantial contribution in Britain to the sociology of science was published several years ago by Cardwell (1957; see also, 1972).

This study is strongly historical, following in detail the development of applied research from the eighteenth century until shortly after World War I. Accordingly, Cardwell relies mainly on documentary material, the historian's customary source of data. He shows that the development in England of applied research on a large scale took place several decades after the emergence of industrial research in Europe. From the 1860s onward, a series of pressure groups were formed in England, whose members had been impressed by the way in which the German educational system appeared to promote effective applied research. These groups attempted, in various ways, to create educational institutions in Britain which would produce a well-trained scientific rank and file as a supplement to the intellectually influential but industrially ineffective amateurs who still dominated British science. Cardwell's central argument is that, although the main reasons advanced historically in favor of scientific growth placed great emphasis on the practical benefits to be gained thereby, professional science was actually brought into being by the formation of a body of science teachers and academic researchers and that industrial science was able to expand only after the creation of this academic community. Much of the subsequent literature has examined how scientists trained within this academic community have fared in the industrial environment.

In the late 1950s Burns and Stalker (1961) examined this problem. Their central objective was to investigate how scientific discovery was exploited by industry. They studied in depth twenty firms in the technologically advanced field of electronics. The method used was to build up an account of the routines of behavior and the codes of conduct in each firm by observation, interviews, meetings, informal talks, and discussions with participants of tentative interpretations. The focus of study was the response by management to the consequences of forming groups of specialists expressly to produce technical innovations. Its conclusions are, accordingly, as much about management as about industrial scientists. I shall concentrate here on the latter.

Most managements in the electronics industry have come to accept that research and development is necessary, if their firms are to remain competitive in a market where economic success is closely related to technical expertise. But technical expertise is more than an essential productive resource. It can also be used by specialists as the basis for claiming power and high status within industrial organizations. These claims are seldom expressed overtly by scientists. Nevertheless, to the extent that scientists influence the processes of manufacture and the general conduct of business, their actions impinge on the established political and status structure—usually to the detriment of other participants. This frequently leads nonscientific management to resist the "incursions" of scientists and to attempt to minimize their impact on organizational affairs. This tendency is made more pronounced by the attitudes of many industrial scientists, who see themselves as members of a distinctive professional group which extends beyond the realm of business into government service and higher education, and who feel to some degree outside the industrial authority structure and exempt from many of the conventions governing their counterparts elsewhere in the firm. The main consequence of this convergence of factors, even in organizations where there is a generally acknowledged need for the fullest cooperation between scientists and nonscientists is that scientists tend to become socially isolated and their information and skills underutilized.

In a later study, Cotgrove and Box (1970) adopt a rather different approach to essentially the same problem studied by Burns and Stalker. Cotgrove and Box (1970:168) apply "the perspectives of the sociology of occupations and the sociology of organizations to an exploration of the increasingly close articulation between science and industry." As a result of their investigations they stress that there must be a revision of what they regard as the simplistic view proposed in much of the prior literature.[5] That literature overemphasizes the difficulties encountered in employing professionals within hierarchically structured business organizations, who have been trained in the ethos of academic science. The main weakness of the literature is its failure to recognize fully that participants develop a range of scientific identities. These identities involve differing degrees of commitment to science, and there are processes of differential adaptation and selection. Consequently those least committed to the ideals of academic science are most likely to enter applied research.

In order to investigate these problems, two main surveys were carried out. A postal questionnaire survey of several hundred undergraduate and postgraduate chemistry students at three universities and questionnaires from a similar number of research chemists and administrators in nine industrial laboratories were obtained.[6] The majority of respondents, both research scientists and students, were then divided into three categories on the basis of their expressed commitment to the norms of disinterestedness, organized skepticism, universalism and, in particular, communism.[7] Those who regarded themselves as committed to science and as eager to publish their results were termed *public scientists*. Those who saw themselves as committed to scientific research but who were much less concerned with communicating their findings were called *private scientists*. Finally those who regarded their training primarily as a means of career advancement were called *organizational scientists*. Having established these categories, Cotgrove and Box go on to show that among final year chemistry students there was a significant association between career choice and scientific identity. For example, 36 percent of the public scientists preferred academic employment compared with 13 percent of the organizational scientists, while 57 percent of the latter and 65 percent of the private scientists preferred industry, compared with 39 percent of the public scientists. These differences between career choices of the various types of scientists were not a result of differing perceptions of conditions of employment in universities and industry. There was general agreement that, whereas salaries and technical equipment are better in industry, universities allow greater freedom to choose research projects and to publish. The authors suggest, therefore, that students tend to seek out those careers which appear to them most rewarding. Public, private, and organizational scientists have different views about what constitutes an attractive career.

But the match between scientific identity and career choice was far from complete. For instance, 64 percent of undergraduate public scientists did *not* prefer academic employment. There must, therefore, be other factors at work. Cotgrove and Box suggest that one of the most important is students' estimates of their chances of getting the job desired and they show that those public scientists who do not expect to do well academically tend to express a preference for a career in industry. Thus to a considerable extent the variance in undergraduates' choices between employment in industry, government, and university can be explained by reference to three main variables: scientific identity, evaluation of conditions of employment, and expected academic achievement.

The evidence furnished by Cotgrove and Box provides little support for the simple view that potential applied scientists acquire, during their university education, attitudes and values which are unsuitable for the social context of industrial research. Instead their findings indicate that, as a result of processes of socialization, social definition and self-selection, those whose values and aptitudes are more suited to applied research (i.e., private and organizational scientists) are much more likely to wish to go into industry. Accordingly it is not surprising that, when they examined the responses of scientists in industry, they find that the majority do not report high levels of dissatisfaction. Dissatisfactions do exist, of course. In particular the lack of supporting personnel and the inadequacy of long-term planning, as well as salaries, career prospects, and the question of rewards for productive researchers are problematic. But these areas of dissatisfaction are connected in no obvious way with commitment to an academic ethos. The actual complaints appear to be more those of industrial specialists concerned with furthering their careers by means of technical work for which limited resources are made available. As we would expect, however, public scientists who do enter industry are more likely to express dissatisfaction than either private or organizational scientists.[8] The authors (Cotgrove and Box, 1970:94) suggest this is because dissatisfaction "is more likely to arise when there is a lack of congruence between role and identity." If this is the case, it follows that the level of dissatisfaction in a research laboratory will depend not only on the scientific identities of those involved, but also on the social environment provided by the laboratory. This inference is confirmed by the analysis of material from eight laboratories. Laboratories with a high proportion of public scientists but little organizational freedom have markedly higher levels of dissatisfaction than laboratories where a high proportion of public scientists is combined with high organizational autonomy.

Cotgrove and Box also examined the productivity of industrial chemists and the strategies which the latter devise to increase the congruence between their own preferences and the requirements of their organization. The *main* findings can be summarized as follows. Many of those most committed to scientific values and best qualified to undertake research do not enter industry. Many of those who, although committed to science, are defined as lacking the abilities necessary for academic research enter industry and accept realistically the limitations imposed in the industrial context. Industrial chemists do not appear to be particularly dissatisfied although a substantial proportion believe that they could be employed more productively. In general, public scientists are the most likely of the three categories to be dissatisfied. But in research settings which allow greater autonomy and active participation in directing research, the level of dissatisfaction of public scientists is appreciably reduced. If there *is* a widespread practical problem associated with the employment of chemists in industry, it is that of the underemployment of skilled men and the relative absence of positive satisfactions. This problem cannot be solved merely by changes in scientific education. It must also involve changes in industrial organization.

The findings of Cotgrove and Box are in no important way inconsistent with those of Burns and Stalker (1961). The latter do place more emphasis on conflict between scientists and management, in addition to the underemployment of scientists and dissatisfaction among scientists that both sets of authors recognize. But this may well be due to their studying different industries. Whereas Cotgrove and Box studied researchers in the chemical field, where scientists have been employed on a large scale for many years, Burns and Stalker investigated firms where, in many cases, R & D laboratories were being established for the first time. Misunderstandings and open conflict seem more likely to occur in the latter situation and this may account for the different emphasis in the two studies. Furthermore, Cotgrove and Box wanted to rectify, not the kind of structural interpretation proposed by Burns and Stalker (which lay outside the scope of their analysis), but the view which attributes the problems of scientists in industry to a clash between scientific and managerial cultures. Their line of argument is also pursued in a paper by Ellis (1969).

Ellis begins by outlining what he calls the orthodox model of the "two cultures" which, he says, has dominated prior research on industrial science (see, e.g., However and Orth, 1963). This model is seen as resting on four main contentions. First, the meanings assigned to research by the scientific culture and by the management culture are in direct opposition. Second, many, if not most, industrial scientists remain committed to the scientific culture. Third, their commitment is maintained by participation in professional organizations. Fourth, this cultural gap is the major source of the conflict and frustration which characterize the relations between scientists and management. Ellis then presents evidence pertinent to this model, gathered by means of interviews with several hundred scientists and technologists in university, government, and industry. He concludes that the great majority of researchers in universities are concerned with making a recognized contribution to knowledge. But his material provides little support for the assertion that this is a major preoccupation of scientists in industry. Very few industrial scientists in his sample embraced the "pure science ethos," and most of them not only accepted the practical constraints on their activities but actually expressed a preference for applied research. Furthermore, Ellis points out, there are very few professional organizations in British science. Consequently, commitment to scientific values is unlikely to be maintained by participation in scientific societies. However, "although it is certainly true that most industrial scientists accept the logic of applied science, this does not mean that they accept management's definition of their role" (Ellis, 1969:200).

Ellis goes on to describe the relations between scientists and management in a way which closely resembles that of Burns and Stalker. On the one hand, higher management attempts to confine scientists to a purely technical role. On the other hand, many industrial scientists believe that they can make their full contribution only if they are allowed greater participation in the formulation of policy. As a result, industrial scientists tend to be significantly less satisfied than university scientists or technologists with the extent to which their abilities are utilized. Ellis does not offer a structural interpretation of this situation. He does, however make an interesting comparison between scientists and technologists. Whereas scientists are trained in relation to the established body of knowledge in a defined academic discipline, such as physics or chemistry, technologists are trained in a specific expertise, such as chemical engineering or color chemistry, associated with a particular industry. Thus, on entering industry, the science graduate finds that much of his knowledge is irrelevant and that he is competing from a disadvantaged position with his fellow technologists. Ellis concludes therefore that, although the actual relationship between the university and industrial science is far from that depicted in the orthodox model, the nature of university education does contribute to the problems facing scientists in industry.

The longitudinal study by Barnes (1971) is also concerned with the values held by industrial scientists and with the sources of conflict and dissatisfaction in industrial laboratories. Barnes concentrates on the changes in values which occur during the first months of industrial employment. His main data are the responses of fifty-four undergraduates who were interviewed twice, once during their final year, and again, between six and twelve months after they had started work. In addition, postal questionnaires were obtained from fifty-one science graduates who were either in their first or second year of employment in R & D. On the basis of the interviews, Barnes shows that commitment to scientific values is likely to be highly unstable. Thus those few undergraduates in his sample who regarded freedom to publish as important in choosing a job, and who subsequently went into industry, had all come to accept restricted communality by the time of the second interview. Similarly, those who in the first interview claimed the right in their future job, either to choose their own projects or to carry them out as they thought best, had considerably modified their views after some months of industrial employment.

These findings are based on very small numbers and are subject to the usual problems of inferring attitudes or values from verbal responses. Barnes suggests, however, that if a pronounced change of attitudes of this kind was found regularly to accompany the movement from university to industrial research, then virtually all prior work in the field would become suspect. The "culture clash" hypothesis, for instance, is based on the assumption that a large proportion of university students are socialized into the scientific ethos and that problems arise because many of them remain permanently committed to scientific values. A similar assumption tends to be made even by critics of this perspective. Thus Cotgrove and Box assume, although their research design does not enable them to prove the point conclusively, that those who are "public" or "private" scientists as students will tend to remain true to type in industry.[9] If, however, the evidence from longitudinal studies were to show conclusively that we cannot assume any degree of stability in professed scientific values then, as Barnes himself suggests, it might be necessary to adopt an entirely different theoretical perspective.

Barnes decided that a suitable perspective is provided by Becker (1964: 163–64).

> Becker's theories offer an approach to this area which assumes neither that overriding general values can determine action, nor that such values are internalized and thereby acquire stability within the individual actor. Instead, the focus is upon the social structure in which the actor participates. Role learning consists of making a number of adjustments to the social situation;

these are determined solely by the desire of the actor to continue to participate in, or to do well in, the situation, and by the consequent demands the situation makes upon him.

Barnes goes on to present further evidence in support of Becker's approach. He shows that his young scientists were highly motivated to participate in the activities of their industrial organizations and to "do well" in terms of its official structure of reward. He also shows that they placed greatest value on those aspects of their training, namely, theoretical knowledge and acquaintance with the research literature, which most clearly distinguish them from other employees and which they saw, consequently, as being especially important in helping them to "get on" in industry. But evidence of this kind does not require us to adopt Becker's framework, because similar results have been presented elsewhere quite adequately without reference to Becker's work (e.g., Ellis, 1969). The finding which is crucial to Barnes's argument is that of the instability of professed values.

In a study by Duncan (1972) the attitudes of scientists toward managerial tasks is explored by means of a questionnaire survey, group discussions, and participation in a management training course for scientific staff. Duncan begins from the twofold premise that in many fields of research, management tasks have become pervasive (see also King, 1968) and that economic success in many industries requires the participation of technically qualified people at all levels of management (see also Cardwell, 1972:234). Of the ninety scientists to whom his questionnaire was given, all but five agree that in order to get on in industry or government service they had to be prepared to accept an increasing amount of managerial responsibility. There appeared, initially, to be a clear division between that half of the sample who approved of this situation and the other half who disapproved. But Duncan found, in the course of discussions with respondents, that this apparent divergence was in some respects misleading, for both "approvers" and "disapprovers" adopted a strongly "technicist" perspective "i.e., a point of view which is permeated by technical interests and which rests on a developed sense of occupational identity as a 'technical man'" (Duncan, 1972:134). "Approvers" were willing to accept administrative responsibility, but on the whole only if it was closely related to the pursuit of technical objectives. They recognized not only that this kind of technical management was unavoidable but also that it could not be undertaken effectively by laymen. "Disapprovers" agreed that *some* scientists had to accept administrative responsibilities, but were more reluctant than "approvers" to undertake such duties themselves. They would have preferred a more flexible system of promotion in which advancement could be achieved with no involvement in organizational management and little participation even in technical management.

Duncan established that the great majority of his sample viewed managerial duties from a technicist perspective, and then he examined in particular the view of section and project leaders, to determine to what extent those occupying transitional roles adopt a different perspective. He concludes that they also "see themselves and each other as essentially technical men engaged in the co-operative exercise of their specialist skills" (Duncan, 1972:137). They are willing to accept managerial responsibilities as the inescapable accompaniment of promotion. But their interests and satisfactions remain mainly technical. Duncan mentions three factors which foster the continuance of a technicist viewpoint among lower scientific management. In the first place, scientists tend to be widely regarded within their organizations as belonging to the "staff" rather than the "line." The persistence of this traditional distinction, particularly among those higher echelons of management concerned with policy formulation, discourages scientists from seeing themselves as potential managers and from seeking managerial posts. Second, research and development tends to be socially and geographically separated from production and marketing. Third, the work of project and team leaders involves sustained interaction with junior scientists who are engaged exclusively in scientific activities. Leaders are, accordingly, under considerable pressure to conform to the values and attitudes current in this technical group. Thus, Duncan concludes, given that the usual route into industrial employment for science graduates in Britain is via R & D, the persistence of this strong technical, though in no way academic, commitment on the part of scientific primary groups constitutes a definite barrier to the effective deployment of scientists throughout industrial management.

There are two ways in which academic science is likely to make a productive contribution to applied science. One is by the provision of suitably trained personnel and the other is by the passage of potentially useful information from the universities to industry. The studies described so far have all dealt with the first of these processes. However, one study has made a focussed attempt to estimate the extent to which information generated in the course of university research has contributed directly to industrial innovation. Langrish et al. (1972), in *Wealth from Knowledge* (see also Carter and Williams, 1957) furnish a detailed "natural history" of the eighty-four innovations cited in the sixty-six Queen's Awards for technological innovation presented in 1966 and 1967. These innovations were chosen for study in order to avoid the possibility of selecting a sample biased in accordance with the investigator's preconceptions. After compiling a complete set of case histories from documents and from interviews with those directly and indirectly concerned in each innovation, the authors tabulated the types of innovation and their sources. The result which is most relevant to this discussion is that they find little evidence of any observable link between university science and technological innovation in industry. For instance, the main technical ideas or concepts were identified for fifty-one of the innovations. Of the one hundred and fifty-eight important ideas involved, fifty-six originated within the firm centrally responsible for carrying through the innovation. Only ten of the remaining one hundred and two ideas from external sources came from universities; and not one of these ten came from the scientific literature. The authors commented: "We have paid particular attention to the relation of basic science to innovation . . . our failure to find more than a small handful of direct connections is the more striking for the fact that we set out deliberately to look for them" (Langrish et al., 1972:xii). They stress, however, that basic science may make substantial contributions in several ways not easy to observe. Academic research, they point out, is frequently the source of new research techniques. It provides people trained in using these techniques and in scientific ways of thought. And basic science has played a part in producing devices, such as the transistor, which are incorporated in many innovations. Nevertheless, despite these reservations, their findings run counter to widespread assumptions about the relationship between basic and applied science. Clearly, further research into this relationship is required.[10]

It seems that, on both intellectual and practical grounds, we need to know more about the actual processes of communication between governmental, industrial, and university research. One study having a bearing on this issue is that by Whitley and Frost (1971a, 1972). Using methods similar to those developed by Allen (1970) in the United

States, Whitley and Frost studied communication networks, management styles, research performance, and so on, in a British laboratory.
It is their conclusion about "gatekeepers" which is of particular interest
here. In the course of his studies, Allen (1970) noted the existence of
sociometric "stars" who had significantly more technical discussion
contacts with colleagues and who also read more scientific journals,
published more papers, and attended more conferences. On the basis
of these findings, Allen suggested that these researchers acted as
"gatekeepers," monitoring the environment for technical information
and passing it on within their own group.

   Whitley and Frost, however, provide only partial confirmation of
this view. They do find "stars" within their laboratory who are generally more in touch with sources of information outside the laboratory.
But further detailed analysis of their data shows that, to a considerable
extent, "any relation between use of external information sources and
acting as an informal information source is coincidental and due to in-
cumbency of positions of formal authority" (Whitley and Frost,
1972:350). In other words, the "stars" are mostly section leaders and it
is their tenure of this position which makes them the focus of the
internal communication structure and the main point of contact with
external sources. Whitley and Frost (1972:352) conclude that section
leaders are less important as sources of technical information than as
mediators between the research team and the project sponsors: "The
importance of access to external information sources by section leaders
appears to be due to the role of the sponsor in the research carried out.
Section leaders have considerable responsibility for obtaining and
managing contracts and so are perceived as the major source of information concerning contract specification." This, of course, is but one
study of one laboratory. Nonetheless, the finding that the system of
communication revolves around access to sponsors rather than to technical sources is clearly consistent with the conclusion of Langrish et al.,
that there are few direct links between applied science and university
research.

   In Britain, then, the sociological study of applied science has concentrated on a number of closely related questions, such as: What factors have, historically, determined the development of applied science? How has management responded to the growth in employment
of scientists in industry? To what extent do science undergraduates
acquire academic values which prevent them from engaging pro-

ductively in industrial research? To what degree are scientists unwilling to abandon technical work in exchange for managerial tasks? How far and in what ways does university research contribute to technological innovation?

These questions are all closely related to the practical issue of whether Britain is making full economic use of its scientific resources. They do not, on the whole, derive from problems of theoretical interpretation, except where there has been some concern with disproving the "orthodox model" of the two cultures. It is not surprising, therefore, that there has been little discussion of theoretical issues. Several of the studies have, of course, made use of particular theoretical conceptions. Burns and Stalker adapt Durkheim's notions of organic and mechanical solidarity in order to characterize the two types of management structure which they observe. Cotgrove and Box adopt an "interactionistic" approach and they consciously apply an array of related conceptions, such as "occupational identity," "role strain," and "role bargaining." Similarly, Barnes attempts to demonstrate the suitability of Becker's approach to occupational commitment. Each of these theoretical perspectives has been applied independently to somewhat different aspects of the social relationships of applied science. Thus, there has so far been virtually no debate about the theoretical notions which should guide future empirical exploration.

Nevertheless, despite the lack of theoretical discussion and analysis, a relatively coherent corpus of information has been produced. The main findings can be briefly summarized as follows. Most of those working in industrial science are trained in the university. The university provides a social and intellectual context markedly different from that of industry and this does create a difficult social transition for that large proportion of scientists who enter industry. But the difficulties have been exaggerated in much of the American literature and often wrongly interpreted. The difficulties facing scientists employed in industry, on the whole, are due neither to their strong commitment to academic values nor to their membership of a distinctive scientific profession. This is so for several reasons. First, while those who profess greatest commitment to scientific values and who are most successful academically tend to enter university research, those least committed to the values of academic science tend to move into industry. Second, industrial scientists are in general keen to contribute to their organizations and to do well in them. Third, those who do bring into industry attitudes more appropriate to university science often modify their views quickly in accordance with their new situation. Problems do arise, however, in the industrial setting. On the one hand, scientists emphasize the crucial importance of their special skills and the need to apply their expertise extensively throughout the industrial concern and, on the other hand, the existence of a scientific status group having control over valuable but esoteric knowledge constitutes a threat to the position of nonscientific management. There is, therefore, a widespread tendency for industrial management to keep scientists outside the main policy-making structure.[11] At the same time, industrial scientists are largely cut off from university science. Thus they are neither integrated into their own industrial organizations nor into the wider scientific community. As a result, there is considerable dissatisfaction especially over their lack of opportunity to exercise their special skills and their limited chances for promotion. It appears likely that this situation could be improved by changes in the nature of scientific training. But it also requires changes in industrial organization and in the links by which information passes between universities and industry.

SCIENTISTS AND SCIENCE IN THE UNIVERSITIES

In Britain, study of the basic research community has been approached in two different ways. On the one hand, some sociologists have developed a theoretical perspective in which Merton's influential analysis of the normative structure of science has been rejected in favor of certain conceptions initiated by Kuhn. This approach, although it has clear research implications, has so far produced little empirical material. On the other hand, there have been several studies of professional rewards and communication networks in science, which have been modeled on prior research carried out in the United States and which stem directly from Merton's writings. I shall begin this section with an account of these empirical studies.

Gaston's objectives in his (1970) paper are, first, to identify some of the social factors which affect the productivity of and the distribution of professional rewards among British high energy physicists

(HEPs) and, second, to compare his results with those of similar American studies. His broad conclusion is that the scientific reward system in Britain is less subject to social influence. His data come from interviews with 203 of the 220 HEPs known to be working in Britain in 1967–68. Although he recognizes that physicists' contributions to science take various forms, Gaston uses the total number of publications as an approximate index of each respondent's scientific productivity. Consequently, his first task becomes that of discerning whether differences between the overall productivity of individual scientists are associated with specific social variables. No significant relationship is found between this measure of productivity and such variables as social class origins, class of first degree, type of university attended for the Ph.D., or the prestige rating of the Ph.D. department. The data do show, however, that there is a strong association between productivity and professional age, that is, the number of years during which a scientist has been engaged in research. Gaston points out that the association betwen professional age and productivity has not been found to be so close in similar studies of the American research community, within which membership of prestigious departments appears significantly to increase the likelihood of high productivity (see Crane, 1965:699–714).

Having found that social factors other than professional age exert a negligible influence on productivity, Gaston examines how rewards are distributed among British HEPs. He takes professional recognition to be the central reward and constructs an index of recognition based on such items as number of papers refereed, number of invitation lectures given, and membership of honorary societies. He finds that there is no relationship between recognition awarded and such variables as type of undergraduate university, prestige of current department, or type of institutional affiliation, that is, whether at Cambridge, Oxford, London, or provincial university. There are, however, strong relationships between recognition and both productivity and professional age. Of these two factors productivity is the more important. That is, the number of an HEP's publications is more significant than his professional age in determining the level of his recognition. The findings described so far indicate clearly that British HEPs are rewarded for their scientific contributions regardless of social factors. However, Gaston also finds that scientists with first-class degrees are more likely to obtain recognition than those with second-class degrees. At first sight this might appear to be a departure from universalistic criteria. But Gaston shows that those with first-class degrees receive more recognition because they are more likely to be theorists. Thus there are two significant findings here. Those undergraduates who are defined as specially gifted tend to become theorists, and broadly speaking, theorists obtain more recognition than experimentalists for an equivalent number of publications. Not all types of theorists, however, are equally recognized. Abstract theorists, whose work is furthest removed from experimental data, are in fact the least recognized group in the whole HEP community. It is the work of the "phenomenologists" and intermediate theorists which receives most recognition, largely because, Gaston suggests, their work is closely linked to the experimentalists' observations and, therefore, widely regarded as valuable. Thus there is no evidence that particularistic criteria significantly affect the award of recognition among British HEPs. The observed differences in the distribution of recognition are consistent with the notion that recognition is awarded primarily in response to the perceived significance of scientific contributions.

The paper by Blume and Sinclair (1973) is a study of the reward system of British chemistry, similar in design to that by Gaston. The data were gathered by means of postal questionnaire sent to the 1,537 members of chemistry faculties in British universities. The 55 percent who responded appear to represent accurately the initial population. Blume and Sinclair use their data to construct indices of productivity and recognition. In addition, they devise an index for the quality of their respondents' work, based on assessment by peers, as well as a measure of "industrial involvement," which they regard as reflecting the conscious orientation of university chemists to applied science.

They find a strong relationship between quantity and quality of research. In other words, a chemist who has produced a substantial number of papers in recent years is more likely, than one who has not, to be regarded by his peers as having made a significant contribution to his field. It appears that chemists who are most concerned with the problems of industrial research are neither particularly productive nor regarded highly by their colleagues. Furthermore, those with a strong industrial orientation tend to receive appreciably less recognition in the university context for a given quantity of published results. This, it should be noted, is within the discipline that has the longest history of contact with industry. For whatever reason, it seems that the British chemical industry has the attention of the least effective sector of the university research community.[12] This finding is entirely consistent with the apparent lack of fruitful communication between industry and university which was mentioned at the end of the previous section.

In the remainder of their paper Blume and Sinclair deal exclusively with the exchange of information for recognition. They show, for example, that quality of research is slightly more important than quantity in determining the level of recognition.[13] They also investigate the influence of institutional affiliation on the receipt of recognition. In contrast to Gaston, they find that the recognition received by chemists does, to some degree, depend on their institutional location. More specifically they show that chemists of low and medium quality at Oxford and Cambridge tend to receive relatively greater recognition. However, it is by no means certain that Oxbridge chemists at the highest quality level receive significantly more recognition than their peers at other universities. The broad conclusion, therefore, is that, although the quality of a chemist's work is the most important determinant of the recognition he receives from the scientific community, those whose research is of the highest calibre receive an "unmerited" increment from working at either Oxford or Cambridge. This finding clearly throws some doubt on Gaston's suggestion that British science is generally more universalistic than American science. In view of the results of Blume and Sinclair as well as other recent findings (see Halsey and Trow, 1971), it seems likely that there is some special factor which prevents institutional affiliation from influencing the exchange of recognition for information in British high energy physics.[14]

In Whitley's (1969) paper an examination is made of how the reward structure of university science impinges on the system of communication. More specifically, Whitley investigates how the distribution of prestige and "power" influences formal communication in American animal physiology. The first step in this study was to identify three classes of authors within the specialty. One class was composed of those animal physiologists who, during 1957–61 had five or more citations in any one year and who were also listed as referees for the "core" American journals. The former criterion was taken to indicate high prestige and the latter as an index of power, that is, the ability to exert some control over other participants' access to the means of communication. This class of scientists was said to have both high prestige and power (HIPP); and was contrasted with that grouping whose members had low prestige, that is, no citations in 1957–61, and no power (LOPP). There was, in addition, a third residual category, the members of which Whitley calls the "middle classes" of animal physiology. But his main concern is with the upper and the lower classes. He wishes to discern in particular whether these latter groupings, identified on the basis of their prestige and power (this index of "power" could equally well be used as an index of "recognition"), operate as distinct strata in the formal system of communication. His central conclusion is that the communication network of animal physiology *is* clearly stratified.

Using the Science Citation Index, Whitley shows that those who had power and high prestige (HIPP) in 1957–61 published significantly more papers in 1960 than did those with no power and low prestige (LOPP), and that HIPP papers were cited significantly more often in subsequent years. He also shows that self-citation rates for LOPP papers were significantly higher than for HIPP papers; that no HIPP people cited any LOPP papers; that HIPP people cited HIPP papers more often than did LOPP people, and that the middle classes provided the majority of citations of HIPP papers. This evidence indicates, Whitley suggests, that the formal communication system of animal physiology is not merely stratified but, indeed, polarized, for there appears to be virtually no formal communication between the top and the bottom strata. He goes on to conjecture that such polarization may be typical of "Big Science." No investigation is made, however, of the extent to which animal physiology is Big Science or of the structural features of this specialty which may be responsible for polarization. Clearly this is a topic requiring further study.

Gaston's (1972) paper is concerned with communication and stratification, in this case in relation to high energy physics in Britain. Gaston concentrates on discovering which factors influence scientists' participation in the *informal* network of communication. He finds, first of all, that significantly more experimentalists than theoreticians regard informal contacts as their most important source of information. This, he suggests, is because theoreticians and experimentalists require different kinds of information. Much of the time experimentalists need to know only who has set up which experiment from among the limited range of likely experiments; and this information can easily be conveyed by word of mouth. Theoreticians, in contrast, require a full and detailed statement of results before they can get to work on a particular topic. Thus theoreticians and experimentalists participate differently in the communication system because they face different kinds of research problems. A second factor which influences the patterns of communication among HEPs is professional age. For instance, older theorists use oral sources considerably more than younger theorists, and older HEPs are more likely to communicate regularly with scientists in other institutions. In addition, those with both high productivity and high recognition are also more likely to communicate informally with scientists of the opposite type, that is, theorists with experimentalists and vice versa.

Having shown that communication in HEP is affected by factors such as professional age, productivity, and the differentiation of roles between experimentalists and theorists, Gaston applied a computational technique which indicates how far scientists choose and are chosen by their colleagues as sources of information. This technique is used to show, first of all, that scientists with high recognition have two to three times the connections, through other scientists naming them, than they have through the scientists they name. Moreover, it appears that phenomenologists are most frequently sought as informal communicants. Both these findings can be seen as following directly from the exchange of information in HEP. Those with high recognition are generally perceived as sources of valuable information and are, accordingly, in particular demand by their fellow researchers. Similarly, phenomenologists are the one group capable of interpreting results both to theorists and experimentalists. Thus they too are valuable sources of information.

Finally, Gaston investigates whether these patterns of informal communication in HEP indicate the existence of an "invisible college." His data show that communication choices by the total HEP community tend to focus on a small number of scientists who are named as regular communicants more frequently than others and that this small group communicates more with its own members than with other HEPs. These findings must be interpreted with care, however. In the first place, the elite group is by no means isolated from the rest of the HEP community. Second, there is the striking fact that the majority of HEPs make no informal choices outside their own institution, and they are not chosen by researchers in other institutions. Thus the dominant characteristic of the pattern of informal communication in British HEP seems to be that it is confined within particular research groups.

Whether this feature is more important than the presence of an incipient invisible college in helping us to understand the nature of the HEP community, can only be decided after further study.

These empirical studies of the distribution of rewards and of the operation of communication networks, although few in number, have produced several useful findings. They have shown that, in the fields studied, productivity and receipt of professional rewards are, on the whole, independent of ascriptive factors; that recognition is awarded in response to the quantity and quality of information supplied; that, at least in some fields, location at Oxbridge improves researchers' chances of being recognized; that both the communication and the reward systems are stratified; that theorists are recognized disproportionately when they occupy a central place in the communication network; that the degree of participation in communication networks is affected by professional age, level of recognition, and by tenure of a distinct theoretical or experimental role; and that those who profess a concern with the utilization of science in industry are less likely to be well integrated into the university reward system. Clearly these results raise further questions. For example, do those university scientists who show an interest in industrial science actually communicate more frequently with industrial scientists? What influence is exerted by members of the top stratum on the development of their specialty? Does institutional affiliation affect the receipt of recognition in some fields but not in others? If so, why? These are just a few of the problems which arise from these studies directly within the Mertonian tradition.

The second approach to the study of university science, involving a definite rejection of certain parts of the Mertonian perspective, was first expressed in papers by Mulkay (1969) and by Barnes and Dolby (1970). Although these papers were written separately, their criticisms of Merton's account of the scientific ethos are so similar that I shall present them here as one argument. The central theme of this argument is that it is misleading to depict the growth of scientific knowledge as a consequence of commitment by scientists to such social norms as organized scepticism, disinterestedness, communality and universalism (Merton 1967:550). In the first place, it is important to distinguish between what scientists say and what they do. Even when there is considerable agreement about the importance of organized skepticism, this agreement does not necessarily find direct expression in institutionalized behavior (Mulkay and Williams, 1971). Second, there is no systematic evidence that scientists generally endorse these norms, even at the verbal level. Third, as abstractions, these norms are by no means confined to scientific disciplines or even to the academic context. To the extent that they operate within science, they are given specific content in relation to the theories and techniques adopted by the members of particular research groupings. But, fourth, the Mertonian approach expressly forbids the introduction into sociological analysis of the substantive concepts and technical standards of science. This unfortunately directs attention away from the fact that the internal structure of the research community is organized around networks which are socially defined in terms of their members' intellectual concerns and scientific perspectives. Moreover, if the Mertonian norms are effectively institutionalized in science, it becomes difficult to account for the frequency of intellectual resistance. If the scientific ethos is genuinely "open-minded," then intellectual resistance must be explained largely by the intrusion into science of extraneous factors. It is not easy, however, to reconcile this view with the growing body of historical evidence that intellectual resistance is recurrent in science and is, indeed, an essential feature of the growth of scientific knowledge.

Having argued that there are difficulties with the Mertonian account of the scientific ethos, Barnes and Dolby, Mulkay and several others (especially King, 1971), suggest that Kuhn's work is a more suitable point of departure. This is so because Kuhn furnishes an analysis which is more dynamic and in which the esoteric culture of science is seen as intimately bound up with its social processes. Kuhn's work is regarded as important because it facilitates the development of a sociology of science which is part of the sociology of knowledge (Dolby, 1971).

The advocacy by British sociologists of Kuhn's analysis has not been uncritical, however. Martins (1972), for example, revises several of Kuhn's basic conceptions. He points out that, although paradigms are located in specialties or subspecialties, the specialty is not the sole locus of social control. There are contacts between specialties which are likely to influence the creation and alteration of paradigms. Furthermore, to the extent that specialties and paradigms are interrelated, it follows that changes of paradigm can be initiated externally as well as internally, and that the more prestigious paradigms may well have a domain in which they exert considerable influence on their less important neighbors. Martins also argues that there is no need to accept in full Kuhn's emphasis on the tight integration of the cognitive and technical assumptions governing normal science. The crux of his argument is, therefore, that a satisfactory approach to the study of scientific development must allow for a wider range of empirical variation than does Kuhn and that the interdependence between research networks must be recognized. Most of the papers in which a modified Kuhnian approach has been advanced are, like that of Martins, concerned with conceptual and theoretical clarification. However a more concrete model of scientific development has been formulated by Mulkay (1969, 1971, 1972a, 1972b) in which elements from both the Kuhnian and the Mertonian perspectives are combined.

The central idea taken from Kuhn is that scientific knowledge and technique has a normative as well as a cognitive dimension. Thus it is argued that scientific propositions portraying the physical world also constitute standards defining how researchers are expected to perceive the world and how they ought to undertake their research. The term "paradigm," however, is dropped because it implies that the members of any specific network are committed to a series of inseparable presuppositions and is replaced by the terms "cognitive and technical norms," which allow for the possibility of variable intellectual commitment and of gradual intellectual development. Conformity to these norms is maintained because, in general, it is the necessary condition for the receipt of professional recognition.

The degree of nonconformity which is allowed varies from one situation to another. Social control is most effective when conformity brings ample recognition, and this is most likely toward the beginning of work in any given area, when significant and solvable problems are relatively abundant. But there is a pronounced tendency for the problems current within any specific research network to decline in interest over time and for control to become less effective. Under certain conditions this reduction in opportunities for achieving adequate recognition may influence those who are at a competitive disadvantage (new entrants to the field, for example) to attempt to redefine the intellectual framework in such a way that new problems become permissible. In other words, a secular decline in the level of recognition available within an established field will sometimes weaken social control and thereby contribute to the occurrence of a Kuhnian revolution. But this is not the usual sequence. Migration is, in practice, more frequent than revolution. As given areas decline in interest, they are often either wholly or partially abandoned in favor of neighboring fields, particularly when the latter contain problems which are perceived to be interesting and potentially solvable. On some occasions migrants move into established networks, bringing about a cross-fertilization of ideas and a redefinition of existing problems. Just as often, however, research initiated in pursuit of one set of problems produces totally unexpected findings and reveals a whole range of issues previously ignored or unsuspected. Where the new problems have not previously been defined there is, of course, no orthodoxy to be overthrown, and growth proceeds by the formation of a new network which is, in turn, destined for eventual dissolution or gradual redefinition. Thus revolutions are likely to occur only under special conditions, for instance, when migration is impeded by specificity of skills and large-scale investment in inflexible technical equipment, when cognitions are sufficiently precise and integrated to prevent gradual redefinition, and when discoveries take place which, instead of revealing new fields of exploration, are clearly inconsistent with current scientific assumptions.

This model must be regarded as highly tentative. It is certain that, at the very least, it will undergo considerable modification in the light of further empirical investigation. So far there have been few detailed sociological studies of particular scientific developments against which to assess this or any other model of scientific development. Several such studies have recently been completed in Britain, however, and others are under way.[15] It seems likely, therefore, that in the next few years there will be greater interplay in this area between theoretical speculation and well-documented case studies.

THE SOCIOLOGY OF SCIENCE in Britain is still in its infancy and there is every indication that the field will continue to grow in the immediate future. Further research is certain to be undertaken into the values and satisfactions of industrial scientists as well as the contribution they make to technological innovation. There will also undoubtedly be more studies of the distribution of rewards within academic disciplines and of the passage of technical information between universities and industry. In addition, the empirical study of the evolution of research networks, with special reference to the connections between social and intellectual factors, will clearly be an area of growth. Finally, there are two related areas which have not yet been mentioned in this review. In the first place, there is the study of the relations between science and government, to which British sociologists have until recently paid little attention (see, however, King, 1968, and Vig, 1968). Second, there is the "reaction against science" on the part of lay groups and certain sectors of the scientific community. This relatively recent phenomenon has also begun to interest sociologists (Sklair, 1971, 1973). In both these fields the central question is how science is, and can be, controlled in highly differentiated societies. Owing to the urgent practical problems which are widely held to be associated with the "unregulated" growth and application of scientific knowledge, it seems likely that the expansion of these areas of sociological investigation will be particularly marked during the next few years.[16]

NOTES

[1]   Owing to limited space, it has not been possible to discuss every item in the text.

[2]   For some recent British work on the social sciences, see *Sociological Review Monograph* No. 16, ed. P. Halmos (Keele, Staffordshire: University of Keele, 1970).

[3]   Not all of these early items are, in fact, by British authors. See, for example, Moulin (1955).

[4]   At the universities of Bath, Edinburgh, Loughborough, Manchester, and Sussex. Two journals have also been founded, *Science Studies* and *Minerva*. The latter journal contains much of the discussion of science policy in Britain which is not covered in this essay.

[5]   The objections voiced by Cotgrove and Box are directed mainly at the American literature. This also applies to the criticisms raised by Ellis (1969), and the several works of Barnes.

[6]   The industrial sample is a heterogeneous one. The limitations which this imposes on the results are discussed by N. Kaplan (1971). Of central importance is the possibility that the scientific "identities" are distributed differentially among the various kinds of research roles included in the sample.

[7]   The measures for researchers and students were not identical. Greater difficulty was experienced in allocating the former to these categories. See Cotgrove and Box (1970:32 and 95).

8   Their table (5.3) of dissatisfactions must be judged carefully, for it includes only extreme public and extreme organizational scientists, i.e., only 27 percent of that proportion of the total sample which could be classified within the three types.

9   The theoretical difference between Cotgrove and Box and Barnes is perhaps not as great as the latter suggests, for Cotgrove and Box use an "interactionist" perspective at many points in their analysis.

10   Particular attention needs to be paid to the time scale involved, as has been shown in similar American work. The general impression given by Langrish et al., that there is little connection between university science and technological innovation may be misleading. There *may* be a definite connection which is obscured because typically it takes several generations to reach completion. Further research in this area is under way at Manchester.

11   This, at least, follows from the existing literature. There has, in fact, been little study of the distribution of those trained as "scientists" throughout industrial management or of the extent to which they influence policy.

12   That is, they are least effective as participants in university research. It may be that active involvement in industrial research itself hinders participation in university research.

13   It is difficult to construct an index of "quality" which could not equally well be used as an index of "recognition."

14   It may be, of course, that if Gaston had been able to control for quality, his results would have resembled more closely those of Blume and Sinclair. The problem is made more complex, however, by the fact that about half of Blume and Sinclair's respondents did not complete the question on "quality."

15   The first study of this kind in Britain, by Jenkins and Velody (1969), has unfortunately never been published. The studies completed recently are of X-ray crystallography, physical-chemistry and radio astronomy (e.g. Edge and Mulkay, 1976).

16   See R. K. Merton, "Preface: 1970" to *Science, Technology and Society in Seventeenth-Century England* (New York: Harper and Row, 1970) p. vii, ". . . sociologists would turn seriously to the systematic study of interaction between science and society only when science itself came to be widely regarded as something of a social problem or as a prolific source of social problems."

References

ALLEN, T. J.
    1970   "Communication Networks in R & D Laboratories." *Journal of R & D Management*, 1(1).

APTER, M. J.
    1972   "Cybernetics: A Case Study of a Scientific Subject-Complex." In P.
           Halmos (ed.), *The Sociology of Science*. Sociological Review Mono-
           graph, no. 18:93–116.

BARNES, S. B.
    1969   "Paradigms—Scientific and Social." *Man* 4:94–102.
    1971   "Making Out in Industrial Research." *Science Studies* 1 (April):
           157–75.
    1972a *Sociology of Science*. Harmondsworth: Penguin Books.
    1972b "On the Reception of Scientific Beliefs." In B. Barnes (ed.), *Sociol-
           ogy of Science*.
    1972c "Sociological Explanation and Natural Science: A Kuhnian Reap-
           praisal." *European Journal of Sociology* 13:373–91.
    1973   "The Comparison of Belief Systems: Anomaly vs. Falsehood." In
           Robert Horton and Ruth Finnegan (eds.), *Modes of Thought: Essays
           on Thinking in Western and Non-western Societies*. London: Faber
           and Faber.
    1974   *Scientific Knowledge and Sociological Theory*. London: Routledge
           and Kegan Paul. This book centers on the problem of explaining the
           manifest variety and contrast in the beliefs about nature held in dif-
           ferent groups and societies. Its basic contention is that the sociologist
           must seek to investigate "correct" or "scientific" beliefs just as he
           would "incorrect" or "unscientific ones."

BARNES, S. B., AND R. G. A. DOLBY
    1970   "The Scientific Ethos: A Deviant Viewpoint." *European Journal of
           Sociology* 11:3–25.

BECKER, H. S.
    1964   "Personal Change in Adult Life." *Sociometry* 27:40–53.

BERNAL, J. D.
    1939   *The Social Function of Science*. London: Routledge and Kegan Paul.

BLOOR, D. C.
    1973   "Wittgenstein and Mannheim on the Sociology of Mathematics."
           Studies in the History and Philosophy of Science 4:173–91.

BLUME, S., AND R. SINCLAIR
    1973   "Chemists in British Universities: A Study of the Reward System in
           Science." *American Sociological Review* 38 (February):126–38.

BLUME, S. S.
    1974   *Toward a Political Sociology of Science*. New York and London: The
           Free Press and Collier-Macmillan. A systematic examination of the
           political dimensions of modern science.

BOX, S., AND S. COTGROVE
    1966   "Scientific Identity, Occupational Selection and Role Strain." *British
           Journal of Sociology* 17:20–28.
    1968   "The Productivity of Scientists in Industrial Research Laboratories."
           Sociology, 2:163–72.

Box, S., and J. Ford
1967 "Commitment to Science: A Solution to Student Marginality."
    Sociology 1:225–38.
Briskman, L. D.
1972 "Is a Kuhnian Analysis Applicable to Psychology?" *Science Studies*
    2:87–97.
Burns, T., and G. M. Stalker
1961 *The Management of Innovation*. London: Tavistock Publications.

Cardwell, D. S. L.
1957 *The Organization of Science in England*. (Rev. ed.) London:
    Heinemann, 1972.
Carter, C. G., and B. R. Williams
1957 *Industry and Technical Progress*. London: Oxford University Press.
Collins, H. M.
1974 "The TEA Set: Tacit Knowledge and Scientific Networks." *Science
    Studies* 4 (April):165–86. A study of communication among scientists
    engaged developing TEA lasers, with special reference to tacit
    knowledge.
1975 "The Seven Sexes: A Study of the Sociology of a Phenomenon or the
    Replication of Experiments in Physics." *Sociology* 9 (May):205–24.
Cotgrove, S.
1970 "The Sociology of Science." *British Journal of Sociology*
    (March):1–15.
1973 "Anti-Science." *New Scientist* 59 (July):82–84. It is argued that the
    growth of opposition to science is more than a criticism of its uses and
    abuses and that it springs from a belief that science as a form of
    knowledge is antithetical to such human values as imagination, spon-
    taneity, and community.
1974 "Objections to Science." *Nature* 250 (August):764–67. This develops
    the theme that the contemporary attack on science springs from fears
    that it threatens to "dehumanize" man.
1975 "Technology, Rationality, and Domination." *Social Studies of Sci-
    ence* 5 (February):55–78. Critical theory on the technological society
    and the place of science is reviewed in the context of Weber's distinc-
    tion between technical and value rationality.
Cotgrove, S., and S. Box
1970 *Science, Industry and Society*. London: Allen and Unwin.
Cotgrove, S., and M. Fuller
1972 "Occupational Socialization and Choice: The Effects of Sandwich
    Courses." *Sociology*, 6:59–70.
Crane, D.
1965 "Scientists at Major and Minor Universities: A Study of Productivity
    and Recognition." *American Sociological Review* 30 (October):699–
    714.

CROWTHER, J. G.
  1967   *Science in Modern Society*. London: The Cresset Press.

DOLBY, R. G. A.
  1971   "The Sociology of Knowledge in Natural Science." *Science Studies*,
         1(1). Reprinted in abridged form in B. Barnes (ed.), *Sociology of
         Science*.

DUNCAN, P.
  1972   "From Scientist to Manager." In P. Halmos (ed.), *The Sociology of
         Science*. Sociological Review Monograph, no. 18:131–46.

DUNCAN, S. S.
  1974   "The Isolation of Scientific Discovery: Indifference and Resistance to
         a New Idea." *Science Studies* 4:109–34. A study of resistance to ad-
         vances in spatial diffusion theory by "human geographers," in which
         an attempt is made to assess the relative weight of specific sources of
         resistance.

EDGE, D. O.
  1974a "Moral Education and the Study of Science." In G. Collier, P. Wil-
         son, and J. Tomlinson (eds.), *Values and Moral Development in
         Higher Education*, pp. 147–59. London: Croom Helm.
  1974b "Technological Metaphor and Social Control." *New Literary His-
         tory* 6 (Autumn):135–47.
  1975   "On the Purity of Science." In W. R. Niblett (ed.), *The Sciences, The
         Humanities and the Technological Threat*, pp. 42–64. London: Uni-
         versity of London Press.

EDGE, D. O. AND M. J. MULKAY
  1976   *Astronomy Transformed: The Emergence of Radio Astronomy in
         Britain*. New York & London: Wiley-Interscience.

ELLIS, N. D.
  1969   "The Occupation of Science." *Technology and Society*, 5:33–41.

FORD, J., AND S. BOX
  1967   "Sociological Theory and Occupational Choice." *Sociological Review*
         15:287–99.

GASTON, J.
  1970   "The Reward System in British Science." *American Sociological Re-
         view* 35 (August):718–32.
  1971   "Secretiveness and Competition for Discovery in Physics." *Minerva*
         9:472–92.
  1972   "Communication and the Reward System of Science: A Study of a
         National 'Invisible College.'" In P. Halmos (ed.), *The Sociology of
         Science*. Sociological Review Monograph, no. 18:25–41.

GIBBONS, M.
  1972   "Some Aspects of Science Policy Research." In P. Halmos (ed.), *The*

Sociology of Science. Sociological Review Monograph, no. 18:187–207.

GILBERT, G. N., AND S. WOOLGAR

1974 "The Quantitative Study of Science." *Science Studies* 4 (July):279–94. A critical review of quantitative studies of science.

GOLDSMITH, M., AND A. MACKAY (EDS.)

1966 *The Science of Science.* (Rev. ed.). Harmondsworth: Pelican Books.

HALMOS, P. (ED.)

1972 *The Sociology of Science.* Sociological Review Monograph, no. 18. Keele, Staffordshire: University of Keele.

HALSEY, A. H., AND M. TROW

1971 *The British Academics.* London: Faber and Faber.

HILL, S. C.

1974 "Questioning the Influence of a 'Social System of Science.'" *Science Studies* 4 (April):135–63. A questionnaire study of applied scientists' values. The general conclusion is that there is no single scientific ethos, but rather a combination of several classes of values from which scientists select in accordance with their social situation.

HOLLOWAY, D.

1974 "Innovation in Science—the Case of Cybernetics in the Soviet Union." *Science Studies* 4 (October):299–337. An examination of the way in which the development of cybernetics in Russia was affected by the existence of a locus of scientific authority and legitimating values outside the specialist research community.

HOWEVER, R. M., AND C. D. ORTH

1963 *Managers and Scientists.* Cambridge, Mass.: Harvard University Press.

HUTCHINGS, D.

1963 *Technology and the Sixth Form Boy.* University of Oxford, Department of Education.

1967 *The Science Undergraduate.* University of Oxford, Department of Education.

HUTCHINSON, E.

1971 "Government Laboratories and the Influence of Organized Scientists." *Science Studies* 1:331–56.

JENKINS, W. I., AND I. VELODY

1969 "Behavioural Science Models for the Growth of Interdisciplinary Fields: The Cases of Biophysics and Oceanography." OECD Background Paper. Loughborough, End.: University of Loughborough.

JEVONS, F. R.

1973 *Science Observed.* London: Allen and Unwin. A general discussion of science as a social and intellectual activity.

JOHNSTON, R. D.

1972 "The Internal Structure of Technology." In P. Halmos (ed.), *The*

Sociology of Science. Sociological Review Monograph, no. 18:117–30.

KAPLAN, N.
  1971   "Truth and Cliché in the Sociology of Industrial Science." *Minerva*, 9, (July):430–34.
KING, M. D.
  1968   "Science and the Professional Dilemma." In J. Gould (ed.), *Penguin Social Science Survey 1968*. Pp. 34–73.
  1971   "Reason, Tradition and the Progressiveness of Science." *Science and Theory* 10:3–32.
  1973   "Scientists as Moralists." *Technology and Society* 8 (April):15–18.
KING, P.
  1972   "The Development of Ovonic Switches: A Case Study of a Scientific Controversy." *Science Studies* 2.

LANGRISH, J.; M. GIBBONS; W. G. EVANS; AND F. R. JEVONS
  1972   *Wealth from Knowledge*. London: Macmillan and Company.
LAW, J.
  1973   "The Development of Specialties in Science: The Case of X-Ray Protein Crystallography." *Science Studies* 3 (July):275–303. A study of the social and intellectual development of a research area. Distinctions are drawn between "technique," "theory," and "subject matter" specialties.
  1974   "Theories and Methods in the Sociology of Science: An Interpretive Approach." *Social Science Information* 13 (August/October):163–72. Some critical reflections on theoretical and methodological aspects of the author's own work in the sociology of science. Certain problems are raised in connection with the use of a "normative" approach.
LAW, J., AND D. FRENCH
  1974   "Normative and Interpretive Sociologies of Science." *Sociological Review* 22 (November):581–95. A contrast is made between two basic approaches to the sociological study of science. An "interpretive" approach is recommended.

MCCORMICK, K.
  1972   "Models and Assumptions in Manpower Planning in Science and Technology." In P. Halmos (ed.), *The Sociology of Science*. Sociological Review Monograph, no. 18:147–85.
MARTINS, H.
  1972   "The Kuhnian 'Revolution' and Its Implications for Sociology." In Nossiter, Hanson, and Rokkan (eds.), *Imagination and Precision in the Social Sciences*. London: Weidenfeld and Nicolson.
MEIER, R. L.
  1951   "Research as a Social Process: Social Status, Specialism and

Technological Advance in Great Britain." *British Journal of Sociology* 2:91–104.

MERTON, R. K.
1968 "Science and Democratic Social Structure." *Social Theory and Social Structure*. (Rev. ed.). New York: Free Press.

MOULIN, L.
1955 "The Nobel Prizes for the Sciences from 1901–1950: An Essay in Sociological Analysis." *British Journal of Sociology*, 6:246–63.

MULKAY, M. J.
1969 "Some Aspects of Cultural Growth in the Natural Sciences." *Social Research*, 36:22–52. Reprinted in abridged form in B. Barnes (ed.), *Sociology of Science*.

1970 "A Study of Some Prospective Scientists." *The Canadian Review of Sociology and Anthropology*, 5:181–91.

1971 "Some Suggestions for Sociological Research." *Science Studies*, 1:207–13.

1972a *The Social Process of Innovation: A Study in the Sociology of Science*. London: Macmillan and Company.

1972b "Conformity and Innovation in Science." In P. Halmos (ed.), *The Sociology of Science*. Sociological Review Monograph, no. 18:5–23.

1974a "Methodology in the Sociology of Science." *Social Science Information* 13 (April):107–19. Some reflections on methodological issues, arising out of the study of the emergence of radio astronomy.

1974b "Conceptual Displacement and Migration in Science: A Prefatory Paper." *Science Studies* 4 (July):205–34. An examination of some of the ways in which the movement of researchers between research networks gives rise to scientific innovation.

MULKAY, M. J., AND D. O. EDGE
1973 "Cognitive, Technical and Social Factors in the Growth of Radio Astronomy." *Social Science Information* 13 (December):25–61. A case study of the emergence and growth of a scientific specialty.

MULKAY, M. J.; G. N. GILBERT; AND S. WOOLGAR
1975 "Problem Areas and Research Networks in Science." *Sociology* 9 (May):187–203. A general analysis is presented of the dynamics of development within research networks. An attempt is made to show the connections between intellectual and social processes.

MULKAY, M. J., AND B. S. TURNER
1971 "Over-production of Personnel and Innovation in Three Social Settings." *Sociology*, 5:47–61.

MULKAY, M. J., AND A. T. WILLIAMS
1971 "A Sociological Study of a Physics Department." *British Journal of Sociology*, 22:68–82.

PALMERMO, D. S.
   1971 "Is a Scientific Revolution Taking Place in Psychology?" *Science Studies* 1:135–55.
POLANYI, M.
   1958 *Personal Knowledge*. London: Routledge and Kegan Paul.
PYM, D.
   1964 "A Manpower Study: The Chemist in Research and Development." *Occupational Psychology* 38:1–35.

RAVETZ, J.
   1971 *Scientific Knowledge and Its Social Problems*. Oxford: Clarendon Press.
ROSE, H., AND S. ROSE
   1969 *Science and Society*. London: Allen Lane. The Penguin Press.
ROTHMAN, R. A.
   1972 "A Dissenting View on the Scientific Ethos." *British Journal of Sociology* 23 (March):102–08. A brief note to the effect that the Mertonian norms are widely transgressed in science.

SELMES, C.
   1969 "Attitudes to Science and Scientists: The Attitudes of 12–13-Year-Old Pupils." *School Science Review* 51:7–14.
SKLAIR, L.
   1971 "The Sociology of the Opposition to Science and Technology: With Special Reference to the Work of Jacques Ellul." *Comparative Studies in Society and History*, 13:217–35.
   1972 "The Political Sociology of Science: A Critique of Current Orthodoxies." In P. Halmos (ed.), *The Sociology of Science*. Sociological Review Monograph, no. 18:43–59.
   1973 *Organised Knowledge*. London: Hart-Davis, MacGibbon.

VIG, N. J.
   1968 *Science and Technology in British Politics*. Oxford: Pergamon Press.

WALTERS, G., AND S. COTGROVE
   1967 *Scientists in British Industry*. Bath: Bath University Press.
WARREN, N.
   1971 "Is a Scientific Revolution Taking Place in Psychology? Doubts and Reservations." *Science Studies* 1:407–13.
WERSKEY, P. G.
   1971 "British Scientists and 'Outsider' Politics, 1931–1945." *Science Studies*, 1 (1).
WHITLEY, R. D.
   1969 "Communication Nets in Science: Status and Citation Patterns in Animal Physiology." *Sociological Review* 17:219–34.

1972 "Black Boxism and the Sociology of Science: A Discussion of the Major Developments in the Field." In P. Halmos (ed.), *The Sociology of Science*. Sociological Review Monograph, no. 18:61–92.

1974 *Social Processes of Scientific Development*. London: Routledge and Kegan Paul. A wide-ranging collection of papers, with authors from Europe, the United States and Britain, which were presented at an I.S.A. conference in London in 1972.

WHITLEY, R. D., AND P. A. FROST

1971a "Communication Patterns in a Research Laboratory." *Journal of R and D Management* 1:71–79.

1971b "The Measurement of Performance in Research." *Human Relations* 24:161–78.

1972 "Authority, Problem Solving Approaches, Communication and Change in a British Research Laboratory." *Journal of Management Studies*, pp. 337–39.

WUNDERLICH, R.

1974 "The Scientific Ethos: A Clarification." *British Journal of Sociology* 25 (September):373–77. A comment on the Mertonian norm of "disinterestedness."

ZIMAN, J. M.

1968 *Public Knowledge: Essay Concerning the Social Dimension of Science*. Cambridge: Cambridge University Press.

ZINBERG, D. S.

1971 "The Widening Gap: Attitudes of First-year Students and Staff Towards Chemistry, Science, Careers and Commitment." *Science Studies* 1:287–313.

THE SOCIOLOGY OF SCIENCE IN

France

Paul Frank

IN FRANCE, AS ELSEWHERE, the sociology of science is not a well-defined subject. Consequently, articles and books have been selected for review whose origins are diverse, sometimes falling within related sociological specialties. These works have been chosen because they seem to have relevance for the future development of the field. This chapter will indicate some lines along which the sociology of science is developing in France; it will not review critically the work which has already been done. The references section includes publications which deal with the sociological aspects of French scientific institutions, specialties, and communities, and have been written by sociologists, whether or not the authors are French.[1] The discussion primarily concerns articles and books dealing with distinct problem areas that have been studied by several sociologists of science. Unpublished work, work in progress, and work by scholars in other disciplines is discussed only if they speak directly to a controversial issue in sociological studies that has already been published.[2]

Because the French community of sociologists of science is just emerging and there is as yet little consensus among the various groups of researchers in the field concerning its major problems, the discussion will be organized in terms of problem areas that have generally tended to be considered central to the sociology of science in recent years. Three such areas are represented to some degree by studies of French science or social science. For example, the relationship between scientific institutions and the society in which they emerge has been an important topic for study in the sociology of science. Working from the premise that factors internal to scientific knowledge itself cannot fully explain its growth, sociologists of science have attempted to show how the development of scientific knowledge has been shaped by social factors affecting the organization and character of scientific institutions. One strand in the sociology of science in France has been a series of sociohistorical studies of the development of research traditions in sociology. Paul F. Lazarsfeld, then Quetelet Professor of Social Science at Columbia University and for two years (1962–63, 1967–68) at the Sorbonne, played an important role in the genesis of some of these studies. He was interested in the factors affecting the institutionalization of empirical social research and encouraged his students to undertake such studies in England and Germany, as well as in France.[3] Under his guidance, two of his students, Terry Clark and Bernard-Pierre Lécuyer, began studies of the institutionalization of sociological research in France and the development of traditions of empirical research in the social sciences.

A second area that has attracted the attention of sociologists of science concerns ways in which the growth and development of scientific disciplines and specialties are influenced by their social organization and cognitive structures. These problems are just beginning to be studied in France, but the difficulties which sociology has faced in becoming institutionalized in France have produced both a number of theoretical articles which examine the development of sociological theory from the perspective of the sociology of science, and, more recently, empirical studies of the organization of the social sciences.

A third area is the study of the organization of research laboratories and its effects on the productivity of researchers. This subject has received considerable attention in other countries and is beginning to be studied in France.

In addition, another line of inquiry will be discussed, that of the factors affecting the popularization of scientific knowledge, which has received much attention in France. No attempt will be made to review the extensive literature on science policy that has been produced in international organizations located in France (Organisation for Economic Cooperation and Development, 1964–73, 1972–75; Salomon, 1970; UNESCO, 1965–72). That research, properly speaking, belongs in a review of the sociology of science in international organizations.

When French sociology began to expand after World War II, it neglected the sociology of science for the most part, with the exception of a few papers on the sociology of sociology. In the late 1960s, the interest of the French agencies that funded scientific research in the problems of science policy led them to finance studies in the sociology of science.

In 1970, an informal association of British and French historians and sociologists of science called Parex (Par[is-Sus]ex) was created. This group now includes researchers from other countries and has played an important role in stimulating interest in the sociology of science in France and in providing a forum where researchers can present and discuss their ideas.[4]

The French governmental organization for scientific planning, the General Delegation for Scientific and Technological Research (Délégation Générale à la Recherche Scientifique et Technique) has surveyed the state of "research on research" in France and brought researchers together for a series of informal meetings to discuss their work and their mutual problems. A tangible outcome of the discussions was a special issue of Le Progrès Scientifique devoted to the subject of "research on research" in France ("Recherche sur la Recherche en France . . . ," 1973).

To date, however, there is only one center for sociological studies of science,[5] although there are several for the study of science policy and research administration. Also, at present, there are no courses in the sociology of science being given for students in the social sciences although there are a few courses on science policy.

FRENCH SCIENTIFIC
AND EDUCATIONAL INSTITUTIONS
IN THE NINETEENTH CENTURY

One of the most interesting questions for sociological study in France is the effect of the organizational structure of French educational institutions on the development of French science. The educational system, which provides the setting for scientific activities in France, has several features that make it unlike the educational systems of other Western countries. In order to understand the studies that have been done and to appreciate the differences in their interpretations, we must describe briefly the French educational system as it existed between the French Revolution and the mid-1960s.

Perhaps the most unusual feature of this system was the existence of a sizeable group of institutions which had greater prestige in the educational system than did the universities. Predominant among these institutions were the *grandes écoles*, designed to train personnel for government service, higher education, and industry. *Grandes écoles* were created in several professional areas. The most prestigious ones were the École Normale Supérieure which trained professors for the universities and for the *lycées* (secondary schools), and the École Polytechnique which trained army officers and higher civil servants.

The universities were not autonomous decision-making units in the American sense. Until the university reforms of 1968, control over the universities was exercised entirely by the central government in Paris. The control extended not only to budgetary matters and to the appointment of faculty, but also to the administration of libraries, laboratories, and even dormitories. In addition, there were other prestigious institutions, such as the Collège de France and the École pratique des Hautes Études, which were not universities. Although these institutions had staffs of professors and programs of lectures and seminars, they did not award graduate degrees.

An important controversy in the literature on nineteenth-century French science centers on whether this system of educational and research institutions functioned to inhibit or to facilitate the development of scientific research in France during the nineteenth century. Ben-David (1970) argues that while the first part of the nineteenth century was the most productive period in French science, this was due primarily to the system of scientific organizations that existed during the latter part of the previous century; it was not a result of the system as it existed in the nineteenth century. This new system was detrimental to the development of science because research as an activity remained separate from teaching. It was primarily an amateur activity, poorly financed and poorly equipped, and not reinforced by the necessity to teach new generations of scientists. Instead, the content of most of the teaching had little to do with scientific research; it was designed to train students to take special examinations or to reach unspecialized audiences (as at the Collège de France).

According to Ben-David, the failure of this system to adapt and reform itself as conditions favoring scientific activity changed, was due to the excessive centralization and bureaucratization of French institutions. Instead of changing existing organizations, the French tended to create new ones. One such institution was the École pratique des Hautes Études created in 1868 to provide courses and seminars in scientific work. But because the institution was designed to complement rather than compete with or replace existing institutions, it was denied the resources that would have permitted it to perform the role of training research workers in an outstanding fashion. It was not allowed to give advanced degrees and therefore the prerequisite for a French academic career remained the *agrégation* (an examination covering a broad range of materials) rather than the preparation of an advanced piece of research.[6]

Ben-David argues that while science in other countries during the late nineteenth century became increasingly professionalized and collaborative, French science remained a highly individualistic activity in which scientists trained successors only as "personal apprentices." Concomitantly, the French scientist was isolated not only from other scientists in his own country but also from the emerging international scientific community. Organizations which could assist the scientist in negotiating with the powerful central government failed to emerge.

Ben-David covers a couple of centuries in his essay which is more speculative than empirical. A somewhat different interpretation of the development of French science in the nineteenth century is presented by Fox (1973), an historian of science, who argues that it was the norms and values of the French scientific community itself rather than French scientific institutions which were responsible for the poor state of French science in the nineteenth century. After the Napoleonic period, the majority of French scientists became more concerned with success in literary and political circles than with dedication to scientific research. Shinn (1974a), in his detailed analysis of the *École Polytechnique*, shows that French academic science was definitely in a state of decline during much of the nineteenth century but that around the 1880s, the faculties of science in the French universities were reorganized, leading to a rejuvenation of French scientific research. Shinn (1974b) has recently attempted to test Ben-David's hypotheses systematically by examining the productivity of university scientists from 1808 to 1930 and the organization of scientific research in the universities during the same period.

The French system of educational institutions can also be examined in terms of its influence upon the institutionalization of scientific disciplines. Gilpin (1968) argues that the emphasis in university education upon preparing students for national examinations such as the *agrégation* and for qualifying as teachers in secondary schools inhibited the development of new specialties in the natural sciences. The distribution of chairs among scientific disciplines changed very little during the nineteenth century and even in the twentieth. Strong leadership that could have reformed the university failed to develop because these organizations were not permitted to pursue policies which were independent of those of the central government bureaucracy.

Clark (1973) describes how the French educational system affected the institutionalization of the social sciences in France. He stresses that the structure of higher education in France made it difficult to institutionalize new lines of scientific work. In Clark's view, the French university's role in producing teachers for the *lycées* was a crucial factor in inhibiting the introduction of new specialties in the universities. The institutionalization of new specialties was retarded when there was no demand for the teaching of such specialties in the *lycées* and hence no need for university professors or lecturers in special subjects. The fact that sociology never became a subject taught in the *lycées* meant that it could obtain only a precarious foothold in the university.[7]

Within each discipline, only the small number of posts at the University of Paris possessed prestige so that there was little competition within disciplines. Instead, disciplines were organized into groups or clusters, consisting of patrons who were the current occupants of the prestigious posts at the Sorbonne, surrounded by their disciples and followers. Other members of the cluster were located in less important institutions, such as provincial universities, *lycées*, or research institutes. These individuals depended for advancement, and often for the means to do their research, upon the patron and his influence in the system. Thus a few powerful patrons influenced affairs not only within their own departments but also in their disciplines and in the surrounding network of laboratories, research institutes, journals, government advisory boards, and fund-granting committees. As a result, they could effectively control the activities and the opportunities to produce innovative work of virtually all other members of their disciplines.

While Ben-David ([1970] 1971) and Oberschall (1972), in their respective studies of the German and American universities at the end of the nineteenth century, were describing academic systems that contributed to scientific innovation or at least to the proliferation of knowledge, Clark was describing a system in which only innovations of the highest order had a chance to succeed. Both the German and American systems during that period were in the process of expansion. Numerous posts were available in each field and there was a lively competition for them, which in turn produced innovative work in each field. In the French system, Clark shows how the extreme paucity of posts entailed such severe competition that members of different disciplines competed with each other. Failure in this competition could mean not only a personal loss but also the absence of a secure institutional environment and financial support for an academic discipline.

The ways the institutions described in these studies function is so complex that much more work needs to be done if they are to be understood. The recent studies have developed interesting and somewhat controversial theses, but the difficult task remains of gathering detailed empirical information about the great number of organizations and professionals involved. Some work of this kind continues to be under way.[8]

CHANGES AND DEVELOPMENTS IN FRENCH SCIENTIFIC INSTITUTIONS IN THE TWENTIETH CENTURY

The controversy over the effects of the French educational system upon French scientific and social scientific institutions continues in studies of these institutions in the twentieth century. A number of changes have taken place. Since World War II, the National Center for Scientific Research (Centre National de la Recherche Scientifique), founded in 1939, has developed an additional system of support to researchers both through salaries and funds for research. The C.N.R.S.

supports research institutes which are independent of the traditional university faculties, although some researchers in these institutes also teach part time in a university. Many researchers supported by the C.N.R.S. work in research institutes which are associated with a university.

The educational system has changed, to some extent, as a result of the reforms of the late 1960s. The huge University of Paris has been divided into thirteen institutions. Attempts have been made to strengthen the provincial universities, and some are emerging as important intellectual centers. During the last decade, graduates of the École Polytechnique have begun to enter scientific research.

In *France in the Age of the Scientific State*, Gilpin (1968) attempts to explain why French technological achievements were relatively mediocre in the twentieth century. In tracing the development of French educational institutions, he emphasizes the absence of mobility between scientific and practical institutions. Physicians could not teach in the university and scientists could not teach in medical and engineering schools. He suggests that this inhibited the circulation of ideas between these institutions and produced a kind of "intellectual sclerosis." The prestige of the *grandes écoles* had the unfortunate effect of attracting the most gifted students who preferred to study there and go on to administrative careers rather than to pursue scientific careers in the universities. Finally, Gilpin indicts the system of awarding professorships, and in recent years, research grants, regardless of scientific competence and achievement.

Although the reforms undertaken in the 1950s and early 1960s strengthened the organization of science, they were primarily calculated to increase the role which science could play in military defense. The fields emphasized in French science policy were those which had "prestige, military utility, and economic value." Gilpin saw the solution to French problems in the development of science and technology in terms of increasing cooperation with other European countries, but he showed clearly the political obstacles to such a course of action. As it happens, the decline in government support for scientific research in the late 1960s makes some of Gilpin's analysis seem dated today.

Ben-David (1968) showed that the factors which tended to inhibit the development of innovative scientific research in France since World War I were common to other European countries as well. Drawing upon his studies of academic environments for scientific research in

France and Germany, he shows that the organization of European universities was too rigid to permit the introduction of new disciplines or the exploitation of scientific results. The development of existing disciplines was impeded by inefficient organizational units. Chairs representing entire disciplines, and institutes attached to chairs, where one individual directs the activities of a group of researchers in a broad area of knowledge for a generation, constituted an inefficient system. Departments of autonomous teachers representing different specialties within a discipline were more efficient and productive. Finally, the universities had little autonomy or policy-making power because financial and administrative control was vested in central governments. This minimized the possibilities for innovation and experimentation on the university level.

Monique de Saint-Martin (1971) suggests an alternative explanation for the fact that the sciences have been the poor stepchildren of the French academic system for centuries. She argues that it is not so much university or bureaucratic structures that have inhibited the development of French science but that the most powerful social groups in France seldom considered that scientific knowledge was important or potentially useful to them in maintaining their dominant position. Classical and literary studies have always been privileged in comparison with scientific education and have attracted the largest proportion of students from the upper classes. While a certain value is placed on technical expertise, basic research is neither valued nor respected. It is this social context which has greatly affected the development of science in France.

Saint-Martin shows that the most prestigious positions in French society tend to be occupied by graduates from upper- or middle-class social origins. Social origin, rather than academic achievement, is the criterion for success in the social system because graduates of prestigious schools who have lower-class origins derive less benefit from attendance at such schools than graduates from middle- or upper-class origins. A study by Karady (1972) of teaching careers between 1900 and 1914 yielded similar results for that period. Professional achievement was closely linked to social class origins.

Bourdieu and his associates (1971) in their examination of the evolution of the French educational system since World War II found that in both the arts and the sciences, the numbers of students and teachers have greatly expanded during the last twenty years. They argue that this expansion in the number of university posts has produced a decline in the quality of those who obtain the most prestigious positions, "quality" being defined here by reference to the qualifications and educational achievements represented among those who occupy higher teaching positions. At the same time, there is a growing conflict in the social sciences between norms concerning styles of recruitment and academic careers derived from the traditional disciplines[9] and those derived from the exact sciences. The traditional disciplines, which have tended to predominate in the French university, have placed the greatest emphasis upon the *agrégation* as the criterion for entrance into a teaching career rather than the production of a piece of research as represented by a thesis. The thesis as a mode of certification of candidates has come to be accepted in the sciences but is not yet accepted in the social sciences (Bourdieu et al., 1971:74, 77). The continuing predominance of the *agrégation* is explained by the fact that the most important administrative posts in the university are held by members of the traditional disciplines who resist attempts to modernize the university (Bourdieu et al., 1971:62–63).

In the social sciences, Bourdieu and his colleagues see on the one hand the emergence of a group of professional researchers and on the other hand the continuation of the system of patrons surrounded by their followers, as described by Clark (1973). Researchers who wish to enter teaching careers depend more upon their personal relationships with influential professors than upon their scholarly performance. The conflict between these orientations is most severe in sociology where there is the greatest diversity of members drawn from different types of educational backgrounds and where the variation in types of careers is greatest. As a result, "the crisis takes a form at once more intense . . . more personalized than in any other discipline" (Bourdieu et al., 1971:86).

These studies preceded the educational reforms of 1968. Ronald Brickman (1973), an American researcher, has examined the effects of the reforms of 1968 on the policies of French universities toward scientific research. Although changes in law gave French universities greater control and autonomy in research, Brickman found that, on the whole, the universities were not availing themselves of their new powers; instead they were putting the new laws into action in such a way as to leave the situation relatively unchanged compared to the period before 1968. Financial dependence upon the central government, 'which is also unwilling to translate the new laws into action, coupled with the weakness of university administrations at the higher levels, mean that in effect the universities in most cases fail to develop a policy for research. His study suggests that with strong leadership (which has appeared in some instances), the French university could gradually evolve into a more nearly autonomous institution capable of influencing the direction of higher education. However, there remain many of the constraints that have historically inhibited the development of the French university.

Another report on the reformed French university (Gaussen, 1973) also indicates that many of the problems of the old system have not been eliminated in the new one. Overcrowding, control of appointments and other decisions by a small group of "mandarins," and an acute shortage of positions leading to inequities in the allocation of rewards for intellectual achievements continue.

An underlying theme can be discerned in the various studies discussed in this and the preceding section: that French educational institutions, more often than not, have impeded rather than facilitated the development of scientific and social scientific knowledge. A theme in the literature to be discussed in the next section is that an intellectual community having its own norms and values and being somewhat independent of the universities occasionally produces superior intellectual achievements (see, for example, Bourdieu and Passeron, 1967). As important advances in the natural sciences, the social sciences, and the humanities increasingly require rational organization and considerable funding, the central question for further research is how this style of intellectual work can be integrated with the university system in such a way as to make continued progress possible in these fields.

DEVELOPMENT OF SCIENTIFIC DISCIPLINES AND SPECIALTIES

Although the study of the development of scientific disciplines and specialties has begun to attract the attention of researchers in France (such studies are under way at the present time),[10] the articles which have been published deal primarily with problems in the development of sociology as a discipline. An exception is the study of the development of disciplines in the natural sciences by Lemaine, Matalon, and Provansal (1969). Using the results of questionnaires that examined the decisions made by two hundred researchers to undertake research, the authors developed a model of how the scientific community functions. The system for allocating rewards in the scientific community, which places a premium on originality and which therefore encourages competition, leads to a process of social differentiation not only during periods of revolution, but also during periods of "normal science." This process can be seen in a tendency on the part of some researchers to pursue less important but safer topics and in their attempts to differentiate their own research from that of others by producing original ideas, leading to the continual development of new scientific fields.

Perhaps because of the difficulties which sociology has encountered in France, first in the process of institutionalization in the university and later in maintaining its identity as a discipline, articles examining sociological theory from the perspective of the sociology of sociology appeared in France before such an approach became fashionable in the United States. As early as 1959, a colloquium on the "Social Settings of Sociology" was organized by a group of eminent French sociologists. In summarizing the conclusions of the conference, Gurvitch (1971) noted that sociology more than any other science is self-critical. He saw a tendency to attempt to define the boundaries of the field more precisely and to attempt to become truly scientific, and suggested that in order to do so, an analysis of the sociology of sociological knowledge is necessary. At the same time he warned of the dangers for sociology of government demands for technical expertise, a particular kind of sociological influence that can lead to a loss of autonomy by the discipline.

In 1967, Bourdieu and Passeron published an outline of a sociology of French theoretical sociology. Their aim was to show how intellectual positions in the discipline were influenced explicitly or implicitly by philosophical attitudes. They stress that the development of sociology in France has been influenced by the close links which have always existed between French sociology and French philosophy, and describe the intellectual environment in Paris which facilitated the diffusion of ideas between the two disciplines. In the process they describe some of the unique features of French intellectual life that explain both the special qualities of French intellectual writings and their relative isolation from foreign influences. For example, the physical concentration of French intellectual life in Paris and the requirement that an intellectual speak to a wide range of philosophical and historical issues are important features of this milieu.

A recent influence upon the development of French sociology has been its contact with American empirically-oriented sociology starting in the 1950s. According to Bourdieu and Passeron, those who accepted this orientation toward sociology had for the most part had little contact with the French intellectual milieu and tended to reject its concerns as irrelevant to theirs. Somewhat later a period of economic expansion and affluence in France led to a demand for an applied sociology, particularly on the part of the French government. Consequently, some sociologists began to produce sociological work that reflected the expectations of government administrators rather than producing work that used a truly sociological approach. This trend, which is also seen in other disciplines, has gradually changed the character of the intellectual world so that "those in the traditional intellectual occupations have decreased in proportion . . . to those in the intellectual occupations more directly linked to industry or large-scale administration" (Bourdieu and Passeron, 1967:188).

While Bourdieu and Passeron are concerned that sociologists will lose control over the direction of their discipline as a result of demands placed on it from government and industry, Mendras (1971) maintains that in spite of increased external demand for sociological research, French sociological findings and recommendations have had virtually no influence upon practical decisions in France. In general, Mendras concludes that in France neither organizations nor mechanisms exist for the exchange of ideas which could provide the necessary links between researchers and potential users of sociological knowledge.

Until very recently, there were no empirical studies of the organization of social science research in France in spite of a recommendation by three eminent sociologists (Chombart de Lauwe, Mendras, and Touraine, 1965) that, since many aspects of research organization were dysfunctional, such studies should be undertaken. A study of the organization of research in the social sciences has been carried out under the direction of Elisabeth Crawford (1973, 1974, 1976) as part of an international collaborative project by social scientists in England, France, Germany, and Denmark.[11]

Crawford has tabulated basic data concerning about four hundred research institutes and has engaged in an intensive study of fifty of them. In France, organized or collective social science research is conducted largely in research institutes rather than in university departments. From the beginning of the analysis of data, it became evident that French social science research is heavily influenced by the contract mode of financing used mainly by government departments having functional and operational responsibilities and, to a lesser extent, by the National Center for Scientific Research as a means of orienting research to specific problem areas, usually those relating to socioeconomic planning and management (economic forecasting, urbanization, regionalization, educational development, environmental problems, etc.). Contracts are the major sustaining force of many research institutes, some of which were created as arms of government departments with government subsidies. The contract system has had the effect of replacing general disciplinary-based research institutes with much smaller units whose work is tailored to the narrow pragmatic concerns of a specialized government department or a market consisting of a number of public bodies having similar functional responsibilities and representing a somewhat broader but still largely pragmatically-oriented clientele for social-science information.

From the point of view of the individual researcher, the situation brought about by the change to the contract mode of financing is demoralizing. It has led to the creation of an important category of staff in the research institutes whose possibilities for research careers, and even their chances of maintaining themselves in active research employment, are directly dependent on the vagaries of the market for the kind of specialized social-science knowledge and skills which they possess. The career prospects of this group of researchers are particularly unfavorable when compared to those of their colleagues—often working in the same institutes—who hold appointments in universities or the National Center for Scientific Research and, hence, have access to tenured positions.

For the disciplines as a whole, the consequences of this mode of generating organizations and knowledge are also largely negative because knowledge fails to cumulate around broad theoretical concerns.

The results of contract research are most often communicated in technical reports. Institutes depending on contracts can rarely afford to have their staff rework these reports for publication in scientific journals. In other words, the effect of recent funding policies in the social sciences in France is to turn these disciplines increasingly toward research and concerns defined by persons outside the disciplines who are unfamiliar with the knowledge base of the disciplines. The findings of a group of economists at Grenoble (Mallein, 1973; Palluy, 1974) and of a recent O.E.C.D. (1975) report on the social sciences emphasize the negative effects of contract research upon both the research and the researchers. The O.E.C.D. report recommends extensive reforms in the organization of the social sciences in France.

Many other studies remain to be done. In addition to studies of communities of scientists in research areas in the natural sciences, a number of studies of the social sciences, using a combination of qualitative and quantitative methodologies, would be particularly valuable. For example, a detailed examination of the influence of Marxism on the development of French sociology and of the resistance to the social-science approach among non-Marxist scholars in the humanities would be of considerable interest. Similarly, the French scientific community as a whole provides an unusually interesting opportunity to study the relationships between disciplines, and especially the reasons for and effects of the key role played by philosophy in this community.

STUDIES OF RESEARCH
LABORATORIES:
ACADEMIC AND INDUSTRIAL

Although the sociology of work is highly developed in France, owing in large part to the influence of Marxism upon French sociologists in the 1950s and 1960s, industrial research laboratories have hardly been studied. The American literature on industrial research has emphasized the conflict between scientific and commercial values and the problems this poses for the applied scientist who needs to be autonomous in pursuing his research interests. In the mid-sixties, a series of articles in *Sociologie du Travail* (Benusiglio, 1966, 1967; M. Moscovici,

1966, 1967) explored the American literature on this topic and reached somewhat similar conclusions to those obtained on the basis of studies of applied researchers in England (see Mulkay's chapter in this book). In a small study of scientists in two industrial laboratories, Benusiglio (1966, 1967) found that there is generally no great difference between the values of applied scientists and those of industrial managers. He argues that applied research in industry is often inefficient and unproductive because it takes place in narrowly specialized units. He suggests that these groups ought to be reorganized to have more contact with one another and also with university scientists. Surprisingly, this line of research has not been continued in France.

Lemaine, Lécuyer, Gomis, and Barthélémy (1972) have conducted a significant study of successful and unsuccessful academic laboratories in physics and biology. Their objective was to understand why certain scientific laboratories function well and others function badly by comparing laboratories of research teams which varied in terms of scientific quality. They chose two specialties, one in physics and the other in biology, but made comparisons between laboratories only within each specialty. For each specialty, six laboratories which varied in terms of success were chosen for intensive study. While the authors found a number of correlations between the quality of a scientific laboratory and characteristics such as size and relationships with foreign scientists, they attempted to go beyond a static picture of the situation in these laboratories in order to give an idea of their development and to attribute their quality to decisive events in their history. At the end of their report, they draw a number of conclusions that apply to both physics and biology.

1) The organization of the laboratory ought to be considered less as an independent variable and more as a dependent variable. In other words, the mode of organization is a response to constraints imposed on the one hand by the nature of the scientific problems selected for study and on the other hand by the characteristics of the environment (infrastructure, techniques, quality of available scientific personnel, etc.).

2) A director of a laboratory who wants to raise his laboratory to the level of the international standard probably has to disrupt the structure of his laboratory in order to do so. These changes are apt to be opposed by researchers who are content with a less risky enterprise, one that is sufficient to assure an acceptable career.

3)   In the best laboratories, both in biology and in physics, one can identify a strategy of choosing important but risky research problems. The appropriate organizational structure is one that permits the team to take risks which are compatible with its resources, and depends upon the nature of the objectives which have been set by the members of the laboratory.

The conclusions of Lemaine and his associates differ considerably from those of Pelz and Andrews (1976). The latter consider organizational structure to be the most important variable affecting scientific productivity while the former emphasize the strategies and objectives of the laboratory director which, in different contexts, lead to the creation of organizational structures that are best adapted to scientific productivity.

DIFFUSION AND POPULARIZATION OF SCIENTIFIC KNOWLEDGE

Several French researchers have studied the popularization of scientific knowledge. The diffusion of scientific knowledge to the public has been examined from two points of view: first, how social relationships and structures affect the diffusion of scientific knowledge to the public, and second, how scientific ideas are changed or modified as a result of this process.

This line of inquiry began in France with studies by S. Moscovici (1966) of the transmission of knowledge about psychoanalysis to the general public. His study belongs both to the sociology of knowledge and to social psychology. A basic hypothesis of the sociology of knowledge has been that intellectual productions and ideologies are conditioned by social groups or structures. However, the sociology of knowledge has been oriented toward history and has shown little concern with the measurement and control of variables. The objectives of social psychology are more limited but also more concrete. The empirical methodology of social psychology permits an analysis of the process of intellectual change and of the cognitive system itself.

S. Moscovici (1966) adopted a double approach. He surveyed more than 2000 persons and analyzed the contents of approximately

1500 articles which appeared in 230 newspapers (daily, weekly, etc.) during a period of fifteen months. The survey provides a detailed description of how psychoanalytic concepts are assimilated by different social groups (middle classes, professionals, workers, students, etc.). The study indicates what they know about psychoanalysis, their attitudes toward it, and how those attitudes are affected by their political orientations and religious affiliations. Moscovici also describes how psychoanalytic concepts are transformed in the process of transmission and how new meanings are constructed around them. The cognitive activities of those who receive the information are analyzed in an attempt to show the cognitive processes which they use to comprehend the material (e.g., the use of analogy). The content analysis of articles in the press begins with a categorization of publications (Communist, Catholic, information, etc.), and attempts to show how themes are organized in the process of communication.

As a whole, Moscovici's study shows that in order to understand the assimilation of a body of knowledge, it is necessary to examine not only the nature of the ideas themselves but also their social function in society. In the process of diffusion to a wider audience the ideas acquire a new interpretation which reflects social realities and social relationships. The analysis of the relationship between a body of knowledge and its social context leads Moscovici to examine the phenomena of popularization in general. One problem is understanding why popularization has variable effects depending upon the nature of the public. A second problem involves the relationship between popularization and "recurrent education." Recurrent education is one of the necessities of our society because the rapid progress of scientific knowledge, and the transformations of the social structures that accompany it, necessitate the continual presentation of new knowledge to the public.

From this study of psychoanalysis, Moscovici has moved in several directions. In *Essai sur l'histoire humaine de la nature*, Moscovici (1968) presents a vast fresco of the role of knowledge in Western civilization as well as a theory of social invention. He has also directed studies by his associates of the diffusion and assimilation of scientific knowledge. The central theme of these empirical studies is that the transmission of ideas involves not only popularization but a shift from one form of knowledge to another. This process is called "social representation," the ways in which scientific ideas are transformed when they pass from scientists to different social groups and the processes whereby these ideas are assimilated by members of these groups.

The research has largely dealt with adults who have just undergone a period of adult education or "recycling" as prescribed in the French law on *"l'education permanente."* The research has been designed to examine in depth the cognitive effects upon the individual of exposure to new ideas. These intellectual processes are always seen in relation to social and psychological factors. For example, the researchers have examined how individuals resist new ideas, the ways in which new ideas are evaluated, and especially the role of ideological influences in the process. They have studied the attitudes of the scientists who are transmitting information (i.e., whether they present knowledge as being more or less accessible, for example), the social environments of individuals who assimilate new information, and the effects of variations in the organization of information.

Research by Boltanski and Maldidier (1970) on the popularization of scientific knowledge differs from that by S. Moscovici and his associates. They focus, not on the intellectual content that is diffused or on its history, but on what the practice of popularization by basic researchers shows about the social norms of scientific disciplines and the relationships between scientists and nonscientists. A survey of 200 researchers (103 physicists and 97 biologists) in the region of Paris showed that a researcher is more likely to engage in popularization when he occupies a central position in his field. Centrality is defined by a scientist's rank in the university hierarchy and by the type of education he has received (*agrégation* makes one more central than the *licence, ancien élève* of a *grande école* more central than a university graduate). The authors argue that the strategy of researchers is aimed toward reaching the center of the intellectual field, toward adding to their own value in relationship to their peers, and toward becoming in some way more "rare," because the central positions are not numerous. It is only when a central and therefore "rare" position is given (by education) or acquired that a researcher can try to conquer a second kind of "rarity" by seeking a public other than the scientific community.

The freedom of researchers who are "central," compared to the constraints which weigh upon researchers who are peripheral, is interpreted in terms of the social control that the community exercises over its members. Popularization is not generally considered as a legitimate scientific activity. If the researchers at the center have a positive attitude and the researchers at the periphery have a negative attitude toward popularization, it is because there is no risk in their eyes or in the eyes of other members of the community that they will be attracted away from the community. Because scientists at the center are more dedicated and better integrated into the community, the community in some way delegates them as representatives to the nonscientific world without risk of seeing its own norms threatened.

Dulong and Ackermann (1972) point out in their survey of the literature that there is still relatively little sociological research on the popularization of scientific knowledge. One interesting problem that could be examined is the paradox that popularization of knowledge, instead of leading to greater social equality, tends to maintain the gulf between science and the public. In other words, those who gain most from adult-education programs are those who are already well educated. The adult-education system increases rather than decreases cultural inequalities. Another question that deserves attention is whether popularization should take place in structures similar to traditional forms of schooling, or whether entirely new types of systems are necessary if esoteric knowledge is to be effectively transmitted to adults.

A RECURRENT THEME in the sociology of science in France is the study of the development of scientific institutions. This may be explained by the difficulties which the structure of French educational institutions has posed for the pursuit of scientific research. Further inquiry is needed on how French educational institutions structure scientific institutions, relationships between scientists, and the development of scientific knowledge.

As the preceding analysis shows, much of the research that has been done in the sociology of science concerns either the historical development of the social sciences, particularly sociology, or the problems these disciplines face in terms of organization and financing. The present crisis of the social sciences in France has contributed to the development of a sociology of the social sciences and to an analysis of policy for the social sciences. Two special characteristics of the social sciences in France, the powerful influence of philosophy and of Marxism, deserve further analysis.

Finally, a distinctive theme in the French literature is the study of the popularization of scientific knowledge. Again, concern in France with the problems of *l'éducation permanente* has provided a receptive environment for studies of the factors affecting the public's assimilation of scientific knowledge and the ways in which such knowledge is transformed in the process.

What are the long-run prospects for the development of the sociology of science in France? Much of the work which has been published in France to date has been done by researchers who do not consider themselves specialists in the sociology of science. Since a core of specialists in the field is now beginning to develop, one can expect that the number of studies in the field will increase in the future. However, it seems unlikely that the field will develop a stable and productive tradition of research unless the larger problems which plague sociology and the social sciences in France are resolved.

NOTES

[1]   Research by French sociologists on science or scientists in other countries would be relevant, of course, but no examples of such work were found.

[2]   Historians of science sometimes use sociological variables in their discussions of scientific institutions but an adequate coverage of this literature would require more space than is available here and be beyond the scope of this book.

[3]   A number of these studies has been published in Oberschall (1972).

[4]   Parex is now under the joint direction of Gérard Lemaine, École pratique des Hautes Études (6th Section) and Roy MacLeod, History and Social Studies of Science, University of Sussex.

[5]   Groupe d'Études et de Recherches sur la Science, École pratique des Hautes Études (6th Section). The Center is under the direction of Gérard Lemaine.

[6]   A lengthy piece of research for the *doctorat d'état* was and still is a prerequisite for the post of full professor but not for lower ranks in the university.

[7]   In the United States, for example, where the university's function was not defined in the same terms, the factors affecting the expansion of new disciplines were quite different. (See the chapter on American sociology by Oberschall in his edited book on empirical sociology [Oberschall, 1972: 187–251].)

[8] See Shinn (1974b), and Lécuyer, with the assistance of Karady (1973). Lécuyer is tracing the emergence of empirical social research in France and the factors which prevented it from becoming fully institutionalized.

[9] Bourdieu et al. define the traditional disciplines (*les disciplines canoniques*) as languages, literature, and history.

[10] For example, Gérard Lemaine has conducted a study of the research area devoted to the psychophysiological analysis of sleep.

[11] This study is representative of an emerging mode of organization of sociological research in Europe, cross-national comparison based on separate but related studies in several countries. In this case, the researchers hold annual conferences and have developed a common orientation, although the research instruments that are used in each country vary. Cf. Crawford, (1976).

REFERENCES

BACHELARD, G.
1938 *La Formation de l'esprit scientifique*. Paris: Vrin.

BEN-DAVID, J.
1968 *Fundamental Research and the Universities*. Paris: OECD.
1970 "The rise and decline of France as a scientific centre." *Minerva* 8 (April):160–79. (Reprinted in *The Scientist's Role in Society*. Englewood Cliffs, N.J.: Prentice-Hall, 1971, chapter 6.)

BENUSIGLIO, D.
1966/1967 "L'integration de la recherche dans l'enterprise." *Sociologie du Travail* 8 (October/December):338–67; (January/March):64–82.

BOLTANSKI, L., AND P. MALDIDIER
1970 "Carrière scientifique, morale scientifique, et vulgarisation." *Social Science Information* 9:64–82.

BON, F. ET AL.
1973 "Les attitudes de l'opinion publique à l'égard de la recherche. *Le Progrès Scientifique*, nos. 165–66 (August/September/October).

BOURDIEU, P., AND J. C. PASSERON
1967 "Sociology and Philosophy in France since 1945: Death and Resurrection of a Philosophy without Subject." *Social Research* 34 (Spring):162–212.

BOURDIEU, P. ET AL.
1971 "La défense du corps." *Social Science Information* 10:45–86.

BRICKMAN, R.
1972 "The Limits of Reform: Power and Decentralization in the French University System." Ph.D. dissertation, Massachusetts Institute of Technology.
1973 "La Politique de la Recherche des Universités Françaises." Groupe

d'Étude sur la Recherche Scientifique. Mimeographed. Strasbourg: Université Louis Pasteur.

CHOMBART DE LAUWE, PH.-H.; H. MENDRAS; AND A. TOURAINE
1965   "Sociologie du travail sociologique." *Sociologie du Travail* 7 (July/ September).

CLARK, T. N.
1973   *Prophets and Patrons: The French University and the Emergence of the Social Sciences.* Cambridge, Mass.: Harvard University Press.

CRAWFORD, E.
1973   "Participation Française à l'enquête européenne sur l'organisation de la recherche en sciences sociales." *Le Progrès Scientifique*, no. 167 (November/December): 29–36.

1974   Social Science as a Career. Paper prepared for the seminar on the Organization of Social Science Research, 25–28 March, at Cambridge University.

1976   "L'identification 'au dehors' et 'au dedans' des centres de recherches en sciences sociales." *Bulletin*, Société Française de Sociologie, 3 (March): 22–28.

DE CERTAINES, J.
1973   La mort des disciplines closes: naissance de la biophysique? Paper presented at the Parex Meeting, Maison des Sciences de l'Homme, Paris.

DULONG, R., AND W. ACKERMANN
1972   "Popularisation of Science for Adults." *Social Science Information* 11: 113–48.

FOX, R.
1973   "Scientific enterprise and the patronage of research in France, 1800–70." *Minerva* 11: 442–73.

GAUSSEN, F.
1973   "The human cost of French university expansion: academics without careers." *Minerva* 11: 372–86.

GILPIN, R.
1968   *France in the Age of the Scientific State.* Princeton: Princeton University Press.

GIZYCKI, R. VON
1973   "Centre and periphery in the international scientific community: Germany, France and Great Britain in the 19th century." *Minerva* 11: 474–94.

GURVITCH, G.
1966   *Les cadres sociaux de la connaissance.* Paris: Presses universitaires de France.

1971 "The Social Settings of Sociological Knowledge." In E. A. Tiryakian (ed.), *The Phenomenon of Sociology: A Reader in the Sociology of Sociology*, pp. 58–64. New York: Appleton-Century-Crofts.

JAUBERT, A., AND J.-M. LÉVY-LEBLOND
1973 *(Auto)Critique de la Science*. Paris: Éditions du Seuil.

KARADY, V.
1972 "Normaliens et autres enseignants à la Belle Époque: Notes sur l'origine sociale et la réussite dans une profession intellectuelle." *Revue française de Sociologie* 13:35–58.
1973 "L'expansion universitaire et l'évolution des inégalités devant la carrière d'enseignant au début de la III République." *Revue française de Sociologie* 14:443–70.

LÉCUYER, B.-P.
1970 "Contribution of the social sciences to the guidance of national policy." *International Social Science Journal* 22:264–300.
1973 "La recherche longitudinale sur les sciences sociales en France." *Le Progrès Scientifique*, no. 167 (November/December):20–28. (With the assistance of V. Karady.)

LÉCUYER, B.-P., AND A. OBERSCHALL
1968 "The early history of social research." *International Encyclopedia of the Social Sciences*, pp. 36–53. New York: Macmillan and Free Press.

LEMAINE, G.; B.-P. LÉCUYER; A. GOMIS; AND C. BARTHÉLÉMY
1972 *Les Voies du Succès: sur quelques facteurs de la réussite des laboratoires de recherche fondamentale en France*. Paris: CNRS.

LEMAINE, G.; B. MATALON; AND B. PROVANSAL
1969 "Le lutte pour la vie dans la cité scientifique." *Revue française de Sociologie* 10:139–65.

MALLEIN, P.
1973 "Le système de la recherche." *Le Progrès Scientifique*, no. 167 (November/December):47–60.

MENDRAS, H.
1968 "Pour une école d'application des sciences sociales." *Analyse et Prévision* 5.
1971 "Du bon usage de la sociologie ou le sociologue et la société française." *Analyse et Prévision* 11 (January):1–25.

MOSCOVICI, M.
1966 "La recherche scientifique dans l'industrie." *Analyse et Prévision* 2 (November):782–800.
1967 "Le laboratoire dans l'industrie: pour une sociologie de la recherche organisée." *Sociologie du Travail* 9 (October–December):438–47.

MOSCOVICI, S.
    1966   *La Psychoanalyse, son image et son public*. Paris: Presses Universitaires de France.
    1968   *Essai sur l'Histoire Humaine de la Nature*. Paris: Flammarion.

OBERSCHALL, A.
    1965   *Empirical Social Research in Germany, 1848–1914*. The Hague: Mouton.
OBERSCHALL, A. (ED.)
    1972   *The Establishment of Empirical Sociology: Studies in Continuity, Discontinuity and Institutionalization*. New York: Harper and Row.
ORGANISATION FOR ECONOMIC COOPERATION AND DEVELOPMENT
    1964–1973   Reviews of National Science Policy. Paris: OECD.
    1972 1974 1975   *The Research System*, vols. 1, 2, 3. Paris: OECD.
    1975   *Social Science Policy: France*. Paris: OECD.

PALLUY, B.
    1974   *Les Chercheurs et la Procédure Contractuelle en Sciences Sociales*. Institut de Prospective et de Politique de la Science. Mimeographed. Grenoble: Université des Sciences Sociales de Grenoble.
PELZ, D., AND F. ANDREWS
    1976   *Scientists in Organizations*. rev. ed. New York: Wiley.
LE PROGRÈS SCIENTIFIQUE
    1973   "Recherche sur la recherche en France: le Club de Gif." no. 167 November–December).

SAINT-MARTIN, M. DE
    1971   *Les Fonctions Sociales de l'Enseignement Scientifique*. Paris: École Pratique des Hautes Études & Mouton.
SALOMON, J.-J.
    1970   *Science et Politique*. Paris: Éditions du Seuil. (translation: *Science and Politics*, London: Macmillan, 1973.)
SHINN, T.
    1974a   "The Formation of a French Elite: The Sociology of the École Polytechnique and the Polytechnique Circle, 1794–1914." Ph.D. dissertation, Indiana University.
    1974b   Les universités françaises et le déclin de la recherche scientifique en France après 1830: essai de vérification et de spécification d'une hypothèse socio-historique. Unpublished. Paris.

UNESCO
    1965–82   *Science Policy Studies and Documents. Nos. 1–27*. Paris: UNESCO.

THE SOCIOLOGY OF SCIENCE IN

Italy

Filippo Barbano

AT FIRST GLANCE, the sociology of science does not seem to be well developed in Italy; yet nowhere has there been a spectacular development in the sociology of science. The problem is partly one of terminology. First, by "sociology of science" I mean not so much a specialized branch of study as an historical and social *activity* which takes as its starting point the "interests" of science. These interests include the means and ends of scientific study, as well as the content and form of "scientific techniques," which differ from other techniques such as the anthropological or "body techniques" or "social techniques."[1] If the sociology of science is interested in the nature and uses of science in society, it is interested above all in studying these as a consequence of the Western rationale or outlook on science.

Thus in discussing the sociology of science I am not concerned primarily with its academic status, its degree of specialization, or its autonomy as a profession or technique (Barber, 1956)—that is, with its place in the division of labor within the social sciences.[2] I hope that this volume, which surveys recent situations and problems in Europe, will reveal that the social status of the sociology of science implies a meeting, and at once a confrontation, between the sociology of labor and organization and the sociology of knowledge and education.

Second, the sociology of science should modify prevailing concepts of science as "system" (whether cognitive or institutional, or "analogous system"[3] in the politico-economic framework) or as "progress" (i.e., a progressive and cumulative "development") with the notion of science as a theoretical and practical "process" in which science and society reciprocally influence each other. This reciprocity differs from the concept of the mechanical or functional interdependence of science and society in conceiving of science as process and practical activity rather than as system or progress.[4]

In viewing the sociology of science as an activity I mean that it is not merely an "operation," and that it entails more than the unilateral consideration of 1) the effects of science on society, such as the social consequences of technological progress; or 2) the effects of society on science, such as the consequences that socioeconomic, political, and cultural structures may have on science. It involves also the contribution which science has made historically to social reality: its socialization, social status, and social structure. In other words, it means the positive, structural, and intentional historic dimensions of science.

Since these concepts determine the main emphases of my review, I shall define them more precisely. By "socialization of science" I refer to the transformation of scientific effort from individual to social activity. This involves not merely specialization but the structure of activity: the organization and use of labor, power relations with labor, competitiveness. In discussing the "social status" of science, which is determined by its socialization, I refer to the absorption of science into the social and cultural structure, and to the dialectical relationship of science and the structure of society. Finally, by the "social structure of science," I mean the composition, organization, interaction, and goals of groups of researchers, scientists, technicians, and scientific intellectuals. The positive, structural, and intentional historic roles or processes of science correspond to these aspects of scientific activity.[5]

My survey will stress themes and problematics in the sociology of science in post–World War II Italy, rather than institutional factors, tracing first the substantive areas of research, and then the major theoretical approaches that have characterized sociological thinking on science and its heightened social status. (For a general description and history of the specialty, see Statera, 1976.)

The earliest theorists of the emerging social sciences were already aware, albeit vaguely, that science would undergo a process of socialization and assume greater social importance.[6] In fact, the birth of "social science" was itself a direct consequence of the socialization of science, according to Comte, having occurred in the age of the scientific-industrial revolution as a result of the dialectical relationship between intellectual and social organization. Marx maintained that "science," incorporated into technology and machine capital, would become the "captive" science of capital, changing the nature of human labor, its organization, and the requirements of a machine society. Yet he did not by this imply a denial of the historic significance of science and the social sciences, even as a "superstructure" dependent on the material conditioning of consciousness. Engels was perhaps more cognizant of the role of science; but Marx, too, foresaw an age of large industry and advanced development of capital where one might see general social knowledge become a productive force. Furthermore, Marx speculated about the extent to which productive social forces are produced, not only in the form of knowledge, but also as immediate organs of social practice and the process of real life.

A line of thought which starts with Saint-Simon, Comte, and Marx—the first to recognize the historic significance of science and its socialization—continues with Durkheim, Weber, and Troeltsch; then with Mannheim and Sorokin, students of the sociology of knowledge; and finally with such scholars as Tawney, Parsons, Merton, and others. This tradition, in the light of present experience, has shown us that one consequence of an advanced stage in the socialization of science is a reawakening of the dilemmas of the period in which that process was born. It is not by mere chance that social science was born at the same time.

SUBSTANTIVE PROBLEMS: TECHNICAL AND SCIENTIFIC CHANGE IN ITALIAN SOCIETY

Although Italy, the "land of contradictions,"[7] suffers more than other European countries from the international division of scientific labor, it has undergone a vast socialization of science. This has not yet led to sharp specialization, but it has affected both the macrofunctional, or institutional, aspects of society, and its microsociological aspects—the role and activity of scientists, researchers, and intellectuals. "Technological progress" has changed in connotation; simply implying machinery in the early 1950s, it came to mean increased mechanization, then automation, finally the passage from traditional automation to electronics.

As "Big Science" (Price, 1963) has manifested itself in typical ways, conditions have become more favorable for probing the relationship between science and society, or more accurately, technology and industrialization. One infers these conditions from graphs indicating the number of researchers in the field, and from the increasing volume of publication. Although this body of literature does not constitute a systematic sociology of science, it provides a base for such study, as well as theoretical perspectives that have often shown originality.

Five principal subjects have been studied. First are the products of technology: cars, appliances, television, the myriad products which "the age of technical reproducibility" creates and continually renews, as well as the various means of their invention, appropriation, use, and consumption.[8] Second, the instruments of technology—machines and their systems—have been analyzed, since these require technical knowledge to apply the scientific knowledge incorporated in these instruments. Pragmatically, the value and significance of information, or knowledge, determine the social status of science in the sense that 1) professional training is required to handle scientific instruments; 2) capacity, or knowledge, is possessed by a number of people who are sociologically identifiable—for example, experts and technicians; and 3) the product of pure and applied science is produced by scientists, researchers, and groups. (Information has a different meaning when one refers to the quantity of data available in a single system, and to information in different systems.) Third, there has been research in the economics and sociology of scientific creativity. In economics, the starting point has been the study of the new kind of entrepreneur. In the area of scientific creativity, the work and role of the researcher, the "scientific intellectual," have been explored. A fourth theme has been innovation, not merely the invention of concrete items, but innovation as a process. Fifth, there has been great interest in the education of personnel, particularly the role of education as both a dependent and an independent variable in technological and economic development.

There are three main lines, discussed in the following sections, along which changes in this field of study have taken place: scientific and technological progress and its impact on industrial and economic development; the reorganization of schools and universities, with particular emphasis on adaptation, modernization, and reorganization; and the growing interdependence within the social system of science and industry, education and government, economy and research, and the national and international systems. These three lines converge and intersect today.

Scientific and Technological Progress

In the early 1950s, sociology in Italy was just beginning to reestablish itself after over fifty years of neglect. The journal *Tecnica ed Organizzazione* launched a new series about then, and was among the first to publish work on the sociological implications of scientific technology.[9] Toward the end of the decade, various research projects were carried out, leading to the 1960 International Congress to Study Technological Progress and Italian Society. The Congress produced a number of interesting studies. Attitudes toward progress and technological innovation in the trade-union press and in factory organizations were studied by Barbano and Marletti (1960) and by Gallino and Barbano (1960); the life and behavior of the labor force in the industrial city were studied by Diena (1960); and rationalization and community by Pizzorno (1960). Martinoli (1961, 1965) examined technical and scientific change in relation to the sociology of organization and social engineering. Acquaviva (1958) produced a sociological study of automation and the kinds of experts it requires, arguing that scientific technology brought about a new stratification of society because it became the province of an increasing number of people. Ferrarotti (1963) produced a different argument, emphasizing some of the classical aspects of "machine society," and considering advanced technology as it affected labor and industrial attitudes. These factors, he said, lead to different notions of the meaning of time, value and duration, and to different intellectual orientations.

Outside the area of professional study, a public image of science was created by articles in the large daily newspapers and by encyclopedias of science and technology. From 1960 on, these stimulated and reflected the popular "demand" for scientific knowledge, as against the requirements of specialists reading technical publications.[10]

Reorganization of Schools and Universities

The enhanced social status of science, reflected in Italian publications, was marked by an interest in the problems of reorganizing, adapting, and modernizing the institutions of a country still caught in the tensions between a traditional agricultural society, on the one hand, and a modern urban-industrial society on the other. A great deal of criticism has highlighted a number of the "dichotomies" of Italian society; yet these dichotomies are produced not so much by Italian society specifically, but rather by the basic problems and contradictions inherent in the "scientific society."

In education, one dichotomy is that between the training which a new system of production has required for industry and the training which the schools have offered. For decades, Italy has been governed by an educational system pursuing an antiscientific policy, conditioned by lay idealism on the one hand and religion on the other, which has collided with the demands of industrial rationalization.

A second dichotomy exists between "know-what"—that is, specialized knowledge—and methodological "know-how"; that is, between formal training in a subject and the development of the ability to redefine work situations continually in the light of innovation. This has meant a widening of the gap (both quantitative and qualitative) between the supply and demand of trained personnel and raised the related problems of finding adaptable people who at the same time are capable of creative thought.

The increased ties between school and industry exacerbated the dichotomy between technological development as autonomous and as dependent on the training of personnel. Thus an attempt was made to determine the demand for trained personnel and at the same time foresee the requirements of graduates.

These problems are well documented in the research done by the I. R. E. S. (1962), including studies by Barbano, Detragiache, and Bodrato. Reports on the subject were also presented to the 1960 Congress on Technological Progress (A.A.V.V., 1963) by Barbano and Griseri, De Rita, and Zappa. The studies on training of personnel in industry, prepared for the I. R. I. (Institute for Industrial Reconstruction) (A.A.V.V., 1964) by Bontadini, De Rita, Glisenti, Martinoli, Saraceno, Visalberghi, and Vita, also address these problems. Further discussion is found in Martinoli (1964) which includes work by Battelli, Gallino, and Glisenti. For the educational point of view consult De Bartolomeis (1965). In A.A.V.V. (1966), Barbano, Miotto, and Martinoli deal with experiences of local training programs, as do a number of journal articles up to the present.

Interdependence of Social Systems

The growing interdependence of science and society had been observed in the early 1960s, particularly with regard to the demands of science and the development of science; see Barbano (1961) and Ferrarotti (1961) on this subject. At the Congress on Sociologists and Centers of Power in Italy (A.A.V.V., 1962), Ferrarotti reported on Parliament, De Rita on Public Administration, Barbano on Parties and Trade Unions, and Ardigo on Education. (See also Gallino, 1962.) Countering traditional educational policies, the requirements of industrial rationalization prompted several conclusions:

1) Government policy should see state education as a social *investment* (see also the 1966 C. E. N. S. I. S. report). Avveduto (1968), developing this argument, pointed out the contradiction in Italian policy regarding technology and science, indicated by the amount of money set aside for scientific research as part of public spending or as a form of redistribution of national income, and the qualitative reorganization of such research.

2) Schools and universities should be modernized and made more efficient in the light not only of manpower need, but of personnel training as an independent variable in technological development.

3) The organization of science should be a matter not only of policy but of power—that is, the actual interrelationship between science, power centers, and government.

The increased sensitivity to the interdependence of institutional sectors was illustrated by the dispute over the "technological gap." In Italy, this debate was provoked by certain policy decisions of the political classes and was further exacerbated by the famous alarm raised in 1967 by the *défi américain* in France. At that time, few observers pointed out the relationship between the technological gap and the international division of labor. But the dispute did serve at least to call attention to another gap—that between national prestige and international politico-economic reality.[11] It also highlighted the gap between scientific research and the practical social nature of science and its institutions.

The latter consideration meant that we had to reexamine the relationship between theory and research in the natural sciences—a relationship very different from the one entailed by the traditional view of research and experiment as aiming primarily at the validation of theoretical scientific statements. Insofar as "research" is more than an "operation" but involves personnel, labor, and publications; insofar as its organization, institutionalization and coordination change; and insofar as it relates to labor in terms of increased levels of specialization, social power, and rivalry, science acquires a heightened social status. Its scope is profoundly transformed and its interests change. Above all, its development is transformed. Most writers today believe that the quantity of science and the type of specialization involved in research today should aim at a new quality of science (see Baracca and Bergia, 1972).

These publications thus identify for us another set of contradictions and dichotomies inherent in the scientific society and reflected in Italy: the dichotomy between basic and applied research; between the private sphere in scientific research, seen in terms of economic development, and the public sphere, seen in terms of policy and the institutionalization of science research; between functional science and developmental research. This problem has greatly interested Italian scholars and has inspired many specialized studies. Some consist of official documents and studies prepared for public bodies involved in scientific research, such as the annual reports of the president of the National Research Committee on science and research in Italy (see Caglioti, 1968, 1970; C.N.R., 1970).[12] Some deal with research into scientific problems and research, and the conditions of researchers.[13] There have also been critical studies of problems in science, research, and education (de Falco, 1968; Zorzoli, 1969, 1970; Silvestri, 1968; and Berlinquer, 1970). Finally, much research has centered on the problems and conditions of scientific research in industry, with two main themes: the position and scope of industrial research and the problems of innovation.[14]

The problems relating to scientific research in industry merit more detailed attention. Earlier concern with problems of individual talent and intellectual resources has given way to studies of the various types of research formations and their composition, organization, and interaction. Some findings are that multinational industry employs specialist researchers on the basis of *line* organization and division of labor, thus solving the problem of the organization of research. Middle industry, especially in electronics, tends to employ a research staff, and thus its researchers are more homogeneous. Small industry has been a neglected area, but would make an interesting site for investigating innovation in light of the prejudices of the "self-made man," the lack of information, and the shortage of manpower.

The relations of science and industry are reflected also in the relatively large amounts of money paid for patents, copyright, exclusive rights, and so forth. These demonstrate the limited development of scientific research in general, and in industry especially, and underscore the contrast between macro- and micro-industry, a dominant factor in industrial growth in Italy.[15] While the large multinational corporations can exploit *ad hoc* national bodies like the IMI, SORIS and the CGI's Commission for Scientific Research, and can acquire foreign know-how and patents more easily, small industry is very often tied to and conditioned by large industry. The government and the state have been unable to reestablish an equilibrium here, not even through the semi-state-owned and nationalized industries, which by now are large enough to make the Italian economy a mixed economy.

THEORETIC APPROACHES: TOTAL STRATEGIES, SOCIALIZATION, AND STRUCTURAL ANALYSIS OF SCIENCE

The contradictions between the system of science, its social status, and the larger social system have often been studied by Italian scholars, who have theorized about them and drawn some practical conclusions. Publications in Italy exhibit two main approaches to these problems. One of these concentrates on the "total strategies" of science. The second orientation tries to define the social status of science and the dialectic of science and society.

The central components of the total strategies approach are: *1)* "systems" and hence functional conceptualizations of the relationship between science and society; and   2) politico-economic concepts of planning and programming based on a cybernetic model. The mutual influence of these two components tends toward the creation of "scientific policy planning" implemented through the strategy and technology of information.

The study of "total strategies" assumes more or less explicitly that science and society are highly integrated "systems," or, rather, a single system. These systems become an independent variable in the social structure of science and the historical development of science. Thus the old concept of a "technological factor" is shored up by a functional concept of "universality," "unity," and "indispensability" of science as a system. This is similar to the process by which the "holistic" theory of functionalism demonstrated the coherence and completeness of society as an integrated system. The complete identification of the system of science with the system of society is a way of conceptualizing science as a "power," a power that in fact serves the system. In other words, science has, and becomes, a function.

Thus the question is raised: "In our scientific society, does science function as the condition *sine qua non* of social integration, just as religion did in primitive society, according to the functionalists, or as war does in military societies?" Criticism of functionalism by structuralists has long shown that even if one accepts this approach to the problem of society and social order, war and religion in earlier societies in fact served only a relative, not absolute, function in integration. In other words, religion, war, and, by extension, science, cannot be defined only in terms of the system, its unity, and its integration.

The "total strategies" approach has enormous implications for the social status of science. By neglecting the possibility of internal contradiction, it exacerbates the consequences of the objectivization, dehumanization, and institutionalization of science and rejects the consequences—or at least understates the significance—of its socialization. This is especially true when research is seen as more than an operation and involves the interdependence of practice and theory. Such interdependence is especially apparent when the need for innovation and creativity in industry, the trade unions, politics, and so forth, touches on problems involving education and self-awareness, rather than simple feedback.

Science is a theoretical and practical process of high educational value, and as such has an implicit capacity for self-correction and self-criticism. However, the process of self-regulation required by the *system* of science often subverts this capacity both in practice and in theory.[16]

Let us examine the system of science more closely. The idea that the "unification" of the sciences can be definitively achieved is continually being contradicted by the perpetual efforts of scholars to unify them and to establish their interdisciplinarity. Moreover, science in fact does not always develop coherently. Technical and scientific development varies enormously with different social contexts; thus its premises, structures, and social consequences differ.

Science as a system must be distinguished from the social status of science. The latter cannot be defined only in terms of the system, its functions, and the need for institutionalization and integration. Moreover, the social status of science must not be confused with its function of technical rationalization in a scientific society. That is, the process of socialization, which determines the status of science, must not be confused with its ability to integrate the products, ends, and means of a technico-scientific society. In short, socialized science does not mean integrated science, though these tended to be confused in the early, visionary days of the social sciences.[17]

There are several factors that help explain why this approach has been popular in Italy. A sort of historically determined pragmatic functionalism has inhered in the technico-cultural industrialization of the 1960s, which conditioned the Italian socioeconomic system and produced an "increasing interdependence" of social functions[18] in the sociology of industry, labor organization, politics, scientific policy, and so on. In describing this increasing interdependence, theoretical functionalism has in fact been very successful. Sociology has not succeeded, however, in developing a functional criticism, or a critical functional analysis.[19]

There are several reasons for this. First, social science is still tied to its "organic" juridical heritage and its teaching about the state, and to neo-organismic social teaching. Second, sociologically, as general systematic theories (e.g., Parsons's) have become more diffused, they have demonstrated that functional theory can be applied to industrial societies precisely because such societies need greater integration as a result of the contradictions they generate. Third, with regard to social policy, many scholars were opposed to a critical neofunctionalism in a period of rapid industrialization, preferring a pragmatic sociology and a perspective of social integration. For these and other reasons, it is not surprising that Marxist literature has shown more interest in the structure and the sociology of science than the more specialized sociological publications.[20]

It is only now that we can fully understand Merton's proposal of 1947 (1968, chap. 18), in which he suggested that social scientists study the machine, the worker, industrial labor, and technology as part of the sociology of science. He suggested this as an evident alternative to the functionalism of the so-called "human relations" school and to the American tendency to turn industrial sociology into a specialized subject. At the time, this suggestion seemed a sophisticated, even visionary, way of approaching the problem of labor in industrial society. Today it seems to be the only way to prevent the sociology of science from becoming a narrow specialty, freeing it from a narrow functionalism and permitting a "structural analysis" suited to the positive, social, and intentional position that science has gained in society.[21]

The second theoretic orientation does concern itself with the social status of science—that is, the socialization and absorption of science into the social and cultural structure, and the dialectical relationship between science and the structure of society and its level of awareness. The research deriving from this approach includes a variety of structural analyses, whose categories are defined in terms other than those of the system and its requirements. Because these themes are linked to historical developments in Italy and to other substantive concerns, they are discussed in the following section.

THE ANALYSIS OF SCIENCE AND TECHNOLOGY: BASIC THEMES

In the early 1960s, Pagani (1960), starting from the problems of "integration" of theory and research, defined the relationship between social science and social policy. Thus the problem of integration became one of thought-action relations, and interest concentrated on the political nature of science, especially its nonneutrality. This was not just an ideological affirmation but a peculiar characteristic of the social status of science deriving from its socialization.[22] Science was examined in terms of its rationality, *Wertfreiheit*, vocation, and ethical responsibilities. (For a description of how scientific objectivity is inherent in the scientific community, see Phillips, 1976.)

Ferrarotti (1965) saw an indication of the "decline of reason" in the "rending" contradictions of these terms. Following Weber's ethos of values, Leonardi (1960) discussed the ideology of sociology in terms of the sociology of ideology and examined the ends and means of social planning. The Marcusian idealistic rejection of science of the latter 1960s, involving a radical critique of Weber, was taken up by the student-protest movement. Among sociologists it was Marletti (1970) who pointed out the continuity of the relations between science and social practice, between theory and empirical research in the "practice of research"; and this led him to examine the rebirth and development of social science after World War II in a study which really falls within the sociology of knowledge.

During the 1960s, Weberian and Parsonsian thinking had caused sociology to be seen as a means by which the industrial society would understand itself. Although Weber and Parsons have lost ground, a sociological school of "strategic thought" has emerged, employing the theory of games, decision theory, general systems theory, cybernetic models, and so forth. They promise that the "scientific society" will find a means of self-regulation through its direction-control system, extended by analogy to social structures and to the sciences of man in society. Thus the conscious structures in society—the awareness, participation, and consent of man and social groups—will become homeostatic, cybernetic, and informative processes. Gallino (1968, 1972a, 1972b), studying the sociology of industry, economy, and education, has repeatedly theorized about the "homologous" person—that is, one in harmony with the industrial system, and tries to find a way out of the dilemma created by this system with its contradictory needs for the "adaptable," the "creative," and the "innovative" man. A long-time student of technology in all its aspects, he attempts in his most recent work to unify the "total strategies" approaches, especially those inspired by new techniques of information, with the democratic method in industry and in society in general.

Acquaviva (1971) has pointed out the growing importance of sociology in "universal planning" which, he says, has come about because the new social status of science changes the relationship between "labor produced" and "labor thought." Acquaviva maintains that science, as a "critical revolutionary way of thinking," conditions social change. Human projects, participation, and conscious structures will be brought into harmony by "homeostatic," "cybernetic" models, along with the self-regulation of the "universal system" (see Simone, 1972).

The idea of "consent" is a reminder to the sociologist of science that Marx and Comte, though aware that science in theory and in practice could "correct" itself, conditioned their ideas of the social status of science by their conceptions of its historical role and its socialization. This socialization determined the "culturalization" of science; according to Comte it would cure the ills produced by the division of labor and the consequences of specialization in science. Ferrarotti (1959, 1972), critical of the "total strategies" approach and aware of the historical dimension of social science, has tried to create an "alternative sociology." Recently he has demonstrated that the social status achieved by science is a "directly productive force" insofar as science is increasingly being taken out of private hands.

Barbano (1967, 1970a, 1970b, 1971a, 1971b) has examined the origins of sociological thought through research into nonconventional sources of social science. He has studied the causes of the historical role and the socialization of science in its origins, as well as the industrial "revolution" and "culture."

At this point, we must cite some of the factors that have impeded the development of the sociology of science in Italy. First, real work in the general history of science has developed late, only within the last decade or so.[23] Second, the false dilemma of the "two cultures" has had to be overcome; it is understandable that this problem should have lasted longer in Italy than in other countries.[24] Third, the sociology of knowledge must go through the phase when its main interest is in ideology and the superstructural aspects of the formation of thought and conscious structures.

Izzo (1970) has examined the reasons for the "boom" and subsequent crisis in the sociology of knowledge. His study is based on the student-protest movement within the social and educational structures of science, and he emphasizes that both "historical role" and social "quality" in the formation of thought are not sufficiently appreciated.[25] Among Italian sociologists, Statera (1967a, 1967b, 1976) has best understood certain problems of sociological knowledge in relation to the sociology of scientific knowledge. Thus he has contributed notably to promoting the sociology of science in Italy.[26]

We leave the subject of the positive historical role of science to discuss its dialectical structure. The contradictions in the "analogous system" and the development of science and technology in the USSR; the lessons of the technical and scientific revolution in countries like Czechoslovakia and Hungary; the student-protest movements of 1968–70; and the new forces of "revisionism" have stimulated among Marxists an increasing interest in scientific problems. Renouncing the Marcusian idealistic and subjective rejection of science, they have reopened the debate on the relationship between science and materialism and historical dialectical materialism, and have begun to show renewed interest in the history of science. Geymonat and his group have inspired an interest, relatively new in Italy, in the historical role of science and the history of scientific thought.[27]

Other interests which involve dialectical structural analysis more specifically include studies of the relationship between Marxism and technological progress;[28] the problem of technicians, researchers, and scientific intellectuals with regard to their collective activity and the division of labor;[29] and the use of science.[30]

A characteristic dynamic of the social status of science in the advanced industrial countries is the fact that the institutions in which science is "produced" and "transmitted," or "applied" and "used," have become battlegrounds for the interaction of social conflicts as well as political and economic conflict; universities, research centers, hospitals, and psychiatric institutions. The institutionalization of science, so dear to functional analysis, is criticized along with the economics of curative medicine and the lack of public funds available for preventive medicine. Bureaucratic inefficiency and blindness in the field of medicine and psychiatry are also criticized; and the false scientific objectivity which depersonalizes both patient and illness is demystified.[31] With regard to the environment, many scholars have asked whether the problem of the urban industrial environment is not becoming an excuse for industrialization to enter the field of pollution as well.[32]

We now move from the subject of the dialectical structure of science to discuss its social structure. The availability of data on the composition, organization, and interaction of the world of researchers, scientists, technicians, and scientific intellectuals now permits the positive structure of science in Italy to be analyzed concretely, where the old image of the individualistic and ideological intellectual did not offer the same possibilities for the sociology of knowledge.[33] It must be admitted, however, that in Italy, contradictory parameters are still being used to analyze the personnel and the organization of research institutions. For example, the continuing confusion of "research" and university "teaching" means that the parameters for the number of researchers and research institutions are not accurate. The question has been raised: "What constitutes a researcher?"[34]

Other subjects of research have included the relationship between economic planning and research planning; and the relationship between scientific-technological development and the so-called post-industrial "services society" with regard to the social interaction of science and the social structure. The concept of a "services society" implies an expansion of the tertiary, and the emergence of a quaternary, sector. The relations between state and "technostructure" have also been studied.[35] Much attention has been increasingly given to new techniques of information in the production and administration of justice, and to the consequences of computerization and the public control of information, which involve rationalizing organization on the one hand and the protection of personal liberties on the other.[36]

The public image of science in Italy has been shaped by an emphasis on technological progress; the dispute over the technological gap; the space exploits and rivalry between the United States and the USSR; and, more recently, by anxiety over pollution of the air, of water, and of the land. Although many have asked, "Why the rush to the moon?" the space exploits, as well as anxiety about pollution, have enhanced the status of scientists, technicians, and researchers, and have augmented the concept of the organization of science and its *modus operandi* as research and development. Finally, the public image of science is enhanced by forecasts and prospects for the future. The revival of esoteric and traditional sciences, however, are evidence of a decline in this favorable public image.

ALTHOUGH STILL VERY FAR from the classical theoretical coordinates of scientific development as they emerged from the industrial and scientific revolutions of the nineteenth and twentieth centuries, Italy since World War II has undergone a vast socialization of science. This process has affected both institutions and the role and activity of scientists, researchers, and intellectuals; it has affected both the nature of the impact of scientific-technological development on society and the social conditioning of scientific thought.

By studying the socialization of scientific activity, the sociology of science may succeed in joining the classical coordinates—the scientific world view and modes of thought—to the new ones. It is in labor and its organization, man's time, and his social formations that the new coordinates find their expression; and it is there that the reciprocity of science and the social structure may be found. If it is true (as I believe it is) that the total-strategies approaches, with their emphasis on the scientific society, represent a "superstructural" method[37] in the sociology of science, the structural analysis of science will be best equipped to bridge the gap between the classical and the new "coordinates" of the relationship between science and society. If this analysis is called the "sociology" of science, the term holds for the division of labor, and even more so for the historical role of science and its past and present social status.

NOTES

[1]   The first person to talk about the "techniques de corp" was Marcel Mauss, the French cultural anthropologist who worked with Durkheim. For social techniques, see K. Mannheim (1935).

[2]   Merton (1959) pointed out that the founders of sociology worked on problems pertaining to the "intellectual legitimacy" of the discipline, while their successors sought to establish its "institutional legitimacy" or autonomy, above all in the universities.

[3]   Friedrichs (1970) talks about a "Marxist analogue" with reference to Marxist social science. We use the term "analogous systems" in a less paradigmatic sense, one that is historically closer to the scientific and technological reality of the socialist countries.

[4]   We agree with Merton's (1959) statement that "until very recently the reciprocity of these relations has received uneven attention, the impact of science upon society eliciting much notice, and the impact of society upon science little." This view relates the theme of theory-research to the problem of the relationship between scientific knowledge and social practice and takes into account historical theses about the development of machinism; see Schuhl (1938). It also takes into account the way in which historically determined socialist societies have appropriated the science of technology and industrialization, as well as past and current debates on the subject in international and intranational socialist discussion.

[5] Typical aspects of the *positive* historical role of science are its cumulative growth; its structure and "paradigmatic" dynamic; its specialization; and its incorporation into the machine society and fixed capital. Typical aspects of the *structural* role of science in society are the social consequences of technical and scientific development, the social conditioning of scientific thought, and the impact of the "scientific society" on the relationship between consciousness and society. Aspects of the *intentional* role include the connection between scientific discovery and the intention of scientists to get the results which they do in fact produce; the nonneutrality of science; the fact that evaluations can be made of it as the activity of individuals and groups; the possibility of an alternative "use" for science; and the fact that economic groupings have taken it over.

[6] Comte's own concept of science implied the notions of historic role and socialization and their reciprocal relationship. Meyerson (1921:357, 369), who correctly criticizes Comte's "science purement legale," does point out that Comte's concept of science, as Bacon's, stressed the importance of experience, and that Comte must be credited with having insisted on the importance of studying the history of science. Here we should recall a now forgotten work by one of the most able sociologists at the turn of the century when sociology was just beginning in Italy: A. Groppali's *La genesi sociale del fenomeno scientifico: Introduzione a una storia critica della contemporanea*, Torino, 1899. In this work, the relationship between social science and the history of science plays a major part.

[7] "Italy is a land of contradictions, as even the least attentive visitor will notice when he travels through this country where antiquity, the Renaissance and the second half of the twentieth century live peacefully together." This statement was made by Professor Harvey Brooks, Harvard University, who directed a group doing research on scientific policy in Italy under the auspices of O.C.S.E.

[8] See Dorfles (1967, 1968, 1970a, 1970b); Lux (1971); Di Nallo (1970).

[9] See Barbano (1952). For a more official view see the journal *Civilta dello macchine*.

[10] Daily newspapers include: *Il Giorno* and *Il Corriere della Sera* published in Milan, and *La Stampa* in Turin. *Scientific American* has for the last five years published an Italian edition called *Le Scienze* which always opens with an article entitled "Science and Society." Mondadori has published a revised Italian edition of the monumental *Enciclopedia della Scienza e della Tecnica*. Einaudi started publishing a series of works on science and the philosophy of science which is now being published by Borighieri.

[11] Some of the more important studies and conclusions concerning the problems of the gap and the sociological aspects of development are: Albonetti (1967); Zagnari (1968); Cacace and Gardin (1968); C.E.N.S.I.S. (1966a); Santuccio (1971); Cotta (1968); Frey et al. (1971); Palmerio (1968); Silj (1968); and Valli (1970).

[12] The National Research Committee is the largest public body in Italy concerned with scientific and technological research. Originally confining its con-

cerns to the natural sciences, it has gradually become interested in "scientific research" in its broad sense and has established special commissions to deal with the social sciences, history, etc. It grants scholarships, awards contracts for research, and operates research centers. Its policy for distributing funds which the government allocates to it for the organization and division of labor in scientific matters is ambivalent. See Ministry for the Coordination of Scientific Research (1970, 1971) and Ministero degli Esteri (1972).

13   See Baracca and Bergia (1972); Quaranta (1965, 1966); Albonetti (1969); Avveduto and Freeman (1972); C.E.N.S.I.S. (1966b); Cortelessa (1971); Costa et al. (1961); Martinoli (1967–68); Martinoli and De Rita (1968); O.C.S.E. (1972); O.E.C.D. (1968); Pacilio and Iorio (1972); Sacco (1968).

14   See A.A.V.V. (1972); Quaranta and Zanarini (1972); Dinelli (1967); C.G.I. (1971). See also, F.A.S.T. (1968, 1969); Bianco (1969); Prodi (1971); Ugolini (1971); Zanetti and Bratina (1971).

15   The structure of this dualism can be seen in the different generations of Italian entrepreneurs. See Barbano (1972) which introduces the study carried out by the Centro di Ricerca della Scuola di Formazione Sociale di Genova for the Central Committee of New Groups in Industry.

16   With regard to this subject, see the critical dichotomy of Rapoport (1964). Literature on the sociology of communications also broached the subject of so-called "strategic thought," i.e., game theory, decision theory, and information theory. See, for example, Braga (1964, 1969, 1970). The theory of information and the general theory of systems have also attracted interest in Italy because of the new interest in science and the "universal strategies" that stimulated it. See, for example, Carlà (1967); Fano (1968); Morelli (1971). These developments in the field of cybernetics have also interested students of jurisprudence. With regard to planning and constitution, see Predieri (1963). Authors like Robert Dahl, David Easton, Gabriel Almond, and Karl Deutsch have had a much greater influence on recent Italian political science; for a discussion of their impact, see Urbani (1971).

As an alternative to the systems and functional implications of the total strategies approach, Italian scholars, rather than criticize systematic functionalism, have tended toward studies of the social consequences of science, e.g., of the impact of new technology on the administration and organization of industry, etc. See Bagnasco (1970). A year earlier the same review, *Ratio*, carried the papers of a round table held in Spring 1969, in Turin on "Organization and Economic Development in Italy," with contributions by the Sociology Group of C.E.R.I.S., Barbano, Gallino, Castronovo, and Bonazzi. See also Merton (1961). An interesting document on planning strategy at the political system level has been issued by the Budget and Economic Planning Ministry (1969). See also Pacini (1969); Valli (1970); Morandi (1969); Ruffolo (1968).

17   The fact that Comte's philosophy of history and its basic component, the famous "three stages law," are now outdated should not permit us to underestimate the theoretical importance of his "coordinates." The conditions which impede or permit the birth of a scientific movement, or takeoff of scientific

development, are just those which favor the reemergence of these coordinates. See, for example, Feuer (1963), who discusses the failure of a scientific movement to develop in China. Schuhl's and Koyre's theses on the scientific knowledge-practical experience coordinate may in some way intersect with the theology-science coordinate; see Needham (1956). Comte's "coordinates," though based more on intuition than research data, are also a valuable prelude to the "variables" studied by Weber and Troeltsch in their analyses of the relationship between religion and economy. Moreover, the "structural reciprocity between religion, economy, technology, war, individual and social advantages and science" was long ago made the subject of empirical analysis by Merton ([1938] 1975). For an analysis of the question "why were machines not used before 1800?" we may cite the old but valuable work by Lombroso (1931).

[18]   We assume that the concept of "growing interdependence" is the same as what Karl Mannheim calls the principle of "interdependence growing" in his *Man and Society in an Age of Reconstruction* (1935). It refers to the functional interdependence of parts in the industrial society system, and the irrational fragility which appears in such a system when it suffers the shocks of growing interdependence.

[19]   See Johnas (1972) on the attempt to transplant to Italy the structural theory of functionalism. Johnas does not distinguish the structural analysis of functions from the holistic version of functional-structural theory in Parsons's analysis. See Barbano (1968) which is based on Merton's criticism of this theory.

[20]   Interest in the structural aspects of science, in its historicity and socialization, may lead Marxist scholars to ask of the history of science what the sociology of science often grants when not considered simply an "outsider science" (see n. 37 below). Most texts in the history of science are surprisingly lacking in data, even simple documentation, about the evaluation of institutions and the organization of research in general. "More attention is usually paid to either the evolution of conceptual structures . . . or the history of the scientific product. In both cases, the underrating of institutional aspects has meant neglect of the concrete evolution of material mechanisms in the context of which the process of acquiring knowledge and the general process of interaction between the productive forces of science and economic forces are developed and synthesized" (Schiavuta, 1971:318).

[21]   There are many connections between "middle range" theories and structural analysis. In this context we have characterized structural analysis according to the determination of the categories which are defined in terms other than those merely of the system and its requirements. "Middle range theories" are not merely "operational" rejections of total comprehensiveness. The possible antecedents of middle range theories, summarized by Merton (1968), ranging from Plato through Bacon, John Stuart Mill, Lewis, Mannheim, Löwe, and Marshall, demonstrate this. Mannheim (1935), who used the idea of the *principia media* to criticize conventional empirical generalizations and historically determined concepts, said that his use of the *principia media* was similar to Mill's use of *axiomata media*: the *System of Logic* which he derives from Ba-

con. Merton (1968) broadened the discussion of middle range theories by examining the literature that has developed on the subject including that of Soviet scholars. One can study the middle range in terms of structural analysis and recognize that it represents, not a refusal to seek comprehensiveness, but rather the classic function of the *principia media*, the positive criticizing of empirical generalizations and abstract universalizing concepts. And one of these universalizing concepts must surely be the concept of "system."

[22] Pagani (1960, 1964).

[23] Bulferetti (1970a, 1970b); Geymonat (1954); Rossi (1971). The group directed by Geymonat produced *Storia del pensiero filosofico e scientifico* in six volumes, Milan, 1970–72. Translations of Koyré's and Kuhn's works, published by Einaudi, Turin, and the series on the history of science published by Feltinelli, Milan, are further evidence of increased interest in the history of science.

[24] See Snow (1965). For the debate on the two cultures in Italy, see *La cultura dimezzata*, Milan, 1965.

[25] See Izzo (1971). For sociology of science, see Izzo (1966, 1968, 1970).

[26] See also Statera (1970, 1972).

[27] Timpanaro (1970); Aloisi and Vaccatello (1967). (The work by Timpanaro is a series of previously published essays to which the works quoted below refer.) Prestipino (1961); Fiorani (1967); Gianquinto (1971); Semerari (1972); Cera (1972).

[28] Donolo (1970); De Feo (1961); Cerroni (1970); Conti (1969); De Palma (1971); Perna (1968); Prato (1970); Sereni (1968).

[29] Ciafaloni (1968a, 1968b, 1969, 1972); Maestro (1972); Bolzani (1969); Bologna and Ciafaloni (1969); Dina (1969); Leonardi (1957); Salvati and Beccalli (1970); Bergia and Salvini (1971).

[30] Badaloni (1961); Conti (1969); Giannantoni (1968); Guiducci (1970a, 1970b); Guiducci et al. (1971); Panzieri (1965); Savelli (1971); Schiavuta (1970, 1971); Zorzoli (1967, 1969).

[31] We cannot give a bibliography here of particular fields or institutions in which science in Italy has produced the interaction of conflict, and which brought about the 1967–68 protest movement and the rejection of science as a function and science as an institution. Nevertheless we should like to draw attention to the very important *Lettera ad una professoressa* by the *Scuola di Barbiana*, and also the *Movimento Studentesco's Documenti della rivolta universitaria*; A.A.V.V. (1968); the Documents of Congress *Scuola, sviluppo capitalistico, alternativa operaia e studentesca*, Rome, 23–24 May 1970, printed by *Il Manifesto*, vol. 1, Rome, 1970 with a bibliography. Gilli's (1971) work is interesting on the subject of science as a function and institution. The student-protest movement has violently criticized the functionalism of the total institutions and also their authoritarianism (Viale, 1968). Also on the subject of the protest movement and science, see Alberoni (1968, 1969) and Barbano (1969c).

[32] Paccino (1972). See also A.A.V.V. (1971).

[33] The principal names in sociology of science in the last decade have been

Corradini, Izzo, Marletti, Spinella, and Tufari. On the sociology of intellectuals, see Izzo (1968–69); Ferretti (1970); Piccone Stella (1972); Prandstraller (1968, 1972).

[34]   Since 1964 more than a hundred answers have been published on the question "What constitutes a researcher?" The complete list of questions was as follows: What is a researcher? What must his brain be like? What must his capacity be? Must he have more than one ability or quality? What must we expect from him? What must his spiritual and human qualities be? In what way must he be special, i.e., different from other people? What is his position in society and in relation to what? See also Farinelli (1965).

[35]   Barbano (1969a, 1969b); Bonanni (1971); Frosini (1967); Losano (1969); Momigliano (1970); Morosini (1970); Ruffolo (1971); Zampetti and Ipscevich (1972).

[36]   Proceedings of the International Seminar on the Social and Political Implications of Scientific and Technological Innovation in the Information Sector, September 1971, Couramyeur. See Rositi and Tosi (1971).

[37]   This does not restrict the concept of "superstructure" and "division of labor" to an "insider-outsider doctrine" discussed by Merton (1972). For an interesting document on the internal contradictions in the superstructure of development and the strategies, see System Dynamics Group (1972).

NOTE: I offer my sincerest thanks to the following people who have helped me enormously with information, documentation, and advice: S. S. Acquaviva, P. Almondo, S. Avveduto, A. Baracca, P. Bisogno, D. Bratina, L. Bulferetti, V. Caglioti, A. Canino, A. Casiccia, P. Delsedime, V. Dore, F. Ferrarotti, L. Fischer, M. Follis, L. Gallino, A. Guala, A. Izzo, G. Martionoli, G. Prodi, E. Rescigno di Nallo, M. Santuccio, G. Statera, D. Barbero, and S. Bergio. The English translation is by Gerald Devlin for whose cooperation the author is deeply grateful.

References

A.A.V.V.
    1962   *Sociologi e centri di potere in Italia.* Bari.
    1963   *Mutamenti della struttura sociale.* Torino.
    1964   *La formazione del personale nell'azienda industriale.* Firenze.
    1966   *L'addestramento e la formazione professionale nelle aziende della Liguria.* Genova.
    1968   *Università, L'ipotesi rivoluzionaria.* Padova.
    1971   *Problemi dell'ecologia.* Roma.
    1972   "La ricerca scientifica e tecnologica." *Le Scienze,* V, 52:4–19.
ACQUAVIVA, S. S.
    1958   *Automazione e nuova classe.* Bologna.
    1971   *Una scommessa sul futuro: Sociologie e programmazione globale.* Milano.

ALBERONI, F.
1968 *Statu nascenti*. Bologna.
1969 *Classi e generazioni*. Bologna.

ALBONETTI, A.
1967 *Divario tecnologico, ricerca scientifica e produttività in Europe e negli Stati Uniti*. Milano.
1969 "La politica della ricerca in Italia negli anni settanta." *Notiziario CNEN* (June):72.

ALOISI, M., AND M. VACCATELLO
1967 "Il dibattito sul materialismo." *Quaderni Piacentini*, VI, 32 (October):107–15.

AMMASSARI, P.
1964 "Ideologia e sociologia nell' Unione Sovietica." *Russegna Italiana di Sociologia*, V, 50 (January–March):69–117.

AVVEDUTO, S.
1968 *La società scientifica*. Milano.

AVVEDUTO, S., AND CH. FREEMAN
1972 *Rapporto Iulla scienza*. Milano.

BADALONI, N.
1961 "La sottomissione del lavoro e della scienze nel Capitale." *Critica Marxista*, VII, 4–5 (July–October):47–55.

BAGNASCO, A.
1970 "Razionalità tecnica e razionalità pragmatica: considerazioni sul problema della organizzazione del lavoro." *Ratio* 5 (January–June):593–627.

BALBO, L.; G. CHIARETTI; AND G. MASSIRONI
1975 *L'inferma scienza*. Bologna.

BARACCA, A., AND S. BERGIA
1972 "Considerazioni critiche sulle scelte e sul metodo della ricerca attuale in fisica delle alte energie." INFN/AE [National Institute for Nuclear Physics] (March 24):31.
1975 *La spirale delle alte energie*. Milano.

BARBANO, F.
1952 "Macchinismo e relazioni umane nell' impresa: il problema sociologico e le sue alternative." *Tecnica ed Organizzazione* (September/October):12–23.
1961 "I sociologi e le richieste del contesto sociale." *Bollettino delle ricerche sociali*, I, 2:99–103.
1967 "Sociologie negativa e sociologie positiva." *Sociologie*, I, 1:31–38.
1968 "Social Structure and Social Functions: The Emancipation of Structural Analysis in Sociology." *Inquiry* 2 (Spring):40–84.
1969a "Burocrazia, tecnocrazia e potere." *Ratio* 4:461–90.
1969b "Società tecnostruttura e potere." In Barbano, Bonacina, and Prini, *Società e tecnologia*, pp. 223–41. Roma.

1969c   "Contestazione, funzionalismo e rivoluzione, il punto di parteza giovanile e studentesco." *Studi de Sociologia* 4:311–66.

1970a   *Lineamenti di storia del pensiero sociologico: Le Origini.* Torino.

1970b   "La sociologia in Italia ieri ed oggi: con riflessioni sulla scienza sociale e il socialismo." In M. Viterbi, *Bibliografia della sociologia italiana 1945–1970,* pp. ix–lxii. Torino.

1971a   *Profilo critico di storia del pensiero sociologico.* Torino.

1971b   "La teorie sociologiche tra storicità e scienza." In R. K. Merton, *Teorie e struttura sociale.* (3d ed.). Pp. vii–xxxiv. Bologna.

1972   *Riflessioni in margine ad una indagine nell'area dell'imprenditorialità italiana.* Genova.

1975   *Struttura e classi sociali, gli studi e le ricerche, 1955–1975.* Torino.

BARBANO, F., AND C. MARLETTI

1960   "Rilievo del progresso tecnologico nella stampa sindacale." In *Atti del Convegno Internazionale di Studio sul Progresso tecnologico e la Società Italiana.* Milano.

BARBANO, F.; F. BONACINA; AND P. PRINI

1969   *Società e tecnologia.* Roma.

BARBER, B.

1956   "Sociology of Science: A Trend Report and Bibliography." *Current Sociology* 5.

BARTOLOMEIS, F. DE

1965   *Formazione tecnico-professionale e pedagogia dell'industria.* Milano.

BERGIA, S., AND G. SALVINI

1971   "Funzione culturale e sociale della ricerca scientifica." In *La Scienza nella società capitalistica.* Bari.

BERLINQUER, G.

1970   *Politica delle scienza.* Roma.

1974   *La ricerca scientifica e tecnologica.* Roma.

1975   *Per la scienza.* Bari.

BIANCO, LIBRO

1969   *Per una politica dell'innovazione scientifica e tecnica.* Milano.

BOLOGNA, S., AND F. CIAFALONI

1969   "I tecnici come produttori e come prodotto." *Quaderni Piacentini,* VIII, 39 (March):52–72.

BOLZANI, P.

1969   "I tecnici verso una coscienza di classe." *Quaderni Piacentini,* VIII, 39 (November):165–72.

BONANNI, M.

1971   "Scienza, industria e organizzazione militare in Italia." *Tempi Moderni,* XIII, 8 (Autumn):33–36.

BRAGA, G.

1964   *La rivoluzione tecnologica della comunicazione di massa.* Milano.

1969   *La comunicazione Sociale.* Torino.

1970   "Il 'sistema di comunicazione' come costrutto mediatore fra società e linguaggio." *Sociologia,* V, 2:17–50.

BUDGET AND ECONOMIC PLANNING MINISTRY
1969   *Progetto '80. Rapporto preliminare al programma economico nazionale, 1971–1975.* Roma.

BULFERETTI, L.
1970a   "Introduzione alle storiografia." In A.A.V.V., *Introduzione allo studio della storia*, vol. I, pp. 5–102. Milano.
1970b   *La scienza come storiografia.* Roma.

CACACE, N., AND P. GARDIN
1968   *Produttività e divario tecnico.* Milano.

CAGLIOTI, V.
1968   *Relazione sullo stato della ricerca e tecnologica in Italia.* Roma.
1970   *Relazione previsionale e programmatica per l'anno 1970.* Roma.

CARLÀ, M.
1967   *Cibernetica e teoria dell' informazione.* Roma.

C.E.N.S.I.S. (CENTER FOR STUDY OF SOCIAL INVESTMENTS)
1966a   *L'idea dello sviluppo nella letterature degli ultima 20 anni, Bibliografia ragionata.* Milano.
1966b   "La ricerca scientifica in Italia, III: La ricerca universitaria." *Quindicinale di Note e Commenti* 2, 16 (February 1):25.

CERA, G.
1972   "Il concetto di natura in Engels." *Aut-Aut* 129–30 (May–August):4–13.

CERRONI, U.
1970   *Tecnica e libertà.* Bari.

C.G.I.
1971   *La ricerca industriale in Italia, 1968–1970.* Roma.

CIAFALONI, F.
1968a   "Le corporazioni della scienza e la lotta nell' universita." *Quaderni Piacentini*, VII, 34 (August–October):79–90.
1968b   "Una corporazione della scienza: il LIGB di Napoli." *Quaderni Piacentini*, VIII, 38 (July):121–46.
1969   "Un collettivo del CNEN: Esperienze e prospettive di lotta nei centri di ricerca." *Quaderni Piacentini*, VIII, 39 (November):173–81.
1972   "Una fondazione per Agnelli." *Quaderni Piacentini*, XI, 46 (March):142–48.

C.N.R. (NATIONAL RESEARCH COMMITTEE)
1970   *Atti del seminario sulla organizzazione e sulla programmazione della ricerca.* Roma.

CONTI, L.
1969   "Il progresso scientifico-technologico in Marx e nel capitalismo maturo." *Critica Marxista*, VII, 4–5 (July–October):20–46.

CORTELESSA, G.
1961   "I lavoratori della ricerca." Documents of the PSI Conference on Scientific Policy and the Development of Society, April 22–23. Roma.

COSTA, M. CORDA; G. GHIARA; AND G. LUZZATO
    1961   "Ricerca e instruzione." Documents of the PSI Conference on Scientific Policy and the Development of Society, April 22–23. Roma.
COTTA, S.
    1968   La sfida tecnologica. Bologna.

DE FALCO, A.
    1968   Scienza e tecnologia in Italia. Padova.
DE FEO, N. M.
    1961   "Cibernetica e dialecttica sociale nella rivoluzione scientifico-tecnologica." Critica Marxista, VII, 4–5 (July–October):76–96.
DE PALMA, A.
    1971   Le macchine e l'industria da Smith a Marx. Torino.
DIENA, L.
    1960   Gli uomini e le masse. Torino.
DINA, A.
    1969   "Condizione del tecnico e condizione operaia nella fabbrica: dalla oggettività alla scelta politica." Classe I (June):89–134.
DI NALLO, E. R.
    1970   "Tecnomorfismo e progresso sociale." Sociologia IV (September 3):5–60.
DINELLI, D.
    1967   Introduzione alla ricerca industriale. Milano.
DONOLO, C.
    1970   "Progresso tecnico-scientifico e lotta di classe." Quaderni Piacentini, IX, 41 (July):42–49.
DORFLES, G.
    1967   Simbolo comunicazione consumo. Torino.
    1968   Artificio e natura. Torino.
    1970a   Le oscillazioni del gusto, L'arte d'oggi tra tecnocrazia e consumismo. Torino.
    1970b   Nuovi riti nuovi miti. Torino.

FANO, G.
    1968   Neopositivismo, analisi del linguaggio e cibernetica. Torino.
FARINELLI, U.
    1965   Il mestiere del ricercatore. Milano.
    1967   Atti del Convegno su I tecnici nella società italiano. Milano.
F.A.S.T. (FEDERATION OF SCIENTIFIC AND TECHNICAL ASSOCIATIONS)
    1968   Per una politica dell'innovazione scientifica e tecnica, Vol. I. Milano.
    1969   Per una politica dell'innovazione scientifica e tecnica, Vol. II. Milano.
FERRAROTTI, F.
    1959   La sociologica industriale in America ed in Europa. Torino.
    1961   "La ricerca sociale e l'industria in Europa." Bollettino della ricerche sociali, I, 2:184–208.
    1963   Macchina e Uomo nella società industriale. Torino.

1965 *Max Weber e il destino della ragione*. Bari.
1972 *Una sociologia alternativa*. Bari.
FERRETTI, G. C.
1970 *L'autocritica dell' intellettualle*. Padova.
FEUER, C. S.
1963 *The Scientific Intellectual*. New York.
FIORANI, E.
1967 *Friedrich Engels e il materialismo dialettico*. Milano.
FREY, L.; V. POSSENTI; V. PETRINI; G. POSSA; AND S. ZAGUINI
1971 *La misurazione del divario tecnologico, I*. Milano.
FRIEDRICHS, R. W.
1970 *A Sociology of Sociology*. New York.
FROSINI, V.
1967 *Cibernetica Dizitto e Società*. Milano.

GALLINO, L.
1962 *L'industria e i sociologi*. Milano.
1968 *Personalità ed industrializzazione*. Torino.
1972a "Le tecnologie dell'informazione in un' organizzazione aziendale democratica." *Quaderni di Sociologia*, 21, 2:138–77.
1972b "La crisi dell' organizzazione del lavoro." *Economia e Lavoro*, VI, 2–3 (May/June):341–52.
GALLINO, L., AND F. BARBANO
1960 "Commissioni interne e progresso tecnologico." In *Atti del Convegno Internazionale di Studio sue Progresso tecnologico e la Società Italiana*. Milano.
GEYMONAT, L.
1954 *Il pensiero scientifico*. Milano.
GIANNANTONI, G.
1968 "A proposito di ricerca scientifica." *Critica Marxista*, VI, no. 6 (November–December):179–82.
GIANQUINTO, A.
1971 *Critica dell' epistemologia*. Padova.
GILLI, A.
1971 *Come si fa una ricerca, guida alla ricerca sociale per non specialist*. Milano.
GUIDUCCI, R.
1970a *Marx dopo Marx*. Milano.
1970b "La contestazione e una rivoluzione terziaria." *Tempi Moderni*, XII, 1 (Winter):50–56.
GUIDUCCI, R.; I. MOSCATI; AND A. GUIDUCCI
1971 "Sull' autocollocazione critica degli intellettuali e dei neocapitalismo." *Tempi Moderni*, XIII, 5 (Winter):119–28.

I.R.E.S. (INSTITUTE FOR ECONOMIC AND SOCIAL RESEARCH)
1962 *Istruzione professionale e mansioni lavorative*. Milano.

ISTITUTO GRAMSCI
1973   *Scienza ed organizzazione del lavoro.* Roma.
IZZO, A.
1966   *Sociologia della conoscenza.* Roma.
1968   "Un tentativo difficile." Introduction to D. Martindale, *Tipologia e storia della teoria sociologica.* Bologna.
1968/1969   "La sociologia degli intellettuali: introduzione al problema." *La critica sociologica* 8 (Winter):6–32.
1970   *Il condizionamento sociale del pensiero: Antologia di scritti sulla sociologia della conoscenza.* Torino.
1971   "The Present 'Boom' and the Crisis of the Sociology of Knowledge." *International Journal of Contemporary Sociology* 8 (April):95–111.

JOHNAS, F.
1972   *Geschichte der soziologie.* A. M. Pozzan; M. Bernardoni; and V. Calvani, trans. *Storia della Sociologia.* Bari.

LABINI, P. SYLOS
1974   *Saggio sulla classi sociali.* Bari.
LEONARDI, F.
1960   "Sociologia della conoscenza e pianificazione sociale: Note su K. Mannheim." *Rassegna Italiana di Sociologia,* I, 2 (April–June).
LEONARDI, S.
1957   *Progresso tecnico e rapporti di lavoro.* Milano.
LOMBROSO, GINA
1931   *Le tragedie del progresso.* Capolago.
LOSANO, M. G.
1969   *Giuscibernetica macchine e modelli cibernetici nel diritto.* Torino.
LUX, S.
1971   *Arte, società e tecnica.* Assisi-Roma.

MAESTRO, M.
1972   "Lavoro professionale, formazione culturale e orientamento politico dei lavoratori scientifici." In Nicola Badaloni (ed.), *Il Marxismo italiano negli anni sessanta e la formazione teorico-politica delle nuovo generazioni,* pp. 563–75. Roma.
MANNHEIM, KARL
1935   *Mensch und Gesellschaft im Zeitalter des Umbaus.* A. Devizzi, trans. Milano, 1959.
MARLETTI, C.
1970   *Sviluppo e struttura.* Roma.
MARTINOLI, G.
1961   "Trasformazioni nell'organizzazione aziendale in funzione del progresso tecnologico." In *Atti de Convegno sul Progresso tecnologico,* pp. 9–39. Bologna.

1964 *La Formazione sul lavoro*. Bari.
1965 "Evoluzione tecnologica e aspirazioni umane in Italia nell'ultimo ventennio." *Economia e Storia* 3:358–91.
1967/1968 "Ricerca ed insegnamento nella Universita." *Studi Sassaresi*, ser. III:519–42.

MARTINOLI, G., AND G. DE RITA
1968 "Le scelte di politica scientifica in una logica di programmazione." Presented to C.N.R. Seminar on Organization and Planning, November. Pugnochiuso.

MERTON, ROBERT K.
[1938] 1975 *Scienza, technologia e società nell'Inghilterra del XVII secolo*. Milano: Franco Angelo Editore.
1949 "The Role of Applied Social Science in the Formation of Policy." *Philosophy of Science* 16:161–81.
1959 "Social Conflict over Styles of Sociological Work." In *Transactions of the Fourth World Congress of Sociology*, vol. 3.
1961 "Limited Perspectives of Staff Specialists." In R. Dubin (ed.), *Human Relations Administration*. Englewood Cliffs, N.J.: Prentice-Hall.
1968 *Social Theory and Social Structure*. (Rev. and enl. ed.). New York: Free Press.
1970 *Science, Technology and Society in Seventeenth-Century England*. New York: Harper and Row; Howard Fertig, Inc.
1972 "Insiders and Outsiders: A Chapter in the Sociology of Knowledge." *American Journal of Sociology* 78, 1 (July):9–47.

MEYERSON, E.
1921 *De L'explication dans les sciences*. Paris.

MINISTERO DEGLI ESTERI
1972 *La cooperazione culturale, scientifica e tecnica*. Città di Castello.

MINISTRY FOR THE COORDINATION OF SCIENTIFIC RESEARCH
1970 *Idee ed appunta per una politica della ricerca scientifica e tecnologica in Italia*. Torino.
1971 *Politica della ricerca scientifica e tecnologica*. 8 vols. Roma.

MOMIGLIANO, E.
1970 "Tecnostruttura e nuovo stato industriale: demande a Galbraith." *Tempi Moderni*, XII, 2 (Spring):28–32.

MORANDI, L.
1969 *Le difficili intese politica e tecnologia a confronto*. Milano.

MORELLI, M.
1971 *Il centro electronico*. Milano.

MOROSINI, G.
1970 "Ideologia e pratica della tecnocrazia pubblica." *Classe* 3 (November):41–71.

NEEDHAM, J.
1956 *Science and Civilization in China*. Cambridge.

O.E.C.D. (Organization for Economic Cooperation and Development)
    1968   *Politiques Nationales de la science: Italia*. Paris.
    1972   *La Politica della scienza e dell' istruzione in Italia*. Roma.

Paccino, D.
    1972   *L'imbroglio ecologico, l'ideologia della natura*. Torino.
Pacilio, M., and M. Iorio
    1972   *Politica e scienze*. Roma.
Pacini, M.
    1969   *Programmazione e società. Le istituzioni e la programmazione economica in Italia negli anni 1970*. Milano.
Pagani, A.
    1960   "Scienza sociale e politica sociale." In A. Pagani (ed.), *Antologia de Scienze Sociali*, pp. 465–90. Bologna.
    1964   *Responsibilità del sociologo*. Milano.
Palmerio, G.
    1968   *Il ruolo del progresso tecnico nello sviluppo economico italiano*. Milano.
Panzieri, R.
    1965   "Uso socialista della inchiesta operaia." *Quaderni Rossi* 5 (April):67–76.
Perna, E.
    1968   "Progresso tecnologica e sviluppo della democrazia." *Critica Marxista*, VI, 6 (November/December):24–34.
Phillips, Derek L.
    1976   "Le comunità scientifiche come garanzia sociale dell'oggettività della conoscenza." *Problemi* 45:23–40.
Piccone Stella, S.
    1972   *Intellettuali e capitale nella società italiana del dopoguerra*. Bari.
Pizzorno, A.
    1960   *Comunità e razionalizzazione*. Torino.
Prandstraller, G. P.
    1968   *L'intellettuale tecnico*. Milano.
    1972   *L'intellettuale tecnico ed altr saggi*. Milano.
Prato, R.
    1970   "Uso capitalistico ed uso alternativo della macchina." *Classe* 4 (June):143–78.
Predieri, A.
    1963   *Pianificazione e costituzione*. Milano.
Prestipino, G.
    1961   "La disputa filosofica sulla scienza della natura." *Critica Marxista*, VII, 4–5 (July–October):56–57.
Preti, G.
    1975   *Storia del pensiero scientifico*. Milano.
Price, D. J. de Solla
    1963   *Little Science, Big Science*. R. Rambelli, trans. Milano.

PRODI, R.
1971 *La diffusione delle innovazioni nell'industria italiana*. Bologna.

QUARANTA, A. ALBERIGHI
1965 "Un ministero per la ricerca scientifica?" *Il Mulino* (November): 1061–66.
1966 "La Formazione dei ricercatori nella università." Documents of the 6th Congress of Biological and Moral Sciences. Roma.

QUARANTA, A. ALBERIGHI, AND G. ZANARINI
1972 *La gestione della ricerca: Innovazione e ricerca nell' impresa*. Torino: Foundazione Agnelli.

RAPOPORT, A.
1964 *Strategy and Conscience*. New York.

ROSITI, F., AND A. TOSI
1971 "L'alternativa pubblico-privato in un contesto urbano." *Studi di Sociologica* IX: 3–50.

ROSSI, P.
1971 *Aspetti della rivoluzione scientifica*. Napoli.

RUFFOLO, G.
1968 *Ricerca scientifica e programmazione economica*. Roma: Centro Studi e Piani Economici.
1971 "L'Europa tra tecno-struttura ed autogestione." *Tempi Moderni*, XIV, 10 (Spring): 82–93.

SACCO, G.
1968 *Il mezzogiorno nello politica scientifica*. Milano.

SALVATI, M., AND B. BECCALLI
1970 "Divisione del lavoro, capitalismo socialismo, utopia." *Quaderni Piacentini*, IX, 40 (April): 18–52.

SANTUCCIO, M.
1971 "Influenza della istituzionalizzazione della scienza e della tecnica sullo sviluppo dell'idea di progresso." *Sociologia* 2 (May): 169–76.

SAVELLI, R.
1971 "Tempo libero e lotta di classe." *Classe* (June 4): 245–76.

SCHIAVUTA, E.
1970 "Sul rapporto ricerca-produzione." *Contropiano* I: 129–39.
1971 "Scienza, Innovazione ciclo: problemi di prospettiva storica." *Contropiano* 2: 313–39.

SCHUHL, P. M.
1938 *Machinisme et Philosophie*. Paris.

SEMERARI, G.
1972 "Materialismo e scienze naturali." *Aut-Aut* 129–30 (May–August): 104–37.

SERENI, E.
1968 "Rivoluzione scientifico-tecnologica e movimento studentesco." *Critica Marxista* VI (November/December): 3–93.

SILJ, S.
   1968   *Il Mercato dei Cervelli*. Milano.
SILVESTRI, M.
   1968   *Il costra della menzogna: Italia Nucleare, 1945–1968*. Torino.
SIMONE, O. A.
   1972   "Il modello di Acquaviva per il combiamento sociale." *Sociologia*, VI,
          3:181–92.
SNOW, C. P.
   1965   *The Two Cultures and A Second Look*. Cambridge: Cambridge Uni-
          versity Press.
SOCIETÀ ITALIANA DE FISICA
   1971   *La Scienza nella società capitalistica*. Bari.
STATERA, G.
   1967a "La sociologia delle scienze in R. K. Merton." *La critica sociologica*
          3.
   1967b *Logica, Linguaggio e sociologia*. Torino.
   1970   *La conoscenza sociologica*. Roma.
   1972   "'Truth' and 'Objectivity': Two socially conditioned metaphysical as-
          sumptions in science." Paper presented to Conference of Research
          Committee on Sociology of Science, I.S.A. London.
   1976   "Origini e sviluppi della sociologia della scienza." *La critica socio-
          logica* 38:41–66.
SYSTEM DYNAMICS GROUP
   1972   "I limiti dello sviluppo." Report to M.I.T. on the Club of Rome's
          Project on the Dilemmas of Mankind. Milano.

TIMPANARO, S.
   1970   *Sul materialismo*. Pisa.
TREBESCHI, A.
   1975   *Lineamenti di storia del pensiero scientifico*. Roma.

UGOLINI, P. (ED.)
   1971   *La nostra cultura e la qualità della vita*. Torino: Fondazione Agnelli.
URBANI, G.
   1971   *L'analisi del sistema politico*. Bologna.

VALLI, V.
   1970   *Programmazione e sindacati in Italia*. Milano.
VIALE, F.
   1968   "Contro l'università." *Quaderni Piacentini*, VII, 33 (February):2–28.

ZAGNARI, M.
   1968   *La sfida europea*. Milano.
ZAMPETTI, E., AND G. IPSCEVICH
   1972   *Burocrazia, mezze maniche, computer*. Milano.

ZANETTI, G., AND D. BRATINA
1971 *L'impresa innovativa, esperienze nell' industria italiana*. Torino.
ZORZOLI, G. B.
1967 "Prefazione." In D. J. de Solla Price, *Sociologia della creativita scientifica*, pp. 5–23. Milano.
1969 *Le dimensioni del potere*. Milano.
1970 *La ricerca scientifica in Italia*. Milano.

THE SOCIOLOGY OF SCIENCE IN

THE

USSR

Gennady M. Dobrov

SCIENCE POLICY, the policy of the State concerning Research and Development, occupies a central place among today's social problems. This problem attracts the increasing attention of scientists in different countries and various disciplines. Soviet scholars strive to form a system of scientific knowledge which would provide a theoretical foundation for the State organization and management of science.

In the USSR, that branch of science has been called "*naukovedniye.*" The Russian term "*naukovedniye*" was adopted as a name for this branch of science in 1966 at the Soviet-Polish symposium in Lvov. It is an equivalent of the word "*naukoznawstwo,*" formerly used in Poland and the Ukraine; correspondingly, "science of science" in English. It is also an equivalent to "science policy studies" adopted in 1972 by the International Commission on Science Policy Studies of the International Union of History and Philosophy of Science. Science policy studies is a discipline theoretically summarizing the functioning of scientific systems in the name of the increasing effectiveness of research and development by means of organizational, economic, informational, and social influence (see Dobrov, 1970).

From the perspective of science policy studies, science management is considered a purposeful process of the formation and implementation of a certain science policy. What does the phenomenon defined by the term "science policy" consist of? Actual experience makes it possible to claim that the term "science policy" is a generalized name for several notions.

1) It includes the whole complex of principles and criteria adopted by a certain social structure which determines the societal attitude toward science and the social role that science is expected to play.

2) It includes the existing social mechanism of science organization and research management.

3) It includes practical actions dealing with the employment and regulation of the relations involving people and organizations directing their activity toward the achievement of science management goals in the sphere of Research and Development.

In other words, science policy consists of the principles, the mechanisms, and the practical actions providing for the achievement of social aims of the development of science.

THE STRATEGIC DOCTRINE

The first of these components of science policy has a particular name in our country. It is called the strategic doctrine of Soviet science. Sooner or later, a State forms its attitude toward scientific progress either explicitly (in the program documents of the ruling political parties, and in the declarations of national leaders) or implicitly (in the spectrum of practical goals for science and in the adopted ways of their achievement and science management principles). Either way, the guiding participation of the State in the development of science on the basis of certain long-term political principles occurs in the social programs of all the countries of the world.

The formation of such a State science policy in the USSR started more than half a century ago, corresponding to the fundamental interests of the new Soviet state. It met the urgent requirements of the native science. The Russian academician and the founder of the Ukrai-

nian Academy of Sciences, V. I. Vernadsky, who contributed much to
the theory and practice of the organization of science in our country,
wrote in 1916 (Vernadsky, 1917:4–5):

> So far we have never discussed the problem of the organiza-
> tion of the research and scientific work, of the State system of
> research institutes. The task, as it is, has never been considered a
> State problem. . . . Such a way of organization is especially
> needed when it is necessary to achieve a result as great as possi-
> ble, as cheap as possible, and as soon as possible.

The urgent objective requirements had been theoretically generalized and implemented in important State action by the founder, V. I.
Lenin, as far back as the first years of the Soviet state. He was the
initiator of drastic and specific measures on the organization and stimulation of the development of science, on the formation of State bodies
for science management, and on the creation of the material and technical conditions for preserving and consolidating the scientific potential
of the country. The State programs of science and technology, developed and implemented according to the primary goals of the State
science policy, involved the exploration and exploitation of natural resources of the country, the development of modern means of communication and radio broadcasting, the technological reconstruction of
the scientific foundations for increasing the fertility of soils, and the
adjustment of the State system of scientific and technical information
(Meleshchenko and Shukhardin, 1969).

The successful implementation of the State's scientific and
technological program for the electrification of Russia developed under
the immediate leadership of Lenin. The program, recorded in the history of science under the name of the "GOELRO plan" (State Plan of
the Electrification of Russia) was of great importance for the fortunes
of scientific and technological progress of the USSR.

The strategic doctrine developed in the early years crystallized
and was generally accepted in Soviet science. The principles included
the following:

1)   Soviet science was to have a national character, serving the
interests of the whole society and deriving its strength from the vast
strata of the population.

2)   Science should have unity of theory and practice. The development of science was to be planned, concentrating efforts on the key problems of scientific and technological progress.

3) The work of scientists would be collective; there would be cooperation and mutual enrichment by the experience of generations of creators of scientific and technological progress.

4) Science would promote internationalism and humanism of science and would strive for fruitful international cooperation.

5) Science and technology policy would be unified, proceeding from the unity of fundamental social interests of the people of our country.

The basis for the strategic doctrine of the State policy in the field of science is its aspiration for the most effective progress of science including the complete transformation of research work, particularly at the frontiers of the various fields of science, into a productive social force for the society to serve the interests of everyone.

Soviet science ranges from the highest abstractions to fundamental matters. Millions of the most gifted people are involved in scientific activity. Considerable resources of the society are spent in scientific activity, and the results obtained are potentially able to transform production and the areas of social, economic, and cultural life in the shortest period of time. The number of scientists in the USSR exceeds one million people. The total number of those working in the field of science and scientific services is four million people. The allocations by the Soviet state for research and development, including the capital construction budget was on the order of 20 billion rubles in 1973. It is estimated that not less than three-quarters of the increase of the effectiveness of production has been achieved within recent years by various intensive factors, and most important of all is the implementation of the results of scientific research.

This gives science-policy researchers the basis for considering science as an organized type of professional activity whose aim and result are the system of knowledge about the objective world, the methods of its cognition and transformation.

The practical experience accumulated in the modern scientific and technological revolution proved the vitality and potentialities of the existing strategic principles of science policy. It also added a number of new important theses. One, of special significance, is the reorientation of the whole scientific effort of the country from extensive methods to intensive methods.

The validity of these new aspects of the strategic doctrine of Soviet science was expressed by the Twenty-fourth Congress of the Communist Party of the Soviet Union.

> To decisively increase the effectiveness of scientific establishments, to ensure concentration of scientific forces, of material and finance resources first of all on the leading directions of science and on the solving of the most important scientific and technological problems, the further consolidation of the experimental base of the research, the employment of self-supporting methods of the organization of scientific research; to improve the planning of scientific research and experiment design works, envisaging all the stages of these works in the plans up to the implementation of their results in production, to intensify the control of the fulfillment of plans; to consolidate the links between science and production; to practice a system of organizational and economic measures for the assimilation and introduction of new technology, the realization of inventions and discoveries within concise periods of time; to increase the stimulating role of patents and patent information (O. P. S. U., 1972:245).

During the preceding years, the growth of the effectiveness of science was achieved by the exponential increase of   1) the number of scientists,   2) the size of allocations,   3) the quantitative parameters of technical equipment, and   4) the size of research collectives. Now the basic task of the organization and management of Soviet science is to provide exponential growth in the effectiveness of the scientific process with the high absolute rate of growth of resources and organizational parameters of scientific systems.

SOCIAL MECHANISM OF SCIENCE ORGANIZATION AND RESEARCH MANAGEMENT

The second component of science policy reflects the existing structure of the scientific community, the social mechanism of the organization and management of Soviet science. Tables 1 and 2 present data on the

TABLE 1. Number of establishments engaged in scientific research in the USSR by the end of 1971

	1940	1950	1960	1965	1970	1971	1971 % of 1950
Total Number of Scientific Establishments (including higher educational institutions)	2359	3447	4196	4867	5182	5307	**154**
Including scientific research institutes, their branches and divisions	786	1157	1728	2146	2525	2648	**229**

NOTE: In 1913, there were 298 scientific establishments.

TABLE 2. Number of research workers in the USSR by the end of 1971 (in thousands)

	1940	1950	1960	1965	1970	1971	1971 % of 1950
Total Number of Research Wkrs.	98.3	162.3	354.2	664.6	927.7	1002.9	**617**
Including:							
Drs. of Science	. . .	8.3	10.9	14.8	23.6	26.1	**314**
Candidates of Science	. . .	45.5	98.3	134.4	224.5	249.1	**548**
Total No. of People engaged in Science and Scientific Services	362	714	1763	2625	3238	3374	**472**

SOURCE: USSR Government (1972: 103 and 347).
NOTE: In 1913, there were 11,600 research workers.

rate of growth of the number of scientific establishments and different categories of people working in the sphere of science. It is interesting to note that the number of scientific personnel in the USSR grew, in the last decades, some three or four times as fast as the number of establishments themselves. This caused growth in the complexity and significance of the tasks of management of the scientific community.

Depending on the specialization and specific role played by different collective bodies in the sphere of science, the general structure of the scientific forces of the USSR is characterized in the following outline.

TYPE OF ESTABLISHMENTS AND ORGANIZATIONS ENGAGED IN RESEARCH, DEVELOPMENT, AND SCIENTIFIC SUPPORT IN THE USSR

1)   Research institutes (RI). – State establishments whose basic type of activity is the accomplishment of scientific research in a certain field of science: Academic RI; divisions and other independent subdivisions of academic RI's; applied RI's according to branches of economy; divisions and other independent subdivisions of applied RI's.

2)   Establishments conducting a complex of research, project planning, and technological works; research and design institutes; project planning and research establishments; research, design and technological institutes; project planning, design and experimental establishments.

3)   Research establishments organizationally and functionally combined with production; research establishments incorporated in the science-and-production associations; research establishments incorporated in the industrial enterprises and production organizations, including production-and-technology associations.

4)   Research establishments organizationally and functionally combined with the training of personnel by higher educational institutions; higher educational institutions as a whole; research institutes of higher educational bodies; problem laboratories of higher educational bodies; research divisions of higher educational bodies.

5)   Establishments carrying out a complex of information works; institutes and centers of scientific and technical information; computation centers conducting information processing; scientific and technical libraries; information services, archives, museums, exhibitions.

6) Establishments carrying out a complex of experimental works; experimental plants and experimental grounds which are economically independent; self-supporting experimental industrial workshops and industrial organizations dealing with the repair, control, assembly and adjustment of scientific equipment; botanical gardens, experimental and strain testing stations, zoological gardens, reservations, agricultural and zoological experimental stations; expeditions, meteorological stations and astronomical observation stations.

7) Establishments carrying out a complex of works dealing with the organization and management of science; science management bodies; scientific councils, commissions, committees.

8) Other research organizations and service establishments not included in the basic classification.

A highly important factor for understanding the social organization of Soviet science is the fact that the process of scientific and technological creative work is exercised in our country not only by scientists, engineers, and specialists working in different State research organizations, but also by a large group of qualified workers in industry, culture, and social management.

Public bureaus for technological and economic analysis, public research laboratories, and groups frequently incorporated in the so-called public research institutes are actively operating many enterprises. They manage the efforts of the engineering and technical staff, as well as the working innovators of production, to solve the urgent problems of technological progress. These are all in cooperation with the professional workers of science. It is essential that the basic stimulus in the work of people acting in the public sector of Soviet science consists mainly of moral factors connected with their inclination for scientific and technological creative work.

The ratios of the main sectors of Soviet science at the present time can be estimated as follows:

Sector of Soviet Science	Ratio
Academic	1
Higher Education	2
Applied	6
Plant	1
Public	10

The structure of the research orientation of scientific personnel of the USSR within the limits of the basic sixteen sections of science is given in Table 3. The data indirectly reflect the existing dynamics of shifts in the structure of the research activity. The structure of the doctorates in science mainly reflects the structure of research activity of the past decade. The data concerning candidates in science reflect the research orientation formed in the preceding five to eight years. The structure of the research orientation reflected in the data on the composition of persons studying at post-graduate courses in many respects corresponds to the structure of the manpower of the candidates

TABLE 3. Distribution of the scientific potential of the USSR among the branches of sciences by the end of 1971 (in thousands)

Categories	Research Workers		Among them				Post-Graduate Students	
			Doctorates		Candidates			
	No.	%	No.	%	No.	%	No.	%
Physics & Math.	103.7	10.3	3.0	11.0	25.7	10.3	11.9	12.0
Chemistry	47.9	4.8	1.4	5.4	14.7	5.9	5.1	5.1
Biology	39.6	3.9	2.6	9.9	18.7	7.5	5.1	5.1
Geology & Minerology	21.3	2.1	1.1	4.2	8.5	3.4	2.4	2.4
Tech. Sciences	450.3	44.9	5.4	20.7	72.9	29.3	39.9	40.2
Ag. & Vet.	37.3	3.7	1.4	5.4	15.7	6.3	5.9	5.9
Hist. & Phil.	39.2	3.9	1.9	7.3	16.2	6.5	5.5	5.5
Economics	65.6	6.5	1.1	4.2	16.9	6.8	10.3	10.4
Philology	49.7	5.0	1.0	3.8	9.8	3.9	2.7	2.7
Geography	7.7	0.8	0.4	1.5	2.8	1.1	0.8	0.8
Law	5.1	0.5	0.4	1.5	2.6	1.1	0.9	0.9
Pedagogy	32.4	3.2	0.2	0.8	4.9	2.0	2.3	2.3
Med. & Pharm.	52.8	5.3	5.4	20.7	30.9	12.4	4.9	4.9
Study of Arts	12.6	1.3	0.2	0.8	1.3	0.5	0.6	0.6
Architecture	2.8	0.3	0.1	0.4	0.9	0.3	0.5	0.5
Psychology	2.1	0.2	0.1	0.4	0.8	0.3	0.3	0.3
Miscellaneous	32.8	3.3	0.4	2.0	5.9	2.0	0.2	0.2
Total	1002.9	100.0	26.1	100.0	249.2	100.0	99.3	100.0

SOURCE: USSR Government (1972: 104 and 108).

in science in the next seven to ten years, and correlates with the future structure (in eight to twelve years) of the manpower of doctorates in science.

This process is controllable. The analysis of these data, in particular, confirms the conclusion that it is necessary to take State measures to stimulate the training of young cadres of researchers in the field of biology.

Table 4 presents data characterizing the dynamics of the financial support of Soviet science 1) from the State budget, and 2) from the funds of the self-supporting industrial enterprises, cooperative and collective farms, and allocations of various public organizations of the country.

As to the structure of the distribution of efforts among fundamental and theoretical research (F), applied research (A), development (D), and the proceeding works dealing with the immediate realization of

TABLE 4. Expenditures on science in the USSR from the State budget and from other kinds of resources by the end of 1971 (in billions of rubles)

	1940	1950	1960	1965	1970	1971	1971, % of 1950
Total expenditures on science (without capital investments in the construction of lab base and dwellings for scientists)	0.3	1.0	3.9	6.9	11.7	13.0	**1300**
Expenditures from State budget of USSR (billions of rubles)	0.1	0.5	2.3	4.3	6.6	7.0	**1400**
% of total State budget spent on science	0.6	1.3	3.2	4.2	4.2	4.3	**331**

SOURCE: USSR Government (1972:481–83).

innovations (I), the following orientation of the science policy of the country in this respect may be considered to be prospective:

$$F : A : D : I$$
$$2^0 : 2^2 : 2^4 : 2^8$$
$$1 : 4 : 16 : 250$$

The typical changes in the cost of completed research reflect the general process of the rise in the cost of research (the number of the engaged personnel, the duration of works, the price and amount of scientific equipment, the materials and other factors) characteristic of the majority of fields of science. This aspect of activity of the scientific forces of the country is an important problem for the management of scientific activity.

In the USSR, a general structure of the scientific activity management levels and bodies has been formed according to the social specificity and structure of the community of scientists (see Fig. 1). The social mechanism for the management of Soviet science is shown as "zones": the legislative power, the executive power at the State level, and the activity of social organizations directing certain research as well as the propagation of scientific and technical knowledge and experience.

PRACTICAL ACTION
TO ACHIEVE MANAGEMENT GOALS

The third structural component of science policy is forming science management goals and realizing their practical implementation. This is done by using possibilities for organizing, stimulating and directing the activity of people, collective bodies, and organizations.

The general goal of the management of Soviet science (at any level of the organizational hierarchy) is to employ effectively the available resources and scientific results to improve the potential for the future requirements of the society within the limitations of the strategy forecast for scientific activity. The solution of three central problems of science management is directed to the achievement of this goal. These central problems (see Fig. 2) are 1) the formation of goals for the

Figure 1.

Organizational Structure of Control Over Science in the USSR

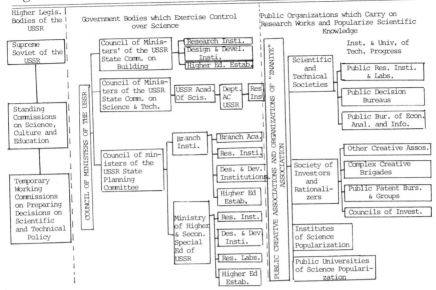

Figure 2

Structure of Goals and Means of Science Management

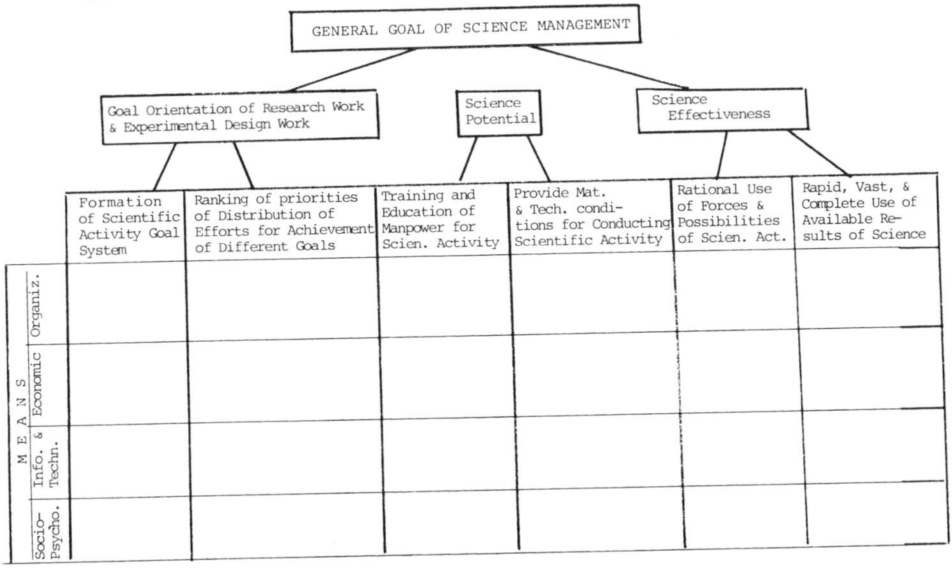

		Goal Orientation of Research Work & Experimental Design Work			Science Potential	Science Effectiveness		
		Formation of Scientific Activity Goal System	Ranking of priorities of Distribution of Efforts for Achievement of Different Goals	Training and Education of Manpower for Scien. Activity	Provide Mat. & Tech. conditions for Conducting Scientific Activity	Rational Use of Forces & Possibilities of Scien. Act.	Rapid, Vast, & Complete Use of Available Results of Science	
M E A N S	Organiz.							
	Economic							
	Info. & Techn.							
	Socio-Psycho.							

research, project planning, and design activity—their orientation in accordance with the strategic goals of the state policy in the field of science ("Goal Orientation of Science"); 2) providing the growth of the national scientific potential whose quantity, structure, and quality would correspond to the requirements of short-term and long-term goals of science ("Science Potential"); and 3) practical implementation of the complex of measures on the increase of the effectiveness of science, both with respect to the employment of its available forces and to the utility of the results of the activity ("Effectiveness of Science").

Each of the basic structural problems of management is a component of the system of goals of science policy in the USSR. It is possible to divide them further into secondary goals and immediate tasks of management. Any specific decision for the implementation of science policy may be aimed at the solution of one or more of the six secondary goals of management.

The goal orientation of science consists first in forming the tasks for research and design activity and in ranking priorities for the distribution of efforts among different areas of R & D. Realizing scientific potential of the country corresponding to the national interests requires solving the tasks of training and manpower and creating material and technological conditions for their research activity. The effectiveness of science is determined by the rational employment of available potential and, more importantly, by the rapid and complete utility of research results available.

The system of science management goals may be analyzed at different levels of control: from the government to the management of a team of individual research workers. In any case, though in different proportions, the scientific specificity of the tasks solved is connected very closely with the social conditions and economic factors determining the character and direction of the scientific activity. This becomes apparent with respect to the *system of the science management means*. The specific measures of influence upon the system are exceptionally diverse. For example, the governing body may for the sake of certain objectives simultaneously change the organizational structure, redistribute the allocations, turn to new methods of research, and establish contacts for this purpose with a new circle of colleagues, and also introduce personal bonuses and other forms of stimulation. All these diverse methods, available at any level of management, may be divided into four main categories: organizational and administrative measures (varying within the regulations, rights, and duties), economic means of management (whose diversity and range of action is determined by economic relations and the level of development of the economy), information and technological means (resulting in immediate influence on the technology of scientific production), and sociopsychological means (varying according to the social situation, standards of ethics adopted by science, and the specific nature of intellectual labor in science).

More than half a century of experience of forming and implementing science policy of the USSR shows that it is impossible to hope seriously for consistent success in the field of the system of goals. Consequently, the regulation and intensification of the research process must include all the groups mentioned and the links between scientists, collective bodies, and organizations.

Economic considerations frequently determine the expediency and character of the employment of certain science management tools. But they are never the only factors taken into consideration. The same thing should be noted about management goals. Their economic substance is indispensable, and they are often the most important component of the six management secondary goals. However, management per se is not brought into Soviet policy only because of economic parameters with respect either to the joint system of goals and means of science policy, or to any of its separate components. One of the main principles of Soviet science policy is the principle of integration of goals and means. The achievement of the whole complex of goals of science policy should be provided in the course of the development of science, and in the process, management acts by using the *complex of means* and measures directing and stimulating the progress of science. Understanding this important factor helps to avoid a number of mistakes in the implementation of science policy.

The role of science policy studies in the system of Soviet science is well reflected in the opinions of the most competent leaders of Soviet science. Millionshchikov (1973), Vice-President of the Academy of Sciences of the USSR, considers that "similarly to the existence of studies of social life, natural history, science policy studies have appeared with the same inevitability. They study their subject in order to give recommendations on optimum ways of development—the development of sciences. This is extremely sophisticated work. The recommendations in this case are of great significance." Gvishiani (1971), the Deputy Chairman of the State Committee for Science and Technology of the Council of Ministers of the USSR, considers that science policy studies

> investigate the general laws of the development of science and technology: the interaction of their economic, social, historical, logical, psychological, structural and organizational aspects. The goal of such studies is to develop both the theoretical foundations of the organization and planning of science and technology and the operating system of practical measures dictated by the objective logics of the development of science and technology. By providing the theoretical basis for making science policy, these studies help ensure an optimum rate of progress and growing effectiveness of R & D.

SCIENCE POLICY AND SCIENCE STUDIES

The cognitive, theoretical, and applied requirements of society and science require that science policy studies be coordinated with cybernetics, informatics, operations research, and other branches of mathematical science. The relations of science policy studies with the logic and history of science are also rather close. These areas contribute new ideas and theories for science policy studies, especially in the process of formulating general concepts for the development of scientific systems. It is important to emphasize that science policy studies and the logic of science use different methods to research two structures which are dialectically connected, but which are essentially different from the point of view of their nature and internal language. They are the social structure of science and the logical structure of scientific knowledge.

There is also a large area of mutual problems between science policy studies and sociology. For sociology, science is a social institution created for acquiring new knowledge and determining the ways of its application in actual practice. Sociology studies science in the interaction of science and society and in the social relations of scientists in the process of scientific research. The results obtained by the sociology of science are important for the development of the strategy of science, science policy foundations, and development of methods for managing all scientific disciplines.

One of the main factors that necessitated science policy studies was the transformation of modern science into an immediate productive force. This accounts for the economic aspects of studying the functioning of science. The development of science policy studies should be enhanced by consideration of the relationship with economics. This enriches science policy studies with the experience of complex problems of economic development, and increases the effectiveness of recommendations developed by science policy studies. The economics of scientific research has become one of the main fields of science policy studies. A considerable number of problems developed by science policy studies that relate to economics include 1) the study of the economic potential of the country and the analysis of the scientific potential; 2) the development of the material and technical base of the society—the study of the rate and level of scientific development; 3) the analysis of the structure of labor resources and reproduction of manpower specialists—the study of the growth of the number, structure, and reserves of scientific manpower; 4) the economic effectiveness of the means of production—the problem of assessing the effectiveness of the work of scientists and the effectiveness of science; 5) the study of the preparatory stage of production—analysis of the implementation of the results of science; 6) planning and forecasting the national economy—R & D forecasting; 7) regional science—the territorial organization of scientific centers; and 8) the history of economic thought—summarizing the experience of the organization of science and the formation of the theoretical foundations of science and technology assessment.

Coordination of science policy studies with psychology and jurisprudence has already begun. The study of problems of scientific creativity by modern psychology can assist science policy studies by providing criteria for assessing the qualities of science manpower resources. Scientific organizations can obtain methods for diagnosing the potentials of people for certain kinds of creative activity; science management can use the contributions of psychologists for improving the formation of scientific groups by taking into account individual characteristics of persons.

Jurisprudence, dealing with the problems of science as an organizational and social system, may be expected to contribute to the development of legislation for controlling relations between scientific bodies and their staffs. An important task is developing a system of basic laws for science through the combined effects of science policy studies and jurisprudence.

There are other areas which could benefit science policy studies, but the main concern governing their use consists in the requirements of the study of science as a controllable system, so that the prospects of complete discovery of the relationship between different components are realized in order for science to increase its effectiveness and functioning.

THE PROBLEMS OF SCIENCE POLICY STUDIES reflect an integrating function in the modern world of science. Research in the economics of science, the sociology of science, technological forecasting, science and technological assessment is within the bounds of science policy studies. The formation of a general theoretical body of science policy studies is of exceptional importance. The general theory for management of science and research plays this role.

There is an old and wise principle uttered by science policy researchers: when cultivating the field, plan seasonal work; when growing an orchard, set yourself tasks for years; when developing science, work out a program for decades.

Theoretical and experimental science policy studies must develop their specific methods. This requires a general theoretical body of science policy studies which are the foundations of a theory of the optimum management of scientific systems. The essential part of this theory is the transition from many science models (information, organizational, economic) to the unit system model of science as a controllable social system.

In the future, science policy studies will turn to projects comprehensively covering the most important aspects of science management (strategy, potential, and effectiveness). An especially great volume of work is to be done by science policy researchers together with the specialists in systems analysis.

The relations formed between science policy studies and science management services are similar to those of science and production in general. A specific task of science policy specialists is participation in the formation and training of personnel for science management services, both by means of a network of special courses and by training specialists in the field of science and technology management, with the help of higher educational institutions and post-graduate courses. In the future, there will be closer relations between science policy studies and the economic analysis of research institutions. At a higher level, this leads to the formation of groups of professional operations researchers, specialized centers and institutes developing the foundations of science policy and methods of managing science.

REFERENCES

ACADEMY OF SCIENCES OF THE USSR
    1960   *Lenin and Science.* Moscow.

C.P.S.U. (COMMUNIST PARTY OF THE SOVIET UNION)
    1970   *V. I. Lenin on Science and Higher Education.* Moscow: Politizdat.
    1972   *Proceedings of the XXIV Congress of the CPSU.* Moscow: Politizdat.

DOBROV, G. M.
    1970   "Science of Science: Introduction to General Science Policy Studies." *Naukova Dumka.* Kiev.

GVISHIANI, D. M.
    1971   "The Revolution of Science and Technology and Problems of Science." *Nauka i Zhizn* 3.

HEMPTINNE, Y. DE
    1972   "Governmental Science Policy Planning Structures." UNESCO, SC/WS/488 (July). Paris.

MELESHCHENKO, Y. S., AND S. V. SHUKHARDIN
    1969   "Lenin and Progress of Science and Technology." *Nauka.* Leningrad.
MILLIONSHCHIKOV, M. D.
    1973   "Logics of Research." *Nedelya* 2 (January): 670.

USSR GOVERNMENT
   1972   USSR National Economy (1922–1972). Moscow: Statistika.

VERNADSKY, V. I.
   1917   "On the State Network of Research Institutes." In *Reports of the Imperial Academy of Sciences, Committee on the Study of Natural Science*.

THE SOCIOLOGY OF SCIENCE IN

Scandinavia

Andrew Jamison

IN THE FALL OF 1973, a leading figure in the sociology of science in the United States gave a seminar in Lund on the "institutionalization of the sociology of science." He attracted four people. To put it bluntly, there has not been a great deal of interest in Scandinavia in what one might call "American-style" sociology of science. That is, the sociology of science that looks at science as a special institution in society, a social role worthy of functional analysis, has not received much scholarly attention.

There are many possible explanations. The various "scientific communities" in the Scandinavian countries are not very large, and, for the most part, they have not had the same degree of autonomy that their counterparts have had in other, larger countries. (The entire population of Scandinavia is around 20 million, and Sweden, the largest country, has only 8 million people.) Science—and scientists—have been fairly well integrated into the total "welfare" system. They have been primarily practical-minded and applied in their orientation. The relatively few "basic" scientists have generally been more interested in establishing contacts with colleagues abroad than in developing a "sense of community" in their own countries. As such, scientists as a group until quite recently have not been a particularly important object of investigation for sociologists.[1]

There is also the nature of Scandinavian sociology itself, which, to a large extent, has served as something of an appendage to the governments' large-scale survey and investigation projects, particularly in Sweden. It has focused primarily on studying problems that are "reformable," that lend themselves to the kind of welfare reforms that have become the hallmark of the Scandinavian governments (Gras, 1970; Eskola, 1971; Gullberg, 1972).[2] This pragmatic, heavily statistical sociology has been slow to single out science—and scientists—for special attention. But, as the state research councils have begun to see the policy implications of such sociological investigations, some tentative first steps have been taken. As we shall see in this chapter, this "sociology of science" has had a number of difficulties. Scandinavian sociologists have tried to use the same statistical methods that they used with success in other parts of the society, but with science they have had some problems. The questions that have been posed have often been unimportant. Rather obvious assertions have been "proved" with statistical surveys. We must still wait for adequate sociological studies of Scandinavian science.

In the meantime, however, a number of other approaches to science have been tried. A new school of critical, Marxist-influenced social scientists has developed in each of the Scandinavian countries. Some of their work on the relations between science and society, the various functions that science serves in society, and the subservience of science to corporate interests is well worth looking at. This work is also at a very preliminary stage, and it is often difficult to separate polemic from social science. I will try, however, to present some of the most interesting studies that have been done by this school of thought.

Finally, I will examine the general area of the "sociology of scientific knowledge" of the "theory of science" and survey some of the research being carried out on the growth of science, the development of scientific ideas, the operation of the "research process," and the relationship of scientific ideas to the larger society. Scandinavian universities are roughly fashioned after the German model and the German theoretical interest has been adopted as well. In recent years, sociologists, and social scientists in general, have been waging a struggle over the theoretical bases of social and natural knowledge. Out of this has come some preliminary work of a Kuhnian-style sociology of science, although the influence of Kuhn has been rather small. Instead, Scandinavian theorists of science got their theoretical bearings from a number of Western European thinkers including Habermas, Althusser, and others.

Because of the nature of the research and writing in Scandinavia, this chapter will survey the sociology of science in a somewhat broad perspective. I will take three different areas of investigation which I have labeled 1) the sociology of the scientific community, 2) the sociology of science policy, and 3) the sociology of scientific knowledge. I have chosen these topics not simply to be able to discuss the Scandinavian activity in a more comprehensive way, but because I feel that all three areas should be included in any worthwhile sociology of science.

I have concentrated primarily on the work done by sociologists, but I have not been overly concerned about academic labels. Labels vary from one country to another, and what a sociologist does in one country might well be the proper concern of a philosopher or a political scientist somewhere else, particularly in a field as fluid and tentative as the sociology of science. I have obviously been somewhat subjective in my selection, totally ignoring the work done by economists and industrial management people on processes of innovation and research efficiency. The work covered is almost totally confined to work published since about 1967. Before then, research in the sociology of science was extremely random and uncoordinated. If it remains somewhat random and uncoordinated today, there is at least more to discuss.

THE SOCIOLOGY
OF THE SCIENTIFIC COMMUNITY

The largest body of work in this area has dealt with the "sociology of sociology" and has centered in a group under the direction of Gunnar Boalt of the Sociology Department at the University of Stockholm. Boalt has developed what he termed "summation theory," through which he sees the scientific role (and other roles in society) as a sum of its components. These components can be quantified and combined in various ways. The approach was initially defined in *The Sociology of Research* (Boalt, 1969), which represents a systematic attempt to break down the scientific, the sociological role, into a large number of different variables which he terms "scientific values."

According to Boalt, the sociologist attempts to satisfy as many values as possible, but is necessarily forced to sacrifice certain values for others. As Alvin Gouldner notes in the introduction to Boalt's book, the conception of the scientific role that Boalt develops is a "tragic" one. It is based on an acceptance of inevitable failure, an inability to fulfill all of the expectations that are forced upon the scientist.[3] The general idea is that certain values complement each other. They form what Boalt calls "clusters," and it is these clusters of values that are always in conflict with each other. Boalt's task, then, is to find, empirically, which values form clusters and what kind of "compensation patterns" emerge.

He and his collaborators have pursued many different strategies. In one study, Boalt looks at the totality of values, dividing them into "planning values," "working values," and "supplementary values" (Boalt and Lantz, 1970). He scrutinizes a number of Swedish doctoral theses, and compares them with masters' theses. He examines papers in the Scandinavian sociology journal, and compares them with papers in the *American Sociological Review*. He tries to discover which values are important and how different values compensate for the lack of attention to other values. He finds thirty-one values breaking down into three clusters: an "empirical" cluster, a "social" cluster, and a "theoretical" cluster. The correlations are extremely well-quantified, but the data do not point to obvious conclusions.

In other research, Boalt has investigated the questions of resource allocation. He found that departments in Sweden that were more interested in "research values" than "teaching values" received larger amounts of money (Boalt and Lantz, 1972). In another study he examined correlations and compensations between "scientific values" and "nonscientific values" (such as time spent with families and in social activities), comparing scientists with nonscientists. Here, his results were largely inconclusive (Boalt and Bergryd, 1973).

Following Boalt, Ribbing (1971) has looked at the matter of recruitment, defining research "effectivity" as a cluster of values that is in conflict with the number of students in the particular department. He attempted to classify the "values" by which the Swedish state council for social research has awarded its grants. An impressive amount of statistical data has been accumulated, but the results are, of course, tentative. It will require more research to determine the specific processes involved (Ribbing, 1973).

The entire enterprise may be constrained by its methodology. Boalt and his collaborators seem to be interested in the "taxonomy" of research, the classification of the scientific role into innumerable values. Clearly, the summation theory "works" in that it can amass statistical data, but the question is how much it can tell us about the scientific process. The discussions that precede the presentation of data in these works are interesting, but it is sometimes difficult to relate these introductions to the data presented. Now that the data have been collected, and the methodological techniques refined, it is possible to progress to a more sophisticated analysis. This process was begun in a recent paper (Boalt and Bergryd, 1972) where data were used to illustrate the fall of the "institutional empire" within Swedish sociology.

The work of Lindbekk (1969) in Norway is primarily an attempt to bring the ideas of American sociologists of science to the attention of Scandinavian sociologists, and to apply them in a preliminary way to the Norwegian "basic science" community. He outlines the historical development of scientific "norms," originality, rationality, and empiricism. He interviewed three hundred scientists to see how they organized the norms and what they think of them. His material is somewhat dated (the interviews were conducted in 1962–63) and not particularly revealing. In the physical sciences, he finds an emphasis on "internationally-oriented team research" and a looser organization within the social sciences and the humanities. He provides a number of personal quotations from scientists to illustrate different kinds of adjustments that they made to the scientific norms, but does not commit himself to any definite conclusions. As with Boalt, the purpose of the project apparently was to establish the existence of norms or values, without providing systematic analysis of where these norms originated and how they are impressed upon young scientists.

A project currently under way may make the situation a bit clearer. The project entitled "The International Comparative Study of the Organization of Research Units," is being carried out in both Sweden and Finland. The idea, from UNESCO's perspective, is to try to determine what produces an effective research unit. The data are being collected by interviewing a representative sample of research units in a number of different countries. In Sweden, the project is led by Rikard Stankiewicz at the Research Policy Program in Lund. A pilot study, involving fifty-five research units in biochemistry and metallurgy has also been partially funded by the Swedish Natural Science Research Council. Stankiewicz is asking members and leaders of the research units questions relating to performance, composition, organization, financing, communication, motivation, and interaction, both within the units as well as with scientists outside, and with the larger social environment. It is too early to discuss results or conclusions, but some significant information on the actual operation of research units may emerge from this large-scale empirical investigation. In the second stage, he will survey two hundred randomly selected academic natural science and technological research units, about 20 percent of all such units in Sweden. Stankiewicz intends to test the hypothesis that the structure of the Swedish academic system interferes with the development of effective research groups, through constraining the mobility of researchers between units, overemphasizing project financing, and limiting the number of "middle-level" research positions.

Aside from these ambitious projects, there has been a number of smaller studies of the scientific community that focused on one particular aspect of the community. Friborg and Annerstedt's (1972) work on the migration of scientists should be mentioned. They attempted to determine the extent of migration, the relationship between science policy and migration, and the motivations that led particular scientists to migrate. This is an ongoing project, that will try to monitor the migration phenomenon through time as it develops in the future. The research will also look at questions relating to return migration.

A number of different approaches have been attempted to study scientific creativity. A variety of models and theoretical perspectives have been developed (Székely, 1967; Nordbeck and Maini, 1970; Ljungh, 1968) and some pilot studies have been undertaken, but the situation remains unclear. It can be expected that research in this area will continue in the years ahead, as the models receive empirical testing, and the theoretical frameworks grow in sophistication. The "Festschrift" to Herman Wold, the Swedish statistician, presented a number of case-histories by Scandinavian, and other scientists, on their own research processes (Dalenius et al., 1970). The haphazard nature of the contributions, because many of the contributors seemed to have little idea of what was expected of them, makes it of somewhat limited value (Dedijer, 1972b).

The special situation of women scientists has also been discussed somewhat in the Scandinavian literature, although an early survey of the literature (Frithiof, 1967) failed to find much empirical research. One study of science students found differences in sex and social background affecting the "realization of research plans" (Bengtsson and Lundmark, 1972). Herlin (1971), using Boalt's summation theory, found differences betwen men and women scientists in terms of the time spent on nonscientific pursuits, such as families (see also Boalt and Bergryd, 1973). As the women's liberation movement develops in Scandinavia, one may expect more work of the kind that tries to analyze discrimination against women in science.

Studies on special groups of researchers are also likely to continue. In Norway the Institute for Studies in Research and Higher Education, associated with the Norwegian Research Council for Science and the Humanities, has undertaken a project on the special career pattern and working conditions of "research fellows" (Skoie et al., 1970). As with the work that has been done under the auspices of the Swedish Committee on Research Organization and Research Economics, associated with the Swedish Natural Science Research Council, the Norwegian studies have been mostly oriented to statistical surveys. There is an absence of either theoretical direction for such work or a perspective into which the empirical findings can be placed.

The Marxist-influenced sociologists who have written on the scientific community, in comparison, have had problems in "proving" their theoretical insights with empirical data. Some interesting work on the changing class nature of scientists and university intellectuals in general has been produced in both Finland (Willner, 1972) and Denmark (Sloth Andersen et al., 1972). This research has become more important as the Scandinavian governments have begun to plan reforms for university education. Aimed at making universities more selective, more training-oriented, and more integrated with the economic system, the reforms have been attacked by many people at the universities, both liberals and radicals. Sociological analyses of the implications of these reforms are just beginning, but one can expect more of these studies in the future.

Alternative approaches to science and education are being tried in Scandinavia and elsewhere. In Norway (at Tromsö) and in Denmark (at Roskilde), new experimental interdisciplinary education and research projects are being conducted. A large-scale sociological evaluation project of the Roskilde University Center is trying to assess the feasibility of such innovative education. It is outside the scope of this study to discuss these in detail.

I finally mention my own work on environmental research in Sweden (Jamison, 1972, 1973). I try to show the ways in which environmental scientists have contributed to research efforts aimed at dealing with the environmental crisis. In a number of case studies of environmental research organization, I show how such research has been steered increasingly by "extrascientific" groups in the government and industry. My work has attempted to link the more policy-oriented work, to be examined in the next section, and the sociological investigations of the scientific community. Most of my efforts have been journalistic rather than academic.

THE SOCIOLOGY OF SCIENCE POLICY

Scandinavian governments, beginning in the late 1950s, have grown interested in science policy. Science and technology have become large items in the national budgets, and the governments have realized that they should have some idea of how the money is being used. They have wanted certain kinds of evaluative tools to make the scientific planning and financing more rational and efficient.

In recent years, these questions of science policy have become of interest also to other groups in the society. They have wanted to know what is being done with state research money, and they have wanted to have some influence on how that money is spent. In Scandinavia these matters have grown in importance rather quickly, receiving a strong impetus from the student movement that flared up in the late 1960s in each of the four countries. I will examine in cursory form some of the more important research efforts that have come out of this trend. Stevan Dedijer calls this trend the "democratization" of science policy.

Dedijer's institute, the Research Policy Program in Lund, was started in 1966. It has been a center for research on science policy. In Denmark, a group of researchers associated with the Danish Student Council has been quite active. In Finland the Society for Science Policy (founded in 1969) has played a key role. Much of this activity has been "political" in the sense that the people involved have shown no reluctance in combining their research with action programs and recommendations for reforms. Discussions of science policy in Scandinavia have been conducted in what might be called a "politicized" climate. Although a good amount of material has been produced, it remains difficult to separate polemic from scholarship.

In 1968, a large group of Scandinavian and foreign social scientists gathered in Lund for a conference on the general subject of "Scientific Research and Politics" (Dencik, ed., 1969). The conference developed into a confrontation between those older academics who sought to bring out the positive, or at least neutral, aspects of scientific research, and the younger breed of social scientists who saw science as intimately connected to the capitalist system. The latter felt that any positive contributions that science could make for social change would require a radically new kind of science.

In the years since then, many of these younger social scientists have tried to develop their arguments with different kinds of empirical data. In one effort, an attempt was made to link practically all of the Swedish government's science expenditures to the largest corporations in an attempt to show that the state served as a willing tool for these corporations by financing the corporations' science and technology (Ambjörnsson et al., 1969). But the empirical grounds on which these assertions were made can be criticized for misrepresentation. No attempt was made to be comprehensive and cases were taken that could serve to prove the hypothesis desired by the researchers.

The next year, the "labor union" for service workers presented the results of a large-scale investigation on science and society (TCO, 1970). The book was a comprehensive treatment of Swedish science, trying to analyze what role science serves in society, and how it could be used more effectively. The report was best in its description of industrial research, but was rather sketchy in its discussion of state research. Its recommendations tried to satisfy everyone, urging more influence for young scientists as well as closer integration between the scientists and private industry.

Annerstedt's 1972 book can be seen, in part, as an answer to the TCO-report. It is a complete statistical description of state expenditures for research and development. It also provides detailed descriptions of the operation of the state research councils. As an OECD-consultant, Annerstedt had produced the most reliable set of R & D statistics for Sweden, and these statistics provided some solid ground on which to discuss further science policy. But his book was not simply statistics. He tried to show which groups in society exercised "power over research," which groups influenced research priorities and the direction of research expenditures. His survey included military research, and particularly the development of the Viggen aircraft, the largest R & D project in Sweden's history. The research raised a scandal in Swedish research circles. Annerstedt, with the meticulousness of a good muckraking journalist, showed that the decisions for the Viggen project had been made by the military industry officials and leading figures in the military over the heads of Parliament and the government. Dörfer (1973), in another study of the Viggen aircraft development project, attempted to explain the situation in a less openly critical way by showing why Parliament had not been interested, and why industry and the military had been able to proceed with their plans.[4]

Critical empirical surveys of science policy have also been produced in Denmark (Juul Jensen and Sloth Andersen, 1972) and Norway. In Norway, an attempt has also been made to combine empirical and analytical research to show what interests science serves in Norwegian society (Kalleberg, 1971).

In 1973, a number of young researchers gathered in Lund to talk about "science policy in Scandinavia" under the auspices of the Research Policy Program and the Scandinavian Summer University, a group that has initiated studies on science in society at all of the Scandinavian universities. The symposium provided an opportunity for a number of people to develop more systematic analyses of the various functions that science serves in contemporary society. Research efforts in this area can be expected to continue and grow in sophistication in the future.

Some of the early signs of historical work in the relations between science and society have begun to emerge in Scandinavia. There has been some theoretical discussion of the history of science (Liedman, 1973) trying to put the history of science into a Marxist perspective. There has also been some study of certain moments in the history of science, trying to show the connections between science and certain needs imposed by the outside society (Ambjörnsson et al., 1968; Ambjörnsson, 1972). Gustavsson (1971) has presented a long dissertation on the development of science policy ideas, tracing the history of the relations of science to society in terms of what different people have thought about them. Andersson's (1973) paper on "science and society" also represents an input into the history of science's relations to society, an area that should grow important in the years ahead.

THE SOCIOLOGY OF SCIENTIFIC KNOWLEDGE

The research done by workers at the Theory of Science Institute in Gothenburg is broadly philosophical but is difficult to classify. It has encompassed sociology, political science, history, and economics. The director, Håkan Törnebohm, has tried to develop a cybernetic approach to science. It takes in philosophical aspects, generally Popper's notions of science's increasing rationalization, with more sociological discussions of the distribution of scientific ideas in society, the writing of research reports, and the institution of scientific norms or "ideals." Törnebohm (1968, 1973) considers science as a model of "inquiring systems" which examine certain "territories" by means of sequences of hypotheses, instruments, and problems. He has sought to elucidate this process, so that research "programs" can be planned as efficiently as possible.

Eriksson (1972) in Upsala has developed another kind of model based on Toulmin's division of knowing into "phenomena" and "ideals of natural order." He has added a third level into the scheme, which includes the strategy of "facticity," "ontological assumptions" and the theory of knowledge. The three levels make up what Eriksson calls a "discursive whole" and take into account different kinds of value assumptions that are held by the individual scientist.

Such abstract theoretical models have had little impact in the Scandinavian discussion of science. A far more important work is that of Radnitzky (1968) who takes up the ideas of Jürgen Habermas and the Frankfurt school of critical theory and tries to synthesize them with Popper's notions of scientific growth. Habermas's central thesis—that one's knowledge of society is determined by one's "interests" or values—has been hotly discussed in Scandinavia. On the one hand, there have been those sociologists and social theorists who have extended this thinking into "action" programs for critical social science (Israel,

1972) and who have tried to put their values for "liberation" into the social science that they produce. On the other hand, there have been the Marxists who have rejected ideas of values, and have discussed instead questions of "partisanship" (Therborn, 1973; Elzinga, 1973; Schmid, 1973). A rather extensive debate on these questions has been carried out in the pages of the *Journal for Critical Studies*, published by a group of "young philosophers" in Stockholm. The debate has generally revolved around the question of what role a critical social scientist can play. Can his science be a tool for liberation unless he aligns himself with the direct political struggle of the working class?

Both sides reject "positivist" notions of social science, and spend a good deal of time criticizing the "bourgeois" ideology that lies concealed in most academic social science. The protagonists have had little to say about natural science, except in Denmark, where the Danish Student Council has produced a number of reports on the "ideological" role that certain kinds of natural science and technology play in late-capitalist society (Sloth Andersen et al., 1972). They have been more interested in the theoretical foundations of their own work. It seems those who are interested in theory find little use for empirical data, and those more interested in empirical "proofs" of capitalism's faulty applications of science show little concern for theory. Discussions on the theoretical level have tended to be abstract, polarizing around differences in how one interprets Marx. The influence of the French philosopher, Louis Althusser, who tries to make a strict distinction between Marxist science and ideology, is evident, particularly in Sweden. In a certain sense, Althusser has served as a kind of justification for the abstractions that are constantly tossed about. This kind of discussion is likely to continue in the future, and perhaps the abstract formulations will someday even receive empirical testing.

FROM THE VANTAGE POINT of the American-style sociologist of science, there has been little "sociology of science" in Scandinavia. At the least, there has been little research on the "standard" problems of the operation of scientific "norms," the institutionalization of scientific activity, or the functional workings of the scientific community. But, from a different perspective, there has been some sociological investigation of science. That it has largely been interested in science's relations to society and in the theoretical foundations of scientific knowledge is due to the special conditions of the nature of Scandinavian science and Scandinavian sociology. In Scandinavia, the sociologist is confronted with small, relatively well-integrated societies. Social science is most concerned with keeping the machine running smoothly, ironing out the "weak links," and providing statistics and survey results that can be useful in the formulation of reforms. Science is primarily of interest, therefore, either in terms of what role it plays in the total social mechanism or it is interesting from a theoretical point of view. One should not underestimate the Scandinavian interest in theory. There is a certain gap between theory and empirical research, and it seems as if one of the main tasks facing Scandinavian "sociologists of science" in the years ahead will be to get their theory and their data together, in some way or another. There are signs tentatively pointing in this direction.

Perhaps even more important, however, is the reluctance that Scandinavian academics have shown in studying the various crises that science and technology have suffered in recent years. Academics have been rather quick in criticizing the uses to which science is put in contemporary society. They have produced a number of solid empirical analyses of science policy and its subservience to what might be called "economic interests." But, and this applies to colleagues in other countries, they have been less ready to discuss possible alternative uses to which science can be put. They have, for all practical purposes, ignored the growing "alternative technology" movement that has sprung up in the last few years. If they are "bourgeois," they pin their faith on the government, and try to do what they can to make science and technology more effective or efficient. They try, that is, to detect the parts of the scientific system that are faulty and propose appropriate cures.

The Marxists, in contrast, seem to be satisfied with showing the domination that large corporations have over science and technology, and the effect that bourgeois ideology has over scientific ideas. They have become so critical of the "system" that no positive change can be conceived without a total transformation of the society, a revolutionary change that will bring on a new socialist epoch.

As a result, the important questions of whether or not science and technology can be used in other ways, whether science policy really can be "democratized," whether small-scale, decentralized scientific and technological activity is feasible, fail to receive academic scrutiny. The attention that these different possibilities have received has been mostly confined to political groups, or to environmental groups. (Some of these groups outside of the academic establishment have begun undertaking their own experiments on a practical level.) The Chinese experience has begun to be considered, but not by sociologists of science (with the exception of Stevan Dedijer).[5]

In each of the four countries, but particularly in Sweden and Denmark, large groups of people have begun attacking the maldistribution of scientific and technological resources. Some of these, mostly labor-union groups, have grown interested in questions of the "working environment," the conditions in which workers carry out their tasks. Political groups and radical student groups also have begun to see the importance of these problems. But their effect on the sociologists of science and on the science policy makers has been minimal.

Environmentalists, too, have begun to see the ways in which science and technology are being used to destroy further the natural environment. They have called for new kinds of science and technology involving qualitatively new forms of scientific activity. But they have also failed to interest the sociologists of science (with the exception of my own journalistic efforts). The changes that these people call for are comprehensive. The problems cannot be solved with minor palliatives. As in other countries, what is required are far-reaching social changes in the direction of science, in the organization of science, in the kinds of science that are being done, and, inevitably, in the organization of society.

Let me comment on the role that the sociology of science can play in these developments. We have developed tools for analyzing society, for studying different aspects of society, and even for reforming society. We know something about how science is organized, how scientific ideas can be produced, and how to produce them most effectively. In a time of change, these insights and these tools can be of great help to the people outside of the academic establishment who need them most. We can study and analyze the alternatives that they are developing, and provide some notions as to how to make those alternatives function more effectively.

These comments are obviously polemical. In an environment in which the sociology of science is as fluid as it is in Scandinavia, at a time when our ideas about science and its functions in society are in doubt and under serious scrutiny, I think it only appropriate to say some words about what the sociology of science *could* be. In Scandinavia, the field is small, groping for direction, and searching for respectability. It is through reviewing this infant field that one is led to thoughts about how the field could be more useful and effective. It is, I think, an appropriate conclusion for the pot-pourri of activity described in this chapter.

NOTES

[1] In the early 1960s, some beginnings can be detected in Segerstedt's (1964) work on "occupational choice" among scientists and a Finnish work on "scientific cooperation" (Törnudd and Valpola, 1963). With the creation of the "Committee for Research Economics" by the Swedish Natural Science Research Council in 1962, a number of other small studies was initiated. But the sociological investigation of science did not really get off the ground much before 1965, and it is only in the last few years that we can seriously talk about an area of interest that could be called the "sociology of science" existing in any coherent form.

[2] In this regard, it is interesting to note that another seminar presented in the 1973 visit to Lund, on the sociology of medicine, by the visiting scholar mentioned at the beginning attracted some forty people.

[3] Gouldner's ideas on the influence that the Swedish character has had on Boalt's perspective are worth consideration. The "special conditions" of the Scandinavian countries—in terms of size and character—are difficult to define, however, and it is even more difficult to analyze the ways in which these conditions have affected the sociology of science.

[4] A journalistic account of the Viggen scandal, and the reactions to Annerstedt's and Dörfer's studies, can be found in Schimanski (1973).

[5] Elzinga has considered the Chinese case in political terms, comparing the Chinese political approach to science to that of Western scientists (Elzinga, 1973). One might also mention the work of Sigurdsson, an engineer, who has investigated rural technology in China (Sigurdsson, 1968, 1973). I might also note the work being done on "alternative uses" of computer technology. An early study on computers in society (Annerstedt et al., 1970) has helped encourage public discussion of computer technology. An important experiment, sponsored by the Norwegian iron and metal workers' union, trying to find ways for workers to make use of computer technology, is the most extensive project in this area. It has also been looked at by academic social scientists, although the main work has been done by engineers (Nygaard and Bergo, 1972).

NOTE: I thank my colleagues at the Research Policy Program, Stevan Dedijer, Jan Annerstedt, and Rikard Stankiewicz, for their suggestions and comments. I particularly express my appreciation to Dedijer, whose work I have not discussed in detail in this chapter. I felt that the international orientation of most of his work made it somewhat out of place in a study of this kind, but I have listed some of his more important papers in the list of references.

REFERENCES

AMBJÖRNSSON, R.
  1972 *Idé och Klass* [Idea and class]. Stockholm: PAN/Norstedts.
AMBJÖRNSSON, R. ET AL.
  1968 *Tradition och Revolution* [Tradition and revolution]. Stockholm: Cavefors.
  1969 *Forskning och Politik i Sverige, Sovjet, och USA* [Research and politics in Sweden, the Soviet Union, and the U.S.A.]. Stockholm: Aldus/Bonniers.
ANDERSSON, G.
  1973 "Vetenskap och Samhälle" [Science and society]. In *Svensk Naturvetenskap 1973* [Swedish natural science 1973]. Stockholm: Swedish Natural Science Research Council.
ANNERSTEDT, J. ET AL.
  1970 *Datorer och Politik, Studier i en ny Tekniks Politiska Effekter på det Svenska Samhället* [Computers and politics, studies in the political effects of a new technology on Swedish society]. Kristianstad: Zenit/ Cavefors.
  1972 *Makten Över Forskningen* [Power over research]. Lund: Cavefors.

BENGTSSON, M., AND P. LUNDMARK
  1972 "Förverkligas Forskarplaner?" [Are research plans realized?], *FEK* (Swedish Committee for Research Organization and Research Economics). Stockholm.
BERGMAN, P. A.
  1974 "Development of a Large-Scale Research Project—Theoretical Studies on an Eco-System Project." *FEK*. Stockholm.
BERNTSEN, H.
  1974 "Studentene, Fagkritikken og Arbejderklassen" [Students, critique and the working class]. *Nordisk Forum* 1–2.
BOALT, G.
  1969 *The Sociology of Research*. Carbondale: Southern Illinois University Press.

BOALT, G., AND U. BERGRYD
1972 "The Decline and Fall of the Departmental Empire." *International Social Science Journal*, no. 4.
1973 *The Academic Pattern*. Stockholm: Almqvist och Wiksell.

BOALT, G., AND H. LANTZ
1970 *Universities and Research*. Stockholm: Almqvist och Wiksell.
1972 *Resources and Production of University Departments*. Stockholm: Almqvist och Wiksell.

BÖÖK, M.
1974a "Forskningsinformation" [Research information]. *Nordisk Forum*, 1–2.
1974b "Arbetarrörelsen och forskningsarbetarna i Italien. Samtal med Pier Luigi Albini" [The workers' movement and research workers in Italy. Conversation with Pier Luigi Albini]. *Nordisk Forum* 4.

DALENIUS, T. ET AL.
1970 *Scientists at Work. Festskrift in Honour of Herman Wold*. Stockholm: Almqvist och Wiksell.

DEDIJER, S.
1966a "Research Policy—From Romance to Reality." In Goldsmith and Mackay (eds.), *The Science of Science*. Harmondsworth, Eng.: Pelican.
1966b "The Sixth Column—A 'Chinese' Appraisal of a Book on Chinese Science." *Science* (August).
1968 "Research Policy Program, A Report from Lund." *Nordisk Forum* 1.
1972a "National R & D Policy as a Social Innovation." In *Management of Research and Development*. Paris: OECD.
1972b "Review of *Scientists at Work*." *American Journal of Sociology* (May).

DENCIK, L. (ED.)
1969 *Scientific Research and Politics*. Lund: Studentlitteratur.

DÖRFER, I.
1973 *System 37 Viggen. Arms, Technology, and the Domestication of Glory*. Oslo: Universitetsforlaget.

ELZINGA, A.
1973 "Objectivity and Partisanship in Science." Gothenburg: Institute for the Theory of Science.
1974a "Två Inlägg om Forskning och Politik" [Two essays on research and politics]. Gothenburg: Institute for the Theory of Science.
1974b "Introduction to Course-Outline." *Nordisk Forum* 4.

ERIKSSON, B.
1972 "Om den Sociologiska Analysen av Kunskap" [On the sociological analysis of knowledge]. Uppsala: Uppsala University Studies in Sociology.

ESKOLA, A.
   1971   "Om Sociologin i Finland" [On sociology in Finland]. Paper presented to the Scandinavian Sociological Congress. Helsinki.

FRIBORG, G.
   1970   "Tendencies of Research on Research in Sweden." *FEK*. Stockholm.
FRIBORG, G., AND J. ANNERSTEDT
   1972   "Brain Drain and Brain Gain of Sweden." *FEK*. Stockholm.
FRITHIOF, P.
   1967   "Women in Science." Research Policy Program. Lund.

GRAS, A.
   1970   "Social Scientists and Other University Teachers in Sweden: Protest or Conformity." *Social Science Information* 11 (6).
GULLBERG, A.
   1972   "Till den Svenska Sociologins Historia" [On the history of Swedish sociology]. Stockholm: Young Philosophers.
GUSTAVSSON, S.
   1971   *Debatten om Forskningen och Samhället* [Debate on research and society]. Stockholm: Almqvist och Wiksell.

HADENIUS, A.
   1974   "Sweden and Cern II—the Research Policy Debate, 1964–1971." *FEK*. Stockholm.
HEISKANEN, I.
   1973   "The State of Science Policy Studies in Finland." Paper presented to the Scandinavian Workshop on Science Policy Studies. Copenhagen.
HERLIN, H.
   1971   "Resursallokering och Rollstruktur bland Manliga och Kvinnliga Forskare samt Parallella Grupper av icke Forskare. Prövning av en Kompensations-modell" [Resource allocation and role structure among male and female researchers, together with parallel groups of nonresearchers. A test of a compensation model]. Stockholm: Stockholm University.
HOLM, R.
   1974   "Sammanhangen mellem den danske forskningsorganisatoriske udvikling og den økonomiske udvikling fra midten af 1960s erne til 1973" [The connection between Danish research organizational development and economic development from the middle of the 1960s to 1973]. *Nordisk Forum* 4.

ISRAEL, J.
   1972   *Om Konsten att Lyfta sig själv i Håret och Behålla Bernet i Badvattnet* [Postulates and constructions in the social sciences]. Stockholm: Rabén och Sjögren.

JAMISON, A.
 1972 "Ecology and Social Change." Research Policy Program. Lund.
 1973 "Science as Control: Environmental Research in Sweden." Research Policy Program. Lund.
JELSOE, E. ET AL.
 1975 "Dansk Forskning: styring, planlägning, interessekamp" [Danish research: steering, planning, and a struggle of interests]. Copenhagen: Danish Student Council.
JUUL JENSEN, N., AND E. SLOTH ANDERSEN
 1972 Rapport om Industri, Stat, og Forskning [Report on industry, state, and research]. Copenhagen: Danish Student Council.

KALLEBERG, R.
 1971 "Vitenskap og Politikk" [Science and politics]. Oslo: Oslo University.
KNUDSEN, J.
 1973 "Science Policy Studies in Denmark." Paper presented to the Scandinavian Workshop on Science Policy Studies. Copenhagen.

LIEDMAN, S-E.
 1973 "Marxism och Idéhistoria. En Skiss" [Marxism and the history of ideas. A sketch]. In Kjerstin Noren (ed.), Människans Samhälliga Vara. Marxistisk Forskningsteori i Humanistisk Forskning [Man's social being. Marxist research-theory in humanist research]. Kristianstad: Cavefors.
LINDBEKK, T.
 1969 Forsknings Organisasjon innen Moderne Vitenskap [The organization of research in modern science]. Oslo: Universitetsforlaget.
LJUNGH, B.
 1968 "En Kreativitetsmodell" [A model of creativity]. Malmö: Council for Personnel Administration.
LUNDQVIST, L.
 1974 "The Case of Mercury Pollution in Sweden—Scientific Information and Public Response." FEK. Stockholm.

NIELSEN, K.
 1975 "Samfundsvidenskabens Samfundsmässige rolle og Fagkritik" [The social role of social science and critique]. Nordisk Forum 1.
NORDBECK, B., AND S. MAINI
 1970 "Critical Moments and Processes in Research Work." Psychological Research Bulletin X: 11. Lund.
NYGAARD, K., AND O. BERGO
 1972 Oppbygging av Kunskaper om Databehandling, Planlegging og Styring innen Norsk Jern- og Metallarbeiderforbund [The building-up of knowledge on computer-programming, planning, and steering in the Norwegian iron and metal workers' union]. Oslo: Norsk Regnesentral.

PETTERSON, A.
    1974 "Organizational and Psychological Constraints in Commissioned
          Evaluation Research." Gothenburg: Institute for the Theory of Sci-
          ence.

RADNITZKY, G.
    1968 *Contemporary Schools of Metascience*. Gothenburg: Institute for the
          Theory of Science.
RIBBING, E.
    1971 "Om Studentrekrytering, Undervisning, och Utbildningsforskning
          vid Naturvetenskapliga och Humanistiska Universitetsinstitutioner.
          En Komparativ Studie" [On student recruiting, education, and edu-
          cational research at natural science and humanistic university de-
          partments. A comparative study]. *FEK*. Stockholm.
    1973 "Statens Råd för Samhällsforskning och Dess Anslagsbeviljande Ver-
          ksamhet. En Fallstudie" [The state council for social research and its
          grant-giving activity. A case study]. Stockholm: Stockholm Univer-
          sity.
ROLL-HANSEN, N.
    1974 *Forskningens Frihet og Nødvendighet* [The freedom and necessity of
          research]. Oslo: Gyldendal.

SCHIMANSKI, F.
    1973 "Swedish Notebook: Another Costly Aeroplane." *New Scientist* (Au-
          gust 9):341–42.
SCHMID, H.
    1973 "On the Conditions of Applied Social Research." Lund: Lund Uni-
          versity.
SEGERSTEDT, T.
    1964 "Naturvetarnas Yrkesval" [Occupational choice among natural scien-
          tists]. Uppsala: Uppsala University Studies in Sociology.
SIGURDSSON, J.
    1968 "Naturvetenskap och Teknik i Kina" [Natural science and technology
          in China]. Stockholm: Academy for Engineering Sciences.
    1973 "The Suitability of Technology in Contemporary China." *Impact of
          Science on Society* 4.
SKOIE, H.
    1969 "The Problems of a Small Scientific Community: The Norwegian
          Case." *Minerva* 3.
SKOIE, H. ET AL.
    1970 "Forskerrekruttering i Norge—Stipendiat og Universitet" [Research
          recruitment in Norway—research fellows and the university]. Oslo:
          Institute for Studies in Research and Higher Education.
SLOTH ANDERSEN, E. ET AL.
    1972 *Kritiske Studier Indenfor Teknik of Naturvidenskab* [Critical studies

on technology and natural science]. Copenhagen: Danish Student Council.

STAKIEWICZ, R.
1969 "The Role of Informal Communication in Research Work." *FEK*, Stockholm.

SZÉKELY, L.
1967 "The Creative Pause." *International Journal of Psycho-Analysis* 3.

THERBORN, G.
1973 *Vad Är Bra Värderingar Värda?* [What are good values worth?]. Lund: Zenit/Cavefors.

TJÄNSTEMÄNNENS CENTRALORGANISATION (TCO) [SERVICEMEN'S CENTRAL ORGANIZATION]
1970 *Forskning och Utveckling* [Research and development]. Stockholm: Prisma.

TÖRNEBOHM, H.
1968 "A Metascientific Model of Research Procedures." Gothenburg: Institute for the Theory of Science.
1973 "Perspectives on Inquiring Systems." Gothenburg: Institute for the Theory of Science.
1974a "Scientific Knowledge-Formation." Gothenburg: Institute for the Theory of Science.
1974b "A Paradigm Shift in Physics. A Case Study." Gothenburg: Institute for the Theory of Science.
1974c "Inquiring Systems and Paradigms." Gothenburg: Institute for the Theory of Science.

TÖRNUDD, P., AND V. VALPOLA
1963 "Vetenskapligt Samarbete och Interdisciplinära Problem" [Scientific cooperation and interdisciplinary problems]. Helsinki: Scandinavian Summer University.

WILLNER, J.
1972 "Om Forskningsorganization och Sysselsättning" [On research organization and occupational practice]. *Finsk Tidskrift* 6.

APPENDIX

INDEX OF NAMES

INDEX OF SUBJECTS

APPENDIX

REFERENCES TO HUNGARIAN RESEARCH IN THE SOCIOLOGY OF
SCIENCE*

BAKOS, I.
1973 "Fiatal kutatók szakmai és társadalmi integrációja" [Professional and
social integration of young research workers]. *Magyar Tudomány* 1.
BERTALAN, I.
"Tudomány és munkafolyamat" [Science and the working process].
Budapest: MTA Szociológiai Kutató Intézet, in press.
BÓNA, E., AND J. FARKAS
1970 "A tudomány mai struktúrájának és fejlödésének néhány ellentmon-
dása" [Some contradictions of the contemporary structure and development of science]. *Magyar Tudomány* 6:435–46.
1973 "Die Lage der Wissenschaftstheorie in Ungarn" [The situation of the
theory of science in Hungary]. *Zeitschrift für allgemeine Wissenschaftstheorie* 4.
BÓNA, E.; J. FARKAS; J. KLÁR; L. LÖRINCZ; AND GY. PACZOLAY
1970 *A tudomány néhány elméleti kérdése* [Some theoretical questions of
science]. Budapest: Akadémiai Kiadó.

CSÖNDES, M.; L. SZÁNTÓ; P. VAS-ZOLTÁN
1971 *Tudománypolitika és tudományszervezés Magyarországon* [Science
policy and science organization in Hungary]. Budapest: Akadémiai
Kiadó.

FARKAS, J.
1971a "A tudományszociológia néhány kérdéséröl" [On some problems of
the sociology of science]. *Filozófiai Közlemények* 1.
1971b "The Science of Science for Science Policies." *Zagadnenia naukoznawstwa* 2.
1973 "A müszaki fejlesztés szociológiai kérdései" [Sociological questions of
technical development]. *Szociológia* 3.
*Ötlettöl a megvalósulásig. A kutatási eredmények alkalmazásának
társadalmi, szervezeti, személyi feltételei a vegyiparban* [From idea
to realization: conditions of social organization and personnel affecting the application of research results in the chemical industry].
Budapest: Akadémiai Kiadó.

*Reprinted, with the kind permission of the authors and publishers, from Sán-
dor Szalai and János Farkas, "Sociology of Science and Research," *Szociológia*
5, Supplement, 1974:105–10.

FARKAS, J.; GY. FUKÁSZ; J. PÁLINKÁS; D. GY. SZAKASITS; AND I. VÁRADI
  1972 "A müszaki alkotómunka, valamint a megszerzett új ismeretek alkal-
         mazásának társadalmi, emberi feltételei" [Social and human condi-
         tions for the applied use of creative technical work and newly ac-
         quired knowledge]. Mimeographed. Budapest: OMFB.
FÖLDVÁRI, T.
  1971 "Társadalomkép, gazdasági—politikai nézetek, elégedettség" [Image
         of society, economic and political views, satisfaction]. Ergonómia 1.
FÖLDVÁRI, T., AND R. MANCHIN
  1972 "A tudományszociológia alapvetö kérdései és jelenlegi helyzete"
         [Fundamental questions and the present situation of the sociology of
         science]. Szociológia 2.
FÖLDVÁRI, T., AND A. SZESZTAY
  1970 "A Szovjetunióban végeztek" [They graduated in the Soviet Union].
         Mimeographed. Budapest: MTA Szociológiai Kutató Intézet.

HEGEDÜS, A., AND M. MÁRKUS
  1970 "Az ipari kutatás néhány szociológiai problémája" [Some sociological
         problems of industrial research]. Tudományszervezési Tájékoztató 6.
  1971 Az alkotómunka életkörülményeinek és hatékonyságának szociológiai
         vizsgálatáról [On sociological research into the conditions and the
         effectiveness of creative work]. Budapest: KGM MTTI.
HEGEDÜS, A. B.
         "Néhány társadalmi jellegzetesség a müszaki fejlesztés folyama-
         taiban" [Some social characteristics related to processes of technical
         development]. Budapest: MTA Szociológiai kutató Intézet.
HELMICH, D.
         "Társadalmi magatartások a müszaki fejlesztés folyamatában" [Social
         behavior and attitudes in the process of technological development].
         Budapest: Szociológiai Kutató Intézet.

KULCSÁR, K.
  1972 A társadalom és a szociológia [Society and sociology]. Budapest: Kos-
         suth Kiadó.
  1973 "A társadalmi tervezés és a szociológia" [Social planning and
         sociology]. In Szelényi (ed.).
KULCSÁR, K., AND J. FARKAS
  1970 "Az MTA tudományszervezeti és irányitó tevékenysége a kutatói
         vélemények tükrében" [Organization and management of science by
         the Hungarian Academy of Science as seen by research workers].
         Magyar Tudomány 7–8.

MTA SZOCIOLÓGIAI KUTATÓ INTÉZET [INSTITUTE OF SOCIOLOGY, HUNGAR-
IAN ACADEMY OF SCIENCES]
         A müszaki kutatás és fejlesztés szociológiai kérdései [Sociological
         problems of technological research and development]. Budapest.

PALÁSTY, I.
1973 "A fiátal kutatók helyzete a Matematikai Kutató Intézetben" [The situation of young research workers in the Mathematical Research Institute]. *Magyar Tudomány* 4.
PETHES, GY.
1973 "A felsöoktatási intézmények fiátal kutatóinak helyzete" [The situation of young research workers in institutions of higher learning]. *Magyar Tudomány* 5.

RÓZSA, GY.
1972 *Tudományos tájékoztatás és társadalom* [Scientific information and society]. Budapest: Akadémiai Kiadó.

SZABÓ, L.
1971 "Az alkotó szellemi munka veszteségforrásai és a vezetés tevékenysége" [The sources of waste in creative intellectual work and the role of management]. *Tudományszervezési Tájékoztató* 2, 3, 4, 5.
SZAKASITS, GY. D.
1971 "A tudományos-technikai haladás maggyorsitásának föbb társadalmi elöfeltételei" [The principal social conditions for the acceleration of scientié and technological progress]. Mimeographed. Budapest: OMFB.
1973 *Magyarország és a tudományos-technikai forradalom* [Hungary and the scientific and technological revolution]. Budapest: Kossuth Kiadó.
SZALAI, S.
1966 "Statistics, Sociology and Economics of Research in Hungary." *Social Sciences Information* 4.
1968 "National Research Planning and Research Statistics: The Case of Hungary." In Anthony de Reuck et al. (eds.), *Decision Making in National Science Policy*. London: Churchill.
1970 "The United Nations System and the Social Sciences." *International Social Science Journal* 4.
1973 "Uj technikák komplex társadalmi hatásainak prognosztikus elemzése" [Forecast analysis of the complex social effects of new technologies]. *Magyar Tudomány* 11.
SZÁNTÓ, L.
1974 "Social Science Policy in the Hungarian People's Republic." In *Social Science Organization and Policy, First Series*. Paris: UNESCO.
SZELÉNYI, I. (ED.)
1973 *Társadalmi tervezés és szociológia* [Social planning and sociology]. Budapest: Gondolat.
SZESZTAY, A.
1970a *Az egyetem után* [After graduation]. Budapest: Akadémiai Kiadó.
1970b "'Schools' of Scholars in Hungary: Zoltan Kodaly and His Disciples." Mimeographed. Budapest: MTA Szociológiai Kutató Intézet.

TAMÁS, P.

"A kutatás-gyártás ciklus rendszerelemzése" [Systems analysis of the research to production cycle]. Budapest: MTA Szociológiai Kutató Intézet, in press.

1971 "La politique scientifique et l'organisation de la recherche scientifique en Hongrie" [Science policy and the organization of scientific research in Hungary]. *Études et Documents de Politique Scientifique* 23.

VARGA, K.

1968 *Magyar egyetemi hallgatók életfelfogása* [View of life of Hungarian university students]. Budapest: Akadémiai Kiadó.

1973 "Teljesitménymotiváció és a kutatás-fejlesztés sikeressége" [Achievement motivation and success in research and development]. *Szociológia* 3.

VAS-ZOLTÁN, P.

1973 *A Brain Drain* [The brain drain]. Budapest: Akadémiai Kiadó.

VEKERDI, L.

1970 "Tudósok világa. A kutatás-szociológia ujabb eredményei" [The world of scholars: new results of the sociology of research]. *Tudományszervezési Tájékoztató* 3–4.

INDEX OF NAMES